D1632414

THE MEDIEVAL BISHOPS OF DUNBLANE
AND THEIR CHURCH

Frontispiece

DUNBLANE CATHEDRAL from South West

THE MEDIEVAL BISHOPS OF DUNBLANE AND THEIR CHURCH

BY

JAMES HUTCHISON COCKBURN

D.D., Theol. D.

Senior Minister of Dunblane Cathedral

Published for
The Society of Friends of Dunblane Cathedral

By

OLIVER AND BOYD

EDINBURGH: TWEEDDALE COURT
LONDON: 39a WELBECK STREET, W.1.

FIRST PUBLISHED .   .   . 1959

Printed in Great Britain by
Robert Cunningham and Sons, Ltd.
Longbank Works, Alva, Scotland

To the Three,
thankworthy and unknown,
members of the Society of Friends of Dunblane Cathedral,
whose generosity,
matching their zeal in all that the Cathedral inspires,
ensured the printing of this volume.

ACKNOWLEDGEMENTS

I AM happy to express my gratitude to many scholars who found time to answer my enquiries. To some I have indicated my debt in various notes to the chapters, but there were others too numerous for individual mention. Several Roman Catholic scholars have been generous in the time and learning which they put at my disposal – Father Walter Gumbley, O.P., Oxford, in my researches into the life of Bishop Clement; Father Gray, of St. Hugh's Charterhouse, Sussex, and the Reverend William James Anderson, Archivist of Blairs College, Aberdeen, in my studies of Bishop William Chisholm the Second. Most of all I thank Mr. Robert J. Adam, M.A., St. Andrews, for his ungrudging guidance. Of course, none but myself is responsible for the views expressed, except when I have named some scholar as the source of my information or the expounder of a particular point.

To Mr. Ian G. Lindsay, O.B.E., Edinburgh, I owe the map of the medieval Diocese of Dunblane. He drew it as the result of many discussions in which he took an equal part.

For the illustrations, and the right of their reproduction, I acknowledge the kindness of H.M. Ministry of Works, Mr. William D. Leask, Edinburgh and Mr. John Dickie, Dunblane. The photograph of the West Door was taken about thirty-five years ago by the late Mr. James Tillie, Dunblane; the photographs by Mr. Leask and Mr. Dickie were taken for this volume.

The generosity of the Society of Friends of Dunblane Cathedral has made it possible for this volume, and the earlier volume on Celtic Dunblane, to be undertaken by me.

Lastly, this volume could not have been published at all, but for the splendid generosity of three members of the Society. To them I have dedicated this volume in deep appreciation.

JAMES HUTCHISON COCKBURN

vii

CONTENTS

viii

ILLUSTRATIONS

DUNBLANE CATHEDRAL

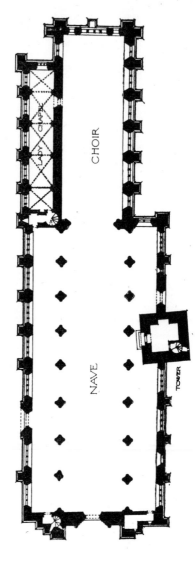

Based on plan in MacGibbon and Ross: *Ecclesiastical Architecture of Scotland*

CONTRACTIONS USED IN REFERENCES

This is not a bibliography of books read. It is merely a list of contractions used throughout to avoid repetition of long references. Other references, if few, to any particular books, are given in full.

A. Aud.	Acts of Lords Auditors of Causes and Complaints, 1466-1494.
ACUP	Auctarium Chartularii Universitatis Parisiensis (Denifle and Chatelain).
ADC or ADCC	Acts of Lords of Council in Civil Causes, 2 vols., 1478-1554.
ADCP	Acts of Lords of Council in Public Affairs, 1 vol., 1501-1554 (Stationery Office).
ADCS	Acts of Lords of Council and Session.
AES	A. O. Anderson: Early Sources of Scottish History.
AP or APS	Acts of Parliament of Scotland (Record Commissioners).
ASA	A. O. Anderson: Scottish Annals from English Chronicles.
ATS	Accounts of Lord High Treasurer of Scotland. Rolls Series.
B.	Boiamund's (Bagimont's) Taxation, 1275- , in T. No. 264.
BA	MS. "Assumptions of Thirds of Benefices". Register House, Edinburgh.
BC	Bain: Calendar of Documents relating to Scotland.
BCPS	J. H. Baxter: Copiale Prioratus Sanctiandree.
BES	W. M. Brady: The Episcopal Succession in England, Scotland and Ireland.
BFDC	Books of the Society of Friends of Dunblane Cathedral. Noted by year.
Brackley.	Charters of Hospital of Ss. James and John, Brackley, Northamptonshire. MS. in Magdalen College Library, Oxford.
BUK	Booke of the Universall Kirk of Scotland. (Bannatyne Club; 3 parts, 1839-45).
CAC	A. I. Cameron: The Apostolic Camera and Scottish Benefices.
CACA	D. E. Easson: Charters of Abbey of Coupar Angus, Scottish History Society.
CAI	Charters of Abbey of Inchaffray, Scottish History Society.
CC	Calendar of Charters. MS. in Register House, Edinburgh.
CCS (or ERS)	Compta Camerarii Scotiae (Accounts of the Great Chamberlain). Bannatyne Club.
CL	Charters of Abbey of Lindores, Scottish History Society.
CMN	Chartulary of Nunnery of North Berwick. Bannatyne Club.
CN	Chartulary of Newbattle. Bannatyne Club.

CPR	Calendar of Papal Registers (Great Britain and Ireland). Rolls Series.
CPR Pet.	Calendar of Petitions to the Pope. Rolls Series.
CR	Registrum Monasterii S. Marie de Cambuskenneth. Wm. Fraser in Grampian Club Publications.
CS	Charters of Burgh of Stirling.
CSA	G. G. Coulton: Scottish Abbeys and Social Life.
CSP	Calendar of State Papers relating to Scotland (Ed. M. J. Thorpe), 2 vols.
CSSR	Lindsay and Cameron: Calendar of Scottish Supplications to Rome (1418-1422). SHS, Third Series, Vol. 23.
CSSR II	A. I. Dunlop: Calendar of Scottish Supplications to Rome (1423-1428). SHS, Third Series, Vol. 48, 1956.
DB	The Douglas Book, edited by Wm. Fraser.
DBS	Dowden: Bishops of Scotland.
DMCS	Dowden: Mediaeval Church in Scotland.
DN	Diplomatarium Norvegicum.
DNB	Dictionary of National Biography.
DSK	A. H. Dunbar: Scottish Kings.
ERS (or CCS)	Exchequer Rolls of Scotland. Rolls Series.
EU	Eubel: Hierarchia Catholica.
Ex.	Extracta e variis Cronicis Scocie. Abbotsford Club.
F.	St. Andrews' Formulary. Stair Society.
FCC.I.	William Fraser: Chartulary of Colquhoun.
FCC.II.	William Fraser: The Chiefs of Colquhoun.
FES	Hew Scott: Fasti Ecclesiae Scoticanae.
FKL	Feu-Charters of Kirk-Lands. MS. in Register House, Edinburgh.
Foed.	Rymer's Foedera.
HB	Hume Brown: History of Scotland.
HH	Herkless and Hannay: Archbishops of St. Andrews.
HMC	Reports of Historical Manuscripts Commissioners.
HS	Haddan and Stubbs: Councils and Ecclesiastical Documents.
IWC	MS. (1782) Inventory of Writs of Cromlix (in care of Messrs Tho. and J. W. Barty, Dunblane).
K.	Bishop Keith: Historical Catalogue of Scottish Bishops.
LA	A. C. Lawrie: Annals of Malcolm IV and William.
LACC	Liber actorum curie consistorialis (dunblanensis). MS in Register House, Edinburgh. 1551-1555.
LAc	Chartulary of Arbroath (Aberbrothoc). Bannatyne Club.
LC	Laing: Charters.
LdC	Chartulary of Kelso. Liber de Calchou. Bannatyne Club.

LESC	A. C. Lawrie: Early Scottish Charters.
LIM	Liber Insule Missarum. Bannatyne Club.
LS	Chartulary of Scone. Bannatyne Club.
M.	Chronica de Mailros. Bannatyne Club.
MCHS	James Mackinnon: Constitutional History of Scotland.
NMS	National Manuscripts of Scotland.
OP	Originales Parochiales Scotiae. Bannatyne Club.
PPN	W. H. Pollen: Papal Negociations with Queen Mary. Scottish History Society.
PSSA	Proceedings of the Society of Scottish Antiquaries.
PSSC	David Patrick: Statutes of the Scottish Church. SHS, 1st Series, No. 54.
RA	Registrum Episcopatus Aberdonensis. 2 vols. Maitland and Spalding Clubs.
Ra.M.S.	Rait: Making of Scotland.
RB	Registrum Episcopatus Brechinensis. 2 vols. Bannatyne Club.
RBG	The Red Book of Grantully.
RBM	William Fraser: Red Book of Menteith.
RCEE	Registrum cartarum ecclesie Santi Egidii de Edinburgh. Bannatyne Club.
RDD	Registrum de Dunfermelyn. Bannatyne Club.
REG	Registrum Episcopatus Glasguensis. 2 vols. Bannatyne and Maitland Clubs.
REM	Registrum Episcopatus Moraviensis. Bannatyne Club.
RESS or SES	Robertson: Ecclesiae Scoticanae Statuta.
RMS	Registrum Magni Sigilli Regum Scotorum.
Rot. Scot.	Rotuli Scotiae. Record Commissioners.
RPSA	Liber cartarum Prioratus Sancti Andree. Bannatyne Club.
RS	Records of Burgh of Stirling.
RSS or RPCS	Registrum Secreti Sigilli Regum Scotorum. Rolls Series.
SBSH	A Source Book of Scottish History, 3 vols., 1952-3-4 (Eds. Dickinson, Donaldson, Milne).
Sc.	Fordun's Scotichronicon. Ed. Goodall, 1775.
SCHS	Scottish Church History Society.
SDI	Stevenson: Documents illustrative of History of Scotland.
SES or RESS	Statuta Ecclesiae Scoticanae. Bannatyne Club.
SHR	Scottish Historical Review.
SHS	Scottish History Society.
SK	W. Fraser: Stirlings of Keir.
T.	Theiner: Vetera Monumenta.
TB	Thirds of Benefices. Scottish History Society.

TV   Transcriptions from the Vatican. MS. in Register House, Edinburgh.

W.   Wyntoun's Orygynale Cronykil of Scotland. Historians of Scotland Series.

WC   Wilkins: Concilia.

CHAPTER I

THE ROMAN CHURCH COMES TO DUNBLANE

THE Culdees, representatives of the Celtic Church in Scotland, continued to labour, and in places to thrive, for some centuries after all hope of ultimate revival had died. Though the Roman Church had penetrated to various parts of Scotland by the ninth century, and in the succeeding centuries made sporadic gains, its advance was for centuries slow, its bishops few, and its impact on the religious life of Scotland little. It was new and foreign, whereas the Culdees had behind them the Celtic tradition and social atmosphere of a predominantly Celtic people, led by a Celtic aristocracy tenacious of the old ways. The struggle between the old and the new was long, but it was without undue bitterness, if also without cordiality[1]; the two Churches lived alongside each other while the old was losing its grip of life slowly, and the new was gathering momentum. It was the spread into Scotland of Norman influence, with its attendant feudalism, which gave to the Roman Church the backing which carried it to domination.

This new power appeared significantly in Scotland with Princess Margaret of England, who became the second wife of Malcolm Canmore. She was a faithful daughter of the Roman Church, who knew no other Church, and held that its canons, worship and discipline should be obeyed and followed without question by all reasonable men. She was a nun at heart, and when she convinced herself that she ought to marry Malcolm and bear him children, she carried the discipline and devotion of an abbess into her family life. Though she laid the Roman ways before the Celtic churchmen with the conviction of a devotee, against whom no argument availed, yet it is on record that she consulted with some of the Celtic anchorites, and that she and Malcolm gifted lands to northern Culdees – which shows at least that the Celtic Church had enough vitality to command the generosity of its opponents. But it was by the acts of her sons, three of whom, as well as a stepson, succeeded to the Scottish throne, that the Church of

Rome came to flourish in Scotland. Edgar (1097-1107) presented lands to Coldingham, St. Andrews and Dunfermline, as well as to Durham. Alexander I (1107-24) was a benefactor of Dunfermline and Durham, and also of Scone, whose monastery he founded c.1113; in his reign, Dunkeld was re-established, and Moray founded, as bishoprics, c.1107. David I (1124-53) reconstituted the See of Glasgow c.1115, before he came to the throne, and set up those of Ross and of Caithness (c.1128), Aberdeen (c.1137) and Brechin (c.1150). When it is remembered that he also founded or re-established nine abbeys,[2] it will be granted, not only that he deserved his nickname of "sair sanct for the Crown", but that he was the supreme builder of the Roman Church in Scotland.

Many writers assume that David I also founded the Bishopric of Dunblane. Of this there is no extant contemporary record, whereas in the five bishoprics already mentioned there are charter references which link the foundation or re-establishment with David and enable an approximate date to be fixed. Absence of record is not determinative; but if Dunblane had been a royal foundation, it is, at least, very unlikely that the King's authorisation would have escaped all notice in contemporary records. Nor is there extant any charter of gift to the Bishopric; that again is not final, but it is very suggestive that the charters dealing with gifts in which the Diocese of Dunblane was interested were granted to Inchaffray Abbey and Inchmahome Priory by two Celts, the Earls of Strathearn and of Menteith, who had espoused the cause of the Roman Church. Strathearn was the more generous of these two earls, and though the medieval Diocese of Dunblane, but for the parishes of Abernethy,[3] and Culross,[4] and perhaps a few others, was wholly within the two earldoms, Strathearn covered the greater area; this was reason enough for the diocese, between 1200 and 1350, varying in name between "the Diocese of Dunblane" and "the Diocese of Strathearn", until the fact that the cathedral of the see was situated in Dunblane determined the name.

The origin of the See of Dunblane seems to be settled in favour of the Earl of Strathearn by two facts:

(1) Several papal letters call the Earl *patronus* of the Church of Dunblane. I have found no other instance of a layman being papally designated patron of the church of a diocese.[5] The Pope

would bestow such title only on one whose generosity was worthy of it, and whose connexion with the see was of the most intimate. It defined the Earl's position in an election to the bishopric, and is a particularly interesting application of the advocate's relation in Germany to religious houses. Whoever founded the See of Dunblane originally, perhaps about 1155, its second and main founder was Gilbert, third Earl of Strathearn, who, according to Fordun, gave, at a date unspecified but perhaps before A.D. 1200, one third of his lands to the Bishopric, and one third to Inchaffray Abbey, near Muthill, within the diocese, retaining only one third for himself. Even if this means only that he gave to these beneficiaries a third of the patronage and teinds (Scottish for tithes) of the churches and chapels on his territory, and not the lands themselves, they were still princely gifts deserving the papal title of *patronus*. But this will be reviewed in a later chapter.[6]

(2) When the Popes intimated to the King of Scotland, to the clergy of the Diocese, and to the people of Dunblane, their appointment of a new Bishop, they also sent intimation to the Earl of Strathearn.[7] This unusual course showed that the title of *patronus* was distinctive.

It was a new form of State and a new form of Church which David I imposed on Scotland. Though born of a Scoto-Celtic father, he was trained in the Norman court of England; he was in effect a Norman knight and a most important earl and landowner in England. He was ignorant of the Celtic tongue and of the Celtic Church and thoroughly given over to English institutions in ecclesiastical and civil affairs. To bring in feudalism, with its system of land tenure from king to baron, from baron to lesser aristocracy and lesser tenant, down to serfs and underlings, each owing allegiance, duties and services to the superior and the highest of them to the king, he relied on Norman[8] friends whose loyalty he received in return for offices and gifts of land. This system was so different from the Celtic that it could not be grafted on to it; the Celtic customs and tenures had to be broken and the new system imposed with the King's authority, supported by his Norman allies. Several fierce campaigns had to be waged by David against his Celtic subjects who counted him, his royal house, and his friends as foreigners. He contrived to subdue the

B

Celts and to destroy their ways and polity, which he regarded as uncivilised and intolerable. In their place he set up the Roman Church after the Norman pattern used in England. Roman Canon Law, Roman worship, bishops with detailed dioceses and parishes, cathedrals with constitutions and statutes copied in places from English examples, monastic brethren, often introduced into their new establishments from England, Norman bishops consecrated to Scottish sees, and clergy of all grades unable in many cases to speak the language of the people throughout the greater part of Scotland – these were among the violent changes of David's encouragement which altered the face of things ecclesiastical. It was a new Church which was created, in which everything was changed except fundamental Christian doctrine. The government of Scotland was feudalised, the Church Romanised, and both of them Normanised – these were David's doings, often at the point of the sword, and always protested against in silence, or in tumult, by the people of the land, till opposition was overborne and reduced to acceptance. The change was inevitable, and though it was not welcomed by many at first, it brought Scotland and its Church into the family of western nations, their civilisation and institutions, and is to be ranked as uplift and advance.

It must be said for David, and for the foreign friends and churchmen whom he brought into Scotland's affairs, that though Scotland was being radically re-formed on an alien model, there was no thought of yielding up Scotland or its Church to English domination. The claims of the English Kings and of the English prelates of York and Canterbury were as fiercely resisted as they had been in the days of Malcolm Canmore. In this the new Church readily availed itself of the prestige of the early Celtic saints, and a cult of S. Ninian, of S. Columba, and of others sprang up in the Roman Church. By this the new Church sought to prove to the world, and to itself, that its roots were deep in the history of Scotland. But this was almost the only use which the Roman Church had for its Celtic predecessor.

Between the Celtic Church and its Roman successor there is a lengthy period of irritating ignorance regarding bishops in Scotland. It is a period of almost total absence of written record, when we have to content ourselves with stray hints of a few names handed down mainly by tradition. It can no longer be asserted dogmatically that at the time of the Norman Conquest there was only one bishop in Scotland, and that he had all Scotland for his diocese.[9] There were probably others, without there being either an uninterrupted succession in the same diocese, or anything that we would call a diocese today, with definite borders. Occasional bishops for undefined areas of influence in a tentative experimental and haphazard scheme would perhaps have fitted the conditions of the centuries before David I which faced the Roman Church; informed surmise cannot take us far into the matter. But in the twelfth century the Roman system begins to emerge, and when the sees of the new Roman bishoprics appear, they are found at the main ecclesiastical sites of the Celtic Church. Records appear in charters for the first time after A.D. 1100, and though they are comparatively few, and omit to tell us so much that we long to know, we begin to touch solid ground. Approximate dates appear, names and titles of grantors and of witnesses are given, places are named, and rights and gifts enumerated; system begins and there are facts to work on. The records were not written for our enlightenment, and give only the bits of information relative to the contemporary transactions; nevertheless they enable us to trace the early stages of growth of dioceses, parishes, rectories, vicarages, parish churches, diocesan benefices, cathedral dignities, and the whole apparatus of the Roman organisation, which later centuries were to know.

This point needs some elaboration, and though we shall see the gradual growth of the system in the case of Dunblane, it will help us to be aware now that we cannot expect the full medieval Church system of bishops, dioceses, parishes, rectors, vicars, canons, prebendaries, officers, and all, to spring before us into life, like mushrooms in a field. These were the results of acts and decisions spread over a long period; no order from Pope or King, bishop or lord, commanded the system to appear, "and it was so". The system emerged through the centuries, but to the last it was only a general system, and many were the details in most of the diocesan regulations which differed from parish to parish and from diocese to diocese. This was due, partly to local history and traditions, partly to unresolved problems between lay landowners, episcopal authorities, monastic rulers and royal superiors, and partly to the use by the Popes of their "plenitude of power", by exercise of which they could disobey, as they often did scandalously, the rules of Councils and of General Statutes set up for the orderly government of the Church. In other words, while the general pattern of the organisation was obvious, there were many particulars in which parishes and dioceses differed from their kind, even from their neighbours. The result was that when the system was in full operation in Scotland, it was confused and confusing. When it is remembered that England and France and other lands harboured the same confusion in Church life, it is most remarkable that the papal system centred in Rome worked as well as it did, for it sought to control the whole of Christendom, even in Scotland which it regarded as at the end of the world's limit.

It would seem that in Dunblane the Bishopric was instituted before the diocese was even roughly delimited. The first recorded Bishop of Dunblane appears in A.D. 1155, in a very early copy of a bull[10] addressed by Pope Adrian IV to the bishops of Scotland, including "M. de Dublan", in which he bids them submit to the Archbishop of York as their metropolitan, or take the consequences. Though the copyist has made two mistakes in the initials of bishops, there seems to be no reason to charge him, as do Lawrie and Bishop Dowden, with a third, when the earliest known record of another Bishop is dated between 1160 and 1162. Nor do I see reason to doubt the genuineness of the bull or of its copy. I accept "M." as first Roman Bishop of Dunblane.[11] It is not known what "M." stands for, though it would be within reasonable chance that it meant Malise, and for these reasons:

(1) Dunblane was chosen as the seat of the Roman Bishopric, doubtless because it was already a centre of the Celtic Church.

(2) As was happening elsewhere in Scotland, and as seems to have happened in the church life of Dunblane, many Celtic churchmen changed their allegiance; M. may have been one of the Culdees of Dunblane or Muthill who decided to give their future service to the Church of Rome, one who had been accepted by the patron and given the Bishopric of Dunblane.[12]

(3) Malise was the chief name of the Earls of Strathearn, whose connexion with the new Diocese was early and intimate. This Bishop may even have been related to the family of Strathearn.

No one can say what the facts of the name M. are; but these are reasonable surmises, consonant with the traditions of the district.

Once the Bishopric was instituted, the way was open for the

creation of the Diocese. Of this act there is no written record till later. But when the Diocese did emerge about A.D. 1200, and more fully about 1234-9, it comprised the lands of the Earls of Strathearn and Menteith. Those of Strathearn covered the area from Aberuthven to Blackford (then called Strogeith) and from Muthill to Comrie, while those of Menteith comprised Aberfoyle, Leny, Port of Menteith, Callander, Kilmahog, Kincardine in Menteith, Kilmadock, Kippen, Dunblane and part of Logie, all of which in due course became parishes in the Diocese of Dunblane. The third Earl of Strathearn was much quicker than Walter Comyn, Earl of Menteith, to adopt the Roman pattern of church life; but up till about 1198, both Earls were Celtic in their sympathies and held to the old Church as decently as they could in the changing times of church loyalties. We shall see later the road travelled by Menteith, but the road taken by the Strathearns is instructive. The first Earl, Malise, without departing from his Celtic traditions, showed interest in the establishment of the Roman Church to the extent of witnessing Alexander I's foundation charter of Scone Abbey,[13] about 1124, and also, with four other Celtic earls, David I's establishment[14] of Dunfermline Abbey in 1128. In his day, the problem of allegiance in the church life of his neighbourhood did not arise, as the See of Dunblane was not ready for development. His son, Ferteth, the second Earl, made a stormy appearance in Scottish history by joining with five other earls in besieging Malcolm IV in his castle at Perth because they distrusted Malcolm's intimacy with Henry II of England, as endangering the freedom both of Scotland's Church and Scotland's kingdom; their lives were spared on the plea of the Scottish clergy, who shared their fears.[15] He and his wife, Ethen, some time after 1160, gave lands and teinds, as one of his son's (Gilbert's) charters[16] states, for the endowment of the Church of S. Catan of Aberuthven. There is no indication in this act that he was endowing a portion of a diocese; it seems to have been simply the re-establishing of an ancient Celtic foundation, without reference to a diocese and without mention that it was now placed by him within the compass of Rome; but the fact that it was given teinds meant that the lands from which the teinds came were its immediate concern, though that would not determine the area of influence or service, which might well be wider. It is worth noting that teinds were regarded as a natural gift, along with "all oblations and obventions of all kinds", the lands and "all things which justly pertain to the Church, with common pasture and all other privileges (easements)" in pure, free and perpetual alms . . . to be enjoyed for ever freely and quietly, fully and honourably, free from all secular service and feudal dues. Ferteth may have given other such gifts, but no record has come down to us. In any case we may count him as the first recorded benefactor of any parish in what became the Diocese of Dunblane.

The early Roman Bishops of Dunblane found the Culdees in a settlement probably on part of the site of the present Cathedral. How many they were, no one can say, or what cells and other buildings they had. All traces of their church and its domiciliary equipments have vanished, but the Celtic cross [17]of the eighth or ninth century still stands, and is now housed within the Cathedral. The four lower storeys of the present Cathedral tower, which is not later than A.D. 1100, and may be much earlier, can be considered only as having been built separate, and at some little distance, from the Celtic church. It does not fit into any scheme for a tower attached to any church, cathedral or other. Its purpose was probably secular and not primarily ecclesiastical, to provide a place of defence for the inhabitants in case of attack, and of guarding the treasures of the church. It is square, but it served the same purposes as the round towers of Brechin and Abernethy, though of later date than they. It may be compared with the square tower of Muthill, for there also, as in Dunblane, the medieval church incorporates the tower awkwardly.

In the second half of the twelfth century, it must be remembered, the district around Dunblane was very different from what it is today, and that in several respects. Its population was very sparse, for the whole of Scotland at the time of the early Roman bishops did not perhaps exceed 350,000 in all.[18] Forests covered much of Scotland; the land was drained only by the rivers, and large areas were under bog; agricultural land to meet new needs had to be won laboriously from the forests. As a consequence of these conditions, and of the absence of foreign trade and of anything that we would call industry today, the inhabitants lived in villages and scattered communities, which were small in the area we are considering. There were no towns (in our modern sense), only groups of people who were self-sufficient in the growing of grains, cattle, fish, horses and wood, and the making of cloth and such utensils of clay and iron as their everyday life demanded. The land was cultivated under feudal tenure.

Also the people of this area spoke a Celtic tongue in probably more than one dialect. During Earl Ferteth's lifetime (he died in 1171),[19] the Celtic traditions and ways were strong; the people were still "the men of Fortrenn" and still looked to Dundurn (the Dun or fortress of the Earn), at the modern St. Fillans, as their stronghold. Though David I, from 1124, began to bring to his court Norman friends of his early days at the English court, it was some time before this invasion gained the prestige and wealth which finally overwhelmed the Celtic tradition in church affairs and in the governing of the country: for instance, King David's witnesses to his founding charter of Dunfermline in 1128 were five earls, all of them Celts, and in the earlier constitution of the church of Glasgow[20] in 1115, the recorded witnesses were for the most part Celts.

Throughout their estates the earls and larger landowners had seen the Celtic Church build, and had helped that Church to build, places of worship for themselves, their families and their dependents, generally in or near a village. So when the Roman Church came to establish itself with bishops, parishes and churches, it found many churches ready for use, some of them perhaps in dwindling use, some in disuse and in need of repair. In the great charter of 1200,[21] Earl Gilbert, son of Ferteth, concedes as of right, and without the permission of the Bishop or any other, to the Priory of Inchaffray, which this charter founds, the Churches of S. Catan at Aberuthven, S. Ethernan at Madderty (Diocese of Dunkeld) S. Patrick at Strogeith, S. Makessog at Auchterarder, and S. Bean at Kinkell. And there were many other such Celtic foundations within the area which became the diocese of Dunblane:

Inchmahome (S. Colm)	Dunblane (S. Blane)
Kilbryde (S. Brite)	Foulis Wester (S. Bean)
Kincardine in Menteith	Logie (S. Serf)
(S. Lolan)	Monzievaird (S. Serf)
Tullibody (S. Mungo)	Strowan (S. Ronan)
Dunning (S. Serf)	Tullieden (S. Serf)
Dupplin (S. Serf)	Balquhidder (S. Angus)
Callander (S. Makessog)	Findogask (S. Findoca)
Comrie (S. Makessog)	Kilmadock (S. Cadog)
Kilmahog (S. Mahon)	Kippen (S. Davie)

When there are added those Celtic centres which are without the names of their founders, such as Muthill, Culross, Abernethy, it will be clear that the Roman Church was built on Celtic foundations, and that the whole Diocese of Dunblane had a pronounced Celtic flavour and history.

It is probable, as it is natural to think, that the Culdee clerics were in many cases persuaded to change over to the Roman Church, when the Bishopric had been set up and clergy were required, especially men who could speak the language of the people and were themselves natives. Many such were given the office of chaplain[22]; for instance, between 1190 and 1200, these eight chaplains bear Celtic names: Gillemure, Malise, Bean, Cormac, Makbeth, Malmure, Gillecrist and Patrick. Such a numerous change must have meant a serious blow to the Culdees of Dunblane and Muthill, though other Culdees carried on the old Church (especially, it would seem, in Muthill) for a hundred years afterwards. Dunblane appears as the seat of Culdees in Silgrave's list written in 1272.

These were the circumstances in which the early Roman Bishops of Dunblane had to labour. The building of the Cathedral was begun, but was seriously hindered; indeed, Bishop Clement (1233-58) changed the whole plan and took down almost the whole of the earlier church and built anew. Parish churches began to appear as such in the records, the earliest being Tullibody, Muthill, Tillicoultry and Kilbryde, with Inchmahome, Kincardine-in-Menteith and Logie following very soon after; all of these have recorded dates between c.1170 and c.1196. But it was 1200 before the Diocese began to take shape, and 1240 before it may be said to have been organised throughout its area.

A third task remains to be mentioned, the setting up of the Cathedral Chapter. In this a good start was made, for there is record of "all the Chapter" c.1170[23]; and in that year the first recorded Archdeacon is met with, as well as the first known Dean and the first Chancellor. But it is about 1196 before more names appear, which perhaps means that the first energetic outburst lost momentum, for only Dean Thomas, Archdeacon Jonathan and a Bishop's chaplain appear between 1170 and 1190. This paucity of clergy may have compelled the Bishop to try to persuade some Culdees to join his staff; in 1190, two appear, a Canon Malgirke and a Deacon Gillemure, and five more with

Celtic names are recorded in 1196 as rectors, priests or Bishop's chaplains. The period 1200-14 is again a lean one for clerical appointments, but the coming of Bishop Abraham, c.1212, brought a new list of chaplains and clerks. But now their names are Norman and no longer Celtic: Luke, William, Peter, John and Ralph, with Galfridus (Geoffrey) as Archdeacon and Matthew as Dean. No other cathedral clergy appear in the records until after Bishop Clement's appointment in 1233, when there are several dignitaries with Norman, or at least non-Celtic, names, but also two chaplains, Gillebaran and Padyn, both Celts, the latter coming from the Culdees of Muthill. In all this, the records themselves may be deficient and so give an inadequate picture; but what we do know, with the mixture of Celt and Norman, and the light and shade of activity and inactivity according to the Bishop's energy and his use of meagre resources, fits in with what was to be expected in the circumstances of the time and the hardness of the Bishop's task in a poor and sparsely populated area.[24]

NOTES

1. The Bishop of Brechin in early thirteenth-century charters speaks of "my Culdees", kindly if a little patronising.

2. Jedburgh, Holyrood, Kelso, Melrose, Newbattle, Dundrennan, Cambuskenneth, Holmcultram (Cumberland), Kinloss.

3. Abernethy's importance in the Celtic period warrants the supposition that it had relations with Dunblane, which led to their diocesan connexion in later medieval times.

4. In BFDC 1934, p. 7n, Dr Black Scott states that an ancient Gaelic writer (unnamed) "had little local knowledge, because he locates Culross in Strathearn". But the Gaelic writer may have been correct; if so, it would explain why Culross came to be in the Diocese of Dunblane.

5. Before A.D. 1000, and in places later, the landowner's authority (dominion) over the parish churches on his lands was almost everywhere claimed and recognised; it was proprietary. This included their patronage. But patronage of a parish church is one thing; patronage of the cathedral church of a diocese is another.

6. See under Bishop Michael Ochiltree's royal charter of 1442/3. Fordun's statement (Sc. VIII, lxxiii) and Earl Gilbert's gifts to Inchaffray must be reviewed in the light of James II's charter.

7. cf. T. Nos. 284 (1284), 355 (1296) and 442 (1322), in which the Earl of Strathearn is called "patron of the Church of Dunblane"; also, Nos. 386 (1307), 576 (1347) and 644 (1361), in which he is notified without being called patronus.

8. In King David I's time, they were Normans and their names in records proclaim their nationality. They were the offspring of those who came with,

or after, William the Conqueror; they were correctly called "*Francigenae*" or "*Franci*", and for long, in Scotland, as in England, kept themselves a separate community as far as possible, a kind of garrison and alien minority in a conquered territory. The native speech was not used by them; they spoke French and their official documents were for long written in Latin. The chief churchmen, and many of the lesser, in Scotland were French; their names show it. Of the early Bishops of Dunblane, Laurence, Symon, W. (if his name was William or Walter), Jonathan, Ralph, Osbert were French and spoke French; they may have learned to speak the Scots tongue, though that is unlikely. Abraham alone (and M. if that initial meant Malise) was a native Celt, if his name is the criterion. Clement was a Scot, and we have to wait till Robert de Prebenda and his successors before we come to bishops to whom the epithet Anglo-Norman is strictly applicable. Until 1250 or so, they had nothing English about them, except that England was in most cases the land in which they or their forebears had settled. See R. L. G. Ritchie: *The Normans in Scotland*.

9. See Gordon Donaldson: Sc. Bishops' Sees before David I, in PSAS, vol. 87 (1955) pp. 106-17.

10. British Museum. Cottonian MSS., Cleopatra C IV, transcribed in HS II i 231-2, and in Wilkin: Concilia I 481.

11. See my article, with reproduction of the MS., BFDC, 1938. cf. LA p. 18 and DBS 193 and n.

12. The early elections to Dunblane were probably made by the chapter on the nomination of the *patronus*, the Earl of Strathearn; at least, the first recorded papal connexion with the provision of a Bishop of Dunblane is found in 1226, when on the resignation of Ralph, elect of Dunblane, "in our presence", Honorius III directs three Scottish bishops to authorise a new election and to confirm it if canonically made. Such papal detachment ended with the provision by the Pope of William, Abbot of Arbroath, in 1284, to Dunblane.

13. LESC No. 36.

14. LESC No. 74.

15. Sc. I ii 430.

16. CAI No. 3.

17. See Romilly Allen: Early Christian Monuments of Scotland.

18. Lord Cooper in SHR Vol. xxvi, pp. 2-9, puts Scotland's population in fourteenth century at 400,000.

19. M. 84.

20. REG No. 1.

21. CAI No. 9.

22. It will save repetition of references, if readers will kindly understand that details given in the text regarding Cathedral clergy are to be found in the appendix so named.

23. CR No. 218.

24. For a general survey of this obscure subject, consult Miss M. Morgan: Organisation of the Scottish Church in the Twelfth century, published in Transactions of Royal Historical Society, 1947. Dunblane, which she does not mention, was true to the general pattern of growth of a diocese north of the Forth, though it had its own peculiarities and exaggerations of detail.

CHAPTER II

BRIEFLY EXPLANATORY

SINCE much of the early history of the Diocese concerns the relationships between bishop and diocese on one hand and abbots and monasteries on the other, it will make for clarity and avoid repetition if briefly the consequences are outlined of the creation of many new monastic houses in Scotland in the twelfth and thirteenth centuries. David I founded Cambuskenneth Abbey in 1147, William the Lion the Abbey of Arbroath in 1178, Earl Gilbert of Strathearn the Priory of Inchaffray in 1200, Malcolm, Earl of Fife, the Abbey of Culross in 1217, David I's grandson David the Abbey of Lindores (in Fife) in 1219, and the Earl of Menteith Inchmahome Priory in 1238. These all became closely connected with Dunblane Diocese and, like the many establishments of various Orders, were inspired by the conviction that the monastic life of praise and prayer of men devoted to these ends was the religious life *par excellence*. The words "religion" and "religious", indeed, came to mean the monastic life and those who entered on its high demands; "conversion" meant entering the monastic life. Monasteries (often called convents) of monks and a lesser number of nunneries sprang up, generally in the more populous and more cultivated places of Scotland, often sited near a royal palace or baronial residence and owing their creation and growth to the religious zeal and gifts of King and barons and lesser landowners. All Scotland shared in the new enthusiasm, and although their institution in all the dioceses brought serious problems for bishops and parochial clergy, the bishops welcomed their coming, for the bishops were as persuaded as the lay landowners that this was the true Christian life. The story of the rise and fall of monasticism in Scotland must be read elsewhere[1]; suffice it to say here that the sheer physical needs of the monks, the necessity of constructing and keeping in repair considerable buildings, often damaged in war and by neglect, and the decline of most of the Orders from their primitive simplicity laid upon abbots the burden of constant search for new gifts, more teinds, larger lands and increase of privileges, which they achieved with remarkable success, if sometimes with loss of popular regard and the serious neglect of their early vows of obligation. By 1275, when Bagimont's taxation[2] was gathered, the Diocese of Dunblane had close ecclesiastical ties with the Abbeys and Priory already noted, and in the end the records show that Cambuskenneth was in possession of four parishes of the Diocese, Inchmahome of four, Inchaffray of ten, Culross two, Arbroath two, while Coupar Angus Abbey, Lindores Abbey, the Nunnery of North Berwick and the Hospital of Sts. James and John of Brackley, Northamptonshire, had each one, twenty-six in all. Only about a dozen parishes in the Diocese were left to the unhindered control of the Bishop and Chapter. G. G. Coulton[3] has calculated that the monasteries in England "drew two thirds of the income from nearly one third of the English parishes". In the diocese of Dunblane nine monasteries drew two thirds of the income from two thirds of the parishes.

Some readers may welcome a brief outline of the medieval church system, with definition of some of the technical terms which steadily recur:

I. *Parish*. This was an area of land attached to a church. Originally it was part of the landowner's domain, on which he or some other had built a church for public worship. At first it had no boundaries of stated extent. Sometimes, in addition to the teinds, the proprietor gave a gift of land, so that the church had an endowment of rent. Also he gave up his rights, real or presumed, to the church income, offerings at worship, fees for services, and such like. Common pasture was another frequent gift. The landowner retained the patronage of the church and much else of the ecclesiastical privileges, and the Church had to strive long and hard to win its spiritual liberty in this regard; when the bishop was gaining ground, often the Pope reserved contested patronal rights to his own decision. All the time the king was eager to assert his authority and the contest became to a large extent one between king and pope, the king, in Scotland, gaining control in the end.

II. *Teinds or tithes*. In establishing a church on his lands, the landowner gave tenths of the produce of his lands within the area

attached to the church, the true parish being the land which paid
tithes or teinds. This system was accepted on both sides as customary and of long standing; the earliest Scottish record of the
creation of a parish and a parish church, Ednam, donates them,
and the first record of the erection of a parish in the Diocese of
Dunblane, Tullibody,[4] c. 1170, mentions them among the gifts.
Teinds were of three kinds:

(1) garbal or predial, derived from the annual crops;
(2) mixed, derived from things nourished by the land, such as
    cattle, wool, milk, cheese, etc.;
(3) personal, the result of labour.

They were before long divided into (i) great teinds, which were
the garbal (garb=sheaf), and (ii) small, lesser or second teinds,
which were the mixed and the personal together.

i. The great teinds, payable on crops, were usually imposed
    on every parishioner who owned crops, and amounted to
    an income-tax of 10 per cent on the produce, without
    allowances for working expenses;

ii. the lesser or second teinds were imposed on as many of
    the mixed and personal sources of income as could be
    drawn within the net. The number of sources varied, but
    were always burdensome; there are records, in one English
    parish[5] in 1290, imposing them on "wool, flax, pot-herbs,
    leeks, apples, cheese, butter, milk, eggs, calves, chickens,
    geese, hens, sucking-pigs, bees and honey, together with
    tithes of servants in Lent, to wit, of hirelings, hawkers
    (caretakers of hawks for hunting), bakers, carpenters,
    quarrymen, masons, coopers, and limeburners . . . of car-
    ters and brewsters" and half a dozen other small dues. This
    was an unusually severe list of teinded income.

In addition to those two classes of teinds, there are instances of
kings, barons and others imposing a voluntary teind on the various
foods which passed to their kitchens; e.g. Earl Gilbert of Strathearn, gave to the Priory (later Abbey) of Inchaffray teinds of the
wheat, meal, malt, grain, cheese, flesh, fowl and fish, etc., which
were used in his kitchen; he even treated as one of his own
servants the Priory's official collector of these dues.[6] These were

the causes of frequent complaints and the tendency was to exchange them into fixed annual payments; in one instance (CAI
No. 113, dated 1283), an exchange dealing with vicar's teinds
was back-dated to 1247.

III. *The rector* (literally, ruler) of the parish was the cleric who
by his induction was vested in, became proprietor of, the great
teinds. His responsibilities included the payment of synodal,
episcopal, and archidiaconal dues, the exercise of hospitality, the
care of the poor, and the upkeep and repair of certain church
buildings. By the law of the Church, repeated in Councils and in
National Synods (e.g. PSSC No. 80) frequently, he should be
resident and perform the duties of his office, especially cure of
souls, for which he required to have advanced to the order of
priesthood. But this law of residence was very soon relaxed,
until non-residence became common practice, for the Popes
in the plenitude of their power allowed what the Councils forbade, non-residence in numberless cases – and this at a price –
to the scandal of many believers and the breaking-down of
discipline. Often, too, the rector was not canonically competent
to discharge his office, being in minor orders only, and licence
for this too was frequently granted by the Popes.

Licence of non-residence led to clerics seeking to obtain from
the Popes, again for money payments to the Papal Court for its
upkeep, more benefices than one; even twenty and thirty are
known to have provided their incomes to one cleric, who never
resided or did a day's work in any of them. Such clerics were
called pluralists. They spent their time in the universities, in
royal courts or in the service of State officials and Church dignitaries. In this way, influential families secured incomes for the
education of younger sons in universities and for their support
throughout their lives. This scandal, too, like that of non-
residence, is amply vouched for in the papal records, and was
denounced often by high-minded Roman bishops in the strongest
language. The vigorous Pope Alexander III called pluralism a
vice of the French Church, and denounced it as "contrary to
Canon Law, and disapproved by us, although the multitude of
offenders renders it impossible to amend it". He was right; in
1237, when the Papal Legate Otho came to a Council for the
system's reform, in St. Paul's, London, he had to have a guard of
nobles and soldiers, armed and numerous, to protect him against

the pluralist clergy who had gathered to resist his attempt to carry out the orders of the Ecumenical Council of 1215. Scotland suffered seriously from this abuse, but not so prevalently as England or France.

IV. *Vicars* were clerics whom the absentee rectors were bound to appoint, and pay, to do their work in the parishes. The vicarial stipends came to be the lesser teinds. They generally amounted to about a third of the rectorial teinds, but were often less, sometimes being below subsistence level. The rectors tried in some cases to pass on to their vicars some of the rectorial obligations; but even if not, the vicar's stipend was generally so mean that little was left for the poor or for repairs of the chancel or for hospitality, after his physical needs had been met. So neglected were the needs of vicars that statutes are common ordaining that their needs were to be more adequately met. It was laid on bishops to ensure that a vicar had a house, a garden and enough to live on. In the thirteenth century, £5 per annum was aimed at by bishops as the allowance for vicars; few had more and many, perhaps a quarter of them, had less, even down to £3. They were on the whole an underpaid and a "sweated" body of men.

V. *Appropriations* added still further to the confusion of Church organisation. To a rectory could be instituted not only an individual cleric, but in his place a corporation, such as a monastery, nunnery, or priory, which then drew the rectorial teinds for its own uses. The same obligations fell on those corporate rectors as on the individual rectors and it is to be feared, as Roman sources declare, that they were in most cases careless of their burdens and came to regard the rectory as providing unobligated income. Indeed the early monastic rules forbade monks to have anything to do with parochial duties and concerns, because these interrupted the life of devotion to which they were pledged. But most of the Orders soon fell from this high decision. The responsibility of serving the parishes was shuffled on to the shoulders of vicars, and often of chaplains and others in minor orders, who were engaged and paid as the abbot could get away with. Chaplains were not instituted into a benefice with security of tenure and a fixed prebend, but held only an office from which they could be dismissed at the abbot's will. And worse even than that stratagem – the abbeys were often allowed to serve their appropriated parishes by their own monks or canons, at no cost to the abbeys. The common contemporary witness is that religious corporations were almost as bad as absentee rectors. Vicars had to reside, and though often they were unlearned and ignorant men, not able to understand the Latin of the services though able to read the words, they were a saving grace of humble and often devoted service in a vast congeries of broken rules and makeshifts which were to the disgrace and confusion of the Church and the often total neglect of the parishioners, especially the poor and helpless. The general testimony to the evil effects of appropriations accords with the passing in 1351 in the English Parliament of the Statute of Provisors. Even that very strict law with its severe penalties against any who obtained a papal appointment to an English benefice (such persons were called provisors), had to be strengthened in 1352, and later still in 1390; even in 1364-5, so many were evading the Statute that Parliament[7] again dealt with the papal impetrations and provisions of benefices which belonged to the King or other patron, and with the benefices which were being appropriated to cathedrals, abbeys, priories, and such institutions. The record asserts that by these acts "the laws, usages and ancient customs and freedoms of the realm are grievously impeded . . . the houses and habitations of benefices ruined and destroyed, divine worship, charity, hospitality and other works of benevolence betrayed and interrupted. In short, many evils and mischiefs follow, and will continue in the future". The King therefore committed the matter "to the prelates, dukes, counts and barons . . . to advise on those mischiefs . . . to take counsel together, in order to safeguard and maintain him and the rights of the crown, the laws and customs of the realm". Bower[8] said that in 1328 the Pope (John XXII) seemed to have reserved to himself the appointment to all the bishoprics in the world.

Such was in rough outline the system as it came to be by the end of the thirteenth century throughout the Christian world. But of hardly any particular can it be said that it was universally practised; the exceptions were multitudinous in variety of details.

The effects of appropriations, absentee rectors, pluralism, and their attendant abuses were serious both in the realm of ecclesiastical discipline and in that of Church organisation. Large areas of dioceses were virtually taken out of the hands of the bishops, though their financial dues were reserved to them; much of the patronage was in others' grant, though the bishop still had power to refuse to institute a nominee, if he were so minded; in some parishes no resident vicars were appointed, the services being given by a monk or canon regular who resided in the monastery which might be several miles away, and in others chaplains supplied the needs of the people. The bishop was not personally impoverished by such practices, except where these made inroads on teinds which he had set aside for his own support, but in Dunblane at any rate that was the least of the matter, for the various Abbots took over from the Bishop not only the care of the people but much of the rule over his clergy. In addition, appropriators, absentee rectors and pluralists deprived the Cathedral Chapter of rectorial teinds, which were the chief source of prebends for the canons of the Cathedral. Indeed, in the case of the parish church of Kippen, and of others, it was the vicarage which became the prebend of one of the canons of Dunblane. The abuses made it difficult for the Bishop to appoint the number of canons which the cathedral worship and services and sacraments and extra masses demanded, or the number of dignitaries of the Cathedral that were requisite. Indeed, the Cathedral of Dunblane only became organised after 1239, and then its Precentor lived at Inchaffray, and three of its other canons at Cambuskenneth, Lindores and Arbroath, all four being *ex officio* members of the Chapter. This undesirable and makeshift chapter was the best that Clement could make of the already appropriated rectorial teinds within the Diocese. Mensal (personal income) prebends for himself, his Dean, Archdeacon, Chancellor, Treasurer and Official were insufficient for their maintenance, after the needs of the parishes assigned to each of them had been met. It was not until after 1443 that the Diocese of Dunblane gives any appearance of having resources adequate to its responsibilities. Past appropriations still held good, but a new source of revenue was donated then, which lifted it above the abuses and scandals, the manipulations and stratagems which have been outlined, and gave Bishop and Chapter an independent income.

A brief description of the organisation of a medieval cathedral, if given now, will obviate the scattering of explanations throughout the book, and may be welcomed by some readers.

I. *The bishop* was the responsible and consecrated head of the

c

diocese, the *judex ordinarius*, "the ordinary" as he is often called. The clergy, both parochial and cathedral, were, except in instances otherwise provided for, under his discipline and rule. He held his consistory court about once a month, for even four days on occasion. Through it he issued decisions in charters, decrees and letters. This ordinary jurisdiction was his by virtue of his office. When, from illness or absence, he was unable to act he could issue commissions, delegating tasks to any whom he chose. He could, in case of lengthy absence, appoint a member of his chapter to be his vicar general; this office, at first temporary, became a permanent appointment about 1400. Vicars general, as also commissioners, exercised only a deputed authority. The bishop was entitled to two fees: (1) synodals, generally 2s.-3s. yearly from each parish, as a recognition of superiority; (2) procurations, i.e., hospitality on his visitation of a parish, once in three years. This latter was burdensome, as he was allowed by Church law a retinue of 20 to 30 horsemen and often took more. By 1275, this was being changed to a yearly grant, as in Aberdeen. In addition, the bishops sometimes asked for a subsidy, a "benevolence". Other sources of income were one parish church or more, designated as mensal (pertaining to his table). In the Diocese of Dunblane the Bishop's mensal churches were Callander (1238), Muthill (1240) and Kilmahog (1259). Bishop Clement also established his mensal claims to Aberuthven and Tullieden against the claims of Inchaffray Abbey and was granted £16 sterling yearly (1234) in lieu of the teinds. In 1266, Bishop Robert de Prebenda leased for five years from the Hospital of Sts. James and John of Brackley, the lease being renewable for five years at a time at the same rent, its Church of Gasknes (Trinity Gask) and all its revenues and lands for 24 marks *per annum*.

When difficult cases came to the bishop, which required detailed knowledge of Canon Law, or which were contentious, the bishop delegated them to

II. *The official*, who heard them in his court and pronounced sentence. Preliminary enquiries and the carrying out of the sentence were outside of the official's competence and were the bishop's responsibility. The official, for instance, could not deprive clergy of office or benefice. But questions arising out of wills belonged to the official's court. This court, the "consistory court", was identical with that presided over by the bishop; in it, the official exercised the bishop's *dominium*, delegated to him, and from its judgments there was no appeal. The official was often a canon; his deputy was called "commissar". It may be noted that CAI No. 135 speaks of "the bishop, dean, archdeacon (of Dunblane) and their officials for the time being", as if each had an official.

III. *The archdeacon* was the chief instrument of the bishop in his parochial superintendence. He had a court of his own, with an archdeacon's official; this court was similar to the bishop's consistory court. He was a canon and had a prebend, often more than one; he had a stall in the choir and he voted in chapter. His duties included yearly visitation of the parishes (except in the year of the bishop's visitation). As he was more of an inspector than a father in God, the archdeacon was rarely popular; he got the reputation everywhere of being greedy and inconsiderate, and in the thirteenth century there were many complaints of undue expense in his unwelcome visits. Very soon his zeal for visitations declined; more and more archdeacons got indult from the Pope to visit by deputy, and parishes were thankful to pay an agreed daily sum instead of procurations. The archdeacon was just "frozen out", and he ended with having little spiritual function; his work, if done, was done by deputy, and his official, one of the parochial clergy, gathered procuration-fees and fines of defaulters. Naturally, archdeacons sought outlets for their gifts, often in state employment, and we shall find examples of Dunblane's Archdeacons who were whole-time officials of the Royal Treasury. Findogask became the mensal church of the Archdeacon of Dunblane. About 1170, Andreas appears as "Archdeacon of Modhel" (Muthill); later the Archdeacon of Dunblane is sometimes designated "of Strathearn".

Until about the end of the twelfth century archdeaconries, if large, were subdivided into areas, each under a

IV. *Rural dean* (sometimes called "dean of Christianity" or "archpriest"), who supervised them for his superior; by the thirteenth century he was appointed by the bishop, instead of by the archdeacon as at first. He was supposed to be resident and had a seal of office. Only two are found in Dunblane's extant records, Martin, Dean of Menteith, 1235, and Donald, Dean of Muthill, 1272.

It will be noted that the official, the archdeacon and the rural dean were in essence officers who enabled the bishop to fulfil his administrative and supervisory responsibilities in the diocese. For the administration of the cathedral, there was another set of dignitaries, of whom the chief was

V. *The dean.* He was elected by the canons and confirmed by the bishop. He was a canon and had a prebend. He presided over the chapter, which consisted of dean, sub-dean, precentor, arch-deacon, chancellor, treasurer and, in some instances, of the official, all of whom were canons with prebends, along with canons, residential and non-residential, and, in the case of Dun-blane, four canons *ex officio*. Among these, the dean was *primus inter pares* (first among equals). The chapter governed the cathe-dral, and, both in that labour and in large areas of diocesan administration, the bishop was careful to do little or nothing in which he had not the assent of dean and chapter. In 1240 Bishop Clement established Muthill as pertaining to his table, though later Muthill seems to have become dean's mensal. The dean had a deputy called the *sub-dean*, who was second in importance in the chapter. He was sometimes called "rural dean", especially in England; very early the office fell into abeyance. In Dunblane, however, the office was first recorded in 1497, when its holder seems to have been also a notary public. A later holder was clerk of the Chapter.

VI. *The precentor*, or chanter, had care of the services, proces-sions, music, training of vicars choral and singing boys in song-schools or less important institutions serving that purpose. After 1240, the precentor of Dunblane was the Abbot of Inchaffray *ex officio*.

VII. *The chancellor's* duties involved the care of the service-books and the writing of new ones, the composition of the chapter's letters and charters, the appointing of duties for choristers and readers, and he was librarian. He had therefore to be a man of learning. Kilmadock was the Chancellor of Dun-blane's mensal church.

VIII. *The treasurer* had charge of the cathedral treasures, vessels, vestments, relics, ornaments. He had to see to the provision of the necessaries of the sacraments, bread, wine, candles, tapers, rushes.

These last four dignitaries (that is, excluding the sub-dean) usually sat in the end stalls of the two rows of stalls, though it would appear that in Dunblane along with the Archdeacon and the Official they occupied the six dignitary stalls still preserved. Those four, as also the Archdeacon and the Sub-dean, held office which included cure of souls (i.e. pastoral responsibility) until 1529, when their offices were declared sinecures (without cure of souls); their offices demanded continual residence.

IX. *The canons* varied greatly in number; e.g. in 1256 Aberdeen had a dean and 12 canons; in 1425, 29 canons. Canons were either

(1) *non-residential*, having a stall and a vote in chapter, which they seldom used, although they were in the enjoyment of prebends in the diocese. A canon could be without a prebend, but only when he received one did he become a member of the chapter. The non-residents generally exceeded in number the residential canons.

or (2) *residential*. These were clerics who had qualified for office by often long and costly training. They lived in nearby manses, named after the prebends they enjoyed, and they shared in the revenues of the chapter, and in the "commons", the daily distribution of food and drink, a privilege which discouraged unnecessary appointments. The vicarage of Auchterarder, worth £10, was "common of Dunblane"; its income endowed the "commons" of the canons residential.

All canons took an oath *de fideli* (of faithful administration), and vowed obedience to bishop and chapter. Each canon, whether residential or non-residential, had to appoint a vicar of the choir, to sing the services in his stead. These had a stall in the choir, and each was supplied by his canon with surplice and a cope of coarse black cloth, and later (1366) with an amice or cape of grey fur. Sometimes those vicars choral were appointed to chaplainries in the cathedral, in which office they served various altars. They, like the residential canons, were bound to daily attendance in the choir, though there may have been a rota of attendance fixed by the chancellor. It is known that in 1799 Dunblane Cathedral had 32 "Ochiltree" stalls; of these only 10 remain.

From the "Records of the Burgh of Stirling" (p. 259), we get a report of the institution of a canon of Dunblane. It runs thus: On the fourth of August, 1476, sir William Ingleram, chaplain, presented letters of collation of John, Bishop of Dunblane, under his round seal, directed to magister John Drummond, Dean of the Cathedral Church of Dunblane, which being received by the said Dean with due reverence, he passed to the choir and chapter-house of the said Church, with said William and witnesses, and assigned William to a stall in the choir and a place in the chapter-house called the canonry and prebend of Cummery (Comrie), and gave him real and corporal possession of the said canonry and prebend.

It remains to mention the strong class-differentiation between the higher clergy and the inferior. Among the latter were vicars, chaplains, and such, who had had little education; they had mostly to be content with poor incomes.[9] The higher clergy were gener-ally men of learning and high professional attainments, often men of aristocratic birth, and by the thirteenth century often bearing university degrees. The younger sons of noble families, the natural sons of kings, earls and landowners had the road to prefer-ment eased for them through papal indult and family influence; they often secured church revenues which enabled them for years on end to study in foreign universities. The higher offices in the Church were often, however, filled by clerics of respectable, if less exalted birth; through an academic training, through service in the royal administration or households of the aristocracy or of bishops, such on occasion even rose to be bishops.

NOTES

1. e.g. G. G. Coulton: *Scottish Abbeys, Mediaeval Panorama*, and *Five Centuries of Religion*; Dowden: *Mediaeval Church in Scotland*; A. Hamilton Thompson: *English Monasteries*, to mention only a few.

2. T. No. 264. SHS, Miscellany VI, pp. 25ff.

3. Coulton: *Mediaeval Panorama*, 168.

4. CR No. 216. See NMS I 14 xi, for Ednam, the first known parish in Scotland, 1107 × 1124.

5. Tadcaster, as quoted in Coulton: *Mediaeval Panorama*, p. 163.

6. CAI Nos. 16, 51, 76.

7. Rotuli Parliamentorum II 284 (Record Office – 7 vols., dated c.1783). The situation was similar in Scotland, but the Scottish Kings fixed the ground of complaint wholly on the questions of patronage and on restricting the trans-ference of Scottish coin to Rome for the "purchase" of benefices – cf. AP II 5, 14, 16 (1428), 144 (1482), 166 (1483/4).

8. Sc, VI c, 45.

9. In medieval times, "stipend", used today of the income of an ordained clergyman, meant the payment made to a cleric in lower orders (e.g. chaplain, clerk, etc.) who held his office only at the will of a superior – it was his hire, he was a stipendiary. A prebend was the parochial income attached to a cathedral canonry or similar benefice; its root meaning was food, fodder, corn. A rector's portion of the teinds, revenues and fruits of a church, including his house, was his rectory; a vicar's portion was his vicarage.

CHAPTER III

THE EARLY BISHOPS

M.	1155 –
LAURENCE	c.1160 – c.1178.
SYMON	c.1178 – c.1196.
W.	c.1196 – c.1197.
JONATHAN	c.1198 – 1210.
ABRAHAM	c.1212 – c.1225.
RALPH	c.1225 – c.1226 (elect only).
OSBERT	c.1227 – c.1230.

OF the early Bishops of Dunblane we have only the little knowledge to be gathered from contemporary charters, which are few until after the coming of Bishop Clement in 1233. Until then the Bishops are very impersonal entities, mainly names with titles in lists of charter witnesses. Many of the early charters are undated, but their dates can be fixed, often only approximately, by internal evidence or by comparison of witnesses, whose dates of office or death happen otherwise to be known. But how these men ruled their dioceses, established the parishes, appointed their clergy, what kind of men they were, where they came from, and what their income, there is very little indeed to tell us. Every episcopal commonplace book, note-book, record and charter, belonging to Dunblane has been lost, and I have failed to trace their present habitat, if any, in Scotland or abroad; every register of the Chapter and of the Cathedral courts has gone; the life of S. Blane written by Archdeacon George Newton (died c.1531) only exists in the writings of two authors who had read it and used it in part; yes, all medieval records are gone, save one, the register or minute-book of the court of the Official of Dunblane Cathedral,[1] and the volume covers only 1551 to 1554. It would be difficult to imagine a scene more historically bare. The Dunblane picture has to be painted from records of other institutions, civil and ecclesiastical, in Scotland and elsewhere.

The early Bishops now demand our attention. The earliest-known, M., has already been dealt with.[2] His date is 1155. He was followed by

BISHOP LAURENCE   c.1160 – c.1178

All we know of Laurence is that he was a witness to two charters, one of Dunfermline,[3] 1160 × 1162, and one of St. Andrews,[4] 1163 × 1169, and that he granted a charter to Cambuskenneth Abbey,[5] c.1170. In this last he gave to the Augustinian Canons of the Abbey of Saint Mary, often called the Abbey of Stirling, the Church of Tullibody with its lands and teinds and all rights pertaining to it, except the rights belonging to the Bishop of Dunblane, this gift to become effective only on the death of the rector of Tullibody, Hugh de Rokesburg, who was also clerk to the Chancellor of Scotland. The Bishop's grant followed the gift, c.1170, by the landowner of Tullibody, Simon, son of Makbeth, of the church of his manor, with lands and teinds, to the Abbey, for the welfare of the souls of himself, his ancestors and his successors; this, too, was to be effected only on Hugh's death. Later the episcopal rights were settled by agreement, the Abbey to pay to the Bishop of Dunblane four shillings per annum.[6] Simon's charter has among its witnesses two interesting clerics: Nicholas, Chancellor of Dunblane Cathedral, the first known holder of that office, and Magister Abraham, "at this time"[7] chaplain to Gilbert, Earl of Strathearn, probably the cleric who became Bishop of Dunblane c. A.D. 1212.

In the agreement fixing the Bishop's dues at four shillings, among the witnesses are "J. de Dunblane and the whole Chapter". It would seem that J. was Dean and witnessed for the Chapter; it is noteworthy that, c.1170-1, there was a chapter, but in the absence of names and titles we do not know its size. It is unlikely that at this period it was large or fully developed.

The Bishop's charter c.1170 has some features worthy of note:

(1) One witness is Andreas, Archdeacon of Modhel; if, as I think, Modhel means Muthill, Andreas is the first known Archdeacon of the Diocese. He may have been designated "of Modhel" if he resided there at this time when the organisation of the diocese was still tentative. Later Muthill belonged to the Bishop of Dunblane's income, and later still, to the Dean's.

(2) This charter of Laurence is the first recorded instance in medieval Dunblane of the appropriation of a rectory or parsonage to an abbey. Within thirty years the Diocese of Dunblane began to be denuded of its parishes, until twenty-six parish churches had been appropriated to nine abbeys, and it was left with about twelve parish churches only, of which it controlled the whole parochial teind.

Before Laurence died about 1178 William the Lion, King of Scots from 1165 to 1214, was captured at Alnwick in A.D. 1174. In December of that year, at Falaise in Normandy, he surrendered Scotland's independence to Henry II of England, as the price of his freedom. King, earls and barons did homage to Henry, but the bishops and abbots refused their homage and Henry had to be content with their oath of obedience.[8] Scottish castles, including Stirling, Edinburgh and Berwick, were surrendered, and Gilbert, third Earl of Strathearn, was among the hostages delivered to the English overlord as sureties of good faith.

It is on record that after the Convention of Falaise, Henry of England gave honours, bishoprics, abbacies and other distinctions in Scotland, "or, let me say rather" says the chronicler, Robert de Torigny[9] "they were given by his counsel". In the same year, other writers[10] speak of the people of French origin in Scotland and Galloway and the numbers of English in Galloway and in the castles and towns of Scotland. The Church likewise was being manned with clergy, many from the English-speaking Lothians and more numerous French from south of the Border. William the Lion, about 1178, founded the Abbey of Arbroath (Aberbrothoc) and dedicated it to St. Thomas Becket, murdered only eight years before. English, that is, at this stage, French rather than Anglo-French, influences were on the increase in Scottish affairs, ecclesiastical and civil.

BISHOP SYMON   c.1178 – c.1196

Symon came from England, and was most probably Norman, like his predecessor. He appears first in a St. Andrews charter,[11] dated 1178 × 1180. He is named a witness in three other charters[12]; in the third, the significance of which will later appear, Earl Gilbert of Strathearn gives three acres to "the brethren serving God at Inchaffray", c.1195. But three charters granted by Symon are immediately noteworthy:

(1) An undated charter, in which he confirmed, as did Bishop Abraham later, the gift, by an unknown predecessor, of the Church of Logie Atheran (Logie Airthrey) to the Nuns of North Berwick.[13] A fascinating list of witnesses includes Jonathan, Archdeacon (later Bishop of Dunblane, probably); Thomas, Dean of Dunblane; Malpol, Prior of the Culdees of Muthill; Michael, rector of Muthill; John, rector of Kilbryde; Gregory, rector of Tullibodevin (Tullibody); Malcolm "our chaplain"; and two Culdees of Muthill, called Sithach and Malcolm. The mixture of Celtic and Norman churchmen argues that the two Churches had come to an amicable working arrangement. Again a church has been appropriated to an institution for its support, this time at a considerable distance. In this case, the vicarage seems to have remained in control of the Bishop.

(2) Perhaps between 1189 and 1196, Symon granted by charter to Arbroath Abbey[14] the Church of Abernethy with its chapels of Dron, Dunbog and Erolyn, and certain lands pertaining to them. Archdeacon Jonathan and Michael, rector of Muthill, are again in the list of witnesses; others are chaplains and clerks of Gilbert of Strathearn and his brother Malise; Malise is himself a witness, which would perhaps indicate a particular Strathearn interest in the lands of Abernethy.

(3) About 1190, Symon gave the Church of St. John of Inchaffray to "Isaac and his successors".[15] The grant included the right of burial there to any who desired it, so long as the dues of their parish cemetery were met. The charter is most interesting; it belongs to the days before Gilbert adhered to the Roman Church and got permission, about 1200, from the Pope to transform "the brethren serving God at Inchaffray"[16] into a Priory of Augustinian Canons. At the date of the charter, Isaac was head of a Celtic monastery at Inchaffray; a church, dedicated in Roman style to St. John the Evangelist, had been built nearby by Gilbert who, still Celtic in his allegiance, now handed it over to Isaac, the chief of the Celtic brethren. Again the witnesses are distinctly Celtic – Malgirhe the canon (the first known canon of Dunblane), Sythack the Culdee (as in charter (1) above), Gillemure the deacon (the first recorded deacon of the Diocese). It looks significant that the only non-Celtic witness, Richard, is designated chaplain of Earl Gilbert. He would almost certainly be a Roman cleric, probably Norman, and as chaplain would play

a significant part in converting Gilbert to the Roman allegiance. Symon's tenure of the See probably ended about A.D. 1196.

BISHOP W.   c.1196 – c.1197

The only appearance of Bishop W. is as principal in an undated charter,[17] by which he confirmed to the Abbey of Cambuskenneth the Church of Kincardine, now known as Kincardine in Menteith (originally founded by the Celt, S. Lolan), with all its chapels and pertinents "as the charter of King William (the Lion) testifies". The witnesses provide no clue even to an approximate date; but c.1196 would appear to be more consistent with the general situation than Fraser's suggestion of 1210 in his "Cambuskenneth Charters". With this Bishop Dowden agrees, "if there was a Bishop W. of Dunblane"; he thinks W. is an error for Symon[18]; Spottiswoode[19] places W. after Bishop Abraham (who died about 1225) and says he was William de Bosco, Chancellor of Scotland. But this cannot be maintained.

I put forward two reasons for the dates above given:

(1) Six of the witnesses are Celts, three of them now Cathedral clergy (Cormac, the Bishop's chaplain; Malise, parson of Dunblane; and Bean, master of Dunblane), and three still designated as "of Muthill" (Malpole, Prior of the Culdees; Michael, parson of Muthill; and his chaplain, Makbeth). The charter belongs therefore to a date before 1200, when some scheme of united labours between the Culdees and the Roman clergy was in operation.

(2) Two of the witnesses, Malpole and Michael above, also appear in Bishop Symon's undated charter confirming Logie-Atheran to the North Berwick Nunnery; but in Bishop Jonathan's charter, c.1200, confirming Tullibody to Cambuskenneth, others holding those offices are among the witnesses.

I cannot share Bishop Dowden's doubt of W.'s existence, because I cannot believe that a bishop who drew up the charter (note "my chaplain, Cormac") would not notice a mistake in his initial, which opened the charter. It is clear however that he can have been bishop for a short time only, and I have tentatively given his dates as c.1196 – c.1197.

During the years of the early Bishops of Dunblane, the Scottish Church was finally delivered from the claim of the Archbishop of

York to be its metropolitan, a claim which had frustrated David I's desire in 1125 to have the Bishop of St. Andrews given the rank of archbishop. The Popes had consistently, from 1122, urged the Scots bishops to submit to York as metropolitan of all churches north of the Humber, but this was as consistently opposed by the bishops, as it was by the King. But in 1175, Pope Alexander III constituted the See of Glasgow "a special daughter of Rome" subject to the Pope alone,[20] and in 1188, Clement III, in a letter to William the Lion, took the Scottish Church under the immediate protection of the Papal See, a decision which was accepted by his successors in the Papacy. Even as late as 1176 at Northampton the claim of York was resisted by the Scottish bishops; twelve years later the Pope wiped it out. Though the bishops were Norman, their patriotism was not in doubt. The final recognition of the independence of Scotland's Church from the claims made by the Church of England came in 1218, when Pope Honorius III issued a bull to that effect, a bull which began with the papal concession to King Alexander II of the independence of Scotland itself (T. No. 18). This was a document of supreme importance to Scotland and its Church in years to come, and gave heart and courage in the long struggle yet to be endured.

In affairs of State, Richard I of England in 1189 acknowledged the independence of Scotland which William the Lion had bartered for his freedom. He also restored the sureties which had been given under the Convention of Falaise (1174). These most welcome gifts were doubtless inspired by Richard's desires to win the support of the Scottish King in the Crusade to which he was pledged, and to leave behind him, when he was fighting in the Holy Land, a peaceful and contented Scotland.

Bishop Jonathan   c.1198 – 1210

Jonathan, in all probability the Archdeacon of the name under Bishop Symon, was a bishop of more than local significance.[21] About 1203 he was papal judge delegate,[22] along with the Bishop of Dunkeld, in an intricate dispute about the teinds of Eccles (St. Ninians, Stirling), between the Abbots of Dunfermline and Cambuskenneth; it began in his consistorial court, though later the Pope committed it to five mandatories because of its peculiar difficulty.

In local church matters of a routine nature, Jonathan confirmed to Cambuskenneth Abbey, c.1200, Bishop Laurence's
grant of the Churches of Tillicoultry and Kincardine "with their
chapels", etc., "saving the rights of the Bishop". This charter
(CR No. 217) is interesting chiefly for its clerical witnesses, who
are again predominantly Celtic; they include Malgegill, Prior of
Muthill; Malise, Prior of Inchaffray; Gillecrist, "our chaplain";
Patrick, son of Gillemanthach, also "our chaplain"; and Gille-
michael, rector of Muthill; another is Maurice, "our chaplain",
Norman as his name shows. The mention of Malise, Prior of
Inchaffray,[23] takes us a long stage further into the growth and
development of the Diocese and its parishes and demands full
explanation now.

Jonathan's episcopate is noteworthy for the rapid growth in
wealth and power of Inchaffray Priory through the munificence
of Gilbert, Earl of Strathearn, who appropriated to it many
parishes of the Diocese of Dunblane. He made the various appropriations by right of his being the landowner, and therefore lord
and patron. The Abbot got the Bishop, the King and the Pope
to confirm separately what the Earl had done in virtue of his
dominium, though the Bishop in the charters of appropriation
was often noted as witness, which was a sign of assent. But
bishops had their dioceses to organise and their canons to provide
with prebends, and they must have been drawn betwixt the two
opposing interests. Earl Gilbert's gifts of parish churches with
teinds, various incomes, and sometimes rents of land or land
itself, to Inchaffray, were of unusual number and frequency; and
each appropriation deprived the Bishop of the control of teinds
which he required as prebends for canons, of patronage, and of
parochial and diocesan responsibilities. But the bishops were
helpless in the face of the monastic enthusiasm pervading the
Church, and of the powerful influence of great founding landowners in their dioceses. They shared heartily in the zeal out
of which the planting of abbeys grew. Nevertheless, it cost
Bishop Clement years of bargaining to undo some of the damage
done to the Diocese with Jonathan's assent by Earl Gilbert, and
the Diocese had to wait for two hundred and forty years before
the opportunist capacity of Bishop Michael Ochiltree enabled it
to rise above its poverty.

Gilbert succeeded to the earldom of Strathearn in 1171, and

died in 1223. The family of Strathearn was Celtic and true to the Celtic Church until the middle of Gilbert's tenure of the earldom. Probably from the first, he conformed to the Norman ways now in full momentum in the land – he married twice into Norman families, adopted the use of charters, and accepted the feudal tenure of land which had displaced the Celtic tenure in Scotland. In spite of this Norman sympathy, however, he supported, as had his forebears, the old and admittedly decaying Celtic Church. Even about 1198, Gilbert presented to "the brethren serving God and St. John at the Isle of Masses (Inchaffray) in Foulis the Church of S. Cathan of Aberuthven", with its teinds, oblations and obventions of all kinds, as well as the land which his father, Ferteth, and his mother, Ethan, had previously given to them.[24] His parents had been content, c.1160, to give an endowment of land to the Church of Aberuthven; Gilbert gave teinds and other gifts as well. Ferteth and Ethan are not recorded as endowing the Church as part of the Diocese but as giving land to the Church; but the original gift may have been given by word of mouth before witnesses, and not recorded in a charter. However, Bishop Clement, later[25] regarded the Church of Aberuthven as having been bestowed on the Bishop for the support of his table. Gilbert's charter was witnessed by Celts and Normans, notably, as we shall see, by Gillecrist, son of Gilbert and his Countess, Maulde (Matilda).

But very soon a change is to be noted. Earl Gilbert by charter,[26] c.1199, granted the Church of Madderty (Diocese of Dunkeld) to the Church of St. John the Evangelist in Inchaffray. This Church of St. John Evangelist, previously given[27] by Bishop Symon to "the brethren serving God at Inchaffray", now stands in its own right and "the brethren" are not explicitly mentioned. Among the witnesses Gillecrist, son of the Earl, does not appear; instead there are "William, Ferthed and Robert, my sons". It was about this time that Gilbert presented[28] to Inchaffray his personal teinds of food used in his kitchen. The way was being prepared for the foundation of the Roman Priory of Inchaffray, in 1200, as an Augustinian House of Canons. To this gift Jonathan was consenting.

The founding charter[29] of Inchaffray Priory tells perhaps the determining reason for the change of allegiance on Gilbert's part. He and his wife, it says, had buried their eldest son's body in the cemetery of the Church (this would be St. John's) when he died

(1198 or 1199). This had made the Church and its cemetery precious to them. This catastrophe brought the resulting change, not unaided perhaps by Gilbert's having already adopted the Norman ways in secular affairs, by his having a Norman wife who shared his grief, and by the fact that his ministering chaplain was Richard, a Norman. It is also possible that St. John's had been built by Gilbert as a church for his retainers. All this is understandable; but even with the erection of the Priory, the break with the Celtic Church was not complete, for Gilbert committed all its possessions to the care and administration of "Sir Malise presbyter and hermit", granting him freedom to call to him whomsoever he desired, [30] and to instruct them in the rules of St. Augustine. Sir Malise, surely a Celt, was perhaps one of the brethren of the Celtic Monastery who had been persuaded to accept the new order of things.

Meantime, an interesting tale unfolds of the Celtic Monastery's endeavours to safeguard its position. Being aware of the changing outlook of the Earl about 1199, the brethren petitioned[31] the Pope, who in response sent forth a bull on 4 December 1200, in favour of "J., hermit and the brethren of St. John of Strathearn", taking under his protection their persons, and their properties, especially those granted to them by Earl Gilbert, which they feared they were in danger of losing. "To no man therefore is it lawful", ends the bull, "to infringe this writ of our protection and confirmation; such would bring down the indignation of God Omnipotent and of the blessed Apostles Peter and Paul." Gilbert, however, having asked for papal confirmation of the change he had brought about in Inchaffray, received from the same Pope, Innocent III, a bull,[32] dated 30 June 1203, taking the Monastery of St. John of Inchaffray under his protection, and confirming it in its many possessions and rights under fifteen heads. There is now no mention of "J., hermit and the brethren"; some of them had doubtless become Augustinian Canons with Sir Malise; if there were others, they were forgotten. The same censures are now uttered on the opposite side. A Pope could not be expected to remember the anathemas and decisions of three years back, when he probably knew nothing of what was happening. The story told him by Gilbert's emissaries would stress the value of the new foundation; was it not supported by three Bishops, and three Abbots? Was not the old Church in decay?

Earl Gilbert's gifts to Inchaffray were generous in the extreme – in 1200, S. Cathan's of Aberuthven, S. Patrick's of Strogeith, S. Mackessog's of Auchterarder and S. Bean's of Kinkell; before 1203, S. Serf's of Dunning; S. Serf's of Monzievaird in 1203-4; in 1210, S. Bean's of Foulis, and later the Churches of Tullieden, Kilbryde, Tullikettle and Holy Trinity, Gask, this last the only one of the lot not known to have been an original Celtic foundation; Strowan was appropriated to Inchaffray in 1282-3, before which it was part of Monzievaird, probably being a dependent chapel. To his personal tithes the Earl added rights of fishing, fowling, cutting of timber, feeding of swine, a mill on the Pow and another on the Earn, tofts, stanks, lands at Stirling, the goods of executed criminals, all money fines in his court of barony, a piece of marsh. The Priory of Inchaffray got off to a good start.

In this formidable list of Earl Gilbert's charters, between 1200 and 1211, certain witnesses of ecclesiastical interest appear[33] for the first time:

Matthew, rector of Dunning; Martin, rector of Monzievaird; Malise, rector of Strowan; Abraham, the Earl's chaplain (often); Brice, rector of Crieff (often); Gilbert, son of the Archdeacon of Strathearn (either Jonathan or John, Archdeacon 1198-1208); Arthur, son of Abraham the Earl's chaplain; Issachar, chaplain of Foulis Wester; Richard, knight of Kinbuck; Malise, rector of Foulis Wester; Malise, rector of Kilbryde. The rectors in this list were probably in some cases the last appointments to those parishes by the Bishop of Dunblane before the parishes were appropriated by Earl Gilbert to Inchaffray Priory.

In 1200, Innocent III confirmed[34] its possessions to Arbroath Abbey, mentioning the Church of Abernethy granted by "our venerable brother Jonathan, Bishop of Strathearn". This Church had chapels at Dron, which later became a parish church, at Dunbog, and at Errol. This gift of Jonathan's had repercussions in 1239 when Bishop Clement's claim on the teinds of Abernethy were settled.

We are given a vivid picture of the state of the Roman Church in England in Jonathan's time. Scottish conditions were neither better nor worse. The Pope gave authority to Peter, Bishop of Winchester, to reform his diocese[35]:

D

to correct abuses in monasteries and churches subject to him;

to revoke alienations made by his predecessors of property belonging to his episcopal income;

to compel archdeacons, deans and others of his diocese to take orders (i.e. ordination befitting their offices) according to the decrees of the Lateran Council;

to compel those who have obtained parsonages (rectories) to appoint vicars to serve them in person;

to restrain those clerks who practise usury or other base gain, adulterers and those who publicly keep women;

to remove the sons of priests who hold churches in immediate succession to their fathers;

to put a stop to the traffic in church patronage.

The Statutes of the Church in Scotland bear similar testimony. The first two hundred pages of the Calendar of the Papal Register, between 1200 and 1240, carry a large number of references to married clerks, mostly in the lowest orders, in which the clerics were hardly differentiated from laymen. In this concern it must be recognised that for hundreds of years the Popes found it difficult to enforce their decrees that chastity was the rule of clerical life. Obedience to those decrees was compromised in Scotland by the fact that the clergy of the Celtic Church was a married clergy. Decrees of General Councils against pluralism were increasingly ineffective, the Popes granting dispensations most freely. The right of vicars even to bare sustenance was often denied, in spite of the thunderings of Councils. While such evils have to be seen in perspective and not over-emphasised, it is yet true that, on the showing of papal mandates, decrees of Councils and episcopal visitations, much was unsatisfactory and damaged the health of the Church and its prestige in the eyes of the people. At the same time the numerous lives of honest and hard-working clergy, high and low, must be gratefully recognised, for they kept the Church in honourable service alike of God and of man.

Fordun informs us that Jonathan died in 1210 and was buried at Inchaffray.[36]

BISHOP ABRAHAM c.1212 – c.1225

Abraham[37] succeeded Bishop Jonathan, c.1211 or 1212. It is natural to assume that he was the cleric who witnessed many of Earl Gilbert's charters, as "Abraham, chaplain of the Earl"; if so, he had a son Arthur.[38] He was himself the son of a priest.[39] He was consecrated Bishop by William Malvoisine of St. Andrews.

His papal appointments show the high esteem in which he was held. On several occasions he was appointed papal judge delegate, to whom the Pope referred causes which had been appealed to Rome. He gave judgment in his Court in 1214 against the Culdees of Abernethy in their dispute with the Abbot of Arbroath about certain teinds.[40] With others he was appointed to settle a teind dispute between Dunfermline and Cambuskenneth.[41] The claim of the latter caused such angry discussion that William the Lion had to interpose and bring about peace. He was one of four bishops mandated to excommunicate and interdict those who had "strippen, beaten, stoned, mortally wounded with a fork, and burnt Adam, Bishop of Caithness".[42]

In local church affairs, he witnessed numerous charters of Earl Gilbert, confirming earlier gifts and granting new donations and privileges to Inchaffray. Being intimate with the Strathearn family, Abraham was frequently called upon; he witnessed charters of Robert, Gilbert's son; of Ysenda, Countess of Strathearn; of Elphin, Prior of Inchaffray; and also of Earl Gilbert.[43] He also himself confirmed[44] his predecessors' grants of churches to Inchaffray, Cambuskenneth, Arbroath, Lindores and the Nuns of North Berwick. These were routine tasks. On one occasion, however, he did try to take a stand in the interests of his diocese; but even with the support of Earl Gilbert, he came badly out of the dispute. Before 1214, Guido, Abbot of Lindores, claimed the Church of Muthill; it was a very thin claim, but intricate, involving the land and Church of Eglesmagril (later a parish church) in the parish of Dron, the Church of Muthill, and teinds of Clavage in the parish of Dunning. Many discussions took place before the papal judges and both parties agreed[45] to accept without appeal the findings of an arbiter, Bishop William Malvoisine of St. Andrews. The verdict was that the Bishop of Dunblane was to possess the Church of Muthill, "as granted by Malise, brother of Earl Gilbert", but had to pay ten marks annually to Lindores. Though Abraham got this reduced to eight by his granting Eglesmagril to Lindores on the death of Patrick its rector, Guido showed by the charters which he caused to be drawn confirming the settlement that he was well satisfied; an impressive array of seals clinched the issue. The decision was so unjust to Dunblane that when Bishop Clement came to the See he immediately complained[46] to the Pope, who, on 3 November 1234, appointed three judges to review the verdict. Their judgment, given on 16 April 1235, is a delightful example of how to say "Yes" and "No" at the same time, and how to save the reputation of a still living bishop and arbiter while condemning his findings as unjust. It runs: "We have diligently examined the case, and although we have found that the decree-arbitral pronounced by the venerable man, the Bishop of St. Andrews, was just, and pronounced in due form, and in good faith, yet we have found that the Church of Dunblane was injured by the Bishop of St. Andrews in the estimate of the payment of the ten marks. Wherefore, wishing that those things which were lawfully done should remain firmly established, and that those things which perchance through error were not quite lawfully done should be recalled to their due state, we have pronounced sentence condemning the Abbot and Convent of Lindores to pay annually to the Bishop of Dunblane and his successors the sum of five marks, the decree-arbitral of the venerable man, the Bishop of St. Andrews, still remaining in force."[47] It was now Clement's turn to lock the door securely on the settlement, which was crucial for him. In several charters Bishop, Abbot and others accepted the new agreement; the whole clergy of the Diocese, and later four abbots, and in a separate charter the Dean and Chapter, ratified it. One of the charters[48] asserted that the Church of Muthill pertained to the table of the Bishop of Dunblane.

After the death of Earl Gilbert, in 1223, there was a remarkable scene in the Church of Strogeith (Blackford) about 1224. Robert, son of Gilbert, was publicly brought to promise loyal obedience to the Abbey of Inchaffray's interests.[49] It was usual for a new earl to be asked by abbots and others to confirm the gifts made to them by his predecessors, and this he did generally by the granting of a charter of confirmation; where there was no argument the charter was routine. It would seem however that Robert had been troublesome after his father's death, perhaps desiring some freedom from the consequences of his father's extraordinary generosity to the Abbey. Therefore he was taken to the Church, and there he promised "in the hand of Abraham,

Bishop of Dunblane, and before witnesses, that he would never in his whole life unjustly harass Innocent, Abbot of Inchaffray, or the Convent, but rather treat them as his most special friends, and, saving his own rights and honour, would, as far as he could, increase the house. He confirmed them in the possession of Gask and Strogeith and all their churches, lands, possessions, liberties, rights, customs, easements and teinds, as his father's and his own charters contained. As patron of their house, he will prosecute their rights as he would his own, will make no peace with the Abbey's enemies without the counsel of the Abbot and Convent and only after securing their rights and their honour." Bishop Abraham doubtless rejoiced that day in the repentance of one of his pupils and in the restored good fortune of Inchaffray; but to make the assurance doubly secure, the Abbey got, on 8 June 1225, a charter[50] from King Alexander II taking the Abbey under his protection.

During Abraham's episcopate, an unusually interesting charter[51] was drawn by *Macbeth rex scolarum de Dunblayn et ejusdem loci scolastici* (Macbeth, king of the schools of Dunblane, and the scholars of the same place). There is only one other known instance of this title, *rex scolarum*, which may mean "governor" and may have included "headmaster". *Rex* and *scolastici* by this charter surrender to Lindores Abbey the conveth[52] which they were accustomed to receive in the township of Eglesmagril; this, in return for two shillings payable each year by the Bishop of Dunblane out of his rents of Drumendufelis (Drumdruils in Dunblane, perhaps). The other instance is found about the same time in a charter in which *Malduveny rex scolarum de Mothel* (Muthill) *et ejusdem loci scolastici* made the same agreement with Lindores, the Bishop again paying two shillings per annum in exchange for the conveth. There were early schools at Stirling, Perth, Abernethy, Linlithgow, Glasgow, Elgin, St. Andrews and elsewhere, of various origin, of which little is known; but it would appear that the schools mentioned in the above charters, Dunblane and Muthill, though Celtic in origin, had continued into the medieval period and were now giving up their separate existence and regularising their affairs, preparatory to their entrance into the scholastic system of the Roman Church.

During Abraham's time support for a Crusade was preached in Scotland by papal legates.[53] It is difficult to be exact about the

Crusade which the Pope desired on this occasion Scotland to support. Dr W. B. Stevenson in his *Crusades in the East* says that only the first, in 1099, can correctly be given a number, and that, though scholars have tried to systematise them as eight in number, there were more than eight, and they formed a continuous stream through most of the twelfth and thirteenth centuries. Crusades, though pressed by Pope on King, baron and commoner, never commanded the zeal of Scotland; not many of the aristocracy volunteered; others did, but not in enthusiastic companies of size. But the papal support of Crusades began, in Scotland and throughout Christendom, and kept in being, a long and testing spell of taxations in the Church, in every parish and office, adding considerably to the burdens of church folk, great and small. These subsidies for the deliverance of the Holy Land from Moslem rule were exacted by papal officers charged with large authority and privileges, which they used to threaten or to cajole the churchmen and the other faithful into obedient generosity.

The date of Abraham's death is unknown. It would appear that he was chaplain in the Strathearn family for many years, and he may have been in his sixties when he became Bishop of Dunblane. His episcopate lasted at least for ten years and maybe for fourteen.

BISHOP RALPH   *elected c.1225; resigned c.1226*

Radulphus is but a shadow of a bishop, for after election he resigned before consecration. An Inchaffray charter (CAI No. 60) informs us that the election of the Bishop of Dunblane belongs to the whole body of the clergy of Dunblane. The patron would present and the clergy in chapter would elect. This was in 1234.

Only two facts are known about him: (1) he witnessed,[54] as *Dominus Rad., electus Dunblanensis* along with *Dominus Innocentius*, Abbot of Inchaffray (the title of *dominus*, lord, is becoming popular with clerics and laymen of superior consequence), an insignificant charter, which cannot be dated more precisely than between 1220 and 1230. (2) On 12 January 1225/6, in a letter[55] to the Bishops of St. Andrews, Moray, and Caithness, Honorius III wrote "our beloved son R. elected Bishop of Dunblane" has resigned in our presence; he directs them to authorise a new election, and to confirm it, if the appointment is canonically in order.

It is not difficult to imagine why he resigned Dunblane, before consecration. The later petition by Bishop Clement to the Pope tells a sorry tale of chaos and poverty. Dunblane was a depressed diocese and Ralph was perhaps not made for such testing. The Diocese was a hopeless proposition to one who perhaps knew only the dioceses of France and the French tongue. His resignation was prudent, if not courageous.

BISHOP OSBERT   c.1227 – c.1230

That Osbert was consecrated Bishop of Dunblane is known from an inspection[56] by the Chapter of Dunblane, in 1240, of the charters of previous Bishops; they name Symon, Jonathan, Abraham, and Osbert, as well as the contemporary Clement. In consideration of its poverty, Osbert allowed Cambuskenneth[57] to supply Kincardine,[58] Tullibody and Tillicoultry by chaplains or clerks or its own canons. There is one dated reference, and only one, to Osbert; in 1230, as "O. Bishop of Stratherne" he witnessed[59] at a Council held in Dundee a settlement of a dispute between Arbroath and Balmerino Abbeys. The Scotichronicon[60] tells that he died in 1231, at Holyrood Abbey, where he had taken the vows of an Augustinian Canon. Thomas Dempster[61] calls him "rhetorician, poet, philosopher and theologian, but greater than these gifts was his sanctity". He also calls him *beatus* (blessed). No more is known of Osbert than this brief paragraph tells. Dunblane was too much for him, as it had been for Ralph; ill-health may have hastened his retiral. But Osbert at least tried to be Bishop of Dunblane.

In its first seventy years the Diocese of Dunblane was only spasmodically organised. Deans, Archdeacons and one Chancellor are known intermittently from c.1170; the other clergy of the Cathedral were chaplains, a deacon, a *sacerdos* (priest), a rector, a magister, several clerks, and three canons c.1214; most of these seem to have been Culdees who had transferred their allegiance to the Roman Church. The same general picture emerges in the organisation of the parishes, where the sparsity of early clerics is in keeping with the slow development of the See, especially after 1200, when the rise of Inchaffray Abbey, while it seriously hampered the Bishop's authority in the Diocese and crippled the resources of the Chapter, yet by the naming and separating of the parishes appropriated to the Abbey, aided the setting up of parish churches and boundaries. The situation degenerated from

1200; no new name appeared among the clergy of the Cathedral between 1214 and 1235, save Alexander, Ada, and Thomas, who though called "servants of Bishop Osbert" were perhaps clerics in minor orders.[62] The See of Dunblane was gasping for life and a bishop of heroic mould was needed to restore it to vigour. In 1233 the man came in the person of Clement, of the Order of Preaching Friars.

NOTES

1. This is LACC. See Appendix 1550-1559, n. 5.

2. Chapter I; also BFDC 1938.

3. RDD 24.

4. RPSA 132-133.

5. CR No. 219.

6. The charter, CR No. 218, states that this sum is "for all episcopal rights which pertained to the bishop, and on account of all debts due to him in connexion with the Church". It was not, therefore, a sum paid for providing a vicar.

7. Gilbert became Earl only in 1171. This fixes the date of CR No. 216, (i.e. Simon's charter), as 1171 or later. CR dates it c.1170.

8. LA p. 193.

9. Quoted in LA p. 203.

10. e.g. Roger de Hoveden II 63; William of Newburgh in No. 82 of Rolls Series I 186/7.

11. RPSA 147. DBS 194.

12. Reg. Vetus de Aberbrothoc I 16; RDD 85; CAI No. 2.

13. CMN 6-7. As well as Logie-Atheran, there is early mention elsewhere of Logie-Woloc, a Celtic foundation named after Woloc, who was trained at Candida Casa, though some identify him as a monk of Iona. But a monk of Iona had no entry to Logie (or to Dunnet, which is also S. Woloc's). Logie-Atheran was probably to the east (cf. Airthrey) and Logie-Woloc to the west of the district. Logie-Woloc was probably absorbed in its neighbour; no ruins of its church can be found, and its name disappears very early. Hutchison's "Menteith" says that one of the two Logie chapels stood in the vicinity of Pendreich. This may be Logie-Woloc.

14. LAc I 145.

15. CAI No. 1.

16. See under Bishop Jonathan.

17. CR No. 122.

18. DBS 194, 195 and n.; CAI 258n.

19. History of the Church of Scotland. (1668) I 214.

20. LA 199.

21. George Mackenzie: *Writers of Scotland* I 394, founding on Dempster: *Hist. Eccles. Gentis Scot.* IX 384, says that, while young, Jonathan travelled to the Holy Land and entered the Order of the Carmelites, founded on Mount Carmel

in Syria, c.1121, and brought under a rule c.1199 by Honorius III. Returning to Rome, he was sent to Scotland with a legate by the pope to gather money for the Holy War. If Dempster is to be trusted Jonathan was the first Carmelite to come west, for it was 1238 before the order began to spread abroad.

22. CPR I 28. Charters of Melrose 135.

23. Inchaffray is Insula Effren, isle of offerings, services, masses. Its Latin name, often used, is Insula Missarum.

24. CAI No. 3.

25. CAI Nos. 60, 61.

26. CAI No. 4.

27. CAI No. 1 (c.1190).

28. CAI No. 5 (c.1199).

29. CAI No. 9 (c.1200).

30. He drew his first canons from Scone.

31. CAI No. 8. This is the Pope's reply, A.D. 1200

32. CAI No. 21.

33. CAI Nos. 10, 14, 23, 26, 27, 30 etc.

34. LAc I 155.

35. CPR I 22-23. Migne II 722-3-4.

36. Sc. VIII 73. This reads as 1210, but LA 377 interprets it as 1211.

37. The nearest we can get to his appointment is CAI No. 28, an undated charter, where he is "elect". The earliest dated record of him as Bishop is in a bull of Innocent III dated 23 Jan. 1214/5, LA 113. But the date of CAI No. 30 may be 1211 or 1212.

38. So designated as a witness CAI No. 26.

39. T. No. 6, in which the Pope on 27 Apr. 1217 admonished Bishop William de Malvoisin (St. Andrews) for his "great audacity of presumption" in confirming the elections of the Bishops of Dunblane and Brechin, both sons of priests, without papal dispensation, and consecrating them bishops. "Our beloved son, Eustatius, canon of St Andrews" had informed the Pope "in our presence" of this and other derelictions of William, both as Bishop of Glasgow and as Bishop of St. Andrews. The Bishops of Glasgow and Moray and a large number of other clerics had been at pains to warn William, etc. He is to be brought to book. Informers were common and were not discouraged at the Apostolic Court; indeed they were often rewarded.

40. Lord Cooper in "Select Scottish Cases of the Thirteenth Century", No. 11, p. 20, analyses this case. Oddly, it was taken before both the King's court, which did not usually deal with teind cases, and the Bishop's. It may be that the King's court delayed judging this ecclesiastical question until the Bishop's court had given its verdict; for then many nobles appointed by the King, including one of the King's secretaries, the Sheriff of Perth, and Brice, the King's Deemster (judex), to hear the episcopal decision, were present when the Bishop's judgment was given. This too was unusual. The matter is also found in DMCS 212; LAc No. 215.

41. CR No. 118.

42. CPR I 89; T. No. 49; CSA 91. See also Chronicle of Melrose, p. 139, and Orkneyinga Saga (Torfaeus and Rolls editions). The Bishop had been pressing for teinds and other rights of the Church. Other references in CPR

leave no doubt of the savagery of this area in the early days of the Roman Church in Scotland.

43. Their references are CAI Nos. 25, 41, 45, 46; CL 33-34, 51/2.

44. CAI No. 30, 31; CR No. 122; CMN 11-12; LAc I 147/8; CL 48-49.

45. Fully described CL 43-60.

46. Clement said that the arbiter "had set equity aside and promulgated an unjust judgment to the very great injury of the Church of Dunblane".

47. Lord Cooper examined this cause in "Select Scottish Cases of the Thirteenth Century" pp. 17-19. But he misses the reason for the equivocative judgment; he says that the original arbiter was by this time dead. But he was still alive. See DMCS 120. He died 9 Jul. 1238, Sc. vi, 42.

48. CL 59-60, xxxviii. In return for an early apostolic (papal) privilege, the Abbey is to pay 6 marks sterling to Muthill Church. The whole case is a good example of how a tangled situation arose from an early papal privilege, and then from an abbot's endeavour to extend his claims and the complacency of a bishop (Abraham). The witnesses to the agreement (1235) still include two Celts, Gillebaran, chaplain, and Padin, presbyter of Muthill.

49. CAI No. 47.

50. CAI No. 53, at Stirling. This also granted to the abbot and his canons the right to seize their neyfs (natives) and fugitive men wherever they could find them outside the royal demesne lands. Neyfs were serfs, not slaves, but unfree labourers.

51. CL No. 46, liiiff. Joseph Anderson: *Scholastic Offices in the Scottish Church of the Twelfth and Thirteenth Centuries.*

52. Skene defines "conveth" as board and lodging for a night, perhaps longer, given by occupiers of land to their superiors when they were passing on a journey; it was due four times a year. Here it may refer to journeys of scholars to Abernethy in their training for the priesthood in Celtic times. Other surrenders of conveth were made about the same time to Lindores by the Chapter of Dunkeld, CL No. 33, and by the clerks of Methven, CL No. 48. The other instance of *rex scolarum* is in CL No. 47. *Scolastici* is a latinisation of Celtic *scologs*; *clerici* (clerks) is a Roman Church term and may inform us that already the Celtic school at Methven, as may the use of "chapter" in case of Dunkeld, that Celtic schools in these places had already been incorporated into the Roman system. Those parallel and contemporary transfers of four neighbouring Celtic institutions are very significant.

53. Sc. I 534. LAc 383. cf. W. B. Stevenson: *The Crusaders in the East.*

54. LAc I No. 87.

55. Quoted in DBS 195-6 from Regesta Vaticana, 13, 105, epistle 152 (Vatican MS.).

56. CR No. 126.

57. CR No. 124.

58. This is S. Lolan's, a Celtic foundation; now Kincardine in Menteith, and not Kincardine on Forth, as some say.

59. SHS Miscellany VIII 6, 7.

60. Sc. IX 48. Ex. p. 93. This Ex. (Extracta e variis cronicis Scocie) published by the Abbotsford Club in 1842 is MS. A. 6-36 in the Scottish National Library. Pages xi and xii record that in 1550 it belonged to Bishop William

Chisholm (I) of Dunblane. It is thought by many to have a close connexion with Dunblane, e.g. it records the death of Earl Gilbert of Strathearn, 1231; it may have been written by some cleric of the Cathedral. Its editor says it may be the work of Alexander Myln, Abbot of Cambuskenneth, who wrote the "Lives of the Bishops of Dunkeld", of which cathedral he had been canon. Myln was *ex officio* canon of Dunblane. The writing of the "Lives" and of "Ex" in MS. are similar, "seem the same" says the editor. Myln died in 1548. Ex. has a reference to Flodden, so the writer must have lived in the reign of James V. Goodall in his preface to Fordun: *Scoticronicon* calls this Extracta *liber Dunblanensis*. But NMS I 49 gives *O de Dublain epis.* as witness to a composition dated 8 Apr. 1236. "O" must be a misreading of C for Clement.

61. Menologium p. 25. In those early days the title of *beatus* was locally bestowed and locally observed. Bishop Jonathan is called, p. 36, a Carmelite and *beatus* (blessed), as is Clement likewise *beatus* on p. 34. David Camerarius advances Clement to *sanctus*, saint, and gives his day (i.e. the day of his death, and therefore of his veneration) as 19 March. When ultimately the Pope governed such titles, beatification was of local veneration and canonisation (or saintship) of universal.

62. There were four minor orders, Door-keeper, Reader, Exorcist and Acolyte; these were often bestowed all together in a composite service. There were three major orders, Sub-deacon, Deacon and Priest. The general term for the four minor orders was *clericus* or *acolytus*; but these men may have been door-keepers, of the lowest clerical status.

CHAPTER IV

BISHOP CLEMENT 1233 – 1258

I F the Diocese was to rise from its low estate, its next Bishop
would require to be a man of stature, courage and dedication.
Otherwise, it would of necessity be divided between other
dioceses or, as the Pope suggested later, be given to a monastery
to supervise and administer. Three years were spent in the search
for the man, and as there was either no electoral college or the
task was beyond them, the Pope gave mandate[1] to the Bishops of
St. Andrews, Brechin and Dunkeld to choose a bishop and provide
him to Dunblane. Their choice fell on Clemens Scotus, of the
Order of Friars Preachers, known otherwise as Dominicans. He
was consecrated at Wedale of Stow, on Sunday 4 September 1233,
by Bishop William Malvoisine of St. Andrews.[2] It was a brilliant
choice; no contemporary bishop in Scotland was more highly
esteemed by King or Pope or rose more capably to conquer
overwhelming difficulties. He saved the Diocese, began to build
the Cathedral, created the Chapter, and played a patriotic role in
Scottish history.

Friar Clement

The "Analecta" of the Dominican Order[3] tells that Clement, a
Scot by birth, was admitted into the Order at Paris in 1219, by
the blessed Matthew, Abbot and first Prior of the Convent of St.
James there, where he was then prosecuting his studies. When,
shortly afterwards, according to the "Analecta", Dominic was
passing through Paris, he sent Clement, along with Laurence the
Englishman and several others, into Scotland; of this company
Clement was "father and leader" when in 1230 the Dominicans
entered Scotland. They came fortified by the goodwill of William
Malvoisine, Bishop of St. Andrews. They had among their company of eight Symon Taylor, an expert in music who taught
church singing skilfully in the cathedrals of the country. In 1230,
Clement and his companions opened three houses of their Order.

Unfortunately the "Analecta" does not give the authorities for its statements, some of which I have questioned in an article[4] published elsewhere. There are grounds for thinking that Clement was educated at Oxford, and not at Paris University, as has generally been supposed. I read the "Analecta" as saying that he was a student in St. James', Paris, when he was admitted to his Order. For present purposes the "Analecta" outline may stand; those who are interested may consult my article. Between 1230 and 1233, Clement founded Priories at Berwick, Ayr, Edinburgh, Perth, Aberdeen, Elgin, Inverness and Stirling (in 1233), some of them (e.g. at Perth and Edinburgh) in houses given by the King, Alexander II. The Order was popular in Scotland with King and bishops; the Friars were of the contemporary monastic zeal, and their vows of poverty made weighty appeal.

Clement cannot have been more than a month or two in his diocese when he found himself at variance with the Abbot and Convent of Inchaffray over the Churches of Aberuthven and Tullieden,[5] and the second tithes of rents and other grants of the Earl of Strathearn. These the Bishop claimed as pertaining to his table by reason of his Church of Dunblane. Coming to deadlock, the parties agreed, "on the advice of men of probity", to submit the dispute to three arbiters, the Bishop of Dunkeld and the Abbots of Lindores and Scone, who, in order to ensure acceptance of their verdict, made conditions which really precluded any refusal to accept the decision. If the Bishop or any of his successors wanted to resile from the finding of the court, he should by way of penalty, before beginning litigation, pay £200 to the fabric of the bridge at Perth; the Abbot likewise, £300.[6] Clement's case was doubtless based on Earl Ferteth's endowment of the Church of Aberuthven about 1160, that is about forty years before his son Gilbert gave it "to the brethren serving God and St. John at the Isle of Masses in Foulis". This appropriation by Earl Gilbert was attested by Bishop Jonathan and other cathedral dignitaries, and was confirmed, c.1211, by Bishop Abraham; against this Clement could make no claim, and made none. It would appear, however, that the Abbey had erected a vicarage with the lesser teinds of the parish, an act which gave to the Abbey the patronage of the vicarage, whether the vicar was duly beneficed or was only a stipendiary cleric or one of the Abbey's canons. The Bishop now claimed that the vicarage belonged to his patronage; he also claimed it for his mensal needs.

The judgment was a compromise; Clement was to abandon the action and give up all the rights he was claiming; the Abbot was to give to Clement and his successors £16 sterling per annum for his *mensa*. In a charter of the same month, August 1234, on the avowal of the Abbot that he had only the garbal teinds of Tullibardine and Kincardine[7] and the fifth part of the teinds of Barderel at his disposal, and that they amounted only to £10, Clement out of compassion for the poverty of the House of Inchaffray remitted the remaining £6, until the Abbot came into full possession of any of these churches, Strogeith, Foulis, Trinity Gask, Monivaird and Dunning.

This settlement was not entirely satisfactory to Clement. He had to give up his rights in return for a fixed payment for all time; whereas teinds tended to increase in value with the development of the land and were largely proof against inflation, a fixed sum remained fixed. If he had to go through a long list of piecemeal settlements like this, he saw irritating legislation before him for years with the abbots of the various monasteries to which so many of his parishes had been appropriated. In the long process the Diocese of Dunblane might well die like a sapless tree. He decided to lay the situation before the Pope, and to Rome he went, with a plan.

This journey must have been made between the springs of 1235 and 1237. On 11 June 1237 Gregory IX commissioned[8] the Bishops of Glasgow and Dunkeld to examine Clement's representations and indicated the actions they should take.

Gregory's commission may be thus translated:

Our reverend brother the Bishop of Dunblane has declared in our presence that, since the Church of Dunblane has been vacant for a hundred years and more, almost all its possessions had been seized by laymen, and although in the course of time several Bishops had been instituted, yet through their lack of wisdom and watchfulness not only were the possessions so seized not recovered, but even what had escaped the marauders' hands had been almost wholly alienated and consumed, so that no suitable person could be persuaded to undertake so heavy a burden and for nearly ten years the church has again lacked the solace of a pastor. We, therefore, having been made aware of its miserable condition, remitted the matter of its provision to our reverend brothers, the Bishops of St. Andrews and Brechin and to you, our brother of Dunkeld. You and the other two Bishops set Clement over the Church, hopeful that by him it could be raised from its sea of wretchedness. Bishop Clement, however, found the Church so desolated that

> there was no place in the Cathedral Church where he could lay his head;
> it had no college of clergy;
> the divine offices were celebrated in a roofless church and by a rural chaplain only;
> and the episcopal revenues were so slender, and had been alienated to such a degree, that they scarcely sufficed to support him for half a year.

Therefore, since the continual care of all the churches is our daily burden, we grant to the said Church, so far as we personally can, and authorise you, if you find the situation to be as described, to assign to the said Bishop, if it can be done without scandal, a quarter of the teinds of all the parish churches of the Diocese of Dunblane, so that under your guidance and that of upright men, he may set aside a suitable portion of them for his own maintenance, and thereafter assign revenues for a dean and canons whom we wish and authorise you to institute there.

Otherwise, the quarter teinds of all the churches of the Diocese assigned to the Bishop, which are held by laymen, you shall transfer with the episcopal seat to the Canons Regular of St. John in the Diocese (i.e. to Inchaffray Priory), who shall have power to elect a Bishop in any vacancy.

Before we examine the various settlements made by the commissioners, there are in the papal mandate certain statements which demand clarification.

(1) *The Church of Dunblane has been vacant for a hundred years and more.* Yet the Bishops are known by name for eighty years before Clement came. Clement may have been referring, though misunderstood by the papal scribe, to the dimly-lit period before the first Roman Bishop (c. 1155), when the Celtic Church in Dunblane would seem not to have had a bishop among its Culdees and the Roman Church had not yet a bishop in Dunblane.

(2) *For nearly ten years the church has again lacked the solace of a pastor.* This is Clement's description of the episcopates of his two immediate predecessors and the vacancy before his appointment.

(3) *Almost all its possessions had been seized by laymen . . . even what had escaped the marauders' hands had been almost wholly alienated and consumed.* This asserts that the possessions of the old Celtic community in its dwindling days had been seized by neighbouring proprietors. The lands of Celtic monasteries like Dunblane belonged to the abbots who were sometimes laymen; the lands were by that fact often detached from their church uses. When the Earls of Strathearn and of Menteith came to give teinds and lands

to the developing Diocese of Dunblane, nearly every church which they so endowed was Celtic in origin. Indeed it is possible, even likely, that some of the teinds at least, if not all, which they appropriated to the Priories of Inchaffray and Inchmahome were from lands which had been the property and endowment of earlier Celtic churches. What had escaped marauding hands may have been alienated by the early Roman Bishops, through lack of wisdom and care; so needy were they that they doubtless leased some of the land, perhaps in perpetuity. So great was the power of landowners in the Church in those days that land so leased was often lost, "alienated and consumed", as the papal commission puts it.

The plan of the Pope and Clement, to exact a quarter of the teinds of all parishes in the Diocese, for the purposes mentioned, was but a partial remedy, for the damage was beyond complete restoration. The quarter teinds were granted only *so far as we personally can* and *if it can be done without scandal*. The plan succeeded only in part. It is clear that Earl Gilbert had attempted too much when he tried to set up at the same time both a diocese and a priory. Doubtless he had the will and the generous heart, but not the resources. To a considerable extent the two establishments had to draw on the same sources of income and these were insufficient, however ample the heart and the plans of the munificent patron. The suggestion of the Pope that in the event of Clement failing to get quarter teinds from all the parishes the See and the Priory should be amalgamated was a natural one and may have arisen from his talks with Clement. But Clement, having put his hand to the plough, returned to Dunblane determined to establish an independent diocese. It says much for the established and fundamentally solid position of the See that the transfer to Inchaffray did not take place. It says as much for Clement's devotion and power of organisation that the See emerged in strength.

The Settlements

Negotiations for the quarter teinds were now undertaken by the Bishops of Glasgow and Dunkeld and long and troublesome were their enquiries before settlements were reached. No enquiry was needed in the unappropriated parishes, which included

Aberfoyle, Balquhidder, Comrie, Dupplin, Glendevon, Kilmahog, Logie-Woloc, Monzie, Strowan, Tulliallan and Tullikettle. In these, the stipend of the rector was simply reduced by a quarter, but probably only at the first vacancy. Muthill had been dealt with in 1235, as the previous chapter tells. Callander was added to the Bishop's revenue in 1238, as we shall later see. In appropriated parishes where little was at stake the Abbeys seem to have yielded the papal imposition without much argument: these were Coupar Angus Abbey, which had Fossoway; Culross Abbey, which had the parish churches of Culross and Tullibole; the Hospital of Ss. James and John, Brackley, in Northamptonshire, which had Findogask (also called Nesgask, Gask, and Gasknes); and the Nuns of North Berwick, who possessed the parish of Logie-Atheray. At least, in these cases no record of dispute survives. But it was very different when issue was joined with the Earl of Menteith, and with the Abbots of Cambuskenneth, Arbroath and Inchaffray. The Abbot of Lindores was reasonable, and the bishops arbiter were not called in.

Walter Comyn, Earl of Menteith, whose property, along with that of the Earl of Strathearn, formed practically the whole of the Diocese,[9] seemed to be one of those laymen referred to in the papal mandate as seizing church lands; it looks as if, in certain of the churches, he had appointed whom he would, when he would, and at what stipend he would, perhaps justifying his actions by the cost of the churches which he had built or repaired. In that way he would pay from the teinds only the stipend of the chaplains whom he appointed. Be that as it may, the Earl refused to obey the papal order, and a heated altercation arose between him and Clement. Reflecting that, while his neighbour Strathearn had built and endowed a Priory, and thereby ensured his eternal welfare through the prayers of the Canons, by granting to the Priory teinds which otherwise would have been used parochially, he had no such guarantees for the next world, or such generous reputation in this. He asked the Pope to allow him to build a priory on Inchmahome; on 16 June 1238 permission was granted.[10]

This description of the Earl's inner thoughts is based on the frank account given by the bishops arbiter, in their letter[11] of 1 July 1238, announcing their decision. "No sooner had the Bishop of Dunblane received this mandate (to collect quarter teinds) than Walter Comyng appeared in our presence; after

E

altercations they submitted themselves to our orders in all the contentions and quarrels between them"; so runs the letter. The judgment was a compromise in which both gained in part:

(1) The Bishop shall renounce all rights, real or presumed, in lands, rents, dues and teinds from the churches of the Earldom of Menteith; in these the Earl holds the patronage. The Bishop shall give up his rights in all the quarrels, exactions and demands between him and the Earl.

(2) The Earl shall be free to build a House of Augustinian Canons on Inchmahome, without opposition of the Bishop or his successors.

(3) The Churches of Leny and of the Island of Inchmahome shall be taken from the Earl's collation and given to "the religious men serving God in the Island".[12]

(4) In the above two Churches, the Bishop of Dunblane shall not be permitted to appoint perpetual (endowed) vicars, but shall accept reasonably qualified chaplains (*honesti capellani*) presented to him, and these clerics shall themselves answer for the cure of souls and for their church and episcopal dues.

(5) The Earl shall assign the Church of Kippen as prebend of a canonry in the Church of Dunblane, the Earl remaining patron.

(6) The Earl shall give up to the Bishop any right he had in the Church of Callander.

The settlement was sealed at Perth in the presence "in council" of many important clerics, among them the Abbots of Arbroath, Cambuskenneth and Inchaffray, who were doubtless eagerly watching against their own coming contentions with Clement. Neither Clement nor Walter can have been fully satisfied with the compromise, but the Bishop fared somewhat better than the Earl.

At a date unknown, the Church of Kilmadock was appropriated to Inchmahome Priory, the vicar's teinds going to the Chapter for the support of the Chancellor; about 1490, Prior David claimed[13] 13 chalders of meal as teinds of Leny and Kilmadock. The Church of Port (i.e. Port of Menteith) was also at some time appropriated to the Priory, for in 1573 the lay commendator of the Priory leased its teind sheaves, with those of Kilmadock, for £6. 13. 4 yearly.[14]

The settlement with Lindores Abbey was agreed to amicably.

The issue concerned lands (Fedale, Beny and Concrag) in the parish of Muthill; in these estates, the Pope had given special privileges to Lindores, including freedom from teinds of fallow lands and the young of flocks. On 7 April 1239 the Abbot admitted[15] that Muthill belonged to the Bishop's *mensa*, and agreed to pay to Muthill six marks sterling yearly in lieu of teinds; also he granted that laymen residing on the same lands should pay to Muthill the oblations due from the living and the dead. The Abbot of Lindores seems also to have been granted an *ex officio* canonry of Dunblane, for as such he took part, in 1307, in the election of Nicolas de Balmyle as Bishop of Dunblane.[16]

Earlier issues were not reviewed on this occasion, for Muthill had been settled between the Abbot and Bishop Clement as lately as 1235, and Exmagirdle had been appropriated to Lindores Abbey by consent of the Bishop and clergy of Dunblane before 1215, an act which was not contested by Clement.[17]

In the case of Cambuskenneth Abbey the quarter teinds of the parish churches of Tullibody, Kincardine-in-Menteith and Tillicoultry were at stake. The agreement was made on 29 January 1239/40, in Dunblane Cathedral, by Bishop and Abbot, and confirmed the day following by Dean and Chapter.[18] It was under four heads, and was negotiated by the bishops arbiter:

(1) Cambuskenneth was to provide four marks yearly (1 mark = 13/4) as the portion of a vicar[19] to officiate for the Abbot in the Cathedral.

(2) The Abbot was to be canon *ex officio* of Dunblane Cathedral.

(3) The Abbey was to pay an additional yearly sum of four marks, to be assigned from Tullibody on the death or resignation of Hugh de Bosco, then vicar; these four marks were to be at the disposal of the Bishop.

(4) No quarter teinds were to be paid from the parishes named, and the Abbey was allowed to present to the Bishop qualified chaplains instead of vicars, the chaplains to answer to the Bishop for all church dues. (Later, *c.* 1495, the Abbey got the rectory of Kippen, on terms.)[20]

The question at issue with Arbroath Abbey dealt with the Church of Abernethy, granted to the Abbey by Bishop Jonathan, with its chapels of Dron, Dunbog and Errol (Erolyn), only Dron, which later became a parish, being in the Diocese. The bishops arbiter[21] ordained in 1240 that

> the Bishop was to receive the revenue of the high altar, along with certain rents;
>
> he was to provide a vicar in his stead for Abernethy, and a vicar of the choir in the Abbot's stead for Dunblane;
>
> the Abbey was to retain certain lands and teinds of Abernethy, and the income of the chapels;
>
> the Abbot was to be a canon *ex officio* of the Cathedral, and be given a toft for a manse in Dunblane.

The income from the high altar, which included the vicar's teinds as well as offerings and rents, was doubtless considerable, for the Bishop agreed in return for them (1) to accept the Abbot as a canon, to grant him a site for a manse, and provide a vicar of the choir in his place, and (2) to provide a vicar in his own stead in the Church of Abernethy.

Three days after Clement accepted the concordat with Cambuskenneth, that is, on 2 February 1239/40, the Dean and Chapter confirmed[22] his agreement (which is not extant) with Inchaffray. Fortunately the Bishop's settlement is given in the confirmation. The main lines of the agreement were dictated by the appropriations already made, and Clement confirmed that ten churches of his diocese (Strogeith, Auchterarder, Kinkell, Aberuthven, Dunning, Gask Christi, Foulis, Monzievaird, Tullieden and Kilbryde) belonged to the Abbey except for

> (1) the vicar's portions "as detailed below" (no such detailed list has however survived);
>
> (2) £16 annually payable to the Bishop from the teinds of lands, as settled in the dispute between Abbot and Bishop regarding Aberuthven[23];
>
> (3) from other garbal teinds, 20 marks were assigned to the Archdeaconry of Dunblane, about to be set up;
>
> (4) certain teinds belonging to Auchterarder Church were assigned to the Abbot for his prebend as canon *ex officio* in Dunblane Cathedral, where his office was to be that of Precentor. In a papal confirmation of 1250[24] (there was an earlier letter in 1248), it is learned that this prebend of the Precentor was worth 10 marks; also, that the arbiters "had assessed moderately the

vicarages of certain churches and authorised certain others to be served by chaplains", because "the Abbey was over-burdened".[25]

Summary of the settlements

Of Clement's six years of struggle for the rights of his diocese and for the quarter teinds it can be said that he brought some measure of order out of measureless chaos. What teinds he did recover were unfortunately mostly in the form of fixed annual payments, subject to every inflationary trend. Also, he had to grant canonries *ex officio* to four abbots, who, if they gave wisdom and experience to the Chapter in high issues, cannot have given attention to the daily administration or regularly served their terms of duty in person. The Dean and Chapter were left with too few rectories for their disposal; many of the vicarages were permitted to be supplied by chaplains or by canons regular. If it had not been for the dozen churches which still remained wholly in the control of the Bishop, Dean and Chapter, none of the objects of the papal grant of teinds could have been achieved and the Diocese would of necessity have been handed over to Inchaffray. The bishops arbiter were given a heavy task, thankless as well; to modern minds they seem on occasion to have yielded too much to earls and abbots; but when the brash exercise of secular power in the Middle Ages is remembered as well as the tidal wave of monastic enthusiasm, it may be admitted that they fulfilled their ungrateful remit with considerable aplomb. They were forced to compromise in a situation that was nearly out of hand. Even the Pope warned them to avoid grievous scandal, and authorised them only "so far as we personally can". On the whole their actions merit commendation. In the end it was the parishes which suffered most, from inadequate attention to the needy and from the lack of resident clergy whose income could enable them to meet their obligations. The authority of the Bishop in his Diocese was reduced, while that of the Abbots was magnified.

In the end Clement made a diocese out of a chaos of churches and monasteries, obtained some income for himself and for his archdeacon and other dignitaries, gained four canons *ex officio* (one of them precentor) for his chapter, set up certain other canonries with prebends, and was able to begin to build his cathedral. His successor complained that the revenues of the See were inadequate, but they sufficed for Clement, who carried into his episcopal office the austerity and poverty to which as a Dominican Friar he had pledged himself.

Clement the Builder

Throughout his episcopate Clement was building his cathedral. Earlier Bishops had begun to build, but had left an unfinished church without a roof. Clement, without a chapter, without the teinds of more than a third of his parishes, without a dwelling, and with no more income than would support him for six months in the year, began to build, with nothing to his hand, nothing save energy, determination, imagination, a sense of beauty, and time.

As well as a church partially built and roofless, Clement found a square tower,[26] four storeys high and Norman in design, with small round-headed windows and some Celtic features, such as mark the round towers of Brechin, Abernethy and Ireland; it is generally dated c.1100, and may be earlier. Its entrance is on the north side, about three feet above ground level. Attached to it, and running north and south,[27] as the roof-marks on the tower show, contrary to the usual orientation, was the unfinished church, its direction probably determined by the nature of the site, which is boggy to the north-east of the present Cathedral.

This unfinished church Clement seems to have taken down. When he pegged out the lines of his proposed church, it is possible that the site stood entirely free from the tower, and to the north of it; if so, the east end would be marked on boggy ground. To avoid this, the pegs would have to be moved some feet to the south, too far to avoid incorporating the towers in part within the nave. This is the likeliest explanation of the very awkward position of the tower, which partly blocks the south aisle; only necessity would enforce such an architectural singularity. But even then, the northern corner of the east end would rest in bog; so Clement would be forced to slew his whole ground plan to the south, some feet out of alignment with the tower. Neither tower nor Cathedral is true east-west.

Clement's first building was the Lady Chapel, also called traditionally the Chapter House, and probably used as both with a curtain between them. Here worship could be carried on while the rest of the Cathedral was being reared. The Chapel's dual purpose may have been determined by the restricted site, but may have been decided after its erection, for the design is a unity. It has fine proportions and the roof is cross-vaulted with central bosses. Above it Clement added a room of equal size, reached by a narrow wheel stair. Here, today, the organ is housed; but it was there that Clement had his private chapel, for the piscina of an altar is still to be seen. It may even have been Clement's living chamber; he had told the Pope that in the Cathedral he had no place to lay his head.

Whether next in building came the choir or the nave has been often argued; but the work of the great restoration (1889-93) revealed the fact that the choir was built before the nave, as the uncovered jointing showed plainly. I mention only a few archi-ectural details[28] : the nave is 140 feet long and has 8 bays, divided by 7 pillars, on north and south; there are north and south aisles, but no transepts; the choir is half the length of the nave. In addition to the great west door, there are entrances to the nave in the south aisle east of the tower, another in the south aisle near the west end, and one near the north-west corner. The only entrances to the Lady Chapel were from choir and nave; the present entrance on the north is modern. The entrance from the nave in the Keir Aisle is a replacement of an original feature, which was lost for about three hundred years during which the nave stood roofless. Above the arches of the nave, triforium and clerestory form one course, with through passages from end to end, reached by a stair in the west wall. The west window is unusual in that on its inside is a passage flanked by pillars, leading to the clerestory passages. Above the great arch between nave and choir there is a series of holes in line, signs that there once stretched across and above it a gallery from which a great crucifix probably rose. The choir has no aisles, the Lady Chapel being on the north side.

It is not likely that the Cathedral was fully built before Clement died, but the design was fixed and in large part completed. It stands today the visible monument of its remarkable creator. "He was no common man who designed that Cathedral of Dun-blane," wrote John Ruskin, "I know not anything so perfect in its simplicity, and so beautiful, as far as it reaches, in all the Gothic with which I am acquainted."[29] Roofless for three hundred years, but outstandingly restored in the nineties of last century, it is, in its stonework, essentially as Clement designed it to be. The building is small when compared with many cathedrals, especially in England and the Continent, no larger than many a parish church; but such are its beauty and dignity of proportion that it impresses the eye as larger than it is. I remember vividly the catch in the breath when first I visited it; forty years of intimate concern and nearly thirty years of almost daily contact, have not staled its appeal. Its various glories never fail to move the discerning worshipper or to inspire the interest of the visitor. Many have been inspired to princely gifts for its adornment; this fact, in itself, is a tribute to its builder, who, out of meagre resources, planned and built a notable sanctuary to the glory of God.

Clement the churchman

Clement's name and title, and on occasions his seal and even his sign manual, are found in various charters, royal, episcopal, monastic and lay, in various collections of records. The Pope sent him few mandates – mercifully, for his hands were full; but, in 1236 he was mandated,[30] with two other bishops, to enquire into the canonicity of Geoffrey's postulation as Bishop of Dunkeld; other more important mandates will fall to be noted.

But once the Diocese was organised there were laid on Clement two important duties, both of which entailed much travel and administrative labour.

(1) William, Bishop of Argyll, was drowned in 1241.[31] Nine years passed before another Bishop of Argyll was appointed, one equipped with Gaelic perhaps and experienced in the ways of the sea. During the vacancy the See of Argyll was administered by Clement, as an Inchaffray charter[32] of c.1247 informs us, for he added his seal and was called "C. by the grace of God Bishop of Dunblane and at the time of this collation having charge of the Bishopric of Argyll". In 1249, he witnessed a charter[33] granting the parish church of St. Bryde in Lorne along with lands and pertinents to the mensa of the Bishop of Argyll. In 1248, with the Bishop of Glasgow, he was given mandate[34] to cancel uncanonical elections to the Bishopric of Argyll, and to appoint and consecrate a Bishop, unless within a given time the canons elected a suitable person. The year following Clement and the Bishop of Glasgow were authorised[35] to transfer the See from

Lismore to some more secure and accessible place, the King having promised his help towards the cost. This transfer was not carried out.

The most interesting monument to Clement's administration of Argyll is still to be seen in the Island of Harris. When MacLeod of Harris about the end of the fifteenth century built a church at Rodil, he dedicated it to St. Clement of Dunblane.[36] I have written an article on the church, with illustrations, and I only add here its significance in measuring the kind of man Clement was. Even down to 1784, it was customary for the natives to swear by "Claiman moir a Rowadill" (the great Clement of Rodil). His visitation of this scattered diocese must have been wide and earnest.

During Clement's administration Alexander II sought to bring the Western and Northern Isles under his rule and to break the Norwegian control of them. This was finally achieved during the reign of his son, Alexander III, at the Battle of Largs in 1263.[37] But in 1249 Alexander II set out on an expedition to the Shetlands with this aim. He died, however, on his way, at Kerrera, on 8 July of the same year. Matthew Paris[38] reports that, according to some, the expedition was undertaken at "the constant urging of a certain indiscreet Bishop of Strathearn, a friar, of a truth, of the Order of Preachers". This derogatory statement may well be true, may equally well be the political verdict of some who were against the expedition. Who can tell, for the death of Alexander brought the expedition to an end?

(2) In 1247, Pope Innocent IV appointed[39] Clement to be collector in Scotland of the subsidy for the Holy Land, that is, for the Crusade which began to be preached in 1246. The tax was a twentieth of all ecclesiastical revenues, fees for redemption of vows, offerings and legacies for the freeing of Jerusalem from the Turks. Clement was instructed to collect these, to conserve them faithfully and to assign to two named crusaders[40] first gatherings up to the value of three thousand pounds of the money of Tours.

The labour involved was immense, including much travel and advocacy of the Crusade. A collector's task in those days was neither easy nor happy. The situation in the Scottish Church (and the Irish) had been bedevilled five months before by another papal command[41] to send as a subsidy to Rome, then troubled by the Emperor Frederick II, "a certain sum of their provision". Clement of course was given helpers – bishops, abbots and prelates were commanded to enforce Clement's orders; in 1250, the Bishops of St. Andrews and Aberdeen were authorised[42] to take over the collection of legacies and offerings, and after making payments to Scottish crusaders to assign the remainder to the King of England, once he had set out on the Crusade. This tax of a twentieth for Crusades was the third imposed on Scotland – a subsidy was ordered in 1213, and a thirtieth in 1238. In the early thirteenth century Rome was at the beginnings of a flood of taxations, and before many years taxation became an important part of the papal machine and led to many abuses and indignities.[43]

Clement the patriot

Bishop Clement was held in high esteem by Alexander II and played an important part in the nation's struggle for independence in the face of Henry III of England's endeavours to bring Scotland under his control. The Bishop's part in the long story began in 1244, when the King of Scots bound himself and his heirs to keep peace with his "liege lord", the King of England.[44] Agreements recently made at York were to be kept, Alexander's only son and Henry's eldest daughter Margaret were to marry, and Alexander abjured military alliance against England, unless injury called for war. In confirmation of his pledge, Alexander caused Alan Durward, the powerful Earl of Atholl, High Justiciar and, as such, the King's chief councillor, and three others of the great nobles, to swear on the King's soul that he would keep his promises; a like oath was taken by the Bishops of St. Andrews, Glasgow, Dunkeld and Dunblane, and by such magnates as Malise of Strathearn, Walter Comyn of Menteith, Robert de Bruis (forebear of King Robert the Bruce) and Henry de Balliol. Their seals were appended.

In five years Alexander II was dead, his son Alexander III, then less than eight years of age, was crowned in 1249 at Scone, and a Council of Regents was appointed, Bishop Clement being one of them. Henry III began immediately to have his feudal superiority over Scotland recognised. He petitioned the Pope to proclaim this, and also to grant him a tenth of Scottish church revenues; both were refused.[45] In 1251, Alexander III and Margaret of England were married at York, and Henry meanly tried to inveigle his son-in-law, though only ten years of age, to do homage to England; but the Regents had warned the boy and he evaded the trap. Henry sent envoys into Scotland as a "fifth column" to undermine the patriotism of the Regents, and in spite of strong opposition by the Bishops of Glasgow and Dunblane they persuaded Alan Durward to lead a pro-English party. Durward's party was strong enough to seize the King and Queen in Edinburgh Castle, take them to Roxburgh, and then to Kelso, to meet the English King, whose presence in the Borders, with troops, was proof of his inspiration of Durward's rebellion. In Kelso Abbey, Henry was acknowledged as the King of Scotland's principal counsellor, with practically supreme power in Scotland. This betrayal the members of the Scottish party refused to sign, especially its leaders, Walter Comyn of Menteith, John de Balliol, the Bishops of Glasgow and Dunblane, and Gamelin, Bishop elect of St. Andrews. These and others were proclaimed at Roxburgh, on 20 September 1255, as "removed from our Council and from their offices, as their demerits demand". New members were appointed to the Council "by advice of Henry III", including the Bishop of Dunkeld and the Earls of Strathearn and Carrick (Robert Bruce's forebear), all three of whom seem to have changed from their political views of 1244.[46] The new Council was appointed for seven years, at the end of which period, when Alexander III would be twenty-one, Henry promised no prejudice to Scotland and its King. Scotland was thus subjected to the will of the English King for at least the next seven years.

But that was not the end. The ruling pro-English party set out to crush the opposition; they brought destruction on themselves instead. They forbade Gamelin's consecration, but William, Bishop of Glasgow, and two other bishops dared to consecrate him on 26 December 1255. They outlawed Gamelin in 1256, as the Chronicle of Melrose says, "both because he refused to acquiesce in their abominable plans, and because he scorned to give a certain sum of money (which the pro-English Council had demanded) as if for the purchase of his bishopric". When Gamelin went to Rome to complain, they seized his revenues. On 22 January 1257, Henry of England ordered his arrest, and in the same year the pro-English Council sent ambassadors to Rome to make charges against him. The Pope investigated the charges and declared Gamelin guiltless of them all.[47] At home, the

Comyns and their Scottish party in 1257 took advantage of the
absence of the King and Queen on a visit to her father in London,
and gained the upper hand. The tide was turning; the Pope excommunicated[48] Gamelin's accusers and commanded Clement
and the Abbots of Melrose and Jedburgh to publish "the sentence
. . . against the King's councillors throughout Scotland with
striking of bells and with lighted candles; in general terms at first,
and afterwards, if they were contumacious, by name". This was
done in general terms at Stirling and then by name in Cambuskenneth Abbey. The Durward party fled to England to save their
skins, if not their heads. Gamelin was recalled by Alexander III
before the end of the year; Henry tried to capture him on his
homeward journey, but without success. The Scottish party
triumphed completely, and if the political strength of the Earl of
Menteith, whose family of Comyn included thirty-two knights
and three earls, was dominating in its sphere, the stout support
of the Bishops of Glasgow, Dunblane and St. Andrews was no
less vital, for it brought moral purpose and papal support, which
finally carried the patriotic cause to its successful issue.

His last days

The excommunication of the pro-English Regents is the last
recorded act of Clement. He died in 1258.[49] His tomb, some
think, is in the choir of the Cathedral, but tradition says that the
effigy and tomb are those of his early fifteenth-century successor,
Bishop Finlay Dermock. McGregor Stirling suggests in his manuscript that the tomb situated in the south-east corner of the nave
stood originally on the south side of the choir and is Clement's;
he says it was removed to its present position to allow a door to
be made in the south wall of the choir. Dempster says that as to
where or when he died, no one, so far as he knows, has left any
writing, but that some think he died in Dunblane. In any case,
Clement's monument lies all around. He was a dynamic man,
outstanding alike as Dominican friar, mitred bishop, courageous
churchman, and stout patriot. The Dominicans held him in deep
affection, for in 1250, when the General Chapter of the Order
met in London, there was adopted this most unusual resolution[50]:

> "Also, we grant to Friar Clement of our Order, a bishop in
> Scotland, after his death, one mass throughout the Order by

PLATE II

ST. CLEMENT'S CHURCH, RODIL, HARRIS

every friar whomsoever who is a priest, and in the Province of England let it be done for him as for other friars."

They looked on him as a shining example of their virtues of poverty, chastity and obedience.

He is credited by Dempster with the writing of four books: *Conciones* (or *Summa concionum*),[51] *Vita sancti Dominici, Ordinis sui in Scotiam ingressus* and, in two volumes, *De peregrinatione ad loca sancta.* These are lost – if they every existed. But in a collection of MSS. in the British Museum (Egerton MS. 655) there is a manuscript,[52] in a contemporary hand, of a sermon, headed "Sermo fratris Clementis", which some authorities think may be by Clement when he was a friar. The "Analecta" of the Order of Preachers describes him as "a notable preacher, skilled in languages, distinguished for his virtue, and worthy". Camerarius gave him the title of saint, his day being 19 March, and though there is no papal authorisation of the canonisation, there were many instances in the early Middle Ages in which a national Church at least allowed an elevation which came from the devotion of people and clergy. Even if lacking in the Pope's approval, the title would seem at this distance to have been worthily bestowed. We may heartily agree with the verdict of Fordun that Clement of Dunblane was a man "mighty in word and deed before God and men".

NOTES

1. This is told in T. No. 91, in explanation of the further steps which the Pope authorised on 11 Jun. 1237. T. 91 will be dealt with later in this chapter.

2. M. p. 143.

3. Analecta Ordinis Fratrum Predicatorum (1906) p. 485.

4. See "Friar Clement" in BFDC 1956.

5. CAI No. 60. The story unfolds in CAI Nos. 3, 10, 13, 30. The temporary remission of £6 is noted in CAI No. 61. The Pope confirmed the settlement at Clement's request, CAI No. 62, 30 Apr. 1237. The location of Tullieden is unknown; I am not persuaded that it is to be identified with Tullykettle (since 1600, incorporated in Comrie), as some think.

6. In modern values these would be in the region of £10,000 and £15,000.

7. This was not a church, but a Strathearn farm or estate, as were Tullibardine and Barderel, which had been given to Inchaffray for the support of the Abbey. There are at least eight Kincardines in Scottish medieval records, and as no regional distinctions are given, the context must decide in each case. Dunblane had three: S. Lolan's of Kincardine (that is, in Menteith), Kincardine

on Forth, which was an estate, its parish church being Tulliallan, and this one, which may be called "K. in Strathearn".

8. T. No. 91. The translation now given varies slightly from that in my article on Bishop Clement in BFDC 1933. That article receives here the corrections which it requires.

9. Robertson: *Early Kings of Scotland*, I 336 n. thinks that the two earls may have been instigated by David I to make their lands the area of the Diocese of Dunblane and that neither earl resigned the church lands in his possession until Menteith waived his claim to the patronage of the See in return for permission to found the Priory of Inchmahome. An interesting suggestion which only the discovery of documents could substantiate. No known facts invalidate it.

10. RBM I 33, 34 and 507ff.

11. *ut supra* II 326-9; *Liber Insulae Missarum*; Macgregor Stirling: *Priory of Inchmahome*.

12. These would be, most probably, the successors of S. Colmoc, who founded a Celtic monastery on the largest island in the Lake of Menteith (hence Inchmahome, called here Inchmaquhomok); see my *Celtic Church in Dunblane*, pp. 115, 116. By c.1196, one witness to a charter of Bishop W. of Dunblane is Malcolm, parson (rector) of the Island of Inchmahome; which means that the Celtic foundation had already become Roman in its allegiance. CR No. 122.

13. ADC p. 184.

14. LC 881.

15. CL No. 54. The witnesses include these Celts, formerly Culdees, now within the Roman service: Gillebaran, chaplain, Padin presbyter of Muthill and sir Andrew, prior of Abernethy. Four years earlier, on 7 May 1235, CL No. 51, sir Andrew had been designated Prior of the Culdees of Abernethy.

16. T. No. 386. CPR II 33.

17. CL No. 45, before 23 Jan. 1214/5, the date of a bull of Innocent III, CL No. 95.

18. CR Nos. 125, 126.

19. Only one rector of Dunblane is known, Malisius, c.1210, CR No. 122. The only vicar of Dunblane known by name is master John Spaldyne 1448, SK 220. After the Reformation the office and its teinds were held in 1567 by John Leirmonth, previously notary and chaplain, RMS IV 1999.

20. CR Nos. 128, 129. RMS II 2306.

21. Reg. Vet. de Aberbrothoc, 1-8, 25, 26.

22. CAI No. 67. The Dean, Precentor and Archdeacon subscribed personally, see reproduction numbered 17 at end of CAI. The double year is necessitated by the fact that till 1600 in Scotland the year ran from 25 March to the next 24 March. The double year shows that to us the year was 1240, but was 1239 to the men of that time.

23. See in Chapter II under Bishop Abraham.

24. CAI No. 80. The letter of 1248 commissioned the Bishop of Brechin to see to its observance, CAI No. 79. CAI No. 81, 23 Apr. 1250, is a papal warning that no one is to molest the Abbot. The Abbot was so satisfied with the settlement, but so afraid of its being broken, that *coram nobis* (in our presence) he or his procurators had asked this papal warning to be given, ten years after the settlement was made.

25. Many of the abbeys and priories in Scotland seemed to be often in that condition. Of course, the buildings sometimes were seriously damaged in war; but the abbots seldom took care of their lands, often disobeying even the Canon Law regarding leases, etc. In 1248, 1252, 1256, 1266, 1274, 1307 and 1317 (CAI Nos. 78, 82, 84, 94, 104, 120, 122) the Pope commissioned certain clerics to recover Inchaffray's property for the Abbey. About 1550, Bishop William Chisholm I of Dunblane had an assedation (lease) of the fruits of the Abbey, ATS X 1551/2; after 1495, the Abbey was held *in commendam*, by laymen or others who, it was thought, could run it better than the Abbot, and who "farmed" it in their own interests, paying a fixed sum to the Abbey for its needs.

26. For a full description of it, see illustrated article by late A. B. Barty, LL.B., the historian of Dunblane, in BFDC 1938.

27. See articles by Mrs Edith Hughes, A.R.I.B.A., in BFDC 1933. William Rae, late custodian of the Cathedral and gravedigger, told me of finding foundation walls when digging on the north of the Cathedral; these ran north and south in the appropriate position. Not every medieval church runs east-west (St. Peter's, Rome, is not E.-W.), though that is customary; strict observance of this architectural canon was not always possible, other directions being dictated by the nature of the site or the compass line of streets in towns. Rievaux Abbey, Yorkshire, runs N.-S.

28. For full descriptions, with drawings, consult McGibbon and Ross: *Ecclesiastical Architecture of Scotland*.

29. Lectures on Architecture and Painting, p. 31 of Vol. XII Library Edition. See also, p. xx, same volume, "far the finest thing I have seen in Scotland", he wrote of Dunblane Cathedral, 2 Jul. 1853, to his father. "The proportion of the whole quite heavenly."

30. CPR I 157. T. No. 85.

31. T. No. 139.

32. CAI No. 74.

33. RMS II 3136.

34. T. No. 139. CPR I 251.

35. CPR I 251.

36. "The Hebrides" in *Reports of Royal Commission on Ancient Monuments*. Also McGibbon and Ross: *Ecclesiastical Architecture of Scotland*. My article on St. Clement's, Rodil, in BFDC 1955, with illustrations. FES says it was the church of an Augustinian monastery, dependent on Holyrood, but gives no authority for this; it also says that the tower (Archdeacon Monro's "steipeill") is older than the church and was called "Tur Mor Chliamain" (Clement's Great Tower). See also *Originales Parochiales* II i 377f.

37. It was 1266 before King Haco recognised defeat and ceded the territory.

38. Chron. Maj. V 89 (Rolls Series).

39. T. No. 128. CPR I 237.

40. Petrus de Cortiniacum and Gualtherus de Iovigniacum, two foreign soldiers, called here *crucesignati* (signed with the Cross).

41. T. No. 124. In this letter, it is added, "the Italian clerics in Ireland and Scotland enjoy their share", that is, they are to pay their share. This indicates that there were a considerable number of Italian clergy in Scotland. In CPR I 286, the Pope said England has so many Italian clergy that their provision to

benefices cost 50,000 marks yearly; this he ordered to be reduced to 8,000 marks. (In this, the Popes themselves had been the chief offenders.)

42. CPR I 263.

43. See my article on "Papal Collections and Collectors in Scotland in the Middle Ages" in BFDC 1945, reprinted there by courtesy of Sc. Church History Society.

44. BC I 1654.

45. CPR I 270.

46. BC I 2013. APS I p. 419a.

47. T. No. 176. Here the Pope says that Gamelin's choice had been supported by Robert de Prebenda, Dean of Dunblane.

48. T. Nos. 201, 202. Also M.

49. M. Sc. II 92 says 1256, but this cannot stand against the recorded dates in the story just told. Trivet: *Annals* says 1250. Sir James Balfour: *Annales of Scotland* says 1257. 1258, the date given in M., fits in with the known facts and with the appointment of his successor.

50. Reichert: *Acta Capitulorum Generalium* I.

51. So called by Quetif-Echard in *Scriptores O. P.* (Paris 1719, 2 vols.).

52. See my article "Friar Clement" in BFDC 1956.

CHAPTER V

BISHOP ROBERT DE PREBENDA
1258 – 1284

W HEN Clemens Scotus died he was succeeded by his Dean, a Frenchman from England,[1] Robert de Prebenda, or "de la Provendir". He belonged to the lesser aristocracy of landowners; in Victorian phrase, he was "a country gentleman". He therefore faced two different loyalties – to the English Crown and laws as a landed proprietor in England, and to the Scottish, as a Bishop in the national Church. These were not always easy of composition, but both were subject to the loyalty he owed to Christ and the Church. He found the Diocese in good order, considering its poverty; the main obstacles to progress in administration had been removed, so far as possible. His cathedral was still incomplete and new sources of revenue had to be discovered. Robert was a different type of man from Clement, with a different background; of necessity he had a different part to play, and he played it not unworthily, according to the climate of his times.

His origins

From a Nottingham assize[2] of 1287 it is learned that his father was Geoffrey de Rotyngton, that he had a brother, Adam, and a nephew, Richard Martel of Rotyngton, who in due course inherited from his uncle the manor of Hokenale Torkard (eight miles north of Nottingham). The Bishop had property also in Chilwell, Clifton and Slapton,[3] which lie to the south of Nottingham, near the Trent. The family of Martels (originally Ruddington, Rotyngton) much later founded a chantry in the Church at Flaworth, at which one of those to be prayed for was "Master Robert Prebend, sometime Bishop of Dunblane". In 1260 he was granted by charter[4] a certain proprietor's "whole rent in the vill of Ruttington"; a list of eleven freemen follows, their rents ranging from two shillings to nine, and one of them named

"Master Ralf de Prebenda". Probably it was from this holding, with its ecclesiastic title of *prebenda* (stipend), that the Bishop called himself Robert de Prebenda. Bain's *Calendar of Documents* has many entries in which the Bishop's English commitments are mentioned – Henry III granted him in 1266 freedom for life from Nottingham suits and from "the wappentake of Risclive" in the same county, by reason of his lands there; letters of protection in travel for three years follow in 1267; liberty to appoint attorneys for seven years to appear for him in all courts, so that he be not fined for absence, in 1267; permission in 1272, against the law, to carry "100 quarters of his own corn to Scotland as a favour"; and, in 1283, a protection for two years as he is "about to set out for Scotland". These and other entries[5] show the travel and responsibilities entailed by the Bishop's property in England.

Before his election as Bishop

In 1255,[6] if not before, Robert was Dean of Dunblane, for in that year the Pope mentions "Master Robert de Prebenda, Dean of Dunblane" and three others as supporting Gamelin's election to St. Andrews against opposition. These four were then present at the Roman Court as proctors of the Prior and Chapter of St. Andrews, and were allowed to contract a loan of £500 new sterling with which to meet their expenses, Gamelin and his clergy being bound by the Pope to repay the loan. This sum has only to be given its modern equivalent of £15,000 or more to show the cost of a plea taken to Rome, where every privilege or benefice granted had its price; out of the exactions all manner of officials took their share, from cardinals to scribes; later the Pope himself took his share. Robert used his visit to Rome to further his interests; in 1256, when he was a papal chaplain, he was granted an indult[7] to hold two benefices with cure in addition to the Deanery, and in 1257, while still in Rome perhaps, another[8] to hold a further benefice with cure of souls, over and above those granted the previous year. Armed with these indults he probably returned to Dunblane; in 1258 he was still a canon of Glasgow. All in all, he was not without the possibility of an adequate income when Dean of Dunblane, holding other benefices. To this plural-ism he was driven, with more excuse than many pluralists, by the meagre stipend of his deanery, and he was perhaps engaged in looking for further benefices when Clement died and he became Bishop elect of Dunblane.

Just when he was elected, and by whom, are not known; but it must have been in 1258, for the Register of Glasgow,[9] on 2 January 1258/9, calls him "Robert, by divine permission elect of the Church of Dunblane and canon of Glasgow". It would appear that he went again to Rome soon after his election, for he is still "elect" on 22 August 1259.[10] His journey to Rome was necessitated by his having to meet the large dues of bulls of consecration; on 13 August of that year the Pope gave him indult for three years to take and use for the payment of the debts of the See of Dunblane the first year's revenue of all benefices and dignities falling vacant in the Diocese. The debts, that is, were to be met by the parishes which fell vacant within three years; for a year, no rector or vicar would be given to a vacant parish.

Under 1259, the Chronicle of Melrose[11] tells a story greatly to the discredit of Robert, who was not only elect of Dunblane, but, if the Chronicle is to be believed, had been consecrated. The story is that Master Nicolas Moffat, Archdeacon of Teviotdale, Bishop elect of Glasgow, went to Rome to ensure his provision, but returned unconsecrated, partly because he refused to pay the fees demanded by Pope and Cardinals – he would not enter the sheepfold save by the door, but partly because he was opposed fiercely by those who went with him ostensibly to support him. The ringleader of these was R., elect of Dunblane, himself a canon of Glasgow, "who was so far blinded in his pride as to imagine that if the election of the other was quashed, he himself might easily be able to mount to the see of Glasgow. In this, however, he was disappointed, for John de Chyum (or Cheam) was consecrated and despatched from the Pope *de latere*, to govern the Church of Glasgow. As for this Robert, he was sent off to the bishopric to which he had been consecrated." When I read this I was willing to believe that Robert, finding his support of Nicolas in vain because of his refusal, honest man, to enter his episcopal office by "another way", saw a chance, and took it, of being provided to Glasgow; but that he was then the newly-consecrated Bishop of Dunblane, I found it hard to accept. My doubts were justified when, six months later, I discovered that, in the original, *electus* had first been written, and had been changed to *consecratus*. Robert's actions *vis-à-vis* Nicolas are not to his credit, but the Chronicle makes them much worse than they probably were. I believe it was only after his disappointment over Glasgow that he went forward to consecration, having met his papal dues by promises of payment out of first year's teinds of parishes which became vacant in the next three years.

His episcopate

Robert de Prebenda, still only elect and at Rome, began to seek improvements in the revenues of his clergy as well as in his own. He persuaded the Pope to allow[12] one of his canons, Richard de Stirling, to hold an additional benefice, and Robert himself to appoint three of his clerks to collegiate or other Churches of his Diocese, the clerks to be ordained and to reside in the benefices, which had cure of souls. The same day, 13 August 1259, the Bishop is given indult, because of his meagre income, to hold to his own uses the Church of Kilmaling[13] in his diocese, of his patronage, worth 10 marks, on the death or resignation of the rector. These, however, are the only records which have been preserved regarding the organisation of the Cathedral in Robert's time; few appointments to Cathedral or parishes occur. Over and above the four canons *ex officio*, two are noted: Richard de Stirling (1266), and William de Lacornere (1263) who was appointed shortly before Richard became Official of the Diocese. It was 1271 before three new canons appeared; a fourth was added in 1273, and a Dean of Muthill, probably a rural dean, in 1272. It was therefore only in the second half of his bishopric that Robert was able to organise his chapter with any completeness.

The Bishop witnessed a number of charters, royal, episcopal and local. The only one of interest is local – Earl Malise of Strathearn in 1270 endowed a chaplaincy in the almshouse of Inchaffray Abbey[14] with four marks from the rent of land called Mukrand; he also gave "the portion of land called Tolauch which Brice of Ardrossan held in the town of Dunblane" to provide a chalice and other gifts to the chapel. Unfortunately for the Earl, Brice had already given Tolauch to the Bishop of Dunblane. To straighten things out, Brice in 1271 granted by deed one mark to the chaplain, and "Tulach" (now so written) remained with the Bishop. A rectifying charter of the same year declared that Brice granted to Inchaffray sixteen acres near the bridge of the Abbey, which Earl Malise had given him in exchange for the land (now written "Cullach") in Dunblane, which the Earl now, with the consent of Brice, assigned to the Church of Dunblane. All's well that end's well. Malise's unwitting gift to the Abbey of another man's property, already bestowed on Dunblane's Bishop, cost him considerably in land and expense of charters; the beneficiary of the mistake was the Abbey; Brice lost one mark yearly; the Bishop finished as he had begun, with the land, variously spelt, but which seems to have been Tulloch or Cullach, somewhere in the city of Dunblane.

Several of the papal mandates laid on Bishop Robert are interesting, if only for the light they throw on the ways of the Vatican. Here are three:

(1) On 10 November 1263, to make provision of two benefices in Scotland[15] to Albert and Boniface, clerks, nephews of V., Cardinal of St. Eustace's, according to papal letters given to the Cardinal. The mandate had first been given to the Bishop of St. Andrews, who had taken shelter behind a papal indult, and impeded and even excommunicated the Cardinal when he tried to force the Bishop's hand. So the mandate was laid on Bishop Robert and on the Archdeacon of St. Andrews. I have not found how the matter ended.

(2) On 9 July 1264, along with Peter Letis, canon of St. Peter's, Rome, now resident in England, to make provision[16] to Peter de Curia, chaplain of "our beloved son John, Cardinal Deacon of Sta. Maria in Cosmedin (Rome)", of a prebend in Glasgow. Peter had been given the second vacancy, but the first had gone to G., canon of Glasgow, now promoted to the Bishopric of St. Andrews. Peter is now willing to resign his church, the second vacancy, and the Pope says he is to have one of the ancient prebends. This too was an ungrateful commission; foreign clerics, many of them Italian, with papal backing, were crowding into Scotland and other lands, and were increasingly unpopular.

(3) On 26 January 1263/4, to recover for several merchants of Florence[17] money which they had lent to certain bishops in Scotland.

But Robert de Prebenda was himself in trouble, for on 10 December 1263 Urban IV issued a mandate against him. He had been Bishop now for at least four years and yet still held on to the canonry and prebend of Dunblane which he held before his episcopal promotion.[18] This was contrary to Canon Law, though in cases of two later Bishops of Dunblane the Pope expressly sanctioned it. The Bishop of Dunkeld was mandated to cause Robert to resign the canonry and all the prebend he had received, the canonry and prebend to be bestowed on William de Lacornere, papal chaplain, who is to be inducted and maintained in possession by Robert himself and the Bishop of Glasgow. Quite a papal joke! This was extremely awkward for the Bishop of Dunblane; the Pope recounts in the mandate how Robert had already given the prebend to his nephew Nicolas, whom he was now advising to resist William, to William's great trouble and expense. The Pope ordered Robert de Prebenda to pay annually to William the equivalent of the prebend until he is put in possession. On the same date the Pope continued to rub the sore spot by mandating[19] the Bishop of Dunblane himself and the Prior of St. Cuthbert's, Durham, to carry out his orders, if the Bishop of Dunkeld is neglectful. Such cases as this, and there were many, might have warned the authorities at Rome that the organisation of the Church needed to be tightened; but matters grew steadily worse. The papal necessities were great, and the allowance, for hard cash, of exceptions to the rules laid down by successive Councils was a temptation which the Popes found too great to resist.

Bagimont's Roll

In 1274, the 20th of September, the Pope made an appointment which was to have severe and lasting effects on the revenues of the Scottish Church and on the economic resources of Scotland. That day he appointed Boiamundus de Vitia as Collector General of the tenths of Scotland for the Holy Land,[20] to enable the Pope to carry on the Crusades. Three days before this he had commanded the Bishops of Scotland to preach a Crusade and to grant a subsidy[21] for immediate relief, and shortly afterwards he laid a like responsibility[22] of preaching on the Dominicans. Bagimont, to give him his Scottish name, was empowered to appoint sub-collectors, and one of these was the Bishop of Dunblane.[23] Bagimont so organised the collection that before the end of 1275 he had surveyed every diocese, detailed the tenth payable by nearly every benefice and office of the Church, from bishop and abbot to prior, rector, vicar, chaplain and cathedral dignitary, and reported fully to the

Vatican.[24] His report, consisting of the taxes payable by the various persons, gathers all facts and figures under dioceses and occupies eight of Theiner's very large pages. It is impressive for its times. The collection was to be made over six years, and the 1275 report gives the sums payable for each of the first two years. The total for the first three years was computed as £7,195 sterling; the final total reported in 1287 was nearly £18,000, equal to about £650,000 in modern values.

Before he explained his plan to the bishops, Bagimont told them that the penalty for non-payment was excommunication, and that, as the existing valuation was out of date, he demanded a new one in keeping with present incomes. The bishops protested to such effect that Bagimont returned to Rome with a petition that the old valuation be accepted; but the Pope was adamant. The details of the taxation give us a rough idea of the incomes and revenues of 1275; if we multiply the tax by ten, we get the yearly incomes; but I say "a rough idea", for these are only the admitted "stipends" and can be regarded as minima. Bagimont's Roll also gives an indication of the parish churches which had been organised at that date, and how they were served.

Examination of Bagimont's Roll will show that at its date the parishes of the Diocese were settled. The only omission from the Diocese of Dunblane is the Abbey of Culross, founded 1217.[25]

It being recognised that Dunblane's own records are lost, we may note the first appearance of the parishes in written records and get some idea of their time of establishment:

c.1170, Muthill, Tullibody;

c.1178, Kilbryde;

c.1196, Inchmahome (parish), Kincardine (in Menteith), Logie, Tillicoultry;

c.1198, Abernethy;

c.1200, Aberuthven, Kinkell, Dunning, Auchterarder, Strogeith, Dupplin, Foulis Wester, Monzievaird, Strowan;

c.1210, Dunblane (parish of);

c.1214, Exmagirdle;

c.1217, Tullibole;

c.1220-3, Tullieden, Trinity Gask;

after c.1233 and before 1274, Aberfoyle, Balquidder, Callander,

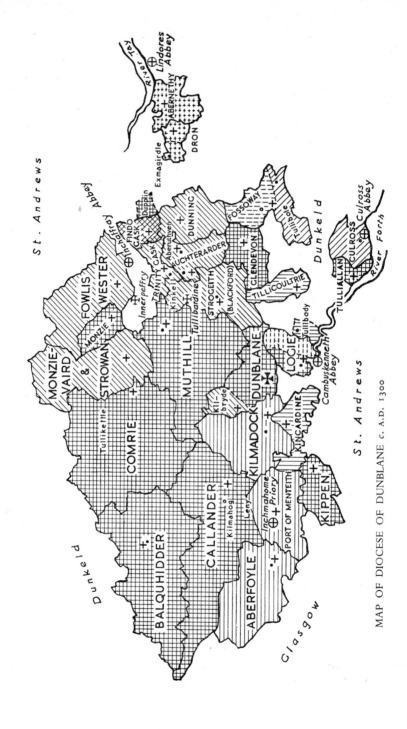

MAP OF DIOCESE OF DUNBLANE c. A.D. 1300

NOTES

1. TULLIEDENE (St. Serf's) was appropriated to Inchaffray Abbey, c. 1220, CAI No. 41, but its locus has not yet been found.

2. LENY, TULLIKETTLE, KILMAHOG. Their loci are indicated, but boundaries and sites are left indefinite, as uncertainly known.

3. INCHMAHOME. There was a church of this name on the island of Inchmahome in Lake of Menteith.

4. CRIEFF. This is not marked, for it was in the diocese of Dunkeld, except the altar and chapel of St. Michael in the parish church, which pertained to Dunblane and provided a prebend. CPR IX441 (A.D. 1445) refers to 'the parish church of Crieff in the dioceses of Dunblane and Dunkeld'.

✠ CATHEDRAL CHURCH

⊕ MONASTERY

☨ COLLEGIATE CHURCH

✝ PARISH CHURCH

• ” ” (ruin)

○ ” ” (site)

CATHEDRAL PREBENDS

▦ Appropriated to Inchaffray Abbey

▨ ” Cambuskenneth Abbey

▤ ” Culross Abbey

▨ ” Inchmahome Priory

▥ ” North Berwick Nunnery

▤ ” Coupar Angus Abbey

▨ ” Arbroath Abbey

▦ ” Brackley, Hospital of Sts. James and John, Northamptonshire

c. 1214

Erratum: Exmagirdle (pp. 37, 53, 73, 76) was appropriated to Lindores Abbey

Comrie, Dron, Findogask, Fossoway, Glendevon, Kilmadock, Kilmahog, Kippen, Leny, Monzie, Port of Menteith, Tulliallan, Tullikettle. These complete the Diocese with the exception of Culross and a small part of Crieff (which was mostly in the Diocese of Dunkeld).

Certain parish churches are not mentioned in Bagimont's Roll, but all of these had been by that date appropriated to an abbey, which then became responsible for the tax on the church. The omissions and their appropriators are:

Inchmahome Priory – Leny and Port
Cambuskenneth Abbey – Kincardine, Tillicoultry, Tullibody.
Inchaffray Abbey – Kinkell, Monzievaird, Tullieden, Tulli-
    kettle.
Lindores Abbey – Exmagirdle.
Culross Abbey – Tullibole, Culross.

The parish of Dunblane is not mentioned in Bagimont's roll. That leaves only Monzie,[26] unmentioned in Bagimont and unappro-priated. Maybe it was too poor, but it has a recorded rector at least forty years before Bagimont's tax.

Bagimont therefore shows that the appropriated parishes which, as noted above, are omitted from his taxation, were supplied with ordinances either by the monastic brethren or by chaplains ap-pointed and paid by the abbey concerned. Other appropriated parishes, which are taxed in Bagimont, had vicars, duly beneficed and "enjoying" the vicar's teinds; such were Aberuthven, Foulis Wester, Strogeith, Dunning, Auchterarder, Logie, Kilmadock, Gask. Dron had emerged from chapeldom.

As there are only two instances in which both the church (meaning the rector) and the vicar are taxed, no deductions can be usefully drawn about the relative stipends. There is some confusion in the roll between churches (rectories) and vicarages; some churches in the first year are vicarages in the second, both with the same tax, and there are instances of the reverse. The roll shows that the Bishop admitted a stipend which in modern values was in the neighbourhood of £10,000 per annum. The tax of the Dean, the Chancellor, the Official and the Sub-dean are not noted; the Precentor would be taxed as Abbot of Inchaffray. The Archdeacon's tax was fixed too high for the first year, and was adjusted the second, to give him an average of about £750 in modern values. The Treasurer's tax for the first year would give him similarly £400, but he is omitted the second year. There are other discrepancies in the two lists, which make exact judgments possible only in some cases.

Robert de Prebenda's Scottish sympathies

Though Robert was a French-speaking Anglo-Norman, he proved his Scottish sympathies. Like the other bishops he supported King Alexander III in his successful opposition to Ottobone, the Cardinal Legate sent in 1267 to make demands on the Church. Ottobone was refused entry into Scotland, and though ultimately he did penetrate into Lothian in 1268 and called the bishops to his counsel, nothing came of it. The bishops decided not to attend, but to send two representatives with a watching brief, lest anything should be decreed by the Legate to the prejudice of the Church; they chose the Bishops of Dunblane and Dunkeld. The clergy likewise sent two, the Abbot of Dunfermline and the Prior of Lindores. Ottobone gave out certain decrees one being a demand by the Pope for a tenth penny of church revenues to be paid to Henry III for the crusade, but these the clergy of Scotland utterly refused to obey. He returned to the more agreeable England, filled with wrath, as Fordun tells.[27]

In 1274 Bishop Robert was a member of the Second Council of Lyons. His seal is attached to its Acts.[28] This was a Council of notable endeavour to reform the abuses of the Church. It had been prepared for by reports from all over Europe of those disturbing features which bishops desired to see amended. There had been a vacancy in the papal throne of more than three years, and the Council heard an opening address from the new Pope, Gregory X, demanding speedier elections by the enclosure of the cardinals and a gradual reduction in food the longer they deliberated, till they were on bread and water. This had little result, for eight years later there was a papal vacancy of seven months. The Pope's memoranda which had been compiled rivalled, and even outdid, says Dr Coulton,[29] the denunciations of Wyclif. Among useful reforms was the introduction of the necessity of a two-thirds majority of votes in all ecclesiastical elections, the rule having been applicable, since 1215, only to the election of the Pope. If the majority was less than two-thirds, the plea of *sanioritas* (the weight of wisdom) might be adopted as validating the election.[30]   Resolutions were passed against pluralism, and the necessary qualifications for parochial clergy were clearly stated – he must be twenty-five years of age, of sufficient knowledge, of sound character, and he must reside; the ordinary, however, might allow absence for a season; all parochial benefices were to be filled within six months, failing which the bishop was to make the appointment; the beneficiary must become a priest within a year, or be deprived of his benefice without warning. Rome never found it possible to obey these Canons of Lyons (1274).   Edward I of England said that the decrees of Lyons did not affect the royal dignity, and as they did not affect the papal plenitude of power, they were broken right and left.   The Council tried to solve the question of usury by declaring it illegal, but this negative attitude left the issue unsolved.[31]   The most notable work of this Council was its effort to reconcile the broken halves of Christendom, East and West, Orthodox and Roman, in face of the advancing Turkish (Mohammedan) domination; but the best endeavours of the members were scorned by the clergy of Constantinople, and the continuing rift allowed the Turks to go on their conquering way.

In 1275 Robert was appointed papal Judge Delegate,[32] with the Bishop of Argyll, in an odd dispute.   Bishop Cheam of Glasgow, appointed when Robert had sought the Bishopric, had bought the lands of Carmyle as endowment of three chaplains in his cathedral, but with money belonging to the Chapter.   Cheam's successor, Robert Wishart, was contesting the transaction.

Twice Robert de Prebenda was appointed by the King ambassador to the English Court: first on 10 April 1279,[33] when, with the Bishop of St. Andrews and Sir Patrick de Graham, he was charged to carry unwritten messages to the King's "dearest friend", Lord Edmund de Almannia, Earl of Cornwall; second, on 10 September in the same year, when Alexander III asked Edward I to give credence to what Robert, Bishop of Dunblane, and two others named, "shall intimate on his behalf *viva voce*"; he also asked Edward "to signify his own and his children's condition, which he hopes is prosperous".[34]

On 5 February 1283/4 eleven bishops of Scotland are recorded, but by titles only, as giving adherence at Scone to Margaret, "the maid of Norway", as heiress-successor of her grandfather, Alexander III.[35]   A few days before, Prince Alexander, the heir, had died, without issue; Prince David had died previously, unmarried. These were but the beginnings of tragedy for Scotland. The only direct heir was Margaret, an infant of weeks, or months at most, daughter of Alexander III's daughter, Margaret, who had married the King of Norway. Alexander III died from a fall from his horse on 19 March 1285/6, and "the Maid of Norway" became Queen of Scotland, aged about two years. In March 1289/90, in a Parliament held at Brigham, near Berwick, "Guillaume, evesque de Dunblain" (Robert's successor), along with the Guardians, bishops, earls, abbots, priors and barons, petitioned Edward I of England to marry his son, Edward, to their Queen Margaret. The Pope gave dispensation to this marriage of children; but Margaret died on her marriage voyage, at Orkney, then belonging to Norway, about 26 September 1290, aged about eight. Scotland's cup of tragedy was full. Thirteen competitors for the Crown appeared, and only in 1306 was the issue settled, after mounting uncertainties and troubles, when Robert I, the Bruce, grandson of one of the competitors, assumed the Kingship.

It is not known when Robert de Prebenda died, but he was alive on 25 March 1283, as an Inchaffray charter (No. 113) proves. It is said[36] that he and his contemporary, Bishop Richard of Dunkeld, outwitted the King, who claimed the right to take the movable estates of deceased bishops, by giving away their goods before death. His successor was confirmed in his election by Pope Martin IV, in December 1284.

His character

Robert de Prebenda was a not unsuitable successor to St. Clement of Dunblane. Though he had not the outstanding qualities of Clement, his saintliness, dynamic vigour, learning or preaching power, he had gifts which fitted him to consolidate his predecessor's development of the Diocese. It is a tribute to Clement's foundations that Robert was able to present to Bagimont a far from hopeless picture of diocesan resources, and though it may be thought that his own declared income was large when compared with the cruelly meagre pittances of the parochial vicars, that was in accord with the views of the times, and there were numerous claims on episcopal revenue. Much of the Cathedral had yet to be built, much of the cost to be met by the Bishop no doubt. To weather the storm of Bagimont's taxation required business ability of no mean order; even in spite of Robert's capacity there were arrears of payment which had to be written off as bad debts. By and large the parishes of the Diocese were in being in Robert's episcopate, though the income of some was very small; two could not be taxed, they were too poor. The population of Scotland in Robert's day was perhaps about 375,000; the Diocese held nothing but small villages and the castles of the great and of the lesser aristocracy; for the most part the people were small farmers and their servants, and tradesmen; the days of larger revenues were still to come. To these circumstances Robert brought the gifts and graces of an educated country gentleman turned bishop, who though Norman in origin and speech proved himself a defender of Scottish rights and privileges, who commended himself to the Kings of Scotland and of England alike, and who moved at ease in the highest circles, whether as bishop, ambassador or papal judge delegate. He had his faults, of course; he was a man of his times, in which self-seeking in church preferment was usual practice. I hope that there are unknown facts and dates in the Melrose story, which would give a more pleasant explanation. As to being a pluralist, that was not only common; it could be achieved only with the Pope's written permission.

It was not usual for Englishmen and churchmen of other nationalities to seek election to bishoprics in Scotland, though there are exceptions. Those sees were not attractive to ambitious men, either in conditions or income, though there were foreigners in plenty eager for the lesser offices of the Church. All in all, Robert de Prebenda was a useful and competent bishop and man of affairs.

NOTES

1. Robert de Prebenda was most probably of Norman descent. But by 1300 it is reasonable to drop "Anglo-Norman" as a designation for such men, for the Normans now regarded themselves as English.

2. Roll No. 671, m. 4; 23 Jul. 1287.

3. Further details in SHR, Vol. VIII, p. 439.

4. BC I 2216. The reddendo (rent for superiority) was "a pair of gilt spurs at Easter, or sixpence". From the Bishop's heirs or assignees, monks and Jews were excepted.

5. BC I 2395, 2439, 2440 (repeated II 65), 2442, 2443, 2656, II 66, 179, 190, 206, 207, 245. They cover 6 Nov. 1260 – 11 Sep. 1283.

6. CPR I 318/9. T. No. 176.

7. CPR I 334. 29 Aug. 1256.

8. CPR I 350. 30 Sep. 1257.

9. REG I 166.

10. CPR I 367. See DMCS, Chapter XX for costs at Rome: also CAC.

11. M. 184-5.

12. CPR I 367.

13. CPR I 367. There is no such parish in the diocese. I thought at one time that the chapel at Malling, attached to, and near, Inchmahome Priory was meant, but it was not in the Bishop's patronage. I finally concluded that this word was a misreading of Kilmahug, near Callendar. From Mr Peter D. Partner, whose assistance I asked while he was working in the Vatican Library, I received this confirmation, 9 Sept. 1954: "I have consulted the original register and I find that your conjecture is perfectly right. The word, quite clear, and repeated twice, is KILMAHUG."

14. The whole series of translations is found in CAI Nos. 97-99.

15. CPR I 414.

16. CPR I 413. T. No. 239.

17. CPR I 395.

18. At that time he was also Dean of Dunblane and canon of Glasgow.

19. CPR I 416 for this and the previous mandate.

20. T. No. 258.

21. T. No. 257.

22. T. No. 260.

23. NMS I 74, dated 1292, the only reference to this appointment.

24. T. No. 264. cf. SHS Misc. VI 25ff.

25. Cambuskenneth does not appear in T. No. 264 as taxed for the first year, but it appears in SHS as above.

26. CAI No. 56, dated 1226 × 1234. Magister C. is given as parson of Mugedha (Monzie).

27. Sc. II 108.

28. Sella and Laurent; I. Sigilli dell Archivio Segreto Vaticano.

29. Medieval Panorama, p. 490.

30. But who is wise enough to weigh wisdom? The Council of Trent introduced secret voting and the plea of sanioritas became invalid.

31. Edward I of England was the first statesman to decree (Statutum de Judaismo, 1275, following the decrees of Second Council of Lyons) that when the Jews were deprived of their business of lending money, they must be granted other openings in trade and commerce. Nevertheless he exploited the Jews and finally expelled them in 1290.

32. REG xxxii and n, 187/8, 190.

33. BC II 157.

34. BC II 164.

35. AP I 82. This looks like a list of Scottish bishoprics, not of individual bishops present and adhering.

36. Chronicle of Lanercost, p. 97. But in the case of Dunblane, it was the Earl of Strathearn who claimed the estate of deceased bishops. It was Bishop William, Robert's successor, who persuaded the Pope to allow him to make a will.

CHAPTER VI

BISHOPS

WILLIAM	1284 – 1296	NICOLAS DE BALMYLE	1307 – 1319
ALPIN	1296 – 1300	MAURICE	1322 – 1347
NICOLAS	1301 – 1307	WILLIAM	1347 – 1361

BISHOP WILLIAM 1284 – 1296

O N 18 December 1284 William, Abbot of Arbroath, was provided by the Pope to the See of Dunblane. The Chapter, of which he was canon *ex officio*, elected him *concorditer* (that is, unanimously), but for some reason the election was contested at the Vatican when William presented himself for confirmation. The opposition may have been based on technical grounds; it did not suit the interests of the Papal Court to have no hand in the election of bishops – very soon the Pope was to reserve such appointments to himself. The Pope sent the election to be examined by three cardinals; William resigned any right he had to the See (this was usual procedure), and the Pope then provided him to Dunblane. Ordonius, Bishop of Tusculum, was directed to consecrate him, and the Pope sent concurrent letters, with news of the appointment, to the Chapter, the clergy of Dunblane, and Malise, Earl of Strathearn, *patronus* of the See of Dunblane.[1]

Of William, formerly Benedictine Abbot, very little is known; but the records give these glimpses of him:

(1) When Master Richard de Stirling, vicar of Strogeith, died, the Bishop believed that the patronage belonged to him and conferred the vicarage, at the request of the Earl of Strathearn, on John de Legerwood, the Earl's chaplain. But the Abbot of Inchaffray produced to an episcopal court appointed *ad hoc* an imposing volume of charters and papal confirmations in his favour. Bishop William withdrew his claim, and the Abbot presented John de Legerwood as vicar; William admitted him and put him

PLATE III

Photograph by the late

WEST DOOR OF THE CATHEDRAL

James Tillie, Dunblane

in corporal possession. The Bishop's public consent to the settlement was dated 21 September 1287, at Arbroath. The final agreement was made at Kenmore[2] a week later.

(2) In 1291 Pope Nicolas IV granted to Bishop William authority[3] to demand from all concerned oaths on the possessions of the churches of the diocese. The Bishop told the Pope that he had been afraid to do this without papal backing. Every form of property was included – gifts of land, values of altars, rights and goods, movable or otherwise, acquired for "the decent and honest expenses of your funeral, or for remuneration of those who served you in life, relatives and others". The object was the payment of debts, "in order that the Church of Dunblane should not remain obligated to its debtors". Unfortunately no details have survived of this useful and evidently necessary investigation. It marked an important step in the ordering of diocesan finance.

(3) The same business acumen is shown in the permission, granted by the Pope,[4] to make a will, disposing of his personal property after payment of debts. The Pope declares that the Earls of Strathearn had by an evil custom taken the personal property of deceased Bishops of Dunblane. The Bishop is told to bequeath his money to the churches from which he derived his income.

In affairs of state, Bishop William was of little consequence. On 12 July 1291, at Stirling, he swore[5] loyalty to Edward I of England as overlord of Scotland. In this, he went with the crowd of clergy and laymen, including Malise, sixth Earl of Strathearn. Bishop William may have salved his conscience in this, if Fordun[6] is right in stating that Dunblane still owned three manors in England which had come down from the time of St. Blane; but even then, his oath was contrary to the main ecclesiastical traditions, and to the interests, of Scotland. To refuse the oath to Edward I, who was in control of Scotland, required heroic courage, and there was little of that in Scotland for the time being. Another day was to dawn.

"Guillame Evesque de Dunblain", and many leaders in Church and State, confirmed in Parliament at Brigham in 1290[7] the Treaty of Salisbury, which arranged the marriage of Edward, eldest son of Edward I, and Margaret, Queen of Scots, perhaps the most far-seeing decision of Scotland's medieval history. On her death before she reached Orkney, thirteen competed for the Crown

of Scotland, eleven of them descended through female line from
earlier Kings, one through male, but illegitimate, line from
William the Lion, and the thirteenth the King of Norway as
representative of his late daughter. In June 1291 the claimants
submitted the choice to Edward I, and on 17 November 1292 he
chose John Balliol, a poor specimen, though genealogically deserving. Balliol had sent forty commissioners to advance his
cause before Edward, and one of them was Bishop William.[8]
John Balliol reigned till July 1296. Though he owed his crown
to Edward, he found sufficient courage in 1295 to make a defen-
sive alliance with France against England. But in April 1296 the
English army defeated the Scots at Dunbar, and that was the end
of Balliol's resistance. He abdicated in July of that year, and
along with the clergy, nobles and other representative Scotsmen,
handed[9] Scotland over to Edward I, who kept him prisoner in
England for three years before releasing him to live in France at
his family estate of Bailleul, where he died in 1313.[10] Edward
then ruled Scotland as if he had conquered it; but William
Wallace took the leadership of the nation and a troubled dawn,
but a dawn of ultimate glory, began to arise for Scotland. Robert
de Brus, grandson of Balliol's opponent, restored Scotland's independence finally at Bannockburn in 1314. He was crowned at
Scone in 1306, when only four bishops and five earls were consenting, along with representatives of the common folk, to his
coronation.

Bishop William died in 1296, probably early in the year, for
his successor was appointed by the Pope before the year closed.
The few records show him to have had business capacity, though
in diocesan rule he would seem to have been a cautious man, who
asked for papal support in actions which were within his own
competence. In public affairs he showed no independent courage
and followed the other bishops and most of the great laymen in
their loyalty to the English King. There was little else he could
do in this regard, for that was the trend of interested expectation
among the ruling aristocracy, many of whom held lands in England
for which they owed feudal obedience. Scotland was waiting for
a leader.

BISHOP ALPIN   1296 – 1300

On the death of Bishop William, the Chapter of Dunblane

decided that they would choose one of their number to be Bishop, and that the method[11] of choice would be *per viam compromissi*, that is, by discussion which might or might not end in unanimity. They chose Canon Alpinus,[12] and were of one mind. The *compromissarii* who had the right to elect are known from Theiner – the Abbots of Arbroath, Inchaffray and Cambuskenneth, canons *ex officio*; the Abbot of Lindores, canon *ex officio*, but absent; John, the Dean; Walter, the Archdeacon; Peter, the Chancellor; Geoffrey, the Treasurer; and two canons, Michael de Dono Dei and William de Gosford. Thomas, Abbot of Inchaffray, is recorded as Precentor.

When Alpin presented himself in Rome with the necessary papers the Pope appointed two cardinals and a bishop to examine the election, and Alpin, diligently. The Pope was satisfied with their report and in his confirmation described Alpin as "a man commended by many for his knowledge of literature, his nobility of race, his honesty of morals, his meritorious walk and conversation, and for other titles of virtue". He appointed the consecration by M(atthew), Bishop of Porto, and he urged Alpin to take the yoke of Christ with reverence and added other scriptural injunctions. The day of consecration was 16 October 1296, and on that day the Pope sent letters of the appointment to the King of Scotland, the Chapter, the clergy of the City and Diocese, and to the Earl of Strathearn, patron.

Of Alpin's brief tenure only one fact has come to light – on 6 November 1296 he promised to the Roman Camera (Treasury) 160 marks in gold florins, and paid the money, the fees of his appointment.[13]

Alpin died about the end of 1300, or, at latest, early in 1301. During his episcopate stirring events took place, even on the borders of his diocese. William Wallace became the intrepid and utterly patriotic leader of Scottish resistance to the domination of Edward I, defeated the English army at Stirling Bridge, on 11 September 1297, invaded England with Andrew de Moravia and laid waste the northern counties towards the end of that year. When, in turn, he was defeated by Edward at Falkirk (22 July 1298), he resigned his Guardianship (he was one of twelve) and with five knights went to France. Later, having returned to Scotland, he was betrayed, handed over to Edward I, condemned as a traitor, though in his defence he asserted that he had never sworn loyalty to the King of England. He was executed at Smithfield in August 1305. Wallace deeply stirred the Scottish people, and without Wallace's inspiring courage it is more than doubtful if Robert the Bruce could have achieved the liberation of the land. But of Bishop Alpin's convictions and actions during this rebirth of the nation, nothing has come down to us. At least we know that he paid his dues to the Papal Treasury.

Bishop Nicolas   1301 – 1307

A letter[14] of Pope Boniface VIII to Nicolas, Abbot of Arbroath, dated 13 November 1301, described the troubled road to his appointment as Bishop of Dunblane. The Dean and Chapter had been unable *per viam scrutinii* to choose a bishop. Several canons of the Cathedral had been proposed, including Nicolas; failing agreement, all the names were sent forward to Rome. Only Nicolas went to Rome to further his candidature; in spite of ample delay, no others or their proctors appeared. An abbot could face the heavy expense; no poor canon of the Cathedral could. In due course, Nicolas resigned any right he had, and the Pope appointed him, out of the fulness of papal power. His credentials were of course scrutinised, and the papal letters detailed his gifts in much the same laudatory terms as were used of his predecessor, for such phrases were common form in ideas, if not in words. Theodoric, Bishop of the Papal City (Palestrina), was appointed to consecrate, and letters were sent to the Dean and Chapter.

Almost nothing is known of this Nicolas. The long struggle against England seriously disturbed the state of Scotland and its Church. This, while it forced acknowledged church leaders, like the Bishops of St. Andrews and Glasgow, into prominence on the political stage, submerged lesser men. Nicolas especially seems to have been content to keep out of politics, finding the times out of joint. Leaders could not avoid playing their part in the raging storms, but the rank and file of bishops and lesser clergy doubtless continued their church work unobtrusively, as do many of the churchmen in Eastern Europe today, while some of their leaders are in the forefront of the struggle for religious freedom. Nicolas appears as witness in several charters[15] of Coupar Angus Abbey. Beyond these there is no mention of him in any church or state document so far published. In 1307, he was dead.

Bishop Nicolas de Balmyle 1307 – 1319

When Bishop Nicolas died, the Dean and Chapter chose to elect his successor *per viam scrutinii* by general discussion, followed by a ballot. They had been instructed, by their patron perhaps, to choose one of themselves, *ex gremio ecclesie cathedralis* (from the bosom of the cathedral), which would also include the serving clergy. The Pope's letter[16] of 11 December 1307, gives the electors – the Dean (nameless); the Abbots of Inchaffray, Lindores and Cambuskenneth, canons *ex officio*; and canons William de Eglisham and Henry de Stirling. They came to the unanimous choice of Nicolas de Balmyle, Abbot of Arbroath, whose name naturally does not appear among the electors, though he was canon *ex officio*. He went to Rome for confirmation, accompanied by the Chapter's procurators and nuncios, who are unfortunately not named, but were members of the Chapter. Again the decree of election was examined by a bishop and two cardinals and Nicolas de Balmyle was appointed with the usual formula of gifts and talents. The Bishop of Ostia, also a Nicolas, was detailed to consecrate. The Dean and Chapter and the Earl of Strathearn were informed.

Before he became a canon of Dunblane Nicolas de Balmyle had been Chancellor of Scotland,[17] his tenure of that high office of state being in that uncomfortable period, 1296-1306, when Edward I subjugated Scotland. In 1296 Edward ordered the clergy by name to give account of their lands that these might be restored to them after homage paid.[18] Among the clergy was "Master Nicolas de Balmyle, rector of the Church of 'Calder Comitis' in the sheriffdom of Edinburgh". He did homage at Berwick-on-Tweed to Edward for his lands on 28 August, and had his temporalities restored on 2 September 1296. Like many another who lived to see happier days in Scotland, he came full circle, when in February 1309/10, at Dundee, he was a party to the famous declaration of the Scottish clergy met in General Council, that of their good will they made vows of fealty to Lord Robert de Bruce, the illustrious King of Scotland, their lawful king, and on the document hung their seals.[19]

The Pope gave the Bishop only two mandates, both of them routine tasks; both were issued on the same day of 1317, and instructed the Bishop and two others to see to it that Robert

Barducii received a canonry and prebend of Glasgow as well as the deanery then vacant.[20] These provisions had been made by the Pope, at the request of Lewis, Comte de Clermont. I mention these mandates as showing the intrusion of another Italian into a Scottish cathedral dignity. This intrusion reached large proportions, and even the Pope, who sponsored many foreign clergy, being made aware of Scottish (and English) resentment, urged moderation of Italian requests for preferment in Britain. In 1312, he gave an excuse for it in a statute establishing a university in Dublin[21] – "doctors and bachelors in theology and masters in grammar or arts have no university of scholars in Ireland, West Scotland or Norway, so that in these parts there are few literate persons". That was true and was a reason for setting up universities in these benighted countries; yet it was 1413 before the Pope confirmed the 1412 foundation of St. Andrews University; 1451 was the date of Glasgow's University, and 1495 of Aberdeen's. Scots in considerable numbers studied at Paris, Cologne and elsewhere on the Continent, often with financial help from monasteries or from benefices to which they had been appointed. Indeed it was the numbers of Scots studying abroad which instigated the founding of Scottish universities, which in their turn greatly increased the learning of the Scots clergy. But in 1300 it was easier to appoint foreign clergy to the cathedrals.

In state affairs De Balmyle seems to have enjoyed the favour of Robert the Bruce and to have been often at court. Among the charters he witnessed were several royal ones which dealt with matters of intimate concern to king and country. In 1315 he witnessed the King's charter[22] giving the barony of Bathgate to Walter the Steward on his marriage to Marjory, "our daughter". When the King in 1316, and again in 1318, took Arbroath Abbey under his protection, Nicolas was at hand to witness, as he had been in 1312, at the King's confirmation of its possession of lands in Tarves.[23] He is also named as a witness in several charters of Coupar Angus Abbey.[24].

It was during De Balmyle's bishopric that the Pope ordered new values[25] to be imposed on parishes and dioceses for the purposes of papal taxation. In 1275, Bagimont on the Pope's order had fixed a new valuation. Now, in 1308, Bagimont's new values had become outdated. In those thirty years Scotland had become more prosperous and had experienced a consequent fall in what money would purchase, and the papal expenses were also rising. Scotland's resources rose and fell according to its political involvements; e.g. when it was faced with meeting the ransom of David II, true values, owing to the long war against England, showed a depreciation from those insisted on by the Bishop of Carlisle, who succeeded Bagimont and stepped up taxation. In spite of occasional rises in the value of money, it falls through the long years, and nations have not yet devised long-term stability in its purchasing power.

During this episcopate the Pope was much concerned with Robert the Bruce's successful resistance to Edward II and several times he urged reconciliation. Three years after Bannockburn, in 1317, he sent Cardinal Legates into Scotland,[26] England and Ireland to bring to peace the King of England and *Robertum de Brus Scotiam regentem* ("R. de B. ruling Scotland," not *regem*, king). When the cardinals presented their letters Bruce told them that they were knocking at the wrong door, for he was *rex*, not merely *regens*. The cardinals then sent a Friar Minor on the same errand; him Bruce refused to receive and on his way back to Berwick he was robbed of his precious documents.[27] But it was in June-August 1320,[28] that the Pope really rose to the height of his self-imposed task:

> on 16 June, Bruce, called to Rome on a promise of safe-conduct, was excommunicated because he did not go;
> on 17 June, the process was continued, with severer penalties against Bruce and all who adhered to him;
> on 29 July, the Pope (John XXII) wrote to Bruce explaining why the title of king was refused to him and urged him to peace, and on the same day he exhorted Edward II to peace with Bruce.

On 16 August, however, he showed by a letter that he was learning from experience, for he suspended Bruce's excommunication and again urged him to peace. By this time he had probably had time fully to digest the letter[29] of the Scottish earls, barons and laymen, written to him in Arbroath Abbey on 6 April of the same year: "If your holiness does not abstain from favouring them (the English) to our confusion, the loss of life, the ruin of souls and other evils that will follow . . . will, we believe, be laid to your charge by the Most High" and "So long as a hundred remain alive, we never will in any degree be subject to the dominion of the English, since it is not for glory, riches or honour we fight, but for liberty alone, which no good man loses but with his life." Even in his conciliatory reply, however, the Pope does not call Robert by the name of King, but refers to him as "that illustrious man Robert, who assumes the title and position of King of Scotland" and thereafter as "the said Robert".[30]

Something of this political struggle must be understood if we would appreciate the difficulties of the Scottish Church. Even after Bannockburn, and in spite of the Scots' capture of Berwick (March 1318) and their invasion of England's northern counties (May 1318), Edward II and his captains, supported by the Pope, were confident of victory. For instance, on 19 July 1319, Edward presented clergy, doubtless English, to 44 churches in the Diocese of Glasgow, to 34 churches in St. Andrews Diocese and to the Church of Kippen in the Diocese of Dunblane.[31] Two months later, the Scots army routed the English, who lost, it is said, 3000 men, including 300 clerics, at Mitton-on-Swale in Yorkshire, and Edward's presentation of Scottish benefices to his friends was reduced to a friendly gesture.

Nicolas de Balmyle was alive on 8 February 1318/19, when he witnessed a Coupar Angus charter.[32] Probably he died very soon thereafter. Bishop Dowden tentatively hints[33] that Nicolas may have died as early as 1318, but charter evidence shows that he was still alive in 1319, and that may be taken as the year of his death.

BISHOP MAURICE   1322 – 1347

It was not until 5 March 1321/2 that the Pope finally provided[34] Maurice, Abbot of Inchaffray, Canon Precentor of Dunblane Cathedral, to succeed Nicolas de Balmyle. The Chapter was divided between Maurice and Master Roger de Balnebrich, rector of Ferrewick[35] in the Diocese of St. Andrews, and as neither party would give way, both men journeyed to Rome. After stating their grounds, both candidates resigned their claims and the Pope committed the case to Arnold, Cardinal Deacon of Sta. Maria in Porticu. The litigation was being stoutly contended by both men, when the King of England, on 30 January 1319/20, gave warrant[36] to his Chancellor, the Bishop of Norwich, to put forward Friar Richard de Pontefract, of the Order of Preachers, "whom the King wishes to be preferred to the vacant See of Dunblane in Scotland". The ecclesiastical conflict was complicated by the political issue between Scotland and England; Robert the Bruce would resent the English King's intrusion and would undoubtedly press the claims of Maurice, his valiant chaplain at Bannockburn, while the Pope had shown his sympathies for England in the national quarrel. After lengthy consideration the Pope chose Maurice, and so informed the patron of the Diocese, the Chapter, the clergy and the people of the City and Diocese – all the usual parties, except the King. He authorised Cardinal Bishop Berengarius of Porto to consecrate Maurice at the Apostolic See, and sent the Bishop to Dunblane with his blessing.

But the date of Maurice's episcopate is complicated by a record in which he is named Bishop of Dunblane in 1318. An Act of the Scots Parliament records "Maurice, Bishop of Dunblane" as present on 18 December 1318, when at Scone Robert the Bruce recalled that in full Parliament on 3 December last, he had reinstated Henry, Bishop of Aberdeen, in the revenues of his see, of which for some reason he had been deprived.[37] This act is found, word for word, in the register of the See of Aberdeen.[38] Bishop Dowden's suggestion that "he was so styled, though only elect", hardly meets the difficulty. He was called "elect" later, on 5 March 1321/2,[39] and the records are usually careful in their use of the word for a bishop before consecration. Dowden also suggests that the date of the charter may be incorrect; but there seems to be no solution there. I suggest rather that some time in 1318 Nicolas de Balmyle may have been stricken with incapacitating illness, during which Maurice acted as vicar general,[40] until Nicolas recovered; that Nicolas recovered sufficiently to witness the Coupar Angus charter of February 1318/9; and that the temporary appointment then lapsed, but not before Maurice in December 1318 had attended in Parliament at Scone (at which his patron, the Earl of Strathearn, was present). Doubtless, Maurice ought to have seen to it that the scribes did not name him Bishop of Dunblane, without some qualifying adjective. But it is unlikely that he ever saw the document, which would be written up after the meetings and which would not in any case be submitted for his inspection. It may well have been that this entry was counted as presumption on his part and brought irreconcilable opposition to his election by some of the Chapter, when Nicolas de Balmyle died, probably soon after witnessing the Coupar Angus charter.

Maurice was more famous as abbot than as bishop, though his episcopal activity was distinctly creditable. As Abbot of Inchaffray he was Canon Precentor of Dunblane *ex officio*, and took part in the election of Nicolas de Balmyle. It is interesting to learn that on 30 January 1312/3, Edward II granted[41] "a safe-conduct till Easter next to Friar (*sic*) Maurice, Abbot of Inchaffray, coming to him in England and returning, with his retinue". Why the Bishop wanted to go cannot now be discovered, but it looks as if Edward was seeking allies in Scotland. Bruce laid waste the north of England in 1311, and the county of Durham in 1312, and, a few days before Edward gave safe-conduct to Maurice, had taken Perth from the English. Before the middle of March of the same year, Edward's troubles were increased by the Scots' capture of Roxburgh and Edinburgh Castles. But if Edward hoped to persuade Maurice to rouse an English party in Scotland, he called the wrong man to his counsels. Maurice may have been faced with awkward requests at Westminster, but his later history showed his staunchness to Robert the Bruce and Scotland. It may be confidently believed that Maurice would not have obeyed a citation to Westminster without Bruce's permission. It is possible that, when he reported to Robert the Bruce, he so impressed the King that he was appointed chaplain to the Scots army.

How Abbot Maurice carried himself on the field of Bannockburn (24 June 1314) is one of the great stories of Scottish history. After hearing the confession of the King, Maurice celebrated mass for the Scots on high ground for all to see and offered brief prayer for liberty and the defence of right, so efficacious, in its result on the Scottish army at least, that a low but happy murmur broke and the soldiers were roused to sudden and incredible audacity. Then, dressed in his ecclesiastical robes, and carrying the Cross, the Abbot passed before the ranks like a captain, and near where the battle was to be joined bade all bend the knee and make their prayers to God. So runs the quaint Latin of Fordun.[42] It is also recorded that Maurice brought to the campaign his Abbey's greatest treasure, the left arm-bone of the Celtic saint, Fillan, visited by numerous pilgrims, for by its ability to give forth light the saint in life could write in darkness. With canny caution, Maurice had left the precious bone at Inchaffray and brought only the silver shrine which housed it. This was so distasteful to the patriotic feelings of St. Fillan that the bone of its own volition made its way across the miles of fields and regained its shrine.[43] Doubtless the Abbot was duly humbled for his deception.

Anyway, the Scots, rising from their prayers, says Fordun, threw themselves impetuously upon their foes and much to the surprise of the English King, his knights and soldiers, won a resounding victory. So sure of victory was Edward that he had brought with him a Carmelite, Baston by name, to record his triumph in Latin verses; but it was of Bruce's victory that he sang,[44] at Bruce's orders.

On his consecration the Bishop found himself in debt to Rome, and in 1322 he was given faculty[45] by the Pope to borrow a thousand florins to meet his expenses at the Apostolic Court.

Bishop Maurice was not long home before he was mandated, 23 May 1322, along with the Bishop of Winchester, to excommunicate and cite to appear at the Roman Curia the Bishops of St. Andrews, Dunkeld, Aberdeen and Moray, who had encouraged Bruce in his resistance to England.[46] The document is of great length (8½ columns of Theiner's *Vetera Monumenta*); it recites the contemptuous refusals of Bruce (called *gubernator*, not *rex*, of Scotland) over a long period to receive nuncios, cardinals and others, even to read their letters or give them safe conduct – one who entered Scotland and denounced the King in broad Scots with a loud voice hardly escaped with his life. The two mandated Bishops are to excommunicate the four Scottish Bishops with ringing of bells and lighted candles, each being expressly named; the Pope promises the four recalcitrants safe conduct for journeys and stay. I can hear the laughter of Maurice as he read his orders, that he, the King's chaplain and confessor, who on Bannockburn's field passed before the ranks like a captain after saying mass and prayers, should curse in the Pope's name his like-minded brethren. Did not the Bruce call one of them, the warrior cleric William St. Clair, Bishop of Dunkeld, "my bishop"? Again the Pope was knocking at the wrong door, and I find it easy to believe that Maurice uttered no fulmination in public or private. Let Winchester see to it!

Three mandates were given him concerning the marriage of persons in his Diocese who had married, or wanted to marry, within the forbidden degrees. It seemed to be not uncommon for those within these degrees (four of consanguinity and four of affinity) to marry irregularly by "holding hands among their relations and friends instead of in church after banns", and later asking the Pope to regularise the marriage and legitimise their children. So it was with John de Graham and Maria de Menteith, in 1334,[47] who are to be given a penance and injunction by oath not to commit again the same offence; also with John de Kyndelochte (Kinloch) and Margaret Rusky, in 1340.[48] With Maurice de Moravia (Moray) and Joanna, Countess of Strathearn, in 1339, the case was different[49]; they asked for papal sanction first, for they wanted to marry but were within the third degree of consanguinity. Besides, they belonged to families at bitter feud, one of Maurice's forebears having been killed in the quarrels, and were afraid of the consequences. Romeo and Juliet in Scotland too! The Pope hoped that the Bishop would agree to their marriage, "if these things are so".

Maurice drew only one charter[50] of which I am aware: between 1322 and 1328, he granted with consent of his chapter the Church of Fossoway to Coupar Angus Abbey in compassion for the Abbey's poverty.

In public affairs Bishop Maurice took due part. He was present in Parliament at Scone, in March 1324/5,[51] and in the following August,[52] when Robert the Bruce confirmed to Scone Abbey charters which the English King had taken away,[53] and Maurice was commissioned[54] with the Abbot of Arbroath to renew charters which they knew had been stolen. In 1326, at Cambuskenneth, in Parliament, along with clergy, nobility and people of Scotland, he vowed loyalty to David, the King's son, then three years old, whom failing in progeny, to Robert, his grandson, the child of Marjorie. In 1326, also at Cambuskenneth, where Parliament was meeting, but perhaps at an extra-parliamentary gathering, a tenth penny of all rents had been granted[55] unanimously towards the King's expenses in the war of liberation; their portion, Maurice and his clergy paid in 1329 – £112. 19. 0[56] out of a total of £3163. 7. 3 for all Scotland; in 1331, they paid £145. 5. 3. Maurice was present in Parliament, held at Edinburgh, on 10-12 February 1333/4,[57] when he was a strangely consenting party to Edward Balliol's subjection of Scotland to Edward III of England, who had demanded it on 1 February of that year. Scotland was at its lowest ebb when patriots like Bishop Maurice were without hope of resisting English domination. Maurice witnessed at least twelve charters,[58] royal and other, between 1324 and 1344, none of them of modern consequence.

The last notice of the Bishop in the records is found in the Pope's answer,[59] 22 November 1347, to a petition to allow two persons to marry who were related in the fourth degree of kindred. These were Robert Steward, the king's nephew, and Elizabeth Mor, "a noble damsel"; she was daughter of Sir Adam Mure of Rowallan. They had evidently cohabited without even irregular marriage and now asked for the legitimisation of their "many children of both sexes". The case needed strong support and the petition was presented by the Kings of France and Scotland, and by seven of the Scottish Bishops, Maurice among them. The Diocesan (Glasgow in this case) was allowed to grant the petition, with discretion to impose on Robert the founding of one or more chapelries. But by the time the petition was granted, Maurice's successor had already been elected and consecrated. At the very latest, to allow time for the election and consequent visit to Rome, Maurice died probably in the early weeks of 1347.

Bishop Maurice has marks of distinct personality. He was a man of action and of affairs, who would have been prominent whatever sphere he had entered. He was a romantic figure in a romantic age, and a patriot in a time of divided and uneasy loyalties. Nothing has appeared to detract from his labours as Bishop of Dunblane, and the records portray him as a courageous man, a worthy chaplain to the Scots army and to the liberator king, and a churchman who for the most part knew where he stood in the conflicting issues of his day.

BISHOP WILLIAM 1347 – 1361

In the elections to the Bishopric of Dunblane after Bishop Clement a pattern emerges. Patron and Chapter seem to have agreed that the See should be held by bishops drawn in turn from the canons ex officio and from the canons of the Cathedral. Canon and canon ex officio alternate as Bishop from 1258 to 1361. True to this pattern came the election of William, one of the Cathedral canons.

In a somewhat florid letter, 23 October 1347, to Bishop William, Clement VI wrote of the election.[60] He described Dunblane as "a church immediately subject to Rome" and "specially reserved to the Holy See". This papal decree of reservation gave to the Pope the patronage of the higher benefices, with the attendant fees; it also gave him a satisfying feeling that he was in command of dioceses to the remote bounds and in control of policy, administration and discipline throughout the whole Church. This was only moderately true and mostly a pious imagination; but it did on occasion enable the Pope to intervene with effect. The Dean and Chapter of Dunblane had made, he says, "an invalid and empty attempt", knowingly or in ignorance, to break down the papal rights, and had elected William with acclamation. William too had consented to the election and come to Rome for confirmation. Clement therefore set the election aside and goes on, rather pompously – in order to provide for the Church of Dunblane, "on whose behalf none but ourselves can take a hand in this regard, and to prevent a long vacancy, and being of studious and solicitous intention, and eager that there be set over Dunblane a person who would know, desire and have power to maintain it in its rights and even to increase it, after diligent deliberation with our brethren . . . we directed the eyes of our mind to you, so skilled in letters, decorous in honesty of life and manners, so prudent in spiritual affairs, and in temporal concerns so circumspect, and in other gifts of virtue, etc. We therefore appoint you. Cardinal John, Bishop of Porto, is to consecrate you at Rome." Similar letters are sent to chapter, clergy and people of City and Diocese, and to the Earl of Strathearn, though he is no longer called patron. No letter was sent to the King, who was at that date in English captivity.

William's tenure lay wholly within the troubled reign of the unfortunate David II, son of Robert Bruce. David came to the throne in his sixth year, already married to Joanna, daughter of Edward II of England. He and his queen were anointed and crowned at Scone in 1331, when he was seven. The honest and wise Sir Thomas Ranulf, first Earl of Moray, the Guardian of Scotland, died the next year, and Donald, Earl of Mar, was appointed in his place. Four days thereafter, John Balliol's son, Edward, invaded Scotland and defeated the Scots at Dupplin, causing a third Guardian to be appointed in thirteen months.

Having been crowned King of Scotland at Scone by the English on 24 September 1332, Edward Balliol ruled the unhappy and reeling country for less than three months before he fled for his life to England. In 1333 the Guardian, the third, was taken prisoner, the Scots were routed at Halidon Hill (near Berwick) and the fourth Guardian killed in the battle. In 1334 King and Queen took refuge in France; two new Guardians were chosen in 1335, and in that year the Scots won one battle, lost another, one of the Guardians was taken prisoner by the English – thus the calamitous tale unfolds. Only a stout-hearted people could have continued to stand, and the end of woes was not yet. David returned in 1341 (he was now seventeen), after an absence of seven years spent mostly in Normandy; but in 1346 the Scots were defeated at Neville's Cross, Durham, and their King was taken prisoner. Again a Guardian was chosen. In 1356, in retaliation for Scotland's attack on England the previous year in the interests of France, Edward III inflicted on Scotland the terrible devastation of the "Burnt Candlemas", in which it is recorded that on the eastern borders his army burned every hamlet and town and destroyed churches, including Haddington Church, the "Lamp of Lothian". It was only in 1357, after eleven years spent in the prisons of his brother-in-law, that David was released, though in 1352 he had been allowed to visit Scotland to try to raise the price of his ransom. His Queen died in 1362; next year he married an extravagant and foolish woman, Margaret Logie, a widow, whom he divorced in 1370; less than a year later, David died, in his forty-seventh year. That was the catastrophic background of Bishop William's life in the diocese. The times demanded from all Scots, churchmen, laymen, nobles and peasants, a dogged dourness of determination if Scotland was to survive.

As if there was not already enough to test the stuff of the Scots, the Black Death reached Scotland in 1349. This "first pestilence",[61] considered the greatest, raged for a year and carried off a third of the people; "the sick hardly survived for two days an inflation of the flesh". The second pestilence[62] attacked Scotland in 1362, from Candlemas to Christmas, and the death-rate was very high of both sexes, of nobles, of rich and of poor. The King retreated to the north; he spent Christmas 1361 in Kinloss.

And yet the work of the Church went on, in parishes, cathedrals and religious houses. Scotland needed all the inspiration which the Church could give, and the comfort in disaster; but these activities do not come down to us in the records, and must be taken as diligently prosecuted, in many areas at least. What even the detached student finds it less easy to endure is the stream of mandates from distant Popes, laying on bishops of Scotland the burden of providing benefices to churchmen, some of them not even ordained to the priesthood, some of them relations of papal favourites, and nearly all of them mulcted of large fees at the Roman Court. The traffic in benefices greatly increased about the time when William began his episcopate, and the hey-day of the pluralist was near. The hunt for benefices in Scotland, as throughout Christendom, was unbelievably shameless – scholars of high learning mingled with the less talented in the miserable scramble, and those who had none to help them were in sore plight. About this time too, the process of obtaining canonries and benefices became more highly organised. Candidates per-suaded king, queen, bishop, university, noble, to petition the Pope in their favour. Rolls of petitions were so presented, and most of them the Pope granted; in one case at least he granted two petitions of two different men for provision to the same church – what did the Pope or his officers know or care about the details? The traffic was heavy, vacancies were many but aspirants many more. Simony was common, often reported to the Pope by disgruntled and unsuccessful candidates, the amount of the bribe being sometimes stated. Mandates were given to bishops to obtain benefices for their friends in the dioceses of other bishops. Such mandates, if obeyed, sent bishops to knock at one another's doors, not by way of friendly request on behalf of a friend, but by way of mandated interference from the Pope himself. Probably the mandates came often too late, the bishop having already appointed whom he desired. The scheme was too clever and brought papal mandates into bad repute.[63]

William of Dunblane had his share of those opportunist mandates:

in 1348, to provide Michael de Monymusk to a canonry of Brechin[64] (this followed William's petition to the Pope to the same effect);
in 1349, to provide David de Fullerton, to a benefice of named value and duties, in the gift of the Bishop of St. Andrews.[65]

again, in 1349, to provide to the Archdeaconry of Dunkeld
reserved to the Pope, Master Walter de Wardlaw, M.A.,
though he is canon and prebendary of Glasgow, and has the
Church of Dunino (St. Andrews), which he is to resign[66];
and eight more such between 1349 and 1354, in which he is
ordered to provide clerics to benefices in dioceses other
than his own.[67]

The Bishop is recorded as witnessing at least six charters, two
of them royal confirmations of a gift to Kelso Abbey and of its
possessions,[68] the others demanding no elaboration. He was appointed[69] to give benediction to James, Abbot of Paisley, on his
installation.

As already noted, David II was allowed to leave his prison in
1352 and visit Scotland. Hostages having been provided, he was
sent to Berwick Castle to raise money for his ransom and was
able to move about, on sufficient security. But, before this visit,
Scottish ambassadors had been granted, on 7 March 1350/1, safe
conduct[70] in order to treat with English ambassadors at Hexam,
and the Scots chosen were the Bishops of St. Andrews, Brechin,
Aberdeen and Dunblane. Later, on 28 June of the same year,
another safe conduct[71] was granted by the English King for certain
bishops and magnates of Scotland to confer at Newcastle on peace;
this time, the Bishop of Caithness took the place of his fellow
Bishop of Aberdeen. These emissaries were allowed 24 horsemen, as well as foot-soldiers, servants and horses, etc. Nothing
came of these talks beyond the permission to David to visit Scotland. It was some time before Scotland could face the vast sum
of a king's ransom; only on 28 September 1357 did several of the
bishops, including William of Dunblane, appoint the Bishops of
St. Andrews, Caithness and Brechin (he was Chancellor of Scotland) as their proctors for the ransom.[72] They were given a papal
grant,[73] on 9 August 1359, of a tenth of revenues of all benefices
in Scotland for three years towards the sum required. The Diocese of Dunblane was valued in 1357 at £376. 13. 4d, plus
£30. 19. 4d from the Bishop's lands. The tenth would therefore
amount to £40 or thereby, for each of the three years.

Bishop William, as the date of his successor's consecration
shows, cannot have lived very far into 1361. He lived in a dis-
tressful time, and in it played an honest and patriotic part. His

H

value was recognised in state affairs and by his brother bishops. It was a time that called for lay leadership and wisdom and for military prowess, rather than clerical guidance, in matters of state; but in those realms of church influence, inspiration, comfort and courage in dire straits, William seems to be the kind of man who would not fail his diocese, clergy or people. Let me call him a useful and fatherly bishop, faithful in his vocation and patriotic, recognised by Parliament as having the gifts and patience necessary in conference with the enemies of his people, not a leader in Church or in State, but possessed of a spirit of devotion and calling which enabled him to play a worthy, if unspectacular part, in the calamitous and stoutly-borne experiences of the Scottish people.

NOTES

1. CPR I 472, 473. T. No. 284.

2. CAI No. 118. The Bishop's Court included John, Abbot of Cambuskenneth; Master W. de Monros, Archdeacon of Dunblane; W. de Stirling, Robert de Dundee, and Alpinus, canons of Dunblane; Dominus N., rector of Crieff; Alan de Kynbuck; Colin, son of Gilleglas; Malcolm de Kinross; Moynache, son of Alpinus (who succeeded William, 1284-96, as Bishop). Patronage, then as later in the Church of Scotland, was a bone of contention.

3. T. No. 343.

4. CPR I 540. T. No. 343.

5. BC II 508.

6. Sc. II 160 (Goodall).

7. All the Bishops are named in French; the document is partly in Latin, partly in French. NMS III 1. SDI I 129. The date is 17 Mar. 1289/90. AP I 441-2.

8. Foedera I 767. Balliol chose also Walter, Archdeacon of Dunblane; the Abbot of Cambuskenneth; Malise, Earl of Strathearn; and William de Moravia de Tullibardine. The Diocese of Dunblane seemed to favour Balliol. Bruce also sent forty, none of them from the Diocese of Dunblane.

9. Ragman Roll, reprinted in BC II 823, dated 3 May – 29 Aug. 1296.

10. This date has been questioned, but Dunbar: Kings of Scotland 117 n.14 gives authorities for 1313.

11. There were three methods of choice: (1) *per spiritum Sanctum*; i.e. by unanimous accord, as Bishop William was chosen, (2) *per compromissum*, i.e. by discussion; a minority of one unyielding person could upset the election, as in case of Alpin, (3) *per scrutinium*, i.e. by ballot, the majority deciding; so in case of Alpin's successor.

12. T. No. 355. SDI II 115-18.

13. This fact I owe to Prof. J. H. Baxter, St. Andrews, who copied it in Rome, from Codex Lateran., 3457, f. 4 in Vatican MSS.

14. T. No. 369.

15. Undoubtedly in CACA I 172 (*c*.1304), 176 (*c*.1304), and I 186 (*c*.1306). But as he was succeeded by another Nicolas as Bishop of Dunblane, it is impossible, because the charters are not dated, to say which of the two witnessed CACA I 160, 161/2, 190/1, 192, 193, 194, 195, 196.

16. T. No. 386. CPR II 33.

17. RPSA 120. In this, 31 Jan. 1300/1, he claimed and discharged fees due while he was clerk in Arbroath Abbey and for his services as Chancellor of Scotland. He alone of Dunblane's Bishops was Chancellor of the realm; cf. Crawfurd: *Lives of Officers of the Crown in Scotland.*

18. Rotuli Scotiae I 25. BC II p. 213. This is the Ragman Roll, 1296.

19. The original is in H.M. Register House, Edinburgh. AP I 100 black, 460 red.

20. CPR II 169, 170.

21. CPR II 102.

22. NMS II 18. CC I No. 77, Parliament meeting in Ayr parish church, 27 Apr. 1315, enacted that if Robert I had no son, the succession should be (1) his brother Edward, or one of his sons, (2) failing them, Marjorie, his daughter.

23. 1316, LAc II 537; 1318, CC I No. 83A; 1312, CC I No. 72A and LAc II 536.

24. CACA Index, cf. note 15 above.

25. T. No. 385, 12 Aug. 1308.

26. T. No. 404.

27. See the amusing account of this in Hume Brown: I 132 (large edition).

28. T. Nos. 427, 428, 429, 430, 431.

29. AP I 114, 115 black, 474, 475 red. Duplicate in Register House, Edinburgh.

30. T. No. 433. CPR II 428. Date 28 Aug. 1320.

31. BC III 653.

32. CACA I 216. The late Dr D. E. Easson informed me that the date given to this charter in CACA I 216, namely 8 Feb. 1319/20, ought to be 8 Feb. 1318/19.

33. DBS 201-2.

34. T. Nos. 441, 442, 443 (23 Mar. 1321/2), CPR II 221, 222.

35. Original reads "Ferrewict". The place may be Ferryport, now Tayport. "Ferrywick" means ferry-bay.

36. BC III 689; but the actual petition, Foedera II 428, is dated 25 Jun. 1320.

37. AP I 118 black, 478 red. DBS 108, 109.

38. RA I 44, 45.

39. T. No. 441; CPR II 221.

40. There is no record of his appointment as such; but the office was of episcopal appointment and usual. I put this forward as a possible explanation of a difficult circumstance.

41. BC III 300.

42. Sc. II 250 (Goodall).

43. Boece.

44. Sc. II ch. 22 (Goodall) gives the poem.

45. CPR II 222.

46. T. No. 445. CPR II 449, 22 Apr. 1322. The Pope personally cited them, 8 Jan. 1320/1, CPR II 192.

47. T. No. 515; CPR II 411. RBM I 103-4.

48. T. No. 547.

49. T. No. 545.

50. CACA I 224-5, 225-7, 228.

51. DBS 203.

52. AP I 122. LS 101. Not 1323 as in DBS 203.

53. AP I 9, year 1292.

54. LS 101.

55. NMS II 22.

56. ERS I 181. The payment in 1331 as given was "for the same peace", the tax was a necessity but also a thanksgiving. ERS I 395.

57. Foedera IV 591. Maurice is not named except as "dunblanensis"; five bishops are given their personal names and titles; only the bishops of Dunblane and Brechin are entered by their titles.

58. RMS I App. I 27, 96. Fraser: *Carnegies of Inveresk* II 483-4. LS 96. REG 241. RBM II 229. "Blackfriars of Perth" 27. CAI No. 130. Liber de Calchou II 366. LAc II 18. CPR II 314, 450.

59. CPR Pet. I 124. This case aroused much controversy regarding the succession of their son, Robert III, to the throne. In Goodall's Sc. there is a long and learned dissertation in 16 closely-printed pages of foolscap in the Latin of John Gordon, advocate. The male petitioner became Robert II.

60. T. No. 576. CPR III 256.

61. Ex. 182. In the Roslin additions to Ex. the date is given as 1350.

62. Ex. 188. Fordun: Annals, 183. Roslin additions to Ex. also give 1362. In 1401, another plague struck Scotland, Ex. 208, when a quarter of the population died.

63. G. Barraclough: *Papal Provisions*, calls this papal procedure in spiritual cases "as impartial and well-balanced as human ingenuity could contrive"; he regards it as "a great achievement and probably an achievement which only a jurisprudence exercised with a consciousness of the nearness of God and of eternity could have produced". This cannot stand as a valid judgment, in the light of the twelfth and thirteenth and later centuries' Roman authoritative condemnation of the practice from Popes down. Hamilton Thompson: *The English Clergy*, 13n, referring to those judgments of Barraclough, asks "But can this be meant to be taken seriously?"

64. CPR III 294. Bishop William's petition is found in CPR Pet. I 142.

65. CPR III 298. CPR Pet. I 152.

66. CPR III 315.

67. CPR III 341, 361, 366, 389 (2), 417, 422, 518. The references to the same, except 417, in CPR Pet. I are 188, 201 (3), 205, 226, 257.

68. *Liber de Calchou* II 385, 387-9. One of the other four is CAI No. 132, in which Nicolas de Kinbuck, Archdeacon of Dunblane, acknowledges, the Bishop adding his seal, Inchaffray's right to 20 shillings of teind from his land of Pettynefive, which was in Trinity Gask, though it belonged to the Church of Nesgask which was Archdeacon's mensal. Trinity Gask belonged to Inchaffray.

The others are in SHS Misc. V 19, 20; CR 255-6; RDD 265-6, dated 18 Feb. 1353/4.

69. CPR III 350.

70. *Rotuli Scotiae* I 740 a.

71. *ut sup.* I 741 a.

72. BC III 1650. AP I 155 (where William is wrongly called Walter, his successor's name). William was present also at a Council held at Inverkeithing, AP, 1354, Supp. 9.

73. TV I 12.

CHAPTER VII

BISHOPS

WALTER DE COVENTRE   1361 – 1371
ANDREW   1372 – 1380   FINLAY DERMOCH 1403 – 1419
DOUGAL   1380 – 1403   WILLIAM STEPHAN 1419 – 1429

BISHOP WALTER DE COVENTRE   1361 – 1371

ON 18 June 1361 Pope Innocent VI wrote to Walter, Dean of Aberdeen, appointing him to the Bishopric of Dunblane. The letter does not seek to hide the papal displeasure; as in their election of Bishop William in 1347, when they were duly rebuked,[1] the Chapter of Dunblane had again tried to by-pass the papal reservation and had elected Walter. In equal ignorance, "as you assert", you, Walter, accepted the See. The Pope declared the action *irritum et inane*, invalid and of no effect. All this was true; the papal reservation was violently disliked as interference and as a means to additional papal income, for in the end, when the papal reservation was challenged by local parties, the Pope in most cases appointed the local choice, who in this case had been elected with acclamation. After declaring Walter's election null and void, the Pope appointed him, and wrote to the Chapter, the clergy and people of the Diocese, and to all the vassals of the Church, to the Earl of Strathearn and to David the King.[2]

This was Walter de Coventre,[3] a superb example of the higher clergy of his day, a scholar of high academic attainments in more than one European university, a diligent and successful pluralist, who won through to the episcopal ring and mitre. He is indeed "a period piece" of ecclesiastical self-seeking, though everything he did was within the practice, if not within the laws of Councils, of the Roman Church of his times, and he ought not to be judged by modern concepts. When he was appointed Bishop of Dunblane, he was Dean of Aberdeen, canon and prebend of Dunkeld and Ross, and rector of Inverarity in the Diocese of St.

Andrews.[4] He was also a canon of Abernethy,[5] and had provision to the Archdeaconry of Dunblane[6] (which he may never have got) and to a canonry of Moray.[7] It is difficult to keep exact account of his moves on the chess-board of clerical promotion, but it is an illuminating tale.[8]

In spite of his English title, Walter seems to have been of Scottish birth. He belonged to a family of notorious pluralists; the student follows the De Coventres through the records, John, William, Walter, Richard, Robert and Thomas, as in the gyrations of an old-fashioned waltz. England, Wales and Scotland were their ample dancing-floor, and while there were individuals like Adam de Tiningham, who struggled through a busy life of petitions till at last he reached the Bishop's throne (Aberdeen), I have not found in the Scottish records of Walter de Coventre's time a family of such numbers so immersed in self-seeking promotion. Later such families were to become fairly common. Walter elevated advancement into a science and had many imitators. More and more the validity of the Church rested on the miserably paid, but often competent, vicars of the parish churches.

On the academic side Walter had high attainments. He is, with the exception of Clement, who was a university *magister*, the first of Dunblane's Bishops to come from the universities adorned with degrees. Others may have studied in Paris and probably Oxford, and some perhaps at Rome, but any degrees they carried are unknown. Walter, however, bursts upon Dunblane like a sudden dawn – Master of Arts, Doctor of Canon Law, Bachelor of Civil Law, all before 1350.[9] He was a determinant in the University of Paris in 1333,[10] that is, an enrolled student intending to take a degree; for more than twenty years he gave himself to academic studies; one of his name, most likely the man himself, was professor in 1350 at the University of Orleans.[11] During that long period he was supported by the prebends of canonries and other benefices which he had obtained for this and no other purpose; even in 1349 the Pope gave him the Deanery of Aberdeen, for five years *in absentia*, to enable him to study Civil Law, Walter being even then only a sub-deacon and therefore canonically unable to fill a deanery even if he had wanted.[12] In modern slang, pluralism was "a racket". The best that can be said for it can be said in Walter's case, that he had high scholastic attainments to show for his pluralism, and what the Church lost in pastoral service it gained in high learning. His training was that of a professor, though Scotland had no university in his day; but the Bishopric of Dunblane, which had little outlet for such vast learning, was his reward.

The loss of the medieval records of Dunblane makes it impossible to fill in the details of his diocesan activities. It would have been interesting to see how his professorial training fitted, or unfitted, him for the administration of his see. Other sources however deal with the larger events of church and of public life, and in these Walter played a part, neither outstanding nor undistinguished.

In church affairs we may note his work on these lines:

(1) In February 1364/5 Walter reduced the top-heavy establishment of the Collegiate Church of Abernethy from ten canons to five.[13] He himself had been a canon there in 1345, shortly after the Church of St. Mary the Virgin and St. Bridget had been transformed into a college (though this may have been done as early as 1326). Though Walter reduced the number of canons in 1364/5, it was 1373, two years after Walter's death, before the Pope commissioned the change,[14] giving the grounds that wars, fire and ruin had reduced the income. The new arrangement received papal confirmation in 1375,[15] and only then is the full story told. It runs: "recently a petition of the secular Prior and Chapter (of Abernethy) for confirmation described how the (Collegiate) Church was founded by lay patrons for a prior and five canons. At a later date some of the patrons were eager to augment its rents, and the number of canons was hopefully raised to ten. No such augmentation took place, and because of wars, fires and ruin the Prior and the Chapter were brought to straits. Bishop Walter, therefore, with assent of the patrons and King David, reduced the canons to five. The Pope asked the Bishop of St. Andrews to make enquiries; he reported that the free income, after payment of the yearly pensions, did not exceed 200 gold florins or 50 marks sterling, and was insufficient for their maintenance if they did not add to it by their industry." The original founders were the Lords of Abernethy, whose lineal descendant, Margaret the elder, Countess of Angus, had added her seal to Bishop Walter's in the original authorisation of reduction made at the Church on 8 February 1364/5.

(2) It fell to Bishop Walter to gather Dunblane's share of the

King's ransom of 100,000 marks, payable in two yearly portions. The miserable son of Robert Bruce was not worth much to Scotland, but independence was worth everything. David II, while visiting London in 1363, offered to acknowledge Edward III, or his son Lionel, as heir to the Scottish Crown, in return for the cancellation of the price of ransom; but the recreant proposal was rejected by the Scots Parliament at the first opportunity. When David died in 1371, only rather more than half the ransom had been paid; only England's need of an ally against France induced her to lower the annual payment to four thousand marks and to sign a treaty of peace for fourteen years. The parliamentary records of 1366[16] give the diocesan dues and payments – Dunblane had paid £407. 12. 8 (which included £30. 19. 4 from the Bishop's portion), and was £200 short.

(3) The Accounts of the Great Chamberlain carry details of many payments made by Walter de Coventre and his Diocese[17] towards the tenth granted to Robert Bruce at Cambuskenneth, July 1326, and continued to his son. In 1361 the Diocese paid £32. 10. 10; in 1362 £15 of arrears; in 1365 the Bishop paid £6 and £21; in 1366 £3 of arrears and £26. 13. 0; in 1368 £13. 5. 11 in 1369 £4, and in 1370 £25. 17. 2. To this tenth, Maurice, Bishop of Dunblane, in 1329 had paid £112. 19 shillings; the difference showed the much greater wealth of the country at that time. These sums were sufficiently large to strain the dioceses already burdened with increasing papal taxation, and now with the cost of the King's ransom.[18] The seriousness of this multiple burden was one of the reasons why so many burgesses attended Parliament at Scone in 1367 and why the business was remitted to a commission which was to hold parliament, while the rest went home to work the harvest. Such commissions, having delegated and stated powers, eased Parliament in the discharge of business and marked a constitutional development of Scotland.

(4) King David II divorced his second wife in 1370, after six years of marriage. She was Margaret Drummond or Logie, daughter of Sir Malcolm Drummond, widow of Sir John Logie of that Ilk. The times demanded restraint and wisdom, and she had neither. In 1371 the Pope, to whom Margaret had taken her cause, commanded the Bishop of Dunblane and two other bishops to compel the King to restore her possessions.[19]

He also wrote to Robert II, now King, urging him to come to an agreement with Margaret, who asserted that she had been ill-treated, expelled from Scotland and despoiled of her property.[20] Evidently Bishop Walter made little headway; Margaret had few friends, though the Pope did his best for her. He appointed a commission in 1374 to hear her complaint for the recovery of her dower land and jewels, "if it cannot be safely heard in Scotland".[21] She won her case, and her divorce was annulled, a few weeks before she died early in 1375.

(5) An Inchaffray charter[22] outlines a suit in which Walter de Coventre appended his seal, as did others, to a surrender of deeds, at the parish church of Perth on 30 November 1365. The others who sealed, in addition to the principals, were important; they included Robert, Steward of Scotland; the Earl of Strathearn; William, Abbot of Scone; Adam, Dean, and Andrew, Archdeacon, of Dunblane; Thomas de Fawsyde, Knight; Maurice de Drummond (ancestor of the Drummonds of Concrag, Stewards of Strathearn); Walter de Moray (Lord of Tullibardine); Tristram de Gorthy (the head of this notable family seems always to have been Tristram); Aythe, son of Thomas, at that time "Baillif" of Strathearn. The principals ("we have procured that the seals of those persons be attached to our present writing") were Nevin MacEwyn and his wife Mariota, daughter and one of the heirs of Malmoran of Glencharny.

To the Court at Perth were brought the terms of a settlement made between them and John, Abbot of Inchaffray, in the Chapel of St. Mary of Innerpeffry at some recent but undefined date, before Bishop Walter de Coventre and an impressive court which included the above Adam and Andrew, all the laymen given above, and in addition Donald and John, perpetual vicars of Strogeith and Muthill, and many others, clerical and lay, called and interrogated as trustworthy.

The matter at issue involved quite large financial settlements, but was quite simple. Some time before, Symon de Scone, a previous Abbot of Inchaffray, had pledged lands "within the shire of Madderty" to Malmoran, father of Mariota, for forty pounds sterling. Now Abbot John desires to get from Mariota and her husband all the papers, letters, writs, instruments, charters connected with the three named lands in Madderty, along with an assurance that Mariota and her husband, their heirs and successors will never claim to succeed to the lands in question. They agree to sell the documents to the Abbot for forty marks, and express themselves as well content.

The legal convolutions seem to sort out something like this:

(a) The Abbot and the MacEwyns came to a settlement, the latter "after solemn conference with relatives and the advice of friends", for their own benefit and the spiritual wellbeing of their predecessors, especially Malmoran and his wife Cecilia, and of their successors. This rather indicates that there was an element of benefaction by the MacEwyns, in return for which prayers were promised; but there is no hint of the amount or nature of the gift; indeed it reads as if they had been pressed into the transaction, or at least to accept less than they thought their due. This possibility is strengthened by the fact that the Abbot took the matter to two courts.

(b) The first court was the Bishop's consistorial court, which on this occasion met in Innerpeffry Chapel. No date is given, but the fact that this and the later court had identical members, except for two local vicars in the first, and a new chairman in the second, seems to show that the consistorial court moved on in a body, very soon after, to Perth.

(c) The court at Perth was presided over by Robert, the High Steward, Marjorie Bruce's only child, who became King Robert II (1370/1-1390); it was therefore of the nature of a royal court. In it the MacEwyns obliged themselves under severe penalties, which included 200 marks to the fabric of the Cathedral and of the Abbey, and the greater excommunication, if they or their heirs or successors sought on any plea in law to invalidate the agreement. They also promised to hand over any further papers which might turn up, and to put themselves under "the jurisdiction, coercion and judgment of the Bishop, Dean, Archdeacon, and their officials for the time being", who were to compel them to observe the terms. If they even tried to upset the settlement, the two hundred marks were to be paid, and the present agreement was to remain irrevocable and in full force.

In addition to the seals noted above, an impressive list of witnesses is given – two Priors (Dominican of Perth and Carmelite of Tullilum, near Perth), a vicar and a chaplain of Perth, one alderman, two baillies and six burgesses of Perth, "and many others".

It will be seen at once that this was a remarkable case. The introduction to *Inchaffray Charters* says "great formality is observed, and a number of important personages, ecclesiastics and laymen, assembled to witness the transaction, probably to protect the act of a married woman parting with her heritage". I cannot accept this as a valid judgment. If the witnesses were there to protect the woman, they only witnessed the imposition by the court of severe penalties, which effectively tied her and her husband and their heirs and successors to impotence and silence.

Here is clearly the background of the transaction. Symon de Scone, Abbot of Inchaffray, being in need of money, pledged to Malmoran, for £40 sterling (in modern values about £1500) three pieces of ground (farms, small estates) in the parish of Madderty. No written pledge has come to light, but there were "well-authenticated instruments", as the Abbot admits, although the transaction was contrary to Canon Law; that the pledge was meant to be as near a sale as could be is shown by all the deeds and instruments of the three properties having been handed over to Malmoran. But Symon de Scone died in due course, and John succeeded him. He also needed money (between 1248 and 1317 the Popes had on seven occasions appointed commissioners at the request of the Abbots to recover for Inchaffray property which had been lost by such uncanonical leases and pledges), and he proceeded to deal with Mariota and her husband. The power of Holy Church prevailed; the Abbot could point out the uncanonical nature of the pledge given and taken; parties came to an agreement; Mariota consented to give back the properties, and for 40 marks sterling to hand over all deeds which might be used to prove ownership. Though Mariota and her husband declare themselves "well content and satisfied", their private thoughts are not revealed. The Abbot promised prayers for their relatives, past and future, and for themselves.

The two MacEwyns are then taken to the consistorial court and swear to this agreement on the Gospels. The penalties already mentioned seem to belong to the semi-royal court at Perth, the actions of which are the basis of the record, those of the consistorial court being recounted as preliminary to the doings at Perth.

The story leaves a distinct impression of ecclesiastical pressure. I do not like thee, Abbot John.

(6) Walter was commissioned[23] on 13 March 1365/6, to grant dispensation for the irregular marriage of John, Steward of Kyle, later Steward of Scotland and Earl of Carrick, and Annabella Drummond of Stobhall in the Diocese of Dunblane. They had married, though within the forbidden degrees. John was the eldest son of Robert II and became King Robert III.

In affairs of state, Bishop Walter witnessed the royal charter of 1368[24] which created the King's nephew, Robert Steward (soon to become the first of the Stewart dynasty), Earl of Carrick. In 1368 and 1369[25] the Bishop was elected to parliamentary committees on general matters and questions of justice; few, if any, of the other members can have been so academically qualified in law. At Scone, on 26 March 1371, after the death of David II, he was present when prelates, earls and barons did homage to King Robert II, all "except the Lord Bishop of Dunblane and Lord Archibald de Douglas, who instead took the oath of fidelity". The point at issue is not clear. The day following he gave his promise to accept Lord John, Earl of Carrick, as heir to the Crown.[26]

His most important civil appointment came in June 1369, when the King authorised the Bishop of Dunblane and four other bishops, along with a distinguished list of barons and knights, to be his commissioners to meet those of the King of England in the interests of peace.[27] A truce for fourteen years was signed on 20 July 1369,[28] and when it was renewed at Westminster in July 1370, "Wauttier de Dunblan" was one of the signatories.

When declaration was made by King and Parliament at Scone, on 4 April 1373, settling the succession to the Crown in the male line,[29] Bishop Walter was dead, and Andrew, Bishop of Dunblane, is noted among those present.[30] Andrew was Bishop elect before the end of April 1372. To allow for the necessary arrangements, Walter de Coventre may be considered as dying in 1371, perhaps in the late autumn.

Bishops during the Papal Schism (1378 – 1429)

I. ANDREW   1372 – 1380

Andrew was Bishop elect when, on 27 April 1372, he was provided by the Pope to the See of Dunblane.[31] He was Archdeacon of Dunblane,[32] and was elected by the Dean and Chapter. He was barely in his episcopal office when a papal mandate, dated at Avignon, 1 July 1372, reached him and his fellow bishops in Scotland, to levy a tenth of church revenues for one year for the recovery and preservation of the lands of the Roman Church.[33] Another such,[34] this time "in aid of the defence of the Pope and the Roman Church in Italy", was imposed in 1374.

The records which mention Bishop Andrew are so few that they furnish excuse for recording them all. They are five in number and they cannot have added greatly to his diocesan labours.

(1) In 1375 Gregory XI wrote[35] to Andrew on behalf of Thomas Stewart. Thomas is described in the letter as a scholar of the Diocese of Glasgow "who desired to join the army of clergy, but suffers from being, as Charles, the King of the Franks, asserts, the son of Robert II, the illustrious King of Scotland". If suitable, he is to be dispensed for illegitimacy to hold office in the Church, even episcopal. He lectured in Paris University for five years, and had so satisfactory an income from his many benefices that in 1401, though elected, he refused the Bishopric of St. Andrews.

(2) On the same day the Pope asked the like of Bishop Andrew for James Stewart, scholar, of the Diocese of Glasgow.[36]

(3) In October 1375 the Pope directed the bishops of Scotland to assist Henry de Sancto Trudone (St. Trond, Belgium – i.e. Limburg), sent to collect the revenues of the Scottish Receptory of the Hospitallers of St. John of Jerusalem, at Torphichen.[37] It was an involved case following on an injudicious lease of land which threatened to be lost to the Hospital. The final settlement was that one Robert Mercer was given a lease for ten years at an annual rent of four hundred gold florins of Florence, to be paid in Paris.

(4) In 1380 the Bishop of Dunblane (unnamed) was commissioned by the Pope to confirm the annexation of the Church of St. Columba in Tiree to the Priory of Ardchattan.[38]

(5) It must have been shortly before his death that Bishop Andrew confirmed the election of William de Culros, vicar of Dunning, as Abbot of Inchaffray.[39]

Bishop Andrew had a kinsman, Michael, to whom he gave the perpetual vicarage of Abernethy. A petitioner[40] to the Pope asserted that the Bishop had previously given it to one who had died after a month, then to another who resigned, and then to his kinsman Michael, who was "under age and illiterate". The petitioner asked the vicarage for himself, and the Pope granted the request.

And that is the whole story of Andrew, so far as printed records tell. In the Diocese, two successive Archdeacons and a Treasurer are known, in addition to the canons *ex officio*. In the parishes no unusual activity is shown. This is very disappointing, for it is difficult to believe that so little was happening through the eight years of Andrew's episcopate. He was perhaps a quiet man and a godly, content with the even course of life during the fourteen years' truce with England, when the Scottish people in Church, State and public life were resting after long wars, dire pestilence and unnumbered woes. Though still burdened with papal and royal taxation, the people were doubtless thankful that they could cultivate their cabbages and chat quietly with their neighbours. Tired folk, left to themselves at last, are happy in doing nothing, and even those in high places, like Andrew, are content to loiter along the paths of easy routine. And who will blame them?

And yet the Papal Schism of 1378 must have created a stir in high ecclesiastical circles at least, though maybe not in the breast of Andrew. In that year, the Roman Church was split in two — so-called "true" Popes residing at Rome, so called "Anti-popes" at Avignon, dividing the allegiance of Christian countries for half a century. The Schism, so scandalous in the spectacle it presented to the world, was largely political in origin and did not, in religious affairs, work the havoc which might have been expected. In their rivalry, each Pope sought to govern the national churches faithful to him, but at times sent nuncios into the territory of his rival. The Avignon Anti-popes were for the most part men of superior stature and moral quality to the Roman Popes; but that was not the reason why Scotland adhered to Avignon. France naturally adhered to the Avignon Popes and Scotland followed her ally, as did Spain, Sicily and Cyprus. England could not side with France, for the issue was not religious but political, and with England stood Italy, Austria, Bohemia and Hungary. This sorry confusion continued till 1429, when Clement VIII, Pope at Avignon, abdicated. But before that date, countries faithful to Avignon began to fall away, until at the last only Scotland remained in the Avignon fold. Benedict XIII (Avignon), deposed in 1409 and again in 1417, had never tried to govern the

Scottish Church, which, having no Archbishop, drifted helplessly; every bishop became a law to himself, abuses grew in number and depth, pluralism entered its heyday, clerical morality declined, the bishops aped the style of living practised by lay magnates, and advanced their relatives to benefices even when under age, unordained and at times uneducated. Only the energy of Bishop Trail of St. Andrews sought to bring his diocese to discipline, as, the "Synodal Statutes of St. Andrews" show. But these had no authority beyond his diocese, and even twenty years after their promulgation, when the Church held a General Council in 1420 at Perth, with the Church tottering, internally at sixes and sevens, and externally in confusion, the only matter on the agenda was the right of bishops to confirm wills and to administer intestate estates. Before that, in 1417, on 2 October, Scotland at last adhered to Rome – there was no Avignon Pope to adhere to; although one such, Clement VIII, was appointed in 1424, no national Church and no country now adhered to him, and he abdicated five years later. Nothing of this stormy and miserable story is to be found in printed records which mention Dunblane, for the Avignon records largely await publication. It has to be recognised that bishops and higher clergy were left to their own devices in large measure, and that the common people of Scotland went about their business unaware of who was Pope and caring as little. Yet vicars and chaplains by their parochial labours held the Church together, and if they could not save it from its distresses, they at least helped to postpone the advancing day of its dissolution.[41]

Bishop Andrew died at some unknown date in 1380, two years after the Schism emerged. In 1381 his name appears in an Inchaffray charter[42] as "Andrew of good memory".

II. DOUGAL   1380 – 1403

Dougal was Bishop elect on 20 September 1380, when he was provided[43] to Dunblane by the Avignon Pope, Clement VII. His father was Sir Andrew Drummond, of Stobhall, an estate which came to him, along with Cargill, Auchterarder, and others, by his wife Mary, eldest daughter and considerable heiress of Sir William de Montefex.[44] Dougal was their fourth son. His sister Annabella, noted for her beauty, spirit and wisdom, as well as

PLATE IV

DUNBLANE CATHEDRAL from South East

for her generosity, married about 1367 John, the eldest son of "the Steward of Scotland", who became Robert II. Her husband became King, by the name of Robert III; they were crowned on successive days in August 1390, the King on the 14th, the Queen[45] on the 15th. Eubel, who had consulted the Avignon records, says that before his election Dougal was a canon of Dunblane.

In the records so far printed there are three Dougals of this period, two of them canons of Dunblane. Here are the known facts:

(1) When Bishop Andrew died, Dougal, a canon of Dunblane, was provided as Bishop of Dunblane, 1380. His family name was Drummond.

(2) In 1380, Dugal de Lorn, priest, of the Diocese of Argyll, admitting that he had canonries and prebends of Argyll and Dunblane, petitioned[46] for a benefice in the gift of the Bishop of St. Andrews. In the same year, Robert, Earl of Fife and Menteith, petitioned[47] for his chaplain and secretary, Dugal de Ergadia, priest, who had studied canon and Civil Law for three years, that he be given a canonry of Dunblane with expectation of a prebend, though already "he has a canonry and prebend of the same and the Church of Kilmorich in Argyll." (To hold two canonries in the same cathedral was against church law.) These two petitions of 1380 doubtless refer to the same man.

(3) In 1394, Bishop Dougal petitioned[48] that a canonry of Lismore, with expectation of a prebend, be granted to "John Dugalli,[49] alias Clark, alias de Lorn, priest, scholar of Canon Law, notwithstanding that he has the Church of Kilmore in the Diocese of Argyll." His name delatinised would be Ian Mac-Dougal of Lorne. He may have been a son of Dougal de Lorn in (2) above, and have followed him as rector of Kilmore.

That sorts out the three clerics who had Dugal in their name. It is interesting to note that Robert, Earl of Fife, who petitioned for Dugal de Ergadia (Argyll), was brother-in-law to Bishop Dougal, and that in a charter (RMS I 908), granted at Dunblane on 29 November 1406 by Earl Robert, then Governor of Scotland, a witness is "John, Seneschal (Steward) of Lorn, our cousin." This witness may have been the above John Dugalli, alias Clark, alias de Lorn.

One item of diocesan history, preserved from Bishop Dougal's

I

time, carries forward the long story of the patronage of Strogeith. On the death of the vicar, Richard de Stirling, Bishop William (1284-96), thinking that he was patron, appointed John de Legerwood, the chaplain and nominee of Earl Malise III of Strathearn. But in a court[50] convened to decide on the objection of the Abbot of Inchaffray, the charters produced by the Abbot convinced the Earl and the Bishop that the patronage of the vicarage belonged to the Abbot, who thereupon nominated John de Legerwood. Later, at a date unknown, the Abbot transferred the Church of Strogeith to the Bishop of Dunblane (perhaps for financial help in necessity). Bishop Walter de Coventre (1361-71) restored the Church to Inchaffray, the transfer to take effect on the death of the rector. The rector died in 1381, and in December of that year the Abbot asked for confirmation[51] of the restoration and the Pope mandated the Bishop of Glasgow "to inform himself and confirm the same according to justice".

Extremely little is known of Bishop Dougal's diocesan labours, partly because he lived his episcopal life wholly within the Great Schism.[52] In public affairs, Dougal does not appear to have taken any part. He lived in a time of confusion in the Church and lawlessness in the realm. "In these days (of Robert III, 1390-1406) there was no law in Scotland; the strong oppressed the weak and the whole realm was a den of thieves. Murders, thefts, arson and other crimes went unpunished and it looked as if justice had been driven from Scotland into exile." So runs the Latin of the register of the Bishopric of Moray.[53] Bishop Dougal's sister, as wise as beautiful, was Queen; she died in 1401 and she must have borne a heavy load of woe. The King, though of high character, was utterly feckless; to aid him to rule, his brother Robert, Earl of Menteith, Duke of Albany, was made Governor of the Kingdom in 1388, a post he held till he died in 1420; in addition the King's son and heir, the Duke of Rothesay, was appointed King's Lieutenant in 1399, for three years. The magnates quarrelled among themselves; England invaded Scotland in 1400, and in 1402 Scotland's army was defeated twice, Homildon being particularly costly. The heir died in 1402, leaving his brother James, eight years of age, heir to the throne. It was a time of misery for Scotland, and only an outstanding ecclesiastic could play a part in public affairs. Only minutiae are recorded of Bishop Dougal — a commission in 1381[54] to allow John de Dairsie, canon of

Cambuskenneth, to study at a university for five years; and the witnessing of two charters,[55] 1381 and 1392. But it is worth noting that four canons appear among the Cathedral clergy in 1380 and 1381, though no new canon of Dunblane is known between 1349 and 1380, with the exception of the two Dougals. This might mean that the Bishop was active in Cathedral administration after a period of slackness on the part of his predecessors. But there is so much we do not know about Dunblane.

By 1403, if not earlier, Bishop Dougal was dead.

III. Finlay Colini, alias Finlay Dermoch 1403 – 1419

It is Spottiswoode who gives Finlay the name of Dermoch, though at his first mention in the records he is Finlay Colini, son of Colin. He was elected[56] to the See of Dunblane on 10 September 1403, provided by Benedict XIII, the last of the Avignon Popes. Before he became Bishop, he had served Dunblane in other capacities – in 1394 Robert, Duke of Albany, petitioned[57] the Pope to grant him a canonry of Dunkeld, and describes Finlay as his chaplain, Bachelor of Canon Law, canon and prebendary of Dunblane, perpetual vicar of Abernethy, rector of Ferlyn[58] and master of the Hospital of Ochtirogle in the Diocese of St. Andrews, valued at a hundred francs. In 1400 and in 1401 he is designated Archdeacon of Dunblane.[59]

Finlay's tenure of the Bishopric, like his predecessor's, belonged in part to the same unhappy reign of Robert III, whose misfortunes continued. James, the King's third son and heir, sailed in 1406 for France and was taken prisoner on 4 April by the English, though the countries were at peace. That very day, his father, Robert III, died. James was by the Scots declared King as James I, though he was a prisoner in England; he was in his twelfth year; it was eighteen years before he was liberated, and then only by giving hostages for £40,000. It was 1424 before he was crowned, in his thirtieth year.[60] Moreover, heresy had made some progress in Scotland, and in 1407, at Perth, the Church burned James Resby, an English priest, who adhered to Wyclif's teaching.

Hopeful signs amid the woes of Scotland were that Donald of the Isles, invading the mainland, was defeated in 1411 at Harlaw near Aberdeen, and internal peace was restored; the University of St. Andrews was founded in 1412, and Scotland at last adhered in 1417 to the Roman Pope, Martin V. But these only served to light the misery of the times in Scotland.

Perhaps unaware that Scotland had enough on its hands, the Pope in 1404 mandated[61] the Bishops of St. Andrews, Dunblane and Dunkeld to preach a Crusade against the Turks; Constantinople had fallen (this was not correct) and Christians, male and female, were being brutally treated. Scotland was never very responsive to the cry for a Crusade, but doubtless the Bishops did their best.

Other mandates were laid upon the Bishop of Dunblane: in 1409, all the Scottish bishops were commanded[62] to deprive and anathematise the cardinals and others who took part in the Council of Pisa; in 1410, the Bishops of St. Andrews, Glasgow and Dunblane were to report on all vacancies in bishoprics, abbacies and other principal benefices,[63] as these are now reserved to the Pope (this meant the abolition of all local elections and the carrying of claims and hopes and fees to the Roman Court); in 1411, with two others, Finlay was mandated[64] to apply a year's income of vacant benefices in Argyll during two years, to repair the Cathedral of Lismore; and in 1415,[65] to take the oaths due to the Pope by the Abbots of Paisley and Crossraguel.

Bishop Finlay Dermoch attended the General Council of the Church, held at Perth, on 17 March 1415/16.[66] "In the chapel beside the great bridge of Perth, in our diocese", the Bishop of St. Andrews, with assent of many, clerical and lay, decreed that the charters of Edward III resigning all claims of sovereignty over Scotland were to be transcribed and "edited in public and authentic form for future memory of the event".

Finlay and the bishops and dignitaries of the Scottish Church were called by the Pope to a Council at Perpignan on 1 October 1408.[67] Preparatory negotiations between the two Popes had taken place, and it was hoped that at Perpignon the Schism would be healed.[68] The Council did not succeed, but it helped to the final solution. Bishop Finlay may have been present; but, if so, he came back quickly, for on 28 October he was at Perth and witnessed a charter of the Duke of Albany.[69] When Scotland adhered to the Roman Pope, Martin V, on his election in 1417, Mr Robert Young, arch-priest of Dunbar, was given indult[70] to hear the confessions of, and absolve, all Scots who had been faithful to Avignon. Nuncios were appointed in 1418 to receive the fealty of the King, the Lords of the Realm and of the Three Estates of Parliament.[71]

Among the canons of the Cathedral in Bishop Finlay's time there appears one of more than local significance: Donald de Bute, Dean from 1394 till 1408, a considerable pluralist, and auditor of the King's accounts, 1406-8. His career is outlined in the Appendix on Cathedral clergy, under the dates 1394 and 1408.

Fordun[72] tells that Finlay Dermoch built the bridge over the Allan at Dunblane, and that he died in 1419. There is insufficient record to enable us to get into close touch with him, but he may well have been a competent bishop. His university degree guarantees a learning greater than marked some who counted for more in Church and State. And let us remember him for his practical skill, foresight and generosity in giving its first bridge to Dunblane.

During the vacancy in the Bishopric there was also a vacancy in the Priorship of Inchmahome, Patrick the Prior having died. The Convent elected one of their number, Patrick de Portu, and he was confirmed in his benefice by the vicar general of Dunblane, the Bishop's deputy. Only one other mention of this officer in Dunblane's Diocese has been found. Any doubts of the validity of Patrick de Portu's confirmation were removed by the Pope on petition.[73]

IV. WILLIAM (STEPHAN) 1419 – 1429

The Church of Scotland adhered to the Roman Pope, Martin V, in 1417, but another Avignon Pope was elected in 1424, and continued in office till he abdicated in 1429 and ended the Great Schism. Scotland sent, to carry its fealty to the Roman Pope, James Haldenstone,[74] Prior of St. Andrews, John Scheves, and William Stephani. It was 1419 before this mission made its journey; the King was a prisoner in England, and it seems to have been some time before the Guardian, earls, barons and representatives of the people of Scotland were ready to follow the decision of the Church. In August of that year the above emissaries of the Church brought from Florence a bull of the Avignon Pope, Benedict XIII, providing one William Stephani to the see of Orkney on 13 November 1415. Some confusion has been caused by emissary and bishop bearing the same name; they were different men. William Stephani, the emissary, was Master of the

Nunnery of North Berwick, rector of Kinross and Pennicuik; he was also probably rector of Restalrig, and, if so, he was a professor in St. Andrews for a considerable period.[75] If the emissary was not rector of Restalrig, then there were three men of the name. Confusion is doubled by the fact that the other William Stephani, whom the Pope, Martin V, translated[76] from the See of Orkney to Dunblane on 30 October 1419, had been Professor of Canon Law in St. Andrews,[77] perhaps the first to hold that chair, before he was provided to Orkney.

In 1408 our William, generally known as William (Stephan), was Bachelor of Canon Law, canon and prebendary of Rhynie, which he held with the Church of Essy and the Hospital of Ednam.[78] After his appointment to Orkney,[79] and even after his consecration, he was given the Church of Gogar, and allowed to hold Essy and Ednam, contrary to Church Law, because he had not been able to gather his episcopal income which was seized by lay appropriators.[80] Until 1472 the See of Orkney was subject to the Archbishop of Trondhjem[81]; it was "far off among the isles of the sea and at the ends of the earth", and Bishop William obtained his church revenues only after troubles and struggles.[82] He visited the Avignon Pope in December, 1415, and gave his promise to pay his fees for common service within three years.[83] Most unfortunately, when rector of Essy, he had attacked a man who had stolen his cattle, hit him on the head with a stick and killed him. For this crime he was dispensed and absolved by the Pope.[84]

William (Stephan) cannot have been happy in the See of Orkney with its foreign allegiance and its revenues having to be torn from the hands of conscienceless laymen. He saw some hope when the Schism ended in 1417, and wrote[85] to Martin V that, having learned that he had attained "the apex of the apostolic heights", he was hastening to Rome to offer his obedience in person. He also stated in the letter, which is dated 15 July 1419, that, having been appointed proctor in the Roman Court for Robert, Duke of Albany, Governor of Scotland, he was being sent to Rome as one of the ambassadors charged with his country's adherence and fealty. It was in this letter that he asked for Essy and Ednam to be continued to him, and the rectory of Gogar, as otherwise he would have no income. The letter was not delivered until after he had arrived in Rome.

This looks a simple and clear mission, but it had deep political

significance, in addition to its straightforward ecclesiastical pur-
pose. Griffin, Bishop of Ross, seems to have been sent before
William (Stephan) on a mission ostensibly of peace; he settled at
Troyes, where he was joined by two cardinals charged by the
Pope to patch a peace between England and France.

But who was Griffin, for he does not appear among the *de facto*
Bishops of Ross? He was probably a Welshman, provided by the
Roman Pope and given the title of Ross. But Pope Martin V, now
having the obedience of Scotland, provided John Bullock in 1418
as *de facto* Bishop of Ross to aid in the return of Scotland to fuller
allegiance. It has been suggested that Griffin was given his
episcopal title at the instance of Henry V, King of England. If so,
it is strange that he was sent on a Scottish mission. But there is
unsolved mystery about Griffin; it may be that he was in the pay
both of Scotland and of England, and was intriguing with both
parties in France, one seeking English, the other Scottish, support. The Battle of Agincourt (1415) had split France into two
parties, and the King's son, ruling for his father, declared insane,
was in sore straits. "For no reason", says one of the records, the
cardinals left Griffin and went to see Albany in Scotland; probably
their reason was that they were not convinced of Griffin's sin-
cerity. In this they may well have been correct; the truce between
England and Scotland expired at Easter 1418, and Albany was now
fishing in the French-English troubled waters. William (Stephan)
was sent to join the embassy and for a time he stayed with the
Duke of Burgundy, the leader of the party opposed to the King.
France needed Scottish help and early in 1419 the Dauphin received from Albany a promise of aid; but Burgundy, the Dauphin's
enemy, was also in such need of Scottish assistance that he ex-
tracted £6000 from Tournai "to buy off the Scots who offer to
come to serve the king". William (Stephan) became embroiled,
probably in innocence, in a piece of political intransigence when
he travelled to Rome on what seemed a plain church mission.[86]
In addition, he had his own ambitions to further in the Church.

This journey to Rome was made in style, as befitted the occasion, and there seemed no reason for haste. For four weeks in
April and May 1419, the embassage rested at the chateau of the
Duke of Burgundy and details have come down even of the
dinners they were given, and the entertainments, by the hospit-
able Duke; they met ambassadors from Brittany and Savoy, and

altogether enjoyed a pleasant interlude in a long journey.[87]   But while William (Stephan) tarried, one John Dalgles posted hard to Rome, and had, even while William and his company were dallying at the chateau, obtained from the Pope, on 27 April, the collation and provision of Essy.[88]   This was awkward for William, who wanted Essy to be continued to him *in commendam*; nevertheless he presented his petition in hope.   The Pope did not fail him; on 6 September, after William had resigned his canonry of Moray and the Hospital of Ednam, the Pope provided[89] him to the See of Dunblane, and allowed him to enjoy for a year the fruits of Essy and Gogar.   The translation to Dunblane was made on 30 October 1419[90]; the Bishop offered, on 24 November, for his common service and the usual five little services, 370 gold florins of the Camera, half within twelve months, half within eight months thereafter.[91]   But after his penury in Orkney, it is not surprising to learn that in April 1422 he was given a respite of six months.[92]

The Great Schism being ended, Scotland was back in the stream of church life, and things were taking a new shape, on the surface at least.   The Scots people from the King down were purged by papal commissioners[93] of their Avignon diversions, and even the fierce "inquisitor of heretical pravity", Laurence of Lindores, who had burned James Resby in 1407, was admonished[94] in 1418 for his lenient dealing with Robert Harding, who at the Church Council at Perth that year had dared to uphold the cause of Benedict XIII, recently deposed.   Perhaps the Pope suspected that Laurence was of the same mind.   In local affairs, Martin V granted on 6 September 1419, the day on which the Pope intimated to William his translation to Dunblane (the actual letter of translation being dated 30 October 1419), an indulgence to Dunblane Cathedral in its need of restoration and rehabilitation in vessels, ornaments and vestments.   In this indult the Pope describes the Church of Dunblane as "of old most sumptuous in its buildings, its glass windows, its ornaments and vestments, its many relics and jewels", but now, because of mortality (that is, the pestilences which struck Scotland in 1349, 1362 and 1401, when on each visitation about a third of the population died), the evils of the times and the meagreness of its revenues, the Bishop, Dean and Chapter could not fittingly maintain the fabric.   To all the faithful who visited the Church on the feast of St. Blane, Bishop and Confessor, or on any of his days, and gave a contribution, the Pope was asked to grant, and did grant, relaxation of penance for seven years and as many quarantines, and to the vicar-in-spiritualities the faculty of absolution to all faithful who confessed to him and helped the restoration of the Church.[95]

On the same day, the Pope granted special privileges to the parishioners of Strogeith,[96] in answer to a petition of the Bishop and of the rector and vicar of the parish. "A great number of the parishioners are distant from their church 10 or 8 or 6 or 5 Italian miles and therefore take no pains to come to the church – nay, some come scarcely once a year, namely at Easter; moreover, many of them come like beasts and are utterly ignorant of the divine offices and the mandates of the Church. They cannot conveniently come on empty stomachs, as it is too much to hear divine offices and afterwards return to their homes fasting." The petitioners make two requests, which were both granted by the Pope: a relaxation of forty days of penance for each day they come to church, whether fasting or not, and hear the divine offices; and "an indulgence, according to the custom of the Papal Chancery, to all who visit their church devoutly on the feasts of the Church, seven of Christ, five of Mary and of St. John Baptist, and who stretch out helping hands".

Those two indulgences were obviously the papal answer to representations made by Bishop Finlay before he died. The new Nuncio and Papal Collector was James de Haldenstone, Prior of St. Andrews, who had led the deputation of submission to the Roman Pope. In fact Martin V was desperately anxious to please all petitioners, thereby to strengthen his authority as the one Pope, especially in Scotland and other countries recently faithful to Avignon. That was understandable; but a stronger man would have seized the chance of beginning the reform of the many irregularities in the Church. The Roman Church needed a bold and reforming Pope; it got Martin V, whose failure to inaugurate Church reform from within led in the end, though 150 years later, to reform from without. But Martin was of his times – neither a prophet with vision nor a reformer with zeal; he was content to work the institution which he inherited. His Papacy was a misfortune; but to his contemporaries he was an agreeable, busy and devoted Pope.

There occur in the records during this episcopate two superb examples of pluralism and its consequences, which even if briefly told will reveal the system of preferment as clearly as a lengthy formal description. The first will show the eagerness to occupy the shoes of dead or dying or resigning men.

(1) John Bowmakar, Bachelor of Decreets, rector of a parish church in the Diocese of Glasgow, supplicated the Pope to be given the Archdeaconry of Teviotdale and was so provided. But he found William Croiser in possession and got the matter referred to a papal auditor. Before the suit was heard, he informed the Pope (4 January 1423/4) that he had decided to proceed with the utmost vigour, and asked him to give mandate to the auditor that if he discovers (as John asserts) that neither William nor John has right to the said Archdeaconry (worth with its annexes £84 sterling) he should provide John to it. John lists the possible reasons for its being vacant:

by death at Rome of Alexander de Foulerton,
or by the death of James Lyon,
or of James Walteri, formerly possessors of the Archdeaconry,
or by the resignation of Edward de Lawedre made before a notary public and witnesses,
or in whatsoever way.

All this, "notwithstanding that he holds the parish church of Munyabro, . . . and is known to be litigating in the Apostolic Palace anent the Chancellorship of Dunblane and the perpetual vicarage of Falkirk, . . . which he does not possess and to which he was provided or had a grant of provision (total fruits, £120 of old sterling)". He is "ready to resign the Church of Munyabro and the Chancellorship or all right thereto provided he obtain peaceable possession of the said Archdeaconry with its annexes and the vicarage – which incompatibles he is sufficiently dispensed to hold". Three such supplications were sent to Rome, just to ensure that one of them reached the Pope and got to his desk with least delay. "Let it be done as asked for all three", wrote the Pope, and John Bowmakar is left to fight it out in the Apostolic Court.[97]

John Bowmakar's hint that he was ready on certain conditions to resign his right, if any, to Dunblane's Chancellorship, roused Nicolas de Atholia, Precentor of Dunkeld, to the hunt for the Chancellorship of Dunblane (£24 of old sterling) when and if it becomes vacant by resignation of John B.; in that case, it would be vacant by the death of Donald Gillisson or by the death of Adam de Port, or in some other way, though a suit is pending between John B. and John Willielmi, who has detained it by the Bishop's collation for two years or more, unlawfully. Nicolas de A. asks for John B.'s right to be transferred to him, notwithstanding that he is Precentor of Dunkeld and vicar of Strathmiglo, and has provision to Fetteresso, which he does not yet possess. He is ready to demit Strathmiglo.[98]

The hint of a possible vacancy in Strathmiglo is enough to bring John de Stanton, vicar of Aberlady, into the scramble; he is ready to resign Aberlady.[99] Now John de Rettre,[100] priest of Dunkeld, wants Aberlady, and as he has only a grant of provision to Cargill and has not yet got possession, he has nothing to resign, and that scramble ends. The Pope has agreed to all the supplications with *Fiat*. But a lesser one begins, for Thomas de Rew, vicar of Falkirk, had lately died, and John Cameron, Lic. Dec., vicar of Levenstoun, supplicates for it (£60 of old sterling) if and when John Bowmakar resigns; but John B. has at court a suit anent the vicarage of Falkirk with the Abbot of Holyrood and his Convent, who retain Falkirk *de facto*. Again the Pope adds his *fiat*.[101]

(2) It is recorded in 1423 that to Griffin, Bishop of Ross (who was only titular, and never resided), a cleric who was mixed up in Scots-French political intrigues, the Pope gave the incomes of ecclesiastical benefices, secular or regular, even of one, two or three priories, up to an income of 500 florins of gold of the Camera. He was permitted to possess these in the Dioceses or Provinces of Rheims and Tours; they were to be accepted within a month, till Griffin got Ross or some other cathedral church. In this way he became Prior of Locmaria (Diocese of Quimper), worth £300, and asked for new provision, though he had two other priorships worth £400, and was litigating in the Roman Court anent two more, whose value was £200 per annum. Within months, 13 April 1424, he was supplicating for Locminé (Diocese of Vannes), worth £120.[102] For all of which income from the Church in France, he did nothing whatever, except knock at the Pope's door and pay the stipulated fees.

If the Pope failed the Church at the centre, so did the Scots bishops at the periphery. The Scottish Church on 16 July 1420, "in the Church of the Friars Preachers at Perth", held one of its infrequent Provincial Synods and General Councils. "After mass and the invocation of the Holy Spirit and sermon to the clergy, there was unanimously elected to be Conservator of Privileges (i.e. Moderator, of sorts) the reverend father in Christ our Lord, William, by the grace of God Bishop of Dunblane" – so runs the account.[103] William (Stephan) took an authoritative part in the proceedings – he proposed the matter for discussion, he "insisted" on the senior clergy making their declarations "on their consciences with an oath on the Holy Gospels of God", and when concord was reached, he ordered the usage to be observed, and asked the bishops to confirm it with their seals. But when revival and reform were the crucial issues, the only business discussed was the traditional customs in the confirming of wills throughout the dioceses.

Bishop William (Stephan) witnessed four charters[104] issued under the Great Seal between 1420 and 1423, but their modern consequence is inconsiderable. In 1422, however, he was judge ordinary[105] in a process of legitimation, on the issue of which depended succession to the property of John de Logy of that Ilk; this must have occupied much time, for the decision runs to nine pages of quarto. Among the members of the court are seven clerics of the Cathedral – the Dean (Master Michael de Ouchtre, who became Bishop); the Treasurer; a canon, three presbyters, and a notary.

In 1425 Bishop William informed the Pope that he did not have sufficient revenue for his support, or, as he put it, that the former rents and profits of his *mensa*, by reason of wars and the evils of the times, were so meagre that the Church of Dunblane for twelve years or thereabout lacked a pastor, they were at present so scant that he could scarcely keep himself in becoming pontifical dignity and maintain his Church which though once flourishing is now ruinous. If the Pope does not help, things will worsen. He asked therefore that the vicarage of Abernethy (£30 of old sterling) be added to his *mensa* on the next vacancy, so that he might have its revenues to his own use, subject to a fitting portion being reserved for a vicar.[106] To this the Pope gave consent, though it may not have been any more clear to him than it is to me what period of twelve years the Bishop was referring to when the Diocese had no pastor. The Bishop may have been making a derogatory judgment on one of his predecessors, without specifying any one by name.

But another claimant appeared on the death of the vicar, Thomas de Tiningham.[107] John Days, M.A., B.Dec., hastened to ask provision from the Pope, which he got in September 1426, promising to pay, because of insufficient mandates, $333\frac{1}{3}$ florins in gold for his common and 5 customary services. The Abbot of Lindores stood surety for him and payment was spread over sixteen months.

However, when John Days tried to take possession of his new vicarage, he found that Bishop William was already drawing the revenue of the benefice. He did not question the Pope's action in uniting the vicarage with the Bishop's *mensa*, but discovering that Thomas de Tiningham had been "a chaplain of honour of the Apostolic See", that the benefices of such a cleric were reserved to the patronage of the Pope, and that (here was the technical error which John founded on) Bishop William had not mentioned this fact in his petition, he held that the Pope's provision was by that fact invalid.[108]

Nothing seems to have come of this; so John Days tried another tack. In September 1427 he informed the Pope that the Bishop had been guilty of misrepresentation – the *mensa* was sufficient to support him and (saving his reverence) his allegations were not true – and that he was actuated by greed. He therefore asked the Pope, "in order to obviate the roguery (*maliciis*) of the Bishop and the intricacies and digressions of lawsuits", to annul the union, declare it invalid, and impose silence on the Bishop regarding the vicarage and its fruits.[109]

No more is heard on this vicious attack; but it was 1463 before the next vicar appeared in the records.[110] John Days was not the kind of man who had any right to complain about another, as his own supplication to the Pope for rehabilitation declared.[111] Celebrating clandestine marriage, dicing, and playing other disreputable games prohibited by law were the least of his faults; he had been excommunicated, suspended, interdicted, and had contracted irregularity. Now vicar of Carnbee, and over sixty years of age, fearful lest some rivals might trouble him in his possession of the vicarage, he asks for absolution from his sins, dispensation from irregularity, release from excommunication and other penalties, and a new provision to Carnbee, in so far as need be.

Several mandates were laid on William (Stephan) in the early days of his bishopric, six in all,[112] between 1420 and 1427. One of these, the second, has an amusing side – in 1420, with two other mandatories, he is commanded to collate to a benefice Andrew de Hawyke, a priest of St. Andrews. But this was not easy, for the papal records show that Andrew was in considerable trouble – he required absolution for irregularity and rehabilitation for continued adherence to the deposed Avignon Pope. The Governor of Scotland, Robert, Duke of Albany, had sent him in 1417 as envoy to the Pope, but Andrew, even after Scotland had given allegiance to Martin V, had presented himself at the papal palace of Avignon. There he learned the facts, and evidently thinking that the Governor shared his ignorance or his determined prejudice, he departed for Scotland primed with the news and left the Roman Pope unvisited. On his return he bribed the rector of Liston to resign in his favour, and, this having been discovered, he is ordered to resign Liston. It would be hard to get a benefice for Andrew, ignorant of his country's new papal allegiance, or unwilling to obey the decree of his Church, feckless in his commission as an envoy of Scotland's Governor and guilty of simony. Andrew's confusion, ignorance or invincible refusal to fall into line is interesting. It may be assumed that the healing of the Great Schism was known to the bishops and the earls and barons, but Andrew's case would seem to indicate that to some of the lower clergy and, more so, to the ordinary folk, the Papal Schism was of little consequence and its healing for a time largely unknown or disregarded. Yet Andrew must have had considerable ability and some flair for business. He was Bachelor of Decreets, having studied at the University of Siena, where in 1423 he was "general rector of the doctors and scholars". In that year also, he described himself as "counsellor and secretary of Murdoch, Duke of Albany, Governor of Scotland", and in another supplication as "counsellor and procurator in the Roman Court of Murdoch" (with the above title and office). Two years later he called himself "first secretary and counsellor of the late Governor of Scotland"; he is now Licentiate of Decreets and "has been in the Roman Court for a long time with much labour and expense". On 22 May of that year (1425) it is recorded that he had died recently at the Roman Court. He was an eager supplicator for wealthy benefices, but was not very successful; of one such, Kincardine in the Diocese of Aberdeen, worth £100 of old sterling, he wrote that "he has not, nor hopes to have, possession".[113]

The only remaining record of a papal duty laid on Bishop William is of more than usual interest. On 1 August 1426 the Pope asked him and the Bishop of Glasgow to advise him on a petition sent by James I of Scotland.[114] The King desired that the University of St. Andrews, founded thirteen years earlier by Benedict XIII, often called Peter de Luna, should be transferred to St. John's Town (Perth) and gave these grounds:

(1) in the wars between England and Scotland St. Andrews was too near England by sea;

(2) because of its mild climate and its abundance of provisions, Perth had advantages over the other places of the realm.

If these statements are true, and if the King will grant privileges and liberties to the University, the Bishops are authorised to make the transfer after enquiring into the whole question. Either the reasons given were not determinative, or the King was not willing to grant further privileges, for the change was not made.

The second half of William (Stephan)'s episcopate of ten years was marked by very considerable service to the State in two offices to which he was appointed by James I and Parliament.

(1) In 1425 he was one of the ambassadors sent to Rome, the others being the Bishop of Aberdeen, the Abbots of Melrose and Balmerino, the Prior of St. Andrews, two knights and three *magistri* (i.e. clerics), ten in all. To them Henry VI of England granted safe-conduct till Easter next,[115] calling them "ambassadors of our dearest cousin and king, the King of Scots". James I had just emerged from eighteen years of imprisonment by Henry V and his son, at a cost of £40,000, the alleged cost of his "maintenance" in England. "Dearest cousin" forsooth! The ambassadors, with fifty men and horses in their troop, were promised protection, going and coming, by sea and by land, "provided they behave themselves honestly and well towards the King of England and his people". This was the Bishop's third journey abroad, one to Avignon (1415), two to Rome (1419, 1425), certainly his most magnificent and probably his most comfortable.

(2) In 1424 Parliament, meeting at Perth, on 26 May, five

days after the King's coronation, appointed Bishop William the chief of ten auditors and receivers of the tax of 10,000 marks for each of five years to pay the King's ransom of £40,000.[116] The other auditors were the Bishop of Dunkeld, two abbots and six earls. The baillies and taxators were charged to tax all men for two years in all goods, corn, cattle and other property, in leases, lands and rents; clergy and laity alike were to pay twelve pence in the pound and the proceeds were to be paid to the Auditors on 12 July 1424, "next to cum". William was reappointed in 1425 and in 1426. According to Fordun,[117] the Bishop and the Abbot of Inchcolm handed to the King in the first year almost 14,000 marks, but in the second year only about 6,000. The tax was beyond the capacity of Scotland; there were many complaints, and the King abolished the tax until 1433. That Scotland was in no better capacity to pay after 1433[118] is proved by the failure of the King to get twopence in the pound for the dowry of his eldest daughter Margaret on her proposed marriage to the Dauphin of France. The discontent of the people was so manifest that the King gave orders for all monies received to be repaid. Scotland had been bled white.

It does not appear that the Bishop was an effective collector. Collection was difficult, but that is hardly sufficient to explain why the Bishop's executors made ten payments to the Treasury in 1435, six years after his death.[119] He is recorded then as Receiver for Inverness, Lanark, Dundee, Perth and Dunbarton, and his executors paid at various dates in that year 100 nobles (a noble was 6/8d), 170 nobles (for Dunbarton), 5000 nobles for the first year, 5000 for the second, and "under his seal and signature", as if these sums were ready to be accounted for before he died, 61 nobles and 501 nobles. It may be that the delay was caused by the unravelling of book-keeping entries or by the inability of the burgesses to pay the amounts while the Bishop was alive and paid as they could to his executors. Most of the sums were noted as nobles but paid over in English pounds.

The pressure of taxation was not only civil; the Church was making heavy demands, that of annates, the first year's income on appointment to a new benefice,[120] being particularly obnoxious. James Haldanestone, already noted in this chapter, was appointed by the Pope Collector General for Scotland in 1419.

To an appeal by Thomas de Camera, Prior of May, against his having to pay annates, Haldanestone gave a savage reply: you are an unfaithful son of the Church, degenerate and ungrateful, and your appeal is frivolous and hypocritical. Annates were serious enough, but they were only one tax among many, both civil and papal. A papal Collector's lot was not a happy one; John de Opizis, appointed in 1425 sole Collector for Scotland as long as he was Collector for England, was violently treated and put in prison by Humphrey, Duke of Gloucester. The Pope was horrified, said he could not believe it, and was very angry.[121] The transfer of papal taxes to the Pope so threatened the economy of Scotland that laws forbade it, and the same kind of regulations were made against transfer of currency in the later Middle Ages as in the mid-twentieth century. Also both Pope and secular rulers were of the same mind – the Church was a cow to be well milked as it sought to go about its natural avocation. In 1422, Murdac, Duke of Albany and Governor of Scotland in succession to his father, petitioned the Pope for reservation to himself of four benefices in each diocese (that is, 44 benefices), to be bestowed on his nominees.[122]

William (Stephan) died probably early in 1429. He was more a politician and ecclesiastic than a churchman and a pastor. His service of the State militated against his service of the Church. The Governor of Scotland recognised his ability in different missions; such a man was precious to Robert of Albany alike in his own ambitions and in the intrigues of statecraft to which he was committed by Scotland's enmity with England and friendship with France. The Bishop's scholarship and capacity led him naturally to high place in Church and State. It appears that in 1425, or earlier, he was a papal referendary,[123] a new title in the history of Dunblane's Bishops. This means that the Pope appointed him to an office for examining and reporting on supplications, requests, and such matters. The appointment may date from the six months of 1419 which he spent at the Apostolic Court, or it may have been an honorary appointment, like that of papal chaplain, somewhat freely bestowed. In any case it was a papal recognition of ability and wisdom. But it is the political aspects of his career which impress, rather than the religious. Doubtless he was a worthy Bishop in times when, because of the State's need of trained civil servants, demands were made on bishops and other learned churchmen which seriously interfered with the full discharge of the duties of their calling.

NOTES

1. 23 Oct. 1347, on election of Bishop William. See chapter VI.

2. T. No. 644.

3. Spottiswoode: Hist. of Ch. of Scotland I 214, calls him "Walter de Cambuslang", which may have been his birthplace; "de Coventre", used in CPR Pet. I 409, was probably his family name.

4. CPR Pet. I 325. DMCS 279.

5. CPR III 148.

6. CPR III 198. CPR Pet. I 89.

7. CPR III 480. CPR Pet. I 241.

8. See his story in Appendix of Cathedral Clergy, under 1345 when he was titular Archdeacon.

9. CPR III 390.

10. Auctarium Chartularii Univ. Parisiensis I 14.

11. "The Scots in the University of Orleans" in SHS Miscellany II p. 101.

12. CPR III 351.

13. CPR IV 215.

14. TV I Nos. 23, 102. 8 Apr. 1373.

15. CPR IV 214, 215. 31 Oct. 1375, by which time Bishop Walter was dead. In Abernethy the Provost of the Collegiate Church was called Prior, a relic of Celtic usage.

16. AP I 141. The comparative figures of some of the dioceses are interesting. The sums due are followed by the sums paid, the latter in brackets; only pounds are here given: Dunblane £607 (£376) Brechin £441 (£321) Moray £1418 (£559) Glasgow £4080 (£2028) St. Andrews £5414 (£3507). Scotland £15,000 (£9,396). The ransom was a very heavy burden.

17. Compta Camer. Scot. I. See index for references to Dunblane.

18. Churchmen, high and low, paying a tenth of income to the King, similar taxes to the Pope, and their share of the King's ransom, were by 1366 burdened as heavily as those today with an income of £2000 under British taxation. They had no allowance and deductions.

19. TV I No. 21.

20. CPR IV 94, repeated in a secret letter CPR IV 99. In CPR IV 104, 1372, the Pope asked the Bishop of St. Andrews to use his influence. T. No. 685.

21. TV I No. 25.

22. CAI No. 135.

23. TV IV 81.

24. CC I No. 143.

25. AP I black 143, 148, 150, 171, red 501a, 506, 508, 531 (where he is present at Scone, 1368), 534.

26. AP I 545 red. NMS II 43b.

27. BC IV 154; two notes confuse the seals of the Bishops of Dunkeld and Dunblane. cf. BFDC 1937 and Birch: *Catalogue of Seals in British Museum.*

28. *Foedera* III 877. *Rot. Scotiae* I 939b.

29. AP I 185 black, 549 red.

30. AP I 549 red, 185 black. NMS II 43b.

31. Eubel: *Hierarchia Cath.* I 229f. Not in T.

32. CAI No. 135.

33. CPR IV 101; repeated 150.

34. CPR IV 153-160.

35. T. No. 709. CPR IV 215. Thomas Stewart (the name is now so spelt) became Archdeacon of St. Andrews, *Rot. Scotiae* II 130; Exchequer Rolls IV, clxvi f. A notorious pluralist. Bower (Sc. VI 47) calls him a man "of the most modest spirit and a dovelike simplicity". That may explain his refusal of a bishopric. Frequent references in CPR Pet. I. For Robert II's family, see DK 169.

36. CPR IV 215. James may have been a brother, also illegitimate, of the above Thomas.

37. CPR IV 110. Also 140, 205. T. No. 708.

38. Highland Papers, SHS IV 138.

39. cf. CPR Pet. I 565.

40. CPR Pet. I 541-2.

41. A summary of the Popes during the Schism may be helpful:

Roman Popes	Avignon Popes
(obeyed by England, Austria, Italy, Hungary, Bohemia)	(obeyed by Scotland, France, Spain, Cyprus, Sicily)
Urban VI 1378-1389.	Clement VII 1378-1394.
Boniface IX 1389-1404.	Benedict XIII 1394-1417 (deposed
Innocent VII 1404-1406.	1409, but continued as Pope; deposed
Gregory XII 1406-1409 (deposed)	a second time 1417; died 1424).
Alexander V 1409-1410.	
John XXIII 1410-1415 (deposed)	
Martin V 1417-1431.	
(Scotland came to his obedience 2 Oct. 1417 by decision of a General Council at Perth).	In spite of Scotland's adherence (1417, and she was the last country to adhere to Avignon), an Anti-pope, Clement VIII, was elected in 1424. His abdication in 1429 closed the Schism of 51 years. The Council of Basle elected another Anti-pope, Felix V, in 1439; he abdicated in 1449. Scotland strongly supported the Anti-popes, until 1417.
Eugenius IV 1431-1447 (deposed by Council of Basle in 1439, which elected Felix V (see parallel column); but he was acknowledged as Pope till he died, 1447.	

Nicolas V, elected 1447, became undisputed
Pope on abdication of Felix V.

42. CAI No. 139.

43. EU., under Dunblane.

44. Wood: Peerage II 359, says Dougal became Bishop about 1398, but died soon after consecration. Both statements must be wrong; Eubel's references and recorded acts are against them.

45. Her eldest son, David, died in 1402, probably starved to death; her second, Robert, died in infancy; her third, James, the Steward of Scotland, became James I (1406-1437). Her husband is the ageing King in *The Fair Maid of Perth*.

46. CPR Pet. I 554.

47. Reference as in n. 46.

48. CPR Pet. I 591-2.

49. The first use of "alias" which I have found. In this same roll there is "William de Forgrund alias Lang".

50. CAI No. 118.

51. CPR Pet. I 565.

52. e.g. CPR V (1396-1404) has but one reference to Scotland (an Irish monk apostatised and fled to "Scotland and lands occupied by schismatics". CPR VI (1404-15) has none. Barely was the Schism healed before Bishop Finlay in 1418 received a mandate from Rome, CPR VII 69.

53. Registrum Epis. Moraviensis (Bannatyne Club) 382.

54. TV No. 46.

55. (1) British Museum: Campbell XXX 19, 13 Feb. 1380/1. (2) Charter Chest of Earldom of Wigtown No. 403, 1 Oct. 1392.

56. Eubel.

57. CPR Pet. I 615, 618.

58. This is Erolyn of Arbroath's "Reg. Vetus" No. 241, and stands for Errol in Diocese of St. Andrews. Finlay was something of a pluralist.

59. CPR Pet. I 615, 618.

60. But even in 1414, the Guardian received from the Pope a grant of one half of all fees due to the Roman Treasury from Scottish benefices vacant in five years, for the ransom of the King and of Murdac, the Guardian's son. TV II No. 64.

61. TV II 79-86.

62. TV II 169-95; 1 Dec. 1409.

63. TV II 48; 6 Jun. 1410.

64. SHS. Highland Papers IV 159-61.

65. BCPS. lxi.

66. AP I 225 black, 588 red.

67. TV II No. 32, 15 Jun. 1408.

68. TV II No. 31 gives a letter from the Avignon Pope inviting him to Perpignan and so declaring, 15 Jun. 1408.

69. RMS I 908.

70. TV II No. 96.

71. CPR VII 6, 1 Mar. 1417/8. T. No. 739, 27 Feb. 1417/8. The Nuncios were also collectors.

72. Sc. II 459. Also Ex. 221. Finlay's original bridge, twice widened in recent years, once on each side, still carries the weight of modern traffic. He was indeed a pontifex.

73. CSSR 257-8.

74. He and John Scheves were important clerics; cf. BCPS.

75. BCPS 54, 413. In one of the records of St. Andrews University, 22 Dec. 1439, he is "vicar of Calendrath"; in CAC 102, he is "vicar of Calatrade". These look like Callander, in the Diocese of Dunblane. He was Professor in Arts, was present at meetings of the Faculty as late as 1439, ten years after death of Bishop William Stephan, who had been Professor of Canon Law in St. Andrews. Professor J. H. Baxter in BCPS has clarified all this.

76. CPR VII 133.

77. Sc. XV 22. SHR VIII (1911) 235, 242.

78. CPR Pet. I 636.

79. 13 Nov. 1415. Both 1415 and 1416 are given in *Diplomatarium Norvegicum* XVII, p. 372 giving the earlier and pp. 285/6 the later. There seems to have been a correction in the MS. from 1415 to 1416. Vol. XVII 302 gives 13 Nov. 1415 and summarises his episcopal tenure in Orkney. Eubel and DBS give 1415. For his consecration, see CPR VII 103.

80. CPR VII 118, 6 Sep. 1419.

81. Pope Sixtus IV, 17 Aug. 1472, T. No. 852, put Orkney Diocese under the Archbishopric of St. Andrews, set up by the same bull. Archbishop of Trondhjem had control of Diocese of Orkney, 1154-1472. Before 1154, Orkney had been claimed by the Archbishops of York and of Hamburg, and by the Bishop of Trondhjem.

82. Reg. Vat. 328 f. 461, in BCPS 397/8.

83. Reg. Avin. 346, ff. 308, 312, in BCPS 398.

84. Reg. Avin. 333, f. 56, in BCPS 398, 401-2.

85. Diplom. Norveg. XVII. 303-4, cf. 980 – in BCPS 398. Details repeated in Pope's reply, 6 Sep. 1419, CPR VII 118.

86. See Beaucourt: *Histoire de Charles VII* i, 306ff.

87. Ernest Petit: *Itineraires de Philippe le Hardi* (Paris, 1888) 446-7. BCPS 398.

88. CPR VII 103.

89. CPR VII 118.

90. CPR VII 133.

91. CAC 2. The common and the five little services are detailed in CAC xlix ff.

92. CAC 4. cf. CSSR 139.

93. These were Griffin, Bishop of Ross, and Finlay de Albania, Friar Preacher, Bachelor of Sacred Theology, promoted Papal Nuncios, 1 Mar. 1417/18. For Finlay, see BCPS 388-9, DBS 384-5.

94. BCPS 282-3.

95. CSSR 121-2.

96. CSSR 122.

97. CSSR II 45-46, 49, 49-50.

98. ib. 86-87.

99. ib. 87.

100. ib. 87-88.

101. ib. 88.

102. ib. 34, 62.

103. PSSC 80-82. SES II 77. RBI 38.

104. RMS II 48, 67, 102. RBM I 265-6.

105. RBG I 148-57.

106. CSSR II 100-1 and n. *Re* suggestion in that note, Bishop Maurice witnessed a charter in 1344, and with 6 other Bishops and 2 Kings sent an urgent petition to the Pope, which though answered only after Maurice's death, would not be long delayed by the Pope. See Chapter VI and its notes 58 and 59.

107. BCPS 405; CAC 7.

108. SCSR II 158-9. Exactness and completeness of details were necessities in petitions.

109. CSSR II 171-2. 19 Sep. 1427.

110. John Bell, M.A., CMN 71.

111. CSSR II x, 192, 29 Feb. 1427/8.

112. CPR VII 148-9, 154, 238, 248 (259), 251, 511.

113. CSSR II 6, 44, 83, 86, 91, xxx.

114. CPR VII 440-1.

115. *Foedera* X 344, 9 Jun. 1425. *Rot. Scot.* II 253. BC IV 979.

116. AP II 5.

117. Sc. II 482.

118. Ex. 227-8.

119. ERS III and IV, Indices.

120. BCPS 75-77, 368, 426, 427.

121. CPR VII 4, 36, 37.

122. TV VI 6. 25 Feb. 1421/2.

123. CSSR II 99, 100-1.

CHAPTER VIII

BISHOP MICHAEL OCHILTREE
1429 – 1447

IN a dispensation granted on 22 June 1429 to Michael Ochiltree as son of unmarried parents, the Pope added that "he intended this day to make provision to him of the See of Dunblane".[1] At that time he was Dean of Dunblane, having been appointed by the Bishop on the death of Donald de Bute, and he was already well-known in papal and Scottish Church circles, as well as to the Scottish royal family. He was a canon of Dunblane and vicar of Strogeith in 1418; before that, he had studied Church Law for three years and had taken the degree of Bachelor of Decreets (Canon Law) of Paris. He was the intimate friend of James I and his Queen, Joan, as he had been of Robert III and his Queen, Annabella Drummond. Indeed he was of noble though illegitimate birth and was brought up in the royal court. In a petition to the Pope on his behalf in 1419, King James I calls him "the familiar, the domestic and commensal of himself, his father and his mother", that is, the intimate friend and household officer, who had his meals at the royal table. He was an eager seeker after benefices and a diligent litigant at Rome, which he consequently visited oftener than was good for his churchly duties and his purse. His struggle for the Deanery began quietly enough, but very soon it became a *cause célèbre* at Rome, where two other contenders appeared. Three years were to pass before Michael got secure possession. In one of his petitions, early in 1421, he said that "on his collation to the Deanery he obtained possession and holds it at present peaceably, or nearly so". That was an understatement, for, as he alleged, John Senescalli (or Stewart), "alleged clerk", had tried to take it from him. No decision was reached by "the Auditor of the Sacred Apostolic Palace of Causes" to whom Michael had contrived to have the dispute remitted. The trouble was that when the Deanery became void, the Pope had given it to John Senescalli, M.A., B.L., illegitimate son of Robert II, and rector of Flysk. John Senescalli began litigation, which demanded Michael's presence at Rome to defend his interests. John's petition, remarkable to our ears, was true to medieval practice: "because exalted and lettered persons ought to be honoured with greater benefices, and the said John is conspicuous for the aforesaid merits", he should be dispensed to hold the Deanery for seven years, along with Flysk. Something of a stalemate arose, but it was broken by a rumour of the Pope's provision of Michael Ochiltree to the See of Sodor. John, who had been repelled in his quest for the Deanery, would experience hope reborn; but others petitioned for Michael's canonry of Dunblane and other benefices, as crumbs from a rich man's table. One of these was John de Keremor, "priest of the Diocese of St. Andrews, Bachelor of Decreets, and abbreviator of apostolic letters", an able and deserving man, but a pathetic figure and now in his middle sixties. He described himself as "a continual follower of the Curia since 1378" (i.e. for 44 years), and as "holding no benefice, seeing that he has, through no fault of his own, been frustrated of all benefices hitherto void in the Curia". He petitioned for any right which Michael had in the deanery at Dunblane, and to be provided to it. "Let it be done as is asked; let it be done", wrote the Pope on the petition. A few days later, on 22 April 1422, as Eubel notes,[2] one Michael Anchire, a priest of Dublin, was provided to Sodor. It seems clear that John de Keremor, from whose petition alone we learn that Michael Ochiltree had been provided to Sodor, had been misled by the talk of the Court; indeed the rumour may have started with this abbreviator of papal letters, who would see the papal decision in first draft. Michael Anchire and Michael Ouchtre (the usual spelling of Ochiltree) were not so different, and Dunblane and Dublin were often mixed up in medieval records. The rumour would soon be killed by the facts. If the Pope had read John de Keremor's petition, he would have seen it stated that he had confirmed Michael Ochiltree's provision to Sodor; but probably he too mixed up Anchire and Ouchtre and Dunblane and Dublin, and his *Fiat ut petitur Fiat* meant no more than a general expression of good will towards a faithful servant of the Curia.

The argument dragged its length along, and though Michael designated himself "Dean of Dunblane" in various documents within the period of litigation,[3] it was only in April 1424 that official judgment was given in his favour. Now he is described as B.C.L. and "Almoner General of James, King of Scots", who had just been released after eighteen years in his English prison. The litigation must have cost Michael a deal of money, and his deanship must have been exercised largely *in absentia*, though it is possible that he visited Dunblane on occasion. In 1425 he was made rector of Inchmagranach (Dunkeld), worth £10 of old sterling; in addition, he held the vicarage of Tibbermore (Dunkeld) for three years, and, when the three years were up, the rectory of Lilliesleaf (Glasgow) for life. On his consecration as Bishop of Dunblane in 1430, he resigned Inchmagranach and his other benefices.[4]

Michael was one of three Ochiltrees, contemporaries if not brothers or otherwise related: James, who described himself as "of noble birth" and illegitimate, and John were both canons of Dunblane in Michael's bishopric. Other families appear frequently in the records of this time, many members of the family, though not all of them, as pluralists: Robert Cranach, Dean of Dunblane, was one of four brothers Cranach, all but William, Abbot of Inchaffray, being diligent seekers of plural benefices; Laurence Piot, Chancellor of Dunblane, occurs so often in the records that it would appear that there was more than one cleric of the name, if all the promotions could be sorted out, and there were also Patrick Piot and Alexander. Alexander de Lichton was Chancellor of Dunblane, 1440, and there were also Duncan, John and Henry de Lichton in the same period, most of them not pluralists to any extent, though the Dunblane Chancellor was. In this chase after church revenues, in which every possible influence was employed and even claims made which the Pope on occasion denied, the needs of the Church were of quite minor significance, even in the eyes of the Popes, who for fees which often hampered the beneficiary for years granted benefices of which they knew little to men whom they hardly knew, and that in spite of the Canons of the Church, the decrees of Councils and even their own bulls.

Though Michael was provided to Dunblane on 22 June 1429, he was still unconsecrated on 9 August following, when a papal letter speaks of his consecration as "forthcoming". On 1 September the Pope granted him faculty to be consecrated by any bishop who shall call two or three bishops to the service. He seems to have been in no hurry to be consecrated, for on 10 May 1430 there is extant a notarial transumpt (or minute) made by authority of "Michael, Bishop elect of Dunblane" of a process of legitimation in which he had played a part in 1422 as Dean.[5]

If he is correctly designated in the transumpt, Michael must have returned to Scotland and taken up his episcopal duties before his consecration, though where and when his consecration took place are unknown; on 24 January 1429/30 he was called Bishop of Dunblane, though still unconsecrated, in his appointment as one of a numerous and important embassy to meet eighty of Henry VI's honest men and make peace.[6] Other ambassadors were the Bishops of Glasgow (Chancellor of Scotland) and Aberdeen, and there was a distinguished array of earls, barons, knights, officials and legal experts. The English King granted safe-conduct to the meeting-place, Hawdenstank, for a company of 800 horses and men, which showed his confidence in the peaceful intentions of the Scots King. James I was in serious conflict with the Lord of the Isles and sought the assurance of peace on his southern borders. The Scottish rebellions, which had their greatest success at Inverlochy in 1431, were ended before England again attacked Scotland. The English were defeated near Berwick in September 1436, six months before James I was assassinated at Perth in February 1436/7, at the instigation of his uncle, Walter, Earl of Athol, and his accomplices, who the next month paid the penalty of treason.

Michael's public duties were both honourable and onerous. His most distinguished honour was to be chosen by the Three Estates of Parliament[7] to anoint and crown in their presence in Holyrood, on 25 March 1437, the child King James II, then only six years of age. In 1439, at Stirling, Michael Ochiltree, along with the Bishops of Glasgow, Moray and Ross, appended his seal to the accord between the "Princess Jehane, Queen of Scotland" (she was James I's Queen) and John de Livingstone and others who had arrested her and her husband, Sir James Stewart, the "Black Knight of Lorn", whom she had just married.[8] Livingstone had kept them prisoners in Stirling Castle for four weeks in August 1439 in an endeavour to gain the advantage over Crichton, custodian of Edinburgh Castle, in the struggle for power during the minority of the young James II. The accord was the settlement for the indignity suffered, but it did not prevent the seizure of several of the Livingstone family in 1449, the forfeiture of their lands and the execution of two of them.

Bishop Michael was a faithful attender of Parliament[9] and was elected to the Council deputed to work as the General Council and do the work of Parliament, this latter having become too unwieldy by the numerous attendance of the growing class of burgesses. The Bishop of Glasgow, also of the Council, and Michael were evidently the most significant of the episcopate in this regard. He was present in the Exchequer Court on 16 June 1441, when auditors of the king's taxes were appointed.[10] He was himself appointed auditor in 1441 and 1442.[11] He witnessed at Stirling in 1444 a royal confirmation of a charter, and two others at Dalkeith in the same year.[12] In 1445 he authenticated a summary of the Church of Aberdeen's charters.[13]

In Scottish church business also Michael Ochiltree played an active part. A few mandates arrived from Rome for his attention.[14] One decision in a case remitted to him by the Council of Basle was appealed against, the appellant asserting to the Pope that Bishop Michael's sentence against him was unjust.[15] This perhaps only meant that he did not like it. On 4 June 1433 the Pope directed a bull[16] to him, which must have involved him in long and boring labour: the Pope has learned that Patrick, Abbot of Cambuskenneth, and his predecessors, had granted teinds, lands, houses, privileges, farms, fishings, castles, towns (that is, farm settlements), cottages, meadows, woods, mills, rents and other property to certain clergy and laymen, to some in life-rent, to some on long lease, to others for ever, to the great injury of the Abbey. The Bishop is ordered to revoke all such grants as he should find to have been illegally made. Cambuskenneth Abbey, like the majority of such establishments, was generally needy of revenues. Monasteries were not set up as economic units with professional advisers and they took many roads to satisfy immediate needs, without counting the ultimate cost. As many of the expedients mentioned in the bull had been forbidden by the general statutes of the Scottish Church and by decrees of General Councils, it is within the credible that abbots broke the statutes, knowing that when the situation became no longer bearable they could appeal to the Pope to annul their illegal acts and restore their possessions to them. Part of the Abbey's difficulties in such cases was that the other party to the transaction knew its illegality and therefore offered less than a just price, not knowing how long he would be allowed to enjoy his illicit bargain.

The difficult case of a disputed canonry of Glasgow was referred to Bishop Michael and two other clerics by the Pope in 1437.[17] Walter Stewart, who claimed it, had thrice appealed to Rome and thrice lost his appeal, being mulcted in 40, 14 and 8 gold florins. The canonry had been given by the Pope's decision to Robert Heriote, and the three mandatories had the task of ensuring Heriote's possession.

In 1443 Bishop Michael achieved a most notable success. He persuaded King James II and Parliament, doubtless at great cost, to present "to God and the blessed Virgin Mary and to the blessed Blaan the Confessor, and to Michael and his successors, and to the Chapter of Dunblane", lands, annual rents and property of very large value. These included the City of Dunblane, no less than thirty estates and farms and a number of rents, "with all pertinents whatsoever, in one entire and free barony and regality of their city, to be held with all accommodations, etc., in pure and perpetual alms, of us and our successors". Woods, plains, meadows, pastures, waters, stanks, hawking, hunting, fishing, common pasture are all included, *cum furka et fossa, sok et sak, tholl et theme, infangantheif, hamesukkin et outfanghandtheif*,[18] and all liberties, etc. This was the granting to the Bishop and Chapter of Dunblane, already a Bishop's Burgh, of the rights of barony[19] and regality, by virtue of which the church authorities were given the appointment of bailiffs, the government of the City and the donated lands, the preservation of liberties and the administration of justice, in fact much of the oversight in civil affairs which falls today to sheriffs and to Town and County Councils,[20] and more extensive powers than a sheriff in criminal jurisdiction.

The lands given to the Bishop by James II were, in the main at least, lands of the Earldom of Strathearn. Malise, eighth Earl, was twice charged with treason and felony because he had, of his own free will, resigned his earldom into the hands of Edward Balliol, crowned King of Scotland by the English and King for about eleven weeks in 1332. On both occasions Malise was acquitted,[21] but as he had given up his earldom to the King, it remained with the Crown. It passed by the King's sanction through several hands, but when Walter, Earl of Atholl, Caithness and Strathearn, Lord of Brechin, son of Robert II, was beheaded in 1437 for the murder of his nephew, King James I, the title passed again to the Crown, where it still rests.[22] Walter left no heir, for one son died in England and the other in battle; his only grandson was beheaded in 1437 as accomplice of his grandfather. So there was no heir. The friendship between James I and Bishop Michael was deep and lasting; "my familiar, . . . commensal of my father and mother and of me . . . Almoner General of the King", these were no empty words.[23] For the first time in its history the Cathedral of Dunblane had the promise of sufficient revenue, and once it had paid the compensation to the royal Treasury, its days of penury were over.

All the lands mentioned in this charter are recognisable today, and all of them, sometimes with varied spelling, occur in other documents. They all lie in Strathearn territory, chiefly in the parishes of Dunblane, Muthill, Crieff and Strogeith. The office of bailiery was granted by Bishop William Chisholm II, in letters dated 30 June 1565, in agreement with the Dean and Chapter, to his brother James Chisholm of Cromlix and his heirs, with powers to create all the officers of court, and to apply all fines and escheats to the bailie's (i.e. bailiff's) own use; this grant was confirmed under the Great Seal on 4 November 1579. Bishop Robert Leighton and the Dean and Chapter granted by charter, 5 October 1659, to General William Drummond (then owner of Cromlix), the offices of hereditary bailie and justiciar of the lordship and regality of Dunblane, and in the charter they founded on James II's original charter and on Bishop William Chisholm II's letters of 1565. Later, in 1748, it is learned from a manuscript in the Register House, Edinburgh, the Court of Session passed an act granting the claim to those above-named offices to Dr Robert Drummond of Cromlix, and specified, in their eighteenth-century spellings, the lands given in the 1443 charter.

In seeking to determine whence came the lands which the King gave to Bishop Ochiltree attention must be paid to the terms of the charter. In its early lines the King states that he is anxious to follow the "precedent of his forebears the Kings of Scotland, of the Earls of Strathearn and other leading and faithful men of our kingdom, who . . . built the Church of Dunblane, endowed it with many possessions and fortified it with privileges. They decreed by statute, and confirmed it, that it was directly from us in chief that the Earl of Strathearn, the lord superior of the

Bishop and Chapter of Dunblane, held his various lands." This is couched in very general terms and could not be founded on to assert the claim, often made, that King David I was a founding father of the Cathedral and Diocese of Dunblane. It is not unknown for kings to be given credit in such instances for acts which involved little if anything more than an acknowledgment that they were the final owners of all land. The only definite statement made is that the Earl of Strathearn, the lord superior of the Bishop, held his various lands in chief from the Crown, as ultimate proprietor.

The charter goes on to state that the lands and rents mentioned "were formerly held in chief from the Earls of Strathearn", that is, as proprietor under the Crown. This is determinative. Especially, must it be so, when the charter goes on to state that "all these the said Bishop and Chapter are to possess as freely and quietly, . . . and in peace as they or their predecessors possessed at any time the said lands or barony, along with the regality of their city, indeed even more quietly, fully and in peace". The Bishop and Chapter "shall render to us . . . such due and customary services as . . . their predecessors were used to render to us". From this it is clear that those lands were not a new gift of Strathearn lands from King James II, but a transfer of the lands formerly held in chief from the Earls of Strathearn, which are now to be held, without intermediary, in chief from the Crown, into whose possession the Earldom and the lands of Strathearn had come.

If this is the correct interpretation, there was justification for Fordun's statement that Gilbert, Earl of Strathearn, gave one part (he says a third) of his lands to the Diocese of Dunblane. On what terms the Bishop of Dunblane held the lands is not known; they may have been free of conditions and annual or other dues, or they may not. But it is clear that Dunblane, as Fordun asserts, was endowed by the Earls of Strathearn.

How else, it may be asked, could the early Bishops have built their Cathedral and the parish churches, and had means with which to provide prebends and incomes and generally to establish the Diocese? Indeed the demands on Bishops starting from scratch were so heavy and the emergencies so urgent as well as continuous, that some of the lands may have been put under pledge or lease. Clement so complained of his predecessors to the Pope. This royal charter of 1443 has the appearance of a tidying-up which had become possible by the passing of the Strathearn lands into the possession of the Crown.

What was involved in the possession of those lands by the Bishop, Dean and Chapter is vividly seen in 1578, when "the native tenants and kindly possessors of the temporal lands belonging to the Bishopric of Dunblane", to the number of a thousand no less, petitioned Parliament to restrain the Earl of Montrose from removing them or changing their "maillis and dewties" into yearly rentals. Mr Andrew Graeme, the first Reformed Bishop of Dunblane, had handed over some of the Bishop's lands by charter to his kinsman, Montrose. An act was passed as the tenants desired, and though the Earl protested the following year that he had never had any such intention, Parliament did not change its decision.[24] This is mentioned at this stage because of the astonishing number of the Bishop's tenants. The figure of one thousand, mentioned in the act, may have denoted more than the tenants, heads of families; it may have included wives and working members of families. Even so, it is an impressive array.

Twice in 1445[25] Michael carried out the exchange of benefices between two clergy who had so agreed. Such episcopal oversight was necessary for the prevention of simony and other irregularities. The second exchange concerned his brother James, who was more than a little restless – he resigned Monzievaird and obtained Muthill, which he exchanged for Kippen, which he exchanged for Strathychtin, which he exchanged for Terwet (Tarves?). This last exchange was cancelled "for certain reasons" and he returned to Strathychtin about 1440, and was in possession on 11 March 1444/5, when the Pope ordered him to resign it. His later history is unknown.

The year 1445 brought upon Bishop Michael (and on the Bishop of St. Andrews) the settlement of the See of Argyll, from which Bishop Finlay had fled.[26] At first the King of Scotland had charged Finlay with treasonably assisting the western rebellion against him; but later he was of opinion that Finlay had refused the rebels the solace of religious offices, and had deserted his See because they had left him destitute. The case came before the Synod of the Church, meeting in Edinburgh on 28 June 1445, and as it concerned State as well as Church, there were present thirty-six deputies of the Three Estates.

The Ochiltree stalls which stand, ten of them, north and south of the Communion Table, are the earliest examples of carving in the Cathedral furnishings. There were once thirty-two such stalls; in recent years two misericords and various other portions have been recovered, and are now exhibited in the Cathedral Museum. The traditional name of them would indicate their date as c.1450, and though one knowledgeable in such matters thought them later than that, when I consulted him, it is possible that (1) the original gift of Michael Ochiltree may have been for a smaller number of stalls than later adorned the Cathedral, (2) Bishop James Chisholm may have added to the stalls when he endowed nine chaplainries of the choir in 1522, or (3) Bishop Ochiltree's stalls may have been given by bequest and been carved after his death. In any case the traditional name is unquestioned and continuous. Michael Ochiltree is credited with building the "Bishop's Bridge" over the Machany between Ardoch and Muthill. Such episcopal gifts were not uncommon; the Bishop of Dunkeld built the bridge over the Tay at Dunkeld, and Bishop Finlay Dermoch the bridge at Dunblane. It is possible, however, that Michael began the bridge when he was Dean of Dunblane, Muthill Church being mensal to the Deanery. He is also traditionally believed to be the builder of Muthill Church.

It was during this bishopric, on 23 July 1433, that Paul Crawar, a Bohemian, a graduate of Prague and Paris and a Bachelor of Medicine of Montpellier,[27] was burned as a heretic at St. Andrews.[28] He had spread the teachings of John Wyclif, whose teaching inspired the doctrine of Jan Hus, the Bohemian reformer. Little contemporary record of this event has survived; the trial seems to have been local, though the Book of Pluscarden records it.[29]

Bishop Michael was followed in the Deanery of Dunblane by Robert de Cranach, one of the Cathedral canons. I call attention to the considerable part he played in the Council of Basle, a Council which continued in session for eighteen years, and which deposed Pope Eugenius IV in 1439 without effect, the Pope continuing to be acknowledged till he died eight years later. The Council of Basle elected Felix V in 1440, so that again, and until Felix abdicated in 1449, there were Pope and Anti-Pope as in the Great Schism. Robert de Cranach was given, on 23 December 1435, the seat and rights of his brother John, Bishop of Brechin. He seems to have attended through nearly four years. He was appointed in 1438 a keeper of the keys of the papal bulls.[30] Dunblane had two others of its clergy among the members of the Council: (1) Donald Macnachtane, canon and prebendary of Logie, who was also Dean of Dunkeld, was incorporated on 8 February 1433/4,[31] (2) William Gordon, canon, who had studied at Louvain in 1434, was incorporated on 9 September 1440.[32] The Council of Basle was the second of the courts of international significance on which the Chapter of Dunblane Cathedral was represented.

Michael Ochiltree died, probably in 1447. There is record of him as witness to a Perth charter[33] in the autumn of 1446, and as it is only towards the end of 1447 that the election of his successor appears, early in 1447 may be taken as the date of his death.

Since Clement, no Bishop of Dunblane had occupied the See with such comprehensive competence as Michael. Trained in the University of Paris, he had sufficient learning, as his degree shows, if he was not so learned as some of his predecessors. He took more than his share of the work of Parliament, which recognised his capacities in his appointment as auditor of accounts and as a member of the Executive Committee with parliamentary powers. His road to the bishop's throne was the road of a struggling pluralist; even his deanery cost him long and expensive endeavour; but in these he was only the child of his times. Once Bishop, he settled to his task with devoted service of both Church and State, as was expected of a bishop in those days. He leaves the impression of a man of energy and capacity, of wisdom, social grace and willingness to labour diligently in his avocations. Whence he got the name of Ochiltree is unknown; but his close friendship with the royal family seems to indicate that his father or mother, or both, was of noble lineage. Such a conclusion is reinforced by his choice to crown and anoint James II, in face of the traditional rights of the Bishop of St. Andrews, and the claims of bishops of more notable sees. His friendship with James II, his parents and his grandparents, must have been paralleled by the regard of the Three Estates, when, the King being only thirteen years of age, Parliament authorised the royal grant of Strathearn lands to the Bishop and Chapter of Dunblane. More than money paid into the royal Treasury was involved in such a transaction. He may be ranked as a founding bishop of Dunblane, second only to Clement, in the long line of Roman diocesans.

L

Michael's struggle at the Court of Rome for the Deanery and for the Bishopric of Dunblane coincided with the beginnings of royal challenge to papal appointments to Scottish benefices, both greater and lesser. Up to about the year 1300 appointments to the greater benefices, that is, bishoprics and abbacies, known as "the prelacies", were in the power of the chapters of cathedrals and of the members of the abbeys concerned; such elections were often only nominal, for local magnates, like the Earl of Strathearn in the cases of Dunblane and of Inchaffray, and in other cases the Crown, used their influence on the electors and very often determined the nominations. The lesser benefices were non-elective and in the gift of the patron (bishop, monastery or layman). About 1300, however, the Popes enlarged their control over both the greater and the lesser benefices; in the former, in which they had always exercised the right to confirm, or to deny, confirmation to an elected cleric, they now asserted a right to "provide", and in the latter, the non-elective benefices, they ruled that, when vacancies of a certain type occurred, they were "reserved" to the Pope for his unfettered appointment. If the Popes had been the heads of a Church in which they or their officers had intimate knowledge of the dioceses, parishes, clerics and abbeys, there would have been some justification for this centralised control; but it is to be suspected that this enlargement of power was dictated by the hope of fees from contestants who thronged the papal court. Its results were not order and speed, but confusion and delay; increased expenses of an enlarged papal bureaucracy were met by many fees and exactions. When the Great Schism of 1378-1417 brought two Popes the situation became worse; and when the Church emerged from schism, Martin V brought all bishoprics and abbacies of more than 200 gold florins per annum under his "reservation".

This system inevitably led to royal opposition: the Kings of Scotland were deprived of patronage (and therefore of money as well as influence), bishops and abbots, who were members of Parliament, were outside of the King's choice, and the numerous visits of Scottish churchmen to the papal market for appointments led often to long absences and to heavy financial drain on national currency. It was not therefore surprising that James I demanded that no cleric might pass to foreign parts without justifying his journey to the King, or might take money furth of Scotland without paying a sixth of its value to the King, the penalty being loss of the gold and silver and a fine of £10. There were other regulations as to exchange (allowed only within Scotland, and only with certain money-changers or merchants within the realm), authorisation for travel (is your journey really necessary?), and sufficient documents, most of them (*mutatis mutandis*) known to us today in the restrictions on foreign travel. By an Act of 1428, to deal with the Papal Court, either personally or by procurator, without licence granted by a bishop and the Chancellor of the Realm, was to commit the crime of "barratry" and incur "the payne of breking of the Act of the Parliament".[34]

This contest of King and Pope for the patronage of vacant sees leaves a trail of Scottish enactments in support of the royal claims and of disputes with Rome. In one of these the King had Croiser, Archdeacon of Teviotdale, whom the Pope favoured, convicted of treason for "barratry", while he supported his secretary, Cameron, who became Bishop of Glasgow and Chancellor of Scotland, and whom the Pope denounced. James I, however, finding the ecclesiastics uncertain in his support, did not press his local advantage. In 1450, however, James II was able to persuade the Bishops, the Provincial Council of the Church, and Parliament to assert his right of patronage in vacant sees which were formerly under the bishop's patronage. This did no more than present the Pope in such a vacancy with an undivided opposition to his claims. How the Pope circumvented the King in the vacancy which first occurred in Dunblane after 1450 can be read in Chapter IX, where it is recorded that Bishop Robert Lawder resigned at Rome on the same day as the Pope provided the new Bishop, John Hepburn.

This clever artifice, which annoyed the King, combined with the disturbed condition of Scotland, led in 1485 to a petition to the Pope that he should delay his provisions for six months until the desires of the King were known,[35] so as to secure, if possible, that the Pope would provide to the prelacies men who were suitable to their place in Parliament and the Secret (or Privy) Council of the King. In 1487 Innocent VIII granted a delay of eight months in appointments to cathedrals and monasteries worth more than 200 florins, gold of the Camera; but he reserved the provision to himself "as we shall think expedient", thus postponing for a while, but not abrogating, his collecting of the fees of promotion.[36]

This papal indult did not work well. Innocent VIII had urged his successors to follow his practice, as the indult states, but the Scottish King and his advisers considered it as a privilege granted for all time. Innocent VIII died in 1492, and the dispute was again wide open. Parliament in 1496 passed an act[37] for the avoiding of damage to the realm "throw the exhorbitant coistis and expensis dalie done be kirkmen upon the impetration and purchessing at the court of Rome beneficis elective and diverse utheris . . . contrair the actis of parliament . . . and contrair diverse faculteis and privilegis" granted by the Pope to the King; it largely re-enacted the Act of 1428 against barratry. It was not till 1519 that Leo X, who had after Flodden acted as if Scottish vacancies were wholly in his control, confirmed the indult of 1487. In 1526 Parliament, asserting that this rule (nomination to vacancies belongs to the King, provision to the Pope) had been violated, enacted that any who took over bishop's places or abbeys without the King's command "sall incur the cryme of tresone and leise majestie".[38] In 1535 the Pope yielded the King's right to nominate and even extended the time for the royal supplication to twelve months. Though this was a victory for the royal *amour propre*, it would be difficult to hold that the King's nominations were always satisfactory, and the papal provisions also were often determined by reasons that had no regard to the religious needs of Scottish dioceses. When, in the 1530s, England threw off the papal yoke, the Pope, in order to retain the allegiance of Scotland, gave up interfering with the nominations of the Scottish King. Consequently King and Pope alike made matters worse and gave added impetus to the rising necessity for reformation. In 1542/13, the surplus of the revenues of the abbeys and priories already granted to the King's sons was converted to the use of the Queen and the realm's necessities.[39]

NOTES

1. CPR VIII 80, where he is called the son of a priest and an unmarried woman.

2. I 481.

3. 1420, CSSR 237; 1421, CSSR 245-6; 1422, HMC Var. Coll. V 10 and RBG I 148-57.

4. All references to the foregoing story of Michael O. are in Appendix of Cathedral Clergy under 1418, n. 1.

5. RBG I 157-59. This Court sat in Muthill parish Church. The 1422 process is in RBG I 148-57. A mandate, 12 Apr. 1431, speaks of him as "now Bishop of Dunblane, at that time elect", CPR VIII 368-9.

6. *Rot. Scotiae* II 269. *Foedera* X 446. BC IV 1032.

7. AP II 31. Sc. II 514. Ex. 237.

8. DK 196, 197, 198.

9. 1439 onwards. AP II, see Index of.

10. ERS III 400.

11. ERS V 108, 112.

12. RMS II 271, 273, 274.

13. DB III 427, 3 Jul. 1445.

14. CPR IX 48-49, 131, 146, 535, 540-1.

15. CPR IX 21.

16. CR 55.

17. CPR VIII 622-3.

18. For this document, see BFDC 1955. The local copy of the Great Seal Charter was once in IWC 114, where it is now marked in pencil as "missing".

19. James II authorised the erection of several baronies: of Dunkeld, of Aberlady, and of Inchaffray Abbey. The last became the barony of Cardenay, which covered the lands of the monastery. It was given to the Abbot and Convent, 27 Jan. 1444/5, CAI No. 146. "Barony" in Scotland means a large freehold estate; right of barony is therefore the privileges of the baron as owner, and (within limits) as ruler and dispenser of justice. Regality in Scotland was territorial jurisdiction of a royal nature granted by the King. A lord of regality had the same civil authority as a sheriff, but in criminal jurisdiction his authority was much more extensive. Regality was abolished in the reign of George II.

20. It has been remarked that this grant of barony and regality does not call Dunblane a burgh; true, but neither does the charter of 1540, which created the city and barony of Glasgow into a regality, call Glasgow a burgh (REG II Nos. 353, 356); neither does the "Golden Charter" of St. Andrews in 1452 (RMS II 1444) style St. Andrews a burgh. Those two instances are noted by Dr Annie Dunlop in her biography of James Kennedy, Bishop of St. Andrews. It would appear that they were recognised as bishop's burghs, and to use the word "burgh" of them would have been confusing. For text and photograph of this charter (8 Feb. 1442/3, AP II 58, RMS II 270) see BFDC 1955.

21. Edward III, Edward Balliol's protector, described Malise in 1334, as "a notorious rebel", that is, against Balliol, whose invasion he seems to have resisted.

22. The late Duke of Connaught was Earl of Strathearn and graciously consented to be the first Patron of the Society of Friends of Dunblane Cathedral.

23. Also, RMS II 18, 8 Mar. 1424/5, James I gave a holding in Perth to "his clerk and familiar, Michael Ochiltree, Dean of Dunblane".

24. AP III 111-12, 165-6.

25. CPR IX 441, 11 Feb. 1444/5; CPR IX 497-8, 11 Mar. 1444/5.

26. RB I 100. DBS 385. BCPS 388/9.

27. BCPS 460.

28. Sc. II 495. Ex. 234. Knox's History I 497-9 (Laing).

29. XI ch. 5.

30. BCPS 487.

31. BCPS 492.
32. BCPS 489. SHR XXV 330.
33. HMC VII 707b, 23 Sep. 1446.
34. AP II 5, 14, 16.
35. AP II. 171.
36. Herkless and Hannay: *Archbishops of St. Andrews* I 157-8.
37. AP II 237-8.
38. AP II 309-10.
39. AP II 424.

CHAPTER IX

BISHOP ROBERT (LAWDER) 1447 – 1466
BISHOP JOHN HEPBURN 1466 – 1486

ROBERT (LAWDER) 1447 – 1466

ON 3 March 1445/6, as appears in the Stirling of Keir charters, Gilbert de Stirling laid before the Precentor and three canons of Glasgow a document[1] drawn by Robert de Laweder, canon of Glasgow and notary public, which stated that the Bishop of Glasgow, by giving a glove, reinvested Gilbert Stirling and his wife Isabella in Easter Cadder, which for some eight years had been in the Bishop's hands. Most of the canons remembered the original transaction. This is the first notice I have found of Robert Lawder, who became Bishop of Dunblane in 1447, on the death of Michael Ochiltree.

But before his election to Dunblane, "Robert de Lawedre, canon of Glasgow, M.A., Bachelor of Canon Law and of noble birth", is intimately concerned in an intricate promotion. He had been provided to the vicarage of Selkirk in the Diocese of Glasgow. The rectory of Selkirk had been appropriated to Kelso Abbey by Pope Eugenius IV (1431-47), transferring it from Jedburgh in whose possession it had previously been. The Abbot of Kelso and Robert could not agree on the vicar's portion and they referred their dispute to the Pope, who delegated the question to one of his chaplains but died before the chaplain could report. The new Pope, Nicolas V (1447-55), annulled all pending suits, and Robert is in doubt whether his provision to Selkirk is valid. The Pope then mandated[2] three clerics to collate the vicarage (now valued at £25 sterling) to Robert, notwithstanding that (a) Robert, lately dispensed to hold for life any two benefices with cure of souls or otherwise incompatible, even if they are parish churches, and to resign them as often as he pleases, holds the perpetual vicarage of Earlston (£8 sterling), (b) is canon of Glasgow and prebendary of Cardross (£9 sterling), and (c) has a yearly pension of £6 out of the fruits of Barlanark (now within the city of Glasgow, to the east).

Robert was not a pluralist on a large scale. He belonged to a clerical family which included, in the same period, George, Bishop of Argyll (1427); Alexander, Bishop of Dunkeld (1440); Thomas, Bishop of Dunkeld (1452); and William, Bishop of Glasgow (1408). Thomas was nephew of William and was the son of an unmarried knight, who was probably related to William de Lawder, Lord of Hatton. It is likely that from the Lord of Hatton came Robert Lawder's claim to be of noble birth.[3]

Six months after Robert Lawder's definite collation to Selkirk he appears, on 27 October 1447, as "Robert, now elect of Dunblane, previously of lower rank".[4] On the same day another papal record speaks of Selkirk as "void by the promotion of Robert elect of Dunblane and by his consecration which is to take place".[5] He was authorised, also on the same day, to receive from the new Bishop of Glasgow the usual oath of loyalty to the Pope and the Roman See.[6] His provision to Dunblane, on that same day, calls him a canon of Dunblane, in priest's orders.[7] The usual concurrent letters were despatched to the Chapter, clergy, people and vassals of the Church, and to the King.

For the vacant Bishopric the Dean and Chapter had elected Walter Stewart, then Archdeacon of Dunblane. Though Walter was related to the King (but out of wedlock), and the King urged his claims, the Pope did not provide him. The provision was made on the same day as the translation of William Turnbull from Dunkeld to Glasgow and the provision of John Raulston to Dunkeld. This triple episcopal settlement on one day, combined with the fact that Robert acted as procurator for the other two, gives the appearance of a plan already made, and this is confirmed by the two instruments of procuratory being drawn by the same notary on 12 September 1447, six weeks before the day of the three episcopal appointments.[8] On 13 November 1447 Robert offered 800 gold florins of the Camera for his common and five customary little services, to be paid in two terms, each of six months, and as their procurator, 2500 florins for William Turnbull and 450 for John Raulston, on the same terms as his own.[9]

Even all these did not exhaust the usefulness of Robert's visit to the Papal Court, for three days later Nicolas V gave to him the extraordinary faculty to provide nominees of James, King of

Photographs: by John

PLATE V

SOUTHERN PILLARS OF THE NAVE

Dickie, Dunblane

PLATE VI

NORTH FACE OF TOWER WITHIN THE NAVE

Scots, to a canonry in each cathedral and collegiate church in Scotland, to reserve for the Bishop's own collation to such persons a prebend and a minor dignity in each such church, as well as 40 benefices, with or without cure of souls, of any value, of any patronage, to be given by the Bishop to 40 other nominees of the King.[10] Of course, the Camera, or the Collector, was to be kept informed, so that the papal dues might be exacted. In 1422 Murdac, Duke of Albany, Governor of Scotland, had petitioned the Pope that four benefices in each diocese be reserved to him by the Pope for bestowal on Murdac's nominees. James II's faculty was an even more monstrous inroad by the State into the liberties of the Church; it allowed the King to appoint friends, or the friends of friends, for financial considerations doubtless, to about 60 benefices; it gave the Bishop of Dunblane an over-riding patronage in every diocese, and it enabled the Pope to satisfy the King and the Bishop without loss of taxes due to him. Bishops and lay patrons were not slow to protest, and in 1450[11] the faculty was withdrawn from the Bishop of Dunblane and given to the Bishop of Whithorn. The reason for the papal change of mind is not stated, but can easily be supplied. The protests were so many and so strong that Robert Lawder could not stand the opposition. Moreover, the Pope realised that not only had he offended the patrons, clerical and lay, but that he himself had not reaped all the taxes inherent in the appointments he had given away. So in the new faculty he made a compromise, authorising the Bishop of Whithorn to reserve all vacant canonries and twenty other benefices, and decreed that as vacancies occur they shall be filled, the first by a papal nominee, the second by a royal, the third by the nominee of a patron, and so to continue. This was still a considerable invasion of diocesan and ecclesiastical free-dom, and it was unfortunate that the Pope should have granted it. The Church of Scotland often protested against such interference. In 1436, for instance, Sir William de Ogilvy, John de Methven, canon of Glasgow, and William Croiser, Archdeacon of Teviot-dale, took it on themselves, by oath to Pope and Cardinals, to try to persuade James II to repeal certain laws which he had made against the liberties of the Church; they promised that despite these laws, which compelled a cleric bound for Rome to prove to the Chancellor of Scotland that his journey was necessary and that he was not exporting coin without permission, the penalty being perpetual exile, they would induce John, elect of Moray, to visit the Roman Court within two years, and would within one year transmit to the Pope and College the repeal of the offending legislation.[12]   One of those who had instigated James II to pass the laws in question was John Cameron, Bishop of Glasgow; for this he was tried by papal commissioners and found guilty, but was pardoned by the Pope in 1430 on the King's petition.[13] In 1440 the King claimed the right to fill all cathedral dignities which fell vacant during a vacancy in the bishopric; the Pope called this a "pretended custom", but agreed to it for this time and limited it to Dunkeld.[14] In 1450 eight bishops, Robert Lawder among them, "bending their knees to our supreme Lord the King", announced in Parliament that they desired their liberties as in previous times[15]; they gave details of the liberties and possessions of cathedral churches. To this appeal, the Queen, Marie de Gueldres, added her influence. The act which gave effect to this powerful appeal reads like the founding charter of a monastery: "for the welfare of our soul and the souls of Marie, Queen of Scotland, our consort, and of our ancestors and our successors, Kings of Scotland", the King grants the liberty asked for, mentioning the copes, golden vessels, etc., which the owner might dispose of, though he was a churchman. An act of common decency was thus elevated to a deed of Christian charity. Two years later Parliament issued a decree,[16] to which Robert Lawder put his name, on the liberties of churches and clerical persons. The days had begun to dawn when spiritual liberty was of moment; as yet, it only meant freedom from inordinate financial burdens and from undue invasions into patronage, church property and ecclesiastical privilege. A hundred years were to pass before the spiritual liberty of the Church was to gather depth of significance and urge.

Further still, Robert Lawder used his visit to Rome to his advantage. On 16 November he was given faculty to grant dispensations to twenty-five couples who had married uncanonically within the third or fourth degree of consanguinity or affinity, and later, another, to dispense twenty-five persons for illegitimate birth, to promote them to holy orders, and grant them to hold two compatible benefices, with or without cure, even if one were a cathedral canonry and prebend.[17] Both faculties were to be exercised within his first year as Bishop, and were meant to provide him with money to meet his debts at the Roman Court, including the 800 gold florins for the services of his provision, within the promised twelve months.

So equipped with faculties of considerable financial weight, Robert Lawder doubtless set out for Dunblane, duly consecrated. There is no record of the date of his consecration, but from 1448 onwards he was an active Bishop; as the secular papers have been preserved better than the ecclesiastical, it is his public rather than his church work which appears.

Thrice in 1449, in August, October and November, the Bishop of Dunblane was one of an important embassage sent into England under safe conduct from Henry VI for the purpose of making peace between England and Scotland.[18] The year before, the English had burned Dunbar and Dumfries, the Scots Alnwick and Warkworth; moreover, the Scots had heavily defeated the English at Clochmaben on the Sarke. Those embassies comprised bishops, abbots, lords, knights, esquires, the Provost of Edinburgh and a Doctor of Decreets; they were allowed a hundred attendants or more and the carriage of money and papers. Little came of this effort, and in 1452 Robert Lawder and others were again sent on a like errand, under promise of safe conduct from the English King.[19] Such truce as emerged was soon broken, for James II invaded England in August 1455. In the rough and tumble of Scots-English attacks, James was killed at the siege of Roxburgh, in 1460, by the bursting of a cannon. He was in his thirtieth year; internal struggles and foreign wars made his reign an unhappy time for Scotland.

The very day of Robert's provision to Dunblane the Pope gave him a mandate. Five such mandates, dated September, October (2) and November (2) 1447, were waiting for his attention when he reached Dunblane. Five others followed, up to 1454. Of these ten,[20] only two call for mention:

(1) A mandate of 1451[21] declared that though the Pope had recently granted a general restitution to those who had been deprived of their benefices for their adherence to the "so-called Councils of Basle and Lausanne", this was not to apply to such of them as had been exiled from Scotland; the Bishops of Glasgow and Moray had been so instructed. Now the Bishops of Dunblane and Spoleto and the Archdeacon of Glasgow are commanded to

defend those who got provision of the benefices of such deprived persons.

(2) In 1454 the Bishop was given an interesting mandate,[22] to investigate a petition from Rankin de Crawford, nobleman, temporal lord, and all the people of Manuel, who desired permission to appoint a clerk minister as local assistant to the priest of Falkirk responsible for services at Manuel, as they found their parish church of Falkirk too distant. Other neighbouring churches or chapels, the petitioners say, have each their own distinct and special clerk ministers to assist the priests and chaplains who serve the said churches and chapels in divine offices; such clerics have been customarily elected and presented by the inhabitants of such places. To them the people of such places are bound to pay those dues which by the law and custom of Scotland are payable to "parish clerks". The people of Manuel have none such, to their great loss. After investigation and binding of the people to pay the customary dues, the Bishop is to grant the request. The Pope adds that the inhabitants, with consent of the chaplain, may elect a clerk minister, for presentation to the chaplain, who shall be bound to admit him, if he is suitably equipped for the duties.

Between 1455 and 1459, four more mandates arrived for the Bishop's attention. Of these, three may be mentioned:

(1) In 1455 he was commanded to ensure very ample promotion to Alexander Preston, canon of Glasgow, who "went lately with a notable company to the Holy Land to fight against the infidels, and whose father and many others of his kin have fought against them . . . and been made knights". He had lately been dispensed as the son of a married baron and an unmarried mother, and is now allowed to hold any number and kind of compatible dignities.[23]

(2) Andrew, Bishop of Glasgow, had petitioned the Pope, asserting that some clerks and laymen of Glasgow, some of them unknown, had stolen certain precious property of the Bishop, both before and after the death of Bishop William, and still detained them. The Bishop of Dunblane and two others are to admonish them publicly, set a term for restitution, which failing, to excommunicate them.[24]

(3) Another mandate followed in the same month, also on a petition from the Bishop of Glasgow: "by reason of the wars and

incursions over the marches of Scotland, the City and Diocese of Glasgow are greatly impoverished", so much so that he cannot visit his churches or people in person without great inconvenience. The Diocese of Glasgow was large and scattered, and included parishes even on the eastern marches. The Bishop of Dunblane and two others named are mandated to allow him for ten years to visit by deputy.[25]

In April 1456, on the petition of Glasgow University, supported by the King, the Pope exempted the University from the jurisdiction of the older University of St. Andrews, and appointed the Bishop of Dunblane, the Abbot of Paisley and the Dean of Glasgow as conservators of its privileges, with the same powers as the conservators of St. Andrews.[26]

That Robert Lawder was a member of the University of St. Andrews, as well as a conservator of privileges of Glasgow University, we learn from St. Andrews records. Richard Wylie, Apostolic Nuncio, found it necessary to intervene, on 23 June 1464, as *commissarius* of the Rector of the University, to demand an oath of obedience from the Bishop as a member of the University. He was charged with absolving one of his diocesan clergy, Gilbert Blawe, parish priest of Culross, who had been excommunicated by the church's Conservator of Privileges. No details of the case are known, nor is the final issue; the Bishop did not agree with the sentence and abolished it.[27]

During Robert Lawder's episcopate, the Pope seems to have had a high regard for the capacities of the Chapter, as well as of the Bishop, of Dunblane. In addition to the fourteen mandates committed to the Bishop, six were sent to the Archdeacon, two to the Official, and two to the Treasurer, all designated only by their dignities. The Bishop had not been able, it would appear, to do enough for Alexander Preston, for in 1458, the Archdeacon and two other clerics are commanded to see to his interests – he "has been engaged for about a year with twelve archers and more in fighting against the infidel".[28] One of the mandates to the Official of Dunblane was to rectify alienations made by a number of Bishops of Dunkeld, it being noted (such was the chaos usual in those days) that some to whom lands had been leased for a long time, or for life, or even in perpetuity, had obtained papal confirmation of their uncanonical leases.[29] The two mandates given to the Treasurer on the same day were complementary; he and two other clerics (the same two in each case) were to execute the exchange between Henry Murref (Murray), Dean of Dunblane, and William Scot, vicar of Stirling, both having resigned their benefices to the Pope through their proctor at the Roman Court.[30]

Robert Lawder had his due share in witnessing charters – most of them transferring lands, some by the King, some by commoners Only one calls for note: a charter of James II in 1449,[31] following a decision of Parliament, granted to the bishops power to dispose of their goods by will. This was conceded on complaints by the bishops that the Kings of Scotland had been in the habit of despoiling cathedrals on the death of bishops; though this had the weight of custom, it is to end.

The Bishop was not in good financial standing with the Papal Camera. His offer of 800 gold florins on his provision to Dunblane proved optimistic; the word "offer" hid what was in reality an assessment. In 1451 Robert was granted a moratorium of eight months, "the term being long past".[32] In 1458 he was reminded that he had incurred penalties for failing to visit Rome once every three years since his provision, that three such periods had passed, that a fourth finished on 3 November, when a fifth will begin.[33] It is clear that the important regulation of Dunblane's property in 1443 had not yet begun to bring financial prosperity; probably neglected repairs to buildings had to be made, and in addition the royal gift "of love and charity" involved heavy payments of hard cash which would burden the Diocese for years.

In this connexion a strange document[34] was issued on 2 April 1487, by Raphael, Vice-chamberlain of the Papal Camera, from the Church of San Lorenzo in Damaso, Rome. It merits large quotation. "For the part of James, elect of Dunblane (i.e. James Chisholm, provided on 31 January 1487), it has been alleged in his promotion that the fruits and rents of the said church do not amount to the annual value taxed in the Apostolic Camera, and that since the said church in one place is found taxed at 370 florins, and the Monastery of Inchaffray, which is in the Diocese of Dunblane, is written immediately after the said church at the said sum of 370, it seems likely that this is the true tax of the church." Hitherto, many provisions have been made to the said church, including two with obligations which were expedited at 370, and two which were obligated at 800, though this had no effect, for nothing was paid. And, in the last place, in the days of Paul II (1464-71) expedition was substituted at the rate of 800, which it is believed so happened because he who was then promoted (he was Bishop John Hepburn, 1466-86), led by some consideration of his private and particular business, did not consider the cause of the church but only his own (this seems to imply that Bishop John Hepburn was so anxious to be Bishop of Dunblane that he accepted an unjust tax rather than complain). "And since by attestation of five trustworthy witnesses, to wit one bishop and four canons, examined thereanent at commission and mandate of the Pope, it was proved that the fruits, rents and profits of the said church in all reach only to 1100 marks in the money of Scotland, which equals 600 ducats and a part, more or less, it seems likely that this is the annual value and that it ought to be taxed at the rate of 300 ducats or according to taxation at 370 ducats. Therefore, after mature deliberation in consistory and taking account of prayers of King of Scotland and of labours and expenses which the said elect has undergone in divers journeys and in other ways for expediting this business, and his great merits, in consistory the Pope and Cardinals have alike ordained and willed that the said James elect, for this time only, pay 500 ducats and at the rate of 500 florins, with remission of remainder, and with mandate to expedite bulls of provision at this rate on account of tenuity of fruits."

This is indeed a strange document. When it says that the over-taxing of Bishops Robert Lawder and John Hepburn at 800 florins "had no effect, for nothing was paid", it is true that Robert paid little and may have died in debt to the Camera, but the whole 800 florins and more were paid by John Hepburn, as the published receipts prove.[35] If the charge of 800 was not an endeavour to get that amount, the correct charge being 370 as the document admits, it seems strange that the charge was fixed at 500 florins. If "tenuity of fruits" was the reason for reducing the tax, the addition that the Camera would accept 500 "for this time only", seems to prove that by the time of Robert Lawder's provision the Camera had heard of Dunblane's additional revenue and had an exaggerated idea of its immediate consequences. Bishop James Chisholm knew the facts, and these were so strong that the

Camera had to re-assess Dunblane. Such a step is never popular with any taxing authority.

It is good fortune, because so unusual in the story of Dunblane Cathedral, that two instances have been preserved of items in the agenda of the Bishop's Court in the days of Robert Lawder.

(1) The charters of the Burgh of Stirling include letters patent by Bishop Robert, which recount that on 21 November 1457, when he sat in judgment in his cathedral church of Dunblane, there compeared a venerable man, Sir John de Atheray, Treasurer of the Cathedral, and John Brady, a burgess of Stirling, procurators and commissioners of the Burgh, and presented a charter of James II to the Provost and Council of Stirling, by which, on 24 June 1456, he bestowed on them the patronage of St. James' Hospital. The Bishop ordained that a copy of the charter be made, and that the copy, confirmed by his seal, be considered as of equal validity with the original. Two canons of the Cathedral, John Cristini and Malcom Drummond, and others, witness the letters patent, and the instrument is certified by John de Spens and John Scot, priests of the Diocese of Dunblane, notaries public.[36]

(2) In 1462 the consistorial court, meeting in the Cathedral, settled a suit brought by the vicar of Fowlis and the Abbot of Inchaffray, who were themselves unable to reach agreement.[37] Tristram de Gorthy in the parish of Fowlis had mortified "100 shillings of usual Scots money" to the Church, and the two contestants agreed to ask the Bishop's court to declare its destination. Parties were heard, the Abbot being represented by his proctor, Fethill, a chaplain; witnesses were examined under oath; Tristram's executors were cited and appeared; the Bishop consulted his assessors and other experts in law, and then gave his judgment. The decision turned on the terms of the foundation of the vicarage (of which we have no record except this), by which undivided bequests, like Tristram's, belonged to the rector, that is, in this case, to the Abbey, whereas bequests, divided and not whole, belonged to the vicar, along with the usual offerings at death. So the unfortunate vicar lost his case, received no part of the legacy, and was mulcted in expenses, the taxation of which was held over. The parallel with modern procedure is striking; even the taxation of expenses was in vogue 500 years ago. The case is fully written out in a legal minute, beginning *In dei nomine amen*, and it ends

thus, in a long attestation in Latin: "I, Johannes Scot, priest of the Diocese of Dunblane, notary public by imperial authority, was present, along with the above-named witnesses, at the moving, ventilation and argument of the above-written cause, and at the decree of definitive judgment, and that I saw and heard all these things done in whole and in part, and that I took notes of them. Therefore this present public instrument I have written with my own hand and now record it in this public form. And I have signed it with my own and customary sign, name and superscription, having been questioned and required to testify on oath to all the foregoing." The document records date, place and hour of the judgment: in the Cathedral, about eleven o'clock forenoon, on 26 January 1461/2; and there are noted as present, and as specially cited and questioned, Malcolm John, Dean of Lismore; John Cristini, Chancellor of Dunblane; Malcolm Drummond, canon of Dunblane; Patrick Ogil and Gilbert Huntar, chaplains; and divers others. The Bishop added his round seal. It is evident that this was regarded as an important issue which would determine precedent. Whether or not, it is interesting to have so full a statement of the various legal steps taken by the court.

We have to wait till the decade before the Reformation before we find, in the only surviving diocesan minute-book of Dunblane's medieval Church, a day-to-day picture of the consistorial court of Dunblane at work. This important and interesting record, consisting of 436 folios, now bound in two volumes, is to be found in the Scottish Record Office, H.M. General Register House, Edinburgh, under the English title of "Commissariot of Dunblane, Act Book". So far no reference to an Official has been found in its pages. It covers the dates 2 January 1550/1 to 5 January 1554/5, a period during which there is no trace of an Official having been appointed in the Diocese. Its original title is given on the original flyleaf, considerably damaged; it reads *Liber actorum curie consisto(rialis)*, Book of Acts of the Consistorial Court.[38] In general the court was presided over by two commissaries of Bishop William Chisholm I; frequently the Bishop himself presided and constituted the court alone, or with one or both of his commissaries, who were often called commissaries general; sometimes the Bishop reserved cases to his own judgment. The Bishop's Procurator Fiscal is frequently mentioned only by title, but it is minuted that the Bishop ratified the

M

appointment of Sir John Leirmonth in that office on 19 October 1554 (folio 405 v). There are frequent references to procurators, that is, proctors or agents, who presented and argued the suits of their clients as in a modern Sheriff Court.

This being only a minute-book, written by the clerk of the court, in this case William Blakwod, as a record of the suits presented, the processes followed and the sentences imposed, there is only rarely any extract of evidence given, and it is often difficult to find what the charges were in any particular case. Doubtless a published transcription of the heavily-contracted Latin, a laborious task which ought to be undertaken, would clear up the details of each case. In many cases the judge heard the case and dealt with it there and then, but in contested cases the stages were gone through in accordance with the rules of plenary procedure – defenders and witnesses were cited, parties appeared at the bar either personally or by their procurators, the libel was produced, answers given, the case argued and all the details of form of proof, admission of witnesses, evidence from other ecclesiastical courts, amending of libels and pleas, objections, and so forth, right until the judge fixed a day when parties were to gather to hear sentence. Few sentences appear in this *Liber*, but there are references to a *Liber Sententiarum* in which the full terms of sentences would be recorded; this book of sentences has not survived.

Matters of the utmost variety were dealt with by the court: teinds, church dues and property, debts, matrimonial causes, slander, contracts fortified by oath, perjury, etc. Usually the court met every week-day, sometimes twice on the same day at different hours. Even on Sundays, occasionally, the court met to deal with one or two cases. Even saints' days and festivals were not excepted, for meetings have been noted on Easter Sunday, Whitsunday and Trinity Sunday. The number of cases dealt with on any one day vary from one to forty, with an average of less than twenty. Often the sentence included excommunication, from which, on petition, and with proof of fulfilment of the rest of the sentence, the court could release the defaulting party. But many of the pleas were for payment of small debts which were dealt with quickly, and quite a number were non-contentious, e.g. for the appointment of curators. Many of the cases involved clerics or tenants of ecclesiastical lands and holdings; but the vast majority were concerned with laymen. Sometimes laymen desired to come to the church court as more convenient or otherwise desirable than the King's courts, and occasionally there are protests in the consistorial court that the case ought to have gone before the civil courts. A small number of criminal cases are recorded, including assaults by, or to the injury of, churchmen. It will be remembered that the Bishop, by reason of his being possessed of the regality of Dunblane, had larger powers in criminal cases than a sheriff and more or less equivalent powers in civil pleas.

The impression left by a less than thorough investigation of the book is that the Bishop's court was active, thorough, competent and eager to do justice in all cases; nobles, landed proprietors, tenants and lesser people resorted to it freely, which is sure proof of its reputation for impartiality and speedy action. The book calls for close study by one who not only has time at his disposal but is expert in law, church affairs, family histories, and social conditions. Examination by such a scholar would be able to make a contribution of value to the working of ecclesiastical courts in Scotland, about which too little is known.

Robert Lawder was chosen as judge arbiter in a case which began "in a council of the clergy, regularly and annually held by ancient and approved custom and by apostolic privilege", at Perth, on 13 December 1464; it was continued for some days before the Bishop of Dunblane. The case was a claim by the Abbot of Arbroath that the teind sheaves of Pitlour belonged to him and not to James Kennedy, Bishop of St. Andrews, to whom they had been leased. The Bishop took seven months before he gave his verdict,[39] again in a council of clergy, that the sheaves in question belonged to the Abbey "except that the farmer folks and inhabitants of the lands of Pitlour[40] have to answer to him (Bishop of Dunblane) and his successors annually, only to the amount of four marks of usual money of Scotland". These four marks constituted one of the annual rents in James II's charter to Dunblane Cathedral, 1443. All parties agreed with this judgment. "These proceedings took place in front of the great stair of the town-house of the Burgh of Perth, about the hour of eleven forenoon", 18 July 1465.

In affairs of state Robert Lawder attended Parliament with diligence. He was present through the several days in January

1449/50,[41] when, among other matters, the bishops appealed successfully to the King for restoration of their liberties; from 1452 to 1460, his name is found frequently in the sederunt.

It is necessary, in an endeavour to get a fuller picture of the times we are travelling through, to remind ourselves of some of the lesser happenings and concerns which helped to make up the life of the people, clerical and lay, and were doubtless the cause of much interest or of heated debate. In Robert Lawder's bishopric, for instance, began a local *cause célèbre* which continued for years.[42] On the death of John, Abbot of Inchaffray, patron and brethren elected George Murray, one of their number, in priest's orders, Bachelor of Theology, and of noble birth on both sides. The Bishop gave him benediction, the Pope confirmed him, and he obtained possession. But one Nicolas Fechil, thought to be an Augustinian Canon, seized the Abbacy, helped, it is said, by certain powerful laymen, and so terrified George that he could not assert his abbatial rights. Fortunately for George, Nicolas died, but George's troubles were not over; for a brother of the Abbey, William de Haddington, who had actually assisted in George's election, brought armed men to gain for him possession of George's office, and by threats and bribery got some of the monks to elect him Abbot. George appealed to Rome, there being not as yet an Archbishop in Scotland, and in the delay William kept possession, wasted the Abbey's revenues "with a certain public concubine of his, by whom he had several children walking the earth", and though excommunicated had treated the sentence with contempt. The enquiry dragged on; in 1468 the Pope admitted that he himself had provided William de Haddington to the Abbey, under a reservation of the Abbey to the Pope by his predecessor. The Pope appointed one of his chaplains to make enquiries and he favoured George. Now William appealed to the Pope, who had provided it to him, but the Pope decided that George be put in possession.

Even that did not end the matter. The Abbey, probably to get rid of him, gave William a pension on certain conditions. George, however, refused to pay the pension till the conditions were observed. So William took the Abbot to the consistory court of the Bishop of Dunblane. Though George denied the right of the local court to try him, he being a papal chaplain, and asserted rightly that William, being still under the greater excommunication, had no canonical right to the pension, which in any case had not been granted by the Pope, and which the monastery could not afford to pay, the judgment went against him, and he also was excommunicated. It was George's turn now to appeal to Rome, and in 1470 the Pope remitted the issue to three mandatories who were to settle the dispute without appeal. It is some satisfaction to learn that George Murray, after such a stormy and lengthy and unmerited dispute, was still Abbot in 1489.[43]

Another common concern of the people and churchmen was the observance of the four forbidden degrees in marriage, in consanguinity and in affinity. One historian has said that in royal and noble circles it was difficult in Scotland, with its frequent warfare and its small population, to marry outside of the forbidden relationships, which ran to about a hundred. A not unusual instance is noted in Dunblane in 1463, when Adam Hepburn of Dunsyre, layman of the Diocese, having married Ellen Hume irregularly, but legally, before witnesses, and had children by her, discovered that he and Ellen were related in the second and third degree of affinity. This troubled him; so he summoned his wife before Bishop Robert Lawder, who pronounced divorce between them. Ellen appealed, "falsely alleging", said the Pope, that this was unjust; but after five months she had not prosecuted the appeal. On Adam's petition the Pope consented to the transfer of the appeal to Scotland, and appointed three Scottish clerics, a bishop and two abbots, as judges.[44]

In the *Records of the Burgh of Stirling* there is to be found (p. 265) an interesting report of a wedding in the Diocese on 25 November 1479. It was a "society" wedding, but there is no reason to think that it differed in essentials from any other wedding. Modern weddings are the same in the main requirements. As it was a church wedding, banns may be presumed as having been publicly read. "In the presence of John, Bishop of Dunblane, Thomas Lord le Erskene, the notary and witnesses, William Lord le Grahame on the one part, and Annabella Drummond, one of the daughters of John Drummond of Cargill, on the other part, for marriage to be contracted between them, past (passed) to the door of the parish church of Muthyll of the Diocese of Dunblane, where Sir Alexander Hyrdman, chaplain, asked the said William and Annabella if they wished to be contracted in marriage, who answered they did; asked if they knew any impediment except consanguinity, which had been dispensed by the said bishop with authority of the Holy See, or if either had made any contract with any other person or were coacted thereto, who answered that they knew of no impediment nor had made contract before, but said they wished spontaneously to complete the said marriage, and gave their corporal oaths thereon on the Holy Gospels. The said Sir Alexander put the right hand of the said William in the said Annabella's hand, and *per verba matrimonii de presenti*, as use is, fully conjoined the said William and Annabella in nuptial covenant and contract of marriage, who in name of matrimony kissed each other. Whereon all and sundry, John Drummond of Cargill, father of the said Annabella, in her name craved instruments (that is, asked for documented proof of marriage). Done in the parish church of Mothill at ten hours before noon or thereabout. Present, the said lord himself, Thomas Lord le Erskyne, Robert Douglas of Lochlevyn, David Grahame of Gargunnok, Master Walter Drummond, Sir Andrew Drummond, vicar of Muthill, Robert Drummond of Ermor, Robert Grahame, Thomas Grahame, Matthew Forestar, Duncan Forestar, Walter Symson, William Chalmer and others."

It is worth noting that it was in the first half of the fifteenth century that Scotland made a significant advance in the arts. Up till then, Scotland's ecclesiastical architecture was largely foreign in inspiration, though there were Scottish adaptations of English and French designs; Scotland's architectural originality belongs to the domestic, the commercial and the military spheres. Likewise her learning was largely foreign, the Church students being sent abroad; the conception of the Scottish monasteries as seats of learning cannot be maintained, and the church schools were few and had few pupils. Few of the nobility about 1400 could write their names. Painting was wholly ecclesiastical; little of it has survived from days before the fifteenth century. Native wood-carving and wrought iron were simple and rough compared with English, French and Flemish examples. Scotland's literature was largely the written chronicle. But about 1375, John Barbour, Archdeacon of Aberdeen, wrote *The Brus*, an epic glorifying the heroic life of Robert I, a poem in several respects unique of its kind in mediaeval literature. Later, and in the early fifteenth century, another churchman, Andrew de Wyntoun wrote his *Original Chronicle*. To note that both Barbour and de Wyntoun were contemporaries of Chaucer is to emphasise the late flowering of Scottish literature compared with that of England. *The King's Quair*, however, written by James I when he was a prisoner in England, or maybe later, breathed something of the spirit of Chaucer and the Renaissance and opened a new day in Scottish poetry. Blind Harry's *Schir William Wallace* is dated by some about 1460, and Robert Henryson was soon to appear. With the establishment of the Universities of St. Andrews (1412) and Glasgow (1451) Scotland had opportunities of study within her own borders. It is mainly to this century that we must look if we would see the Scottish people emerge hesitatingly into a slow and unspectacular dawn of native literature, learning and culture of the arts, though in literature this verdict might be moderated if the works of the Makars lamented by Dunbar were ever discovered.

In 1459, in midcourse of Robert Lawder's episcopate there appears as witness to a charter of James II one "Thomas, Bishop of Dunblane".[45] Keith and Gams both accept him, but this is the only record of him and he cannot be fitted into the succession. The designation of the witness should undoubtedly be "Thomas, Bishop of Dunkeld". His dates are 1452-76, and he too was a Lawder.

A letter from the Pope to Robert Lawder on 12 September 1466, addresses him as "bishop in the Universal Church, sometime Bishop of Dunblane".[46] The letter notes that this day Robert has resigned Dunblane to the Pope by proxy, and it intimates to him a yearly pension of 300 gold florins of the Camera. This retiring allowance, to which his successor has agreed, is to be paid half-yearly at Christmas and Midsummer, and is to come from the revenues of the episcopal *mensa*; default for thirty days will incur interdict, and suspension will follow six months' failure to pay. Concurrent letters were sent to the clergy and people of Dunblane and to the King.

So, after an active episcopate of nineteen years, Robert Lawder goes into honourable retirement. He had taken his duties seriously both in Church and in State, and if he was not brilliant, he was surely competent in every sphere of his activities. Nothing can be charged against him in personal character, and he was sufficiently learned in Canon Law, and businesslike in administration. He impresses me as a man of distinct personality, neither soft nor domineering, but by character, capacity, and grace of manner commending himself to his fellow churchmen as well as to King and barons in Parliament. The tasks committed to him throughout his tenure of Dunblane are proof of his ability and devotion. Before he was promoted Bishop he was modest in his search for benefices, and after his promotion there is no trace of self-seeking. It would appear from his inability to meet his obligations to the Camera without an extension of time that he resisted the temptation to discharge his debts by manipulating the properties regulated by the royal charter of 1443 and was content to consolidate the Diocese and build up its resources. We do not know when he died, but we can happily remember him in honour.

John Hepburn   1466 – 1486

The resignation of Robert Lawder at the Papal Court gave the Pope complete control of the provision of a successor. It enabled him to arrange with the new Bishop a retiring pension for his predecessor. The date of resignation was made to coincide with the granting of the pension and with the provision of the new Bishop, and the whole change-over was neatly accomplished. On 12 September 1466, therefore, the day of Robert's resignation, it was publicly intimated[47] that "at the relation of the Archbishop of Rouen, the Pope in secret consistory provided John Herspolz to the Church of Dunblane, void by the resignation of Robert, last Bishop".

The name Herspolz has so far found no explanation. Scots churchmen seem to have changed it to Hepburn, which was easier on the tongue; or he may have made the change himself. It would seem that his name was Herspolz and that he was of foreign origin. I have found no reference to him in the records of Scotland before he became Bishop of Dunblane. After his provision the papal records simply call him John. All that is known of him before he became a bishop is that he was in priest's orders and of lawful age.[48] His provision at the suggestion of a foreign archbishop, the speed of the change-over, his availability at Rome for the adjustment of the pension and his foreign name seem to indicate that he was a foreign cleric who had influential friends and that he was at the Papal Court waiting for just such a chance.

The speed and secrecy of the arrangement must have irritated the King of Scotland. As soon as James III heard of the coming resignation, he petitioned the Pope on behalf of John Spalding, his counsellor and confessor, Master of the Chapel Royal; but he was too late.[49] His petition had not long been on its way when he received the papal letter informing him of the new appointment. The usual intimations were made to the clergy, the people of the City and the vassals of the Church. John's consecration took place, not earlier than 22 June 1467, and not later than 20 June 1468.[50]

John Hepburn's tenure is lacking in any noteworthy personal activities, and his seems to have been an uneventful episcopate. In diocesan affairs he received the resignation of Gilbert de Camera, Prior of Inchmahome.[51] This resignation caused considerable commotion in the Priory. The Convent elected Thomas Dog (or Dogh) one of a powerful family in Kilmadock in the neighbourhood of the Priory; Bishop John confirmed the election but before Thomas could take possession, Gilbert died, whereupon the Convent took second thoughts and elected John Cawrus, who, unable to obtain possession because Thomas had meantime climbed into the saddle, petitioned the Pope, saying that "from fear of Thomas' power" he cannot meet him in Dunblane. Wisely, the Pope named a third, John, canon of Scone, to be Prior and authorised three dignitaries of Dunkeld to see that he got possession.

In the early years of John Hepburn's tenure four mandates[52] were sent to him — to see that a named priest was received as a canon of Cambuskenneth; to induct to Torphichen William Knolis, though he did not fulfil the general rules; to decide on the allocation of certain utensils and money left by James Kennedy, Bishop of St. Andrews, and claimed both by his executors and by his successor; to keep the peace for ten years between Abbot Patrick and his monks of Newbattle; not a very exciting list, and only the last of them troublesome.

In public affairs, he attended Parliament in 1471,[53] and concurred in a gift of money by the bishops to the King (James III), Dunblane's portion being £100. In 1473, he was appointed the sole bishop among four clergy, along with four earls and four burgesses, as a Committee of Complaints. Parliament went into recess for nearly a year, and gave to this committee powers to implement a long list of decisions including resistance to the Turks, stabilisation of peace with England, and the scantiness of coin in the country.[54] This appointment to Parliament's executive committee with powers shows that the Three Estates held high opinion of his capacities. It is all the more disappointing that further information comprises only his presence at a wedding in 1479[55]; his recovery of a debt of £26. 8. o from William Stirling of Keir, his brother (also William), and one David Arnot[56]; a remit from the Lords of Audit in 1483 to see to the payment of a marriage dowry of £40 wrongously withheld[57]; and, also in 1483, a summons of James Haldar to appear before him, against which James protested to the Lords Auditors.[58] Imagination is needed to fill in the routine of his administration of a diocese which was increasing in parochial organisation and in financial capacity.

Though the Bishop seems to have avoided the light which shines upon an episcopal throne, he may have been able to keep in the background because he had among his clergy the most distinguished set of dignitaries and canons with which Dunblane Cathedral had so far been blessed:

the Dean in 1470 was Sir John Drummond, second son of Sir Walter Drummond of Cargill and Stobhall; he was of considerable note and some notoriety. He is not the first of the family of Drummond to appear among Dunblane's recorded cathedral clergy, for that place belongs to Malcolm Drummond, a canon in 1457; but his holding of the office of Dean began a Drummond monopoly of the Deanship parallel to the Chisholm monopoly of the Bishopric. The name will be often encountered among the Cathedral clergy up to and even beyond the Reformation; and Sir John was still Dean in 1495.

the Archdeacon, Alexander Rate,[59] was a "familiar of the Pope"; but he never had possession of the office, though he was provided in 1474. He was succeeded in 1480 by Duncan Bully, M.A., who, being at Rome in 1481, promised to pay his annates within six months.[60]

the Chancellor was Henry Boys (Boyce, Boece); he visited Rome in 1474, when he carried out commissions for several Scottish clerics[61]; in 1473, Edward IV of England granted safe conduct to him and twelve companions "to pass through England and thence abroad by Calais or elsewhere"[62]; he attended Parliament in 1482.[63]

the Treasurer was William Elphinston, who in 1484 became Bishop of Aberdeen, and was the inspirer of the founding of Aberdeen University (1495) and its first chancellor, a very remarkable man.[64]

two canons were outstanding men: (*a*) in affairs of State, David Luthirdale was one of the auditors of the King's accounts, from 1473 to 1478 (in *Exchequer Rolls of Scotland*, VIII, there are about 25 references to him). (*b*) in Church Law, Sir James Darow, in 1474 chaplain and notary public,[65] later canon, was a lawyer of the highest reputation. His Protocol Book (1469-84), the earliest which Scotland possesses, is in the keeping of Stirling Town Council. He held ecclesiastical titles, but practised as a civilian; he had clients of every rank, including the King and the Queen; as the late Reverend Thomas Miller, of Bonnybridge, his biographer, puts it, "he added dignity to Dunblane Cathedral in his later years by occupying one of the stalls as a canon".

The episcopate of John Hepburn was marked by a generous mortification by William Stirling of Keir, in 1472, for the erection of a chaplaincy attached to the Altar of the Virgin Mary in Dunblane Cathedral.[66] For the welfare of the souls of King James III, John Hepburn, Bishop of Dunblane, Luke Stirling, his father, Margaret, his mother, himself, his wife, children and ancestors and all the faithful dead, William Stirling granted for ever to Almighty God, the Heavenly Choir and the Blessed and Glorious Virgin Mary, and to her altar on the north side of the nave of the Cathedral Church of Dunblane, and to Sir John French, perpetual chaplain at the said altar and his successors serving God there, a toft and croft of the lands of Keir, the lands of Shanrach, the Woodland and Glassingall, an annual rent of forty shillings from the lands of Kippanerayt (Kippenrait), and the mill of Strowe, with three acres of arable land of the lands of Strowe, and the pasture of six beasts in the nether part of the said lands; to be held by the said chaplains in perpetual alms, for performing divine service at the said altar. It is worth recording further details, as this is the first detailed record of an individual's endowment of an altar in Dunblane Cathedral: Sir John French was allowed to hold any benefice or chaplainry during his lifetime, but his successors were bound to reside in the City of Dunblane, absence for two months without leave of the granter and his heirs to entail a vacancy in the chaplaincy. The granter (and heirs) must fill the vacancy within two months under penalty of 20 marks to be paid to the fabric of the Cathedral and the presentation to fall to the Bishop for that occasion. In 1509 William Stirling's son, John, further endowed the chapel in much the same terms,[67] making provision for two chaplains and creating an endowment much ampler than was usual in Scottish chaplainries.

In this bishopric appears John Moffet, "Commissar of Dunblane". He was the deputed representative of the Official of the Cathedral, who gave him authority to act for him in his court. "Elene, Lady Graham", had appealed to the Lords of Audit against "Christian, Lady Graham, and others". Christian seems to have somewhat belied her name in lodging information against her relative, charging that the said Elene should be "under sentence of cursing the Lords Auditors", a not unnatural exercise of human feelings. The Auditors continued the case for a week, and directed the summons to John Moffet, Commissar of Dunblane, and John Scot, who were to summon James Drummond as witness.[68]

John Hepburn died, probably in 1486, while still Bishop, for his successor is "elect" early in 1487. We may think of him as a quiet but effective bishop, probably of Germanic stock. His unobtrusiveness is proved by the scarcity of notices in the records, and his effectiveness by the speed with which he paid the papal charges on his provision, charges which the Roman officers admitted after John's death to have been excessive, by the quality of the clergy whom he gathered into his chapter, and by the confidence which Parliament showed in his wisdom and administrative ability. He mounted the episcopal throne of Dunblane from an unknown past and left it at a date unknown. So it has been with others, whose services like his deserved greater renown.

NOTES

1. SK 217-18.
2. CPR X 310, 311.
3. CPR VII 248, VIII 407. cf. Index CPR X.
4. CPR X 291.
5. CPR X 332.
6. CPR X 299.

7. CPR X 298/9. CAC 39.

8. Mrs A. I. Dunlop: *James Kennedy*, 97 and n. *Reg. Supp.* 421, f. 158, 29 Nov. 1447. CAC 39-40.

9. CAC 40.

10. TV V 70. CPR X 7.

11. CPR X 63-64, 22 May 1450. TV V 100.

12. BCPS 369. CAC 339-41.

13. CPR VII 18-19. DBS 319-22.

14. CPR IX 146.

15. 24 Jan. 1449/50, AP II 37, 62.

16. 24 Jan. 1451/2. AP II 62.

17. TV V 67, and CPR X 6, 7.

18. *Rot. Scot.* II 334, 336. *Foedera* XI 235, 242. BC IV 1218.

19. 22 Jan. 1451/2. *Foedera* XI 306.

20. CPR X 291-2, 363, 324 (2), 183, 294, 400, 89, 669, 691-2.

21. CPR X 89. TV V 194. Those now granted restitution had been excommunicated by Popes Eugenius IV and Nicolas V, as states TV V 54. Nicolas V now limits his general restitution.

22. 4 Apr. 1454, CPR X 691-2. Election by the congrégation will be noted. The parish clerk (clerk minister) was in minor orders.

23. CPR X 158-9, 20 Apr. 1455.

24. CPR XI 270, 4 May 1456.

25. CPR XI 43, 29 May 1456.

26. Mrs A. I. Dunlop: *James Kennedy*, 278/9. She quotes from her researches in the Vatican and gives the reference as *Reg. Supplications*, 490, f. 23v., 22 Apr. 1456.

27. *ut supra*, p. 297.

28. CPR XI 519, 520, 24 Nov. 1458. The Archdeacon was Walter Stewart.

29. CPR XI 378, 12 Dec. 1458. The Official was John Cristini.

30. CPR XI 249, 279-80, 4 Dec. 1455. The treasurer was D. John de Atheray.

31. REG 373, 24 Jan. 1448/9. AP II 37. In RB I 181, 24 Sep. 1451, the concession is again granted.

32. CAC 43.

33. CAC 325.

34. CAC 338-9.

35. See under "Bishop John Hepburn".

36. CS 184.

37. CAI li, No. 150. 21 Jan. 1461/2. CSA 99.

38. LACC. For the description of this MS, I am deeply indebted to Dr C. T. McInnes, Curator of Historical Records, H.M. General Register House, Edinburgh, and his staff. Given the opportunity, I may return to the subject in the Book of the Friends of Dunblane Cathedral.

39. 18 Jul. 1465. PSSC xlii-xliv, 235-7. cf. LAc II 144-5. This annual holding of Church Councils, as here stated, should be noted; it is not borne out by the records which have survived.

40. At that time in parish of Abernethy: now in Strathmiglo. See Butler: *Ancient Church and Parish of Abernethy*, 218.

41. AP II Index.

42. CPR XII 788-90. For the protagonists in this tale, cf. CAI pp. 254, 255, 337, 338. Nicolas Fechil was probably the Fethill, chaplain, who was proctor of Abbot of Inchaffray in a suit before Dunblane Consistorial Court, 1462, see earlier in this chapter, text and note 37 *supra*.

43. CAI p. 150.

44. CPR XI 484-5, 659-60.

45. RMS II 1062.

46. CPR XII 454.

47. Bishop John, 19 Jan. 1466/7, offered 800 florins (gold of the Camera) for his common service and five little services, payable in two terms each of six months, CAC 58; same day, paid 400, CAC 59; 28 Sep. 1467, paid 444 fl. 32 sh. 2d., but got receipt dated 28 Oct. 1467 for 105 fl. less, CAC 61. Brady: *Episcopal Succession*, says that on 19 Jan. 1466/7 he paid 83 fl. at Rome, but does not give any authority for this probably true statement. On 28 Oct. 1467, his receipt states that full payment has now been made for his common and little services. The discrepancy may be due to alteration in the rate of exchange.

48. CPR XII 458.

49. CPR XII 278-9.

50. DBS 206 quotes a Moray document in which 21 Jun. 1469 is noted as "in the second year of his consecration".

51. CAC 161. CPR XII 338-9. 24 Feb. 1469/70.

52. (1) CPR XII 561, 14 Nov. 1466. (2) ut supra, 270, 28 Feb. 1466/7. (3) ut supra, 670, 6 Mar. 1468/9. (4) ut supra, 813, 8 Jun. 1468.

53. AP II 981; *ib*. 103. Dunblane promised £100, Brechin and Ross, £60 etc. No sum is indicated for St. Andrews, Glasgow, Dunkeld, Aberdeen, Moray.

54. AP II 103, 23 Jul. 1473. A. Aud. 23, 8 Apr. 1473. Also, AP II 120, 1 Mar. 1478/9, at Edinburgh.

55. RS 265. CS 203. Date 25 Nov. 1479.

56. A. Aud. 86-87, 13 Oct. 1479.

57. ut supra 128*, 16 Feb. 1482/3.

58. ut supra 131*, 20 Feb. 1482/3.

59. This dignity is valued in 1474 at £32 sterling. CAC 178. Provided 30 Apr. 1474.

60. CAC 203, 3 Aug. 1481. Provided 15 Aug. 1480. Value of dignity £20.

61. CAC 69, 177, 247, 289.

62. BC IV 1403.

63. AP II 136.

64. See note 4, 1474 in Appendix: *Clergy of Dunblane Cathedral*.

65. SK 248-9, 6 Jan. 1473/4.

66. SK 244-6, 26 Apr. 1472. Confirmed by Bishop John 10 May 1472.

67. SK 289-91, 2 Oct. 1509.

68. A. Aud. 34. John Scot was a Dunblane notary, SK 242-3.

CHAPTER X

BISHOP JAMES CHISHOLM 1487 – 1526

AT the relation of the Cardinal of Angers the Pope provided James "Chesom" to the Church of Dunblane, void by the death of John, last Bishop, outwith the Roman Court.[1] The date was 31 January 1486/7, at which date he was Dean of Aberdeen.[2] He may also be the James Chisholm, rector of Ald Roxburgh, who in 1486 gave £20 towards the King's household expenses.[3] But Dunblane was his native parish; he was the eldest son of Edmund Chisholm, the first Chisholm proprietor of Cromlix,[4] an estate in the parish of Dunblane. The family of Chisholm came to Dunblane from the Borders. In his early clerical life, James Chisholm had been a chaplain to James III, who is said to have sent him to Rome.

With James Chisholm's provision to Dunblane there begins a long period during which churchmen of two local families not only dominated the life of the Diocese but possessed, as if by inheritance, the two chief offices in the Cathedral. The Bishops were Chisholms from 1487 till 1573, and the Deans were Drummonds for a comparable period, 1462-1536; members of both of those related families also occupied parochial ministries in the diocese. It was a remarkable burgeoning of local talent and devotion.

When Michael Ochiltree persuaded James II and Parliament to erect the City of Dunblane into a burgh of barony and regality, the cost must have been such as to burden the Diocese for perhaps a generation. But before John Hepburn died the situation had changed; the dignities of the Cathedral had become more attractive and the church accounts more easily balanced. It is significant that Robert Lawder (1447-66) had difficulty in meeting his papal dues, which had been more than doubled without justification, while John Hepburn (1466-86) paid the same inflated taxation within nine months. It must also be remembered that Scottish trade, home and foreign, had much increased, and that the young King, James IV, after a disastrous start, was proving an energetic and capable ruler, to the benefit of the country.

Nevertheless, in spite of the improved financial resources of the Diocese, James Chisholm did not accept the tax of 800 florins, which had been imposed on his two immediate predecessors. A fortnight after his provision, being at Rome when Bishop John died, he paid 380 florins for his common service, by the hands of his bankers, Martellis.[5] This done, he protested that the Camera had recently been over-taxing Dunblane; official enquiry established the validity of his allegations and admitted that 800 had been unaccountably substituted for 370 florins.[6] It was decreed that James Chisholm, elect of Dunblane, "for this time only, pay 500 ducats and at the rate of 500 florins, the Vice-chamberlain justifying the remission of the rest on account of tenuity of fruits". James may have persuaded the Vice-chamberlain of this, but the Diocese was no longer poor. However, it gave the Camera an escape from the overcharge, which has all the appearance of a deliberate act, and not of a mistake.

James Chisholm was consecrated in the latter half of 1487 or the first half of 1488. The exact date is unknown,[7] but he was still "elect" when entered as renter of the King's land of Hairtherne in Yarrow, on 4 July 1487.[8]

Little is recorded of James Chisholm's diocesan activities; but his stout fight for Kippen, in opposition to the Earl of Menteith, the Abbot of Cambuskenneth, King James IV and the Pope himself, has been fully recorded and is worthy of relation. The Earl and his heir desired, in 1496,[9] to change the family burying-ground from Inchmahome Priory to Cambuskenneth Abbey, whose cemetery had recently been distinguished by the burials there of James III and his Queen Margaret, all the more perhaps that the Pope had recently set up a commission[10] to report whether Queen Margaret should be canonised. To ease the transfer, the Earl persuaded the King to give Kippen to Cambuskenneth by charter, which was duly confirmed; the Abbot welcomed the gift, and in order to present the Bishop with a *fait accompli* he got a bull of authorisation from the Pope. But James Chisholm was steadfast – Kippen had always belonged to Dunblane and the King's confirmation was of no value; the Abbot was already a canon of Dunblane with the prebend of Kincardine (in Menteith), and he could not be twice a canon and hold two prebends in the same Cathedral. Notwithstanding the formidable opposition and the secrecy of the transaction, of which he probably knew nothing till it was completed, James Chisholm was able to pluck most of the spurious gift out of the jaws of the spoilers. With the King's consent, Bishop and Abbot agreed that the vicarage of Kippen, plus £20 from its rectory, plus the manse of the prebend, should be erected into a canonry and prebend of the Cathedral, the Bishop to be patron; the Abbot was to have the remainder of the rectory.[11]

In 1492, when Glasgow was created an archbishopric, Dunblane and Dunkeld, Candida Casa (Whithorn) and Lismore (Argyll) were apportioned to it as its suffragans.[12] But in 1500, Dunblane was reapportioned to St. Andrews,[13] as was Dunkeld later.

If James Chisholm was little in evidence in church affairs until the turn of the century at least, he had some remarkable men in his chapter:

Archdeacon Henry Alane, at one time rector of Middletoun, and in 1492 rector of Ruthven, was chiefly notable for the variety of offices which he held in the King's household.[14] He was *director cancellarie* (chancery) (1486); clerk of accounts (1488); clerk of the family (1494); Comptroller (1491-96); "clerk of our comptis of our household" (1492); commissioner of the King (1492). In 1498 he was given clothing for Christmas by the King's bounty; in 1499 he was repaid £38 odd which he had lent to the household; in the same year his salary as clerk of the household was £10 – the same as was given to the butcher, tailor, chief cook, barber, furrier, cutler, and to the King's and the household's seneschal or steward; in the same year he got £10 as librarian, and £30 and £45 for his labours in the Exchequer. Also in 1499, he was commissioner of lands; in 1501, Auditor; between 1497 and 1500, he let Crown lands on 18 occasions. From 1496 he was Archdeacon of Dunblane, but if an archdeacon is the eye of the bishop, James Chisholm was blinded in one eye at least.

Maister John Drummond was Dean, and had held the office since 1462, when he matriculated at St. Andrews as a determinant and paid 7/6 as his term fees. He had been given the Deanship to support him at the University.[15] He was still Dean in 1495.[16] In *The Family of Drummond*[17] it is stated that he was the second son of Sir Walter Drummond of Cargill and Stobhall, and that he was rector of Kinnoul as well as Dean of Dunblane. "He was a hardy

N

and bold churchman who thrust himself into the deanery; hence the saying 'you take it as the Drummond took the order'." He was a papal knight. When his brother Malcolm died he became tutor to his nephews. John had several children, one of whom, William, became the "familiar" clerk of James V and rector of Forteviot, and succeeded his father as Dean in 1532, others intervening. John was succeeded in 1497 by his nephew, Walter Drummond, son of Malcolm. Walter was notable in state and university affairs; he was rector of St. Andrews University at various dates between 1487 and 1510, and in the State he held the offices of Clerk of Rolls, Register and Council; Lord Auditor; Lord of Exchequer; and Parliamentary Commissioner. In the Church, he was rector of Forteviot and of Kinnoul, as well as Dean. After Sir John Chisholm, Dean in 1515, there followed as Dean Sir William Drummond, son of Dean John Drummond. His earliest recorded date is 1532, but he may have been Dean at an earlier date; he died in 1536. The reader is referred to the Appendix of the Cathedral Clergy for details of Alane and the Drummonds, and of the other clergy of James Chisholm's time; the notes there will show something of their quality.

But attention should be called to Magister Henry Quhite (White), perhaps the most distinguished of all who held the office of Official of Dunblane. He may have been Official as early as the end of 1498, though his first recorded date is 1506; he continued in that office till 1527 at least. So valuable were his services to the Lords of Council in Public Affairs that in 1540, being now "of aige and subdit (subject) to infirmiteis" he is asked to attend "at his awin plesour" and is granted his full emoluments as pension.[18]

One of the Bishop's priests was of more than local significance, James Gray; he transcribed an early *Chronicle of the Scots and Picts*. His manuscript is in the National Library of Scotland, and although Skene says that Gray copied the original badly and made mistakes in proper names, it was important enough for Skene to reprint in his *Chronicles of the Picts and Scots* under the title of "Brief Chronicle". The Chronicle states that it was written 337 years and 5 months after the Scots had absorbed the Picts, that is, after A.D. 850. Its date is therefore about 1187, and James Gray transcribed it about 1520. The original chronicle of 1187 no longer exists.

James Chisholm was a frequent witness to charters; I have noted fourteen occasions, all at Edinburgh, within seven weeks.[19]

By the accident of public events, the Diocese of Dunblane was more in the public eye now than it had ever been; the Chisholms of Cromlix and the Drummonds of Stobhall and Drummond Castle were not only in control of the Cathedral, but were, especially the Drummonds, active in the political life and intrigues of the country. The Stirlings bought Keir in 1448 from George Leslie of that Ilk, and therefore were not prominent in local history until the second half of the century. But it was more notoriety than fame which in those days brought Dunblane into public notice:

(1) In the war carried on by a strong confederation of lords against James III in the interests of his son, then about sixteen, Sir William Stirling of Keir favoured the son against the father. James III, defeated at Blackness and forced to sign certain articles and to disband his army in May 1488, found himself attacked the following month at Sauchieburn. He was defeated; on 11 June 1488 he was murdered in a cottage at Milton, near Bannockburn. His son had been seized at Stirling Castle in February 1488 by the rebel lords to force him to their side against his father, and he was present both at Blackness and at Sauchieburn.[20] On one occasion the Prince sheltered in Keir, which his father forthwith besieged and burned, driving out the Prince and destroying the family charters. On coming to the throne the Prince gave £100 to William Stirling "to the biggin of his place". William Stirling was said to have been one of three who chased the King from the field of Sauchieburn, and he has been accused of being a participant in his murder. Fraser, who edited the Stirling papers, goes into the matter minutely and makes a strong case for relieving him of the charge,[21] which we may consider as, at least, not proven.

(2) William Stirling of Keir brought a case before the Lords of Council, in March 1489/90, against Laurence, Lord Oliphant, sheriff in these parts, whom he charged with driving away "8 oxen and 22 ky from Lanracky and 6 oxen and 14 ky out of the Coige" and others from elsewhere.[22] The sheriff charged with cattle-thieving would arouse no end of talk; perhaps to let it die down the case was continued for three months. The probable explanation is that the sheriff ordered the cattle to be taken for some tax or debt which William Stirling refused to pay.

(3) Shortly after the accession of James IV (1488) and the provision of Bishop James (1487), they had on their hands the barbaric brutality committed by the Drummonds, led by David, second son of Lord Drummond, who in October 1490 set fire to the thatch of Monzievaird Church in which six score Murrays – men, women and children – had taken refuge. This crime cost David Drummond his life, though his mother and his sister Margaret pled with the King on their knees for his life. Bishop James, Abbot Henry of Cambuskenneth, and three laymen were chosen in 1492 by both families to arbitrate between them; but it was not until 14 January 1500/1 that the Privy Council bade Lord Drummond and Sir William Murray of Tullibardine renounce the quarrel and forgive the crime, the King having ordered an assessment of penalties.

(4) In the second half of 1496, King James fell in love with the Lady Margaret Drummond, whose pleading for her brother David he had refused six years before. He took her from her father's home, and lodged her in Stirling Castle with the Laird of Lundy and his lady, and later in Linlithgow. The story of her death by poisoning is one of the unsolved mysteries of Scottish history. Tradition says that the crime was committed in Drummond Castle, near Crieff, but there is greater likelihood that it was perpetrated in Dunblane, in the town house of the Drummonds. It is recorded that Margaret and her two sisters – Euphemia, who had married John, fourth Lord Fleming, in 1495, and Sybilla, unmarried – who were poisoned with her, were buried on the day of their death in the choir of the Cathedral, of which their uncle Walter Drummond was Dean. Tradition gives the time as breakfast; there is no support for James Grant's description in *The Yellow Frigate* how they were poisoned in the communion cup (which was not offered to lay folk in the mass). *The Family of Drummond* says that James was affianced to Margaret without consent of his Council, and that, as they were related within the forbidden degrees, petition for dispensation was sent to Rome and the reply was awaited. The King's desire to marry Margaret was opposed by the nobles, who may not have desired a third Drummond Queen on the throne. Milder opposition would come from the clergy on grounds of Canon Law. Suspicion for the murder fell on the Kennedys who were among the enemies of the Drummonds. Margaret was known to be a beautiful

woman and James mourned her deeply. He provided £20 annually until he died at Flodden, "to the tua priestis wha singis for Margaret Drummond in Dunblane Cathedral". Her burial in the Cathedral along with her two sisters in 1501, on the same day as they died, must have moved the hardest and stunned Scotland.

(5) Pitscottie and Sir David Lindsay both recount the wild story of John Stirling of Keir's fight in 1517 with Squire Meldrum.[23] The Squire had carried off the Lady of Gleneagles, now a widow, and become father of two children by her. He wanted to marry her, but as he was "sib to her first husband" he required the Pope's licence. It seemed that Lukas Stirling, uncle of the Laird of Stirling, also desired the lady, and to oblige him his nephew, with fifty armed men, attacked the Squire and his company of five, near Holyrood. The Squire fought stoutly, and though he was left for dead, he recovered and lived for fifty years. The Laird of Keir, wounded to peril of life, withdrew leaving twenty-six of his men hurt or slain. He was overtaken at Linlithgow, tried in Edinburgh, convicted and imprisoned in the castle there, "induring the Regent's will". Sir John Stirling, who in 1509 increased the endowment of the chapel of the Virgin in Dunblane Cathedral, was a man ready for a quarrel; he lost his life in a family feud in 1539. His fight with Squire Meldrum set tongues wagging over a large part of Scotland. He was an unruly member of the Bishop's flock.

(6) The murder of an Archdeacon of Dunblane[24] is sufficiently unusual to warrant notice. He was Patrick Blackadder by name, and the uncertainty of his dates as Archdeacon and even of the date of the crime, which took place between 1513 and 1520, shows that his connexion with the Cathedral's work was of the most tenuous. Archdeacons were far from popular in the Middle Ages, but the fatal attack was not perpetrated by any outraged cleric; it was the result of a family quarrel. Patrick's cousin, Robert Blackadder, had been Prior of Coldingham Abbey for a few months only, when he was slain by David Home of Wedderburn, with whom he was at feud. With Home's help, one William Douglas seized Coldingham Priorship, but his right was contested by Patrick Blackadder, who with consent of Regent Albany had been given Coldingham by the Pope. John Home of Wedderburn now enters the quarrel; most probably a relative of David Home, the forcible Prior, and married to Alison Douglas,

through whom he inherited the Blackadder estates, he changed his name to John Home of Blackadder and found himself not unnaturally at enmity with the Archdeacon of Dunblane, who is said to have tried to slay him more than once. John Home was equally hostile, and chancing to meet the Archdeacon one day near Edinburgh, killed him. The probability is that not one of the lot, Archdeacon, Prior, enforced Prior, and murderer, was a cleric; certainly not the last, and doubtfully the first three.

Bishop James Chisholm was interested in land. His renting of the King's land of Hairtherne has already been mentioned[25]; the rent was £6, plus £8 for grassum. As Bishop he was involved in 1491 in a case of teinds of Wester Petlour, which had been held back for six years[26] – such cases were common. He took the Abbot of Lindores to court in 1498 over the teinds of Bennie.[27] In 1505, as a commissioner of lands, he granted a let of Crown lands.[28] He was given in 1516 "ane lettre of tak" over the King's lands of Troringzale[29] (Ayrshire) and of Kirkandriis (Galloway).[30] These lands he still had in 1519 when he took new leases at enlarged rents for five years, in which he was now joined by "James Chisholm, brother (in this case, half-brother) of the said bishop".[31] These were personal interests and transactions, and though he is designed in the records as Bishop of Dunblane they were not episcopal dealings, but individual activities. James was of landed proprietor stock, interested in farming; he was, for Dunblane, a new phenomenon, a farming bishop. At this time farming was enjoying some prosperity, and there were other signs of Scotland's prosperity due to the wise and forceful guidance of James IV, who above all, in 1502, ended the long feud with England which had lasted for 170 years. But for the ghastly mistakes and folly which led to Flodden's disaster eleven years later, peace might have more abundantly blessed Scotland and laid earlier foundations of its prosperity.

There were other signs of Scotland's progress before Flodden. "Justice Ayres", for lack of which "the people are almost gone wild", were extended to the Northern Isles and the Southern Isles (the latter meaning the Hebrides) by the appointment in 1503 of justices and sheriffs. The same Parliament instituted a daily Council chosen by the King to sit without intermission at Edinburgh or wherever the King happened to be in residence, so that causes might not be delayed; this Council was given the same powers as the Lords of Session, who had been appointed in 1426 to sit thrice yearly. The College of Surgeons, now the Royal College of Surgeons, was created in 1505 by the Town Council of Edinburgh. In 1508, the first book was printed in Scotland, *The Maying and Disport of Chaucer*, "imprinted in the south gait of Edinburgh" by Walter Chepman and Andrew Myllar, to whom the King had granted in 1507 the sole right of printing. The Pope, in 1506, sent to James IV a sword (now part of the regalia of Scotland) and hat of honour – "a purple hat variegated with golden flowers, a sword with golden hilt and a golden scabbard studded with precious stones" – and declared him protector of the Christian religion. The Pope congratulated him because when the rest of the Christian princes were engaged in wars and tumults in their country and abroad, he alone stood aloof from war.[32] In 1511 the King built for his navy *The Great St. Michael*, an amazing ship, 240 feet long, carrying 35 big guns, 300 small artillery, 300 sailors, 120 gunners and 1000 soldiers.[33] Scotland had then an admiral of outstanding brilliance, Andrew Wood, whose daring and successes are the pride of Scotland insufficiently known. In letters, the Court poet was William Dunbar, a Franciscan friar, born about 1460. Aberdeen University was instituted in 1495, and Parliament enacted in 1496 that "all barons and freeholders shall put their eldest sons to a grammar school from the age of eight or nine until they be competently grounded and have perfect Latin; thereafter to remain three years at the schools of art and law". The early sixteenth century was indeed the flowering of Scotland.

Few mandates reached James Chisholm; the earliest which I have found directed him in 1494 to allow the marriage of George Douglas, eldest son of the Earl of Angus, and Elizabeth Drummond, who now desired their uncanonical marriage to be made regular.[34] In fact, some of the matters formerly dealt with by papal mandate were now issued by the King in Privy Council; especially was this true of presentations to Scottish benefices, which, since the papal faculties of 1447 and 1450,[35] were in large measure reserved to Pope, King and patron in turn. The records show that increasingly presentations to canonries and lesser benefices were made by the King. Between 1500 and 1518 the King in Privy Council made many presentations of his nominees to the Bishop of Dunblane – to Strogeith, Aberfoyle, Glendevon (both

parsonage and vicarage), Dunning, St. Fillan's chapel near Castle
Doune, and the Chapel of St. Fillan within it.[36]

In 1515 James Chisholm complained to Albany the Governor[37]
that though he had never had or asked for any pension, he had
lately been pestered by one Balthasar, Papal Orator, who was
claiming from him a pension for an Italian "quilk the said reverend
fadir knew nevir of". The Council sent a macer with the famous
Sir John Sinclair, Dean of Restalrig, to Balthasar, to require him
"to decist and ceis fra all executioun opinly or quietly in this
reverend fadiris persone or at any uthir plaice within this realme
. . . because thai understand the samyn is contrar the previlege
of the realme". The same year witnessed a dispute over the Deanery of Dunblane[38] – Sir John Chisholm claimed that he had been
presented by the Bishop, and Master Gilbert Strathauchin that he
had papal bulls. These, Sir John asserted, had been obtained by
Gilbert's proctor by "sinister informacioun and in contrar our
soverane lordis previlege". John Chisholm, a chaplain of Dunblane and a notary public, and probably a relative of the Bishop,
had a stronger claim and became Dean. Early in 1516 James
Chisholm and other churchmen and nobles were given safe conduct for six months by Henry VIII as Scotland's ambassadors to
Westminster[39]; they were allowed a company of 100 or less. Six
months before this John, Duke of Albany, son of Alexander, Duke
of Albany, and grandson of James II and heir presumptive of the
throne, had been made Governor of Scotland while James V was
an infant. The embassage was required to work out a new
relationship with England.

If James Chisholm had had no other interest or call upon his
energy, he could hardly have attended Parliament with greater
zeal. The entries are numerous[40] and the appointments honourable – six times elected to the Committee of Articles, the chief
body to which Parliament delegated powers, once to the Commission for calling Parliament, and once, with five others, "to
remain with the king" for a season.[41] In 1517 he was Clerk
Register of Council.[42] He was one of the many of the Council
who wrote to the King of England in 1525, asking that peace by
sea and land be established for eight months; if this is not granted,
the lieges will prepare to defend the realm and hold "wapenschaw-
ings".[43] Previously there had been many calls to arms to defend
Scotland against England; in July 1523, for instance, all prelates

Photographs: by

PLATE VII

THE SIX CANOPIED

William D. Leask, Edinburgh

PLATE VIII

STALLS OF DIGNITARIES

were commanded to make known that all within their dioceses "suld provide and have ready xx dayis victuals on x dayis warning", and two months later "every man within the said boundis suld be reddy of 24 hours charge". That these were not false alarms is proved by the burning of the town and Abbey of Jedburgh in September of that year by the Earl of Surrey and his invading army of 9000 men.

In the internal troubles of Scotland James Chisholm was deeply involved. When James IV fell at Flodden in 1513 (along with one archbishop, one bishop, two abbots, one dean, thirteen earls, as many lords, three Highland chiefs, many lairds, and about 10,000 men slain), his son was crowned James V when seventeen months old, and Sir James Stirling of Keir, Lord Erskine and Lord Fleming were appointed guardians of his person.[44] His mother, Margaret Tudor, sister of Henry VIII, however, assumed the Regency, and eleven months after Flodden made a disastrous marriage with Archibald Douglas, sixth Earl of Angus. To add to the national confusion, John, Duke of Albany, born and brought up in France, but heir to the Scottish Crown, returned to Scotland in 1515 and was declared Governor. Though he thrice visited Scotland, it was only for brief periods and he was deposed in 1524 for continued absence. The Queen Dowager kept her young son in Edinburgh Castle; but her husband, growing in power, insisted that the King be given to a parliamentary Council and this was agreed to in 1525. Four prelates, one of them Bishop James Chisholm, and four earls, one of them Angus, were chosen, one of each quality to keep the boy for three months at a time.[45] When the turn of Angus came, he refused to give him up. The Queen Dowager made matters worse by divorcing Angus, though with entire justification, and married Henry Stuart, son of Lord Avendale. She thereby alienated her brother, Henry VIII, as well as the nobles who had hitherto stood by her, especially James Hamilton, Earl of Arran. Under Angus, the King, now fourteen and no longer a minor, assumed his royal prerogatives; but it was Angus who ruled the land like the domineering person he was. Bishop James sided with the young King and his mother, along with the Archbishop of St. Andrews, the Bishops of Dunkeld, Orkney, Aberdeen and Moray, the Earls of Huntly, Argyll, Morton, Glencairn, Errol and others.[46] The party which opposed her return to Angus, to whom she became reconciled for a time before she ultimately divorced him, consisted of the Archbishop of Glasgow, the Bishops of Argyll and Galloway, the Earls of Arran, Cassillis and Lennox, Lord Fleming, and others. Later, as the State Papers of Henry VIII (IV.456) show, and as Angus himself declared, the Archbishops of St. Andrews and Glasgow, the Bishops of Dunblane and Orkney, the Earls of Lennox, Cassillis, Crawford, etc., were arrayed against Angus. In this political contest, loyalties to individuals counted heavily, and Angus was increasingly opposed. James Chisholm had sent gifts to the King's father – pikes (fish) in 1504, "tua quyk crannis" (live cranes) in 1508,[47] and "ane fed ox" in 1513[48] – and now to the son an ox in 1526,[49] just after his stepfather's divorce. Even then, Angus detained the King by force, and it was 1528 before James escaped from Falkland Palace and took over Stirling Castle, a free man. In that year Angus, his brother George and their uncle Archibald were declared forfeited by Act of Parliament. The intimate relationship of the Bishop of Dunblane with the royal family was continued and deepened by Bishop James' half-brother William, who succeeded him.

In four directions James Chisholm actively set himself to equip and enhance the Cathedral:

A. *The endowment of altars*

(1) John Stirling of Keir considerably increased in 1509 the endowment of the Altar of St. Mary in the North (or Keir) Aisle of the nave.[50] His father had given the original endowment in 1472 for one chaplain,[51] John now added £20 Scots, enabling two chaplains to be appointed.

(2) In the same year,[52] Walter Drummond, Dean of Dunblane, "the familiar clerk" of James IV, endowed the chaplain of the Altar of St. Nicholas, "in the aisle lately repaired by him between the entrance of the south door and the choir" (that is, in the S.E. corner of the nave). In 1532, Dom. Robert Akinheid, chaplain of this altar, feued to Robert Leirmouth, citizen of Dunblane, "lands and ruinous dwellings within the city of Dunblane in the high part of it near le Holme-Hill"; the lands adjoined Robert Leirmouth's garden and he wanted to enlarge his holding somewhere between the croft of the Archdeacon called Glenwhommie (Glenquhome) and Ramoyle, and extending down to Kirk Street.[53]

(3) In 1511 the uncle of one Finlay Reid granted to the Bishop

fifteen pence yearly, and to Dom. John Lauder, perpetual (endowed) chaplain of the Atlar of St. Stephen the Martyr, and his successors, six shillings and eight pence per annum.[54]

It will save confusion if at this point the story is told of the other altars which were founded and endowed in Dunblane Cathedral. In addition to the High Altar in the choir, situated about where the Communion Table stands today, and the altar in the east end of the Lady Chapel, several other altars were placed in the North (or Keir) Aisle, and in the South (or Drummond) Aisle of the nave. Each of these latter was in a small chapel marked off by wooden screens; their size was dictated by the space available in the aisles, between pillars. The cuts in the stone where the screens joined the pillars are still to be seen. The date of the founding of these side-altars is known only in one instance, which is described later[55]; for the most part our knowledge of names and sites of the side-altars derives from charters which provided endowment for one or more chaplains of particular altars. The first of these in 1472 has been fully explained, and there is no reason to assume that this was an original erection of an altar; it was the endowment of a chantry priest to serve an altar already erected, which had been previously served by one of the Cathedral priests. Neither the altar nor the chapel which the Pope ordered Lady Margaret Graham and her third and her fourth husband to erect and endow in Dunblane can be traced. The orders may have been compounded.

In addition to the altars already mentioned, there is record of the erection of the Trinity Altar on 1 June 1530 by Henry Quhite, canon of Moray, Dunblane and Brechin, Official of Dunblane, and rector of "Sanct Modoc". Besides possessing those ecclesiastical offices and revenues, he is described as hereditary lord of Auchnaguff, and lord of a third of Kintuloch and of a third of its mill with pertinents (in Dunbarney parish). He was one of the first members of the Court of Session, instituted in 1532 by James V as the College of Justice. The thirds named he handed over to Cambuskenneth Abbey, with instructions to provide 17 marks to a chaplain of the Trinity Altar in Dunblane, the first being Sir Stevin Culros, charged to say masses for ever for Henry Quhite's soul.[56] In 1533 and 1535 Bishop William Chisholm I, with consent of Chapter, of Master Henry Quhite and Sir Stevin

Culros (first chaplain of the altar), issued letters that a chaplain had been instituted to serve the altar "situat within the cathedral kirk of Dunblane, foundit be the said maister Henry". These letters "ar hungin at Dunblane".

In addition, the records tell of these altars: St. Blais', at west end of the north aisle, and St. Michael's, at east end of the south aisle. Of the side-altars, the Bishop was patron of those of St. Stephen the Martyr, of St. Blais and of Trinity; the Stirlings of Keir of St. Michael's and of the Virgin Mary's; and John, Lord Drummond (1536), of St. Nicolas'.

By the middle of the fifteenth century portable altars were greatly desired and the lesser aristocracy were petitioning in increasing numbers for papal indult. The first papal permission to magnates of the Diocese of Dunblane was granted, on 10 April 1466, to "Patrick de Grahame, nobleman, knight, lord of the place of Grahame in the Diocese of Dunblane" (Kilbryde Castle, perhaps). He was allowed to have masses celebrated thereon by his own or other fit priest, "provided that he make a sparing use of the grant to have mass before daybreak". On the same day, "William Strewyling, nobleman, knight, lord of the place of Ker", is given the like indult.[57] Such altars were a great convenience in rough weather and on the frequent feast days and fast days, especially if the house was at a distance from the parish church. They were also useful on journeys. The desire to have them may have been tinged in cases with social satisfaction in the smaller gentry, who were thus given privileges comparable with those of the greater nobility who had private chapels in or near their castles. Understandably they were not popular with the clergy, especially with vicars; they detached their owners from the ordinances of the parish church, and "hurt the collections".

B. *Chaplainries of the Choir*

Out of the growing resources of the Cathedral James Chisholm was able in 1522 to endow no less than nine chaplainries in the choir. Those chaplains had been paid out of the general income of the Cathedral; now they were paid from endowments.[58] He collated Sir Thomas Watson to the first chaplainry of Keir within the choir. This was done in chapter about eleven o'clock forenoon on 14 May 1522, before witnesses, and its importance is vouched for by the presence of no less than three notaries public.

In 1532, in Bishop William Chisholm I's time, the chaplains of the choir increased their endowment by the purchase of further lands from John Stirling of Keir, with money bequeathed by Dom. George Newtoun, Archdeacon of Dunblane, for a daily mass at the High Altar.[59] This bequest enabled the Chapter to enlarge the number of chaplains of the choir to twelve.

C. *Ceremonial occasions*

James Chisholm was called with others of the neighbourhood,[60] the Bishop of Dunkeld, Lords Oliphant and Drummond, and others from a distance, to the baptism of the King's son and heir, James, born at Holyrood House, 21 February 1506/7. This son (as likewise a daughter and another son) died in infancy. About 1523, on the authority of his metropolitan of St. Andrews, he dedicated a chapel of the Blessed Virgin Mary which one of the rectors of the Diocese of St. Andrews had built and endowed at his own expense in his parish church.[61] When the famous Gavin Douglas was consecrated Bishop of Dunkeld in 1520, the Archbishop of St. Andrews was assisted by his suffragans of Dunblane and Brechin.[62] The most noteworthy occasion occurred when James Chisholm in 1521, commissioned by the vicar general of St. Andrews, "dedicated with due solemnities the Abbey Church of Cambuskenneth and its two cemeteries, at the east and west ends, with the chapter-house and enclosure" (i.e. the cloister and garth). A distinguished company was "present and concurring". The Bishop was "assisted by his Archdeacon and the Prebendaries of Kippen and Glendevon"; John Tulydaf, warden of the Minorite Friars of Stirling, preached the sermon, after mass, on the efficacy of the dedication.[63]

D. *Adornment of the Cathedral*

(1) In 1501 and 1502 Bishop James added parapets to the tower and the choir, thereby enhancing their dignity and line. Both bear his coat of arms, "a boar's head erased".

(2) At a date unknown he adorned the choir with six canopied stalls for the dignitaries of the Cathedral. These, now too frail for use, are preserved at the west end of the nave; they are remarkable for the depth of the carving, which seems to some to mark them as of foreign, perhaps Dutch, origin. But the appearance of the Scottish thistle, then coming into use as an appropriate

Scottish symbol, inclines me to think that they are of Scoto-French design and execution. Two of the misericords bear the Bishop's coat of arms.

On 6 June 1526 Pope Clement VII provided to the Church of Dunblane William Chisholm,[64] James Chisholm's half-brother. The arrangement was most unusual; James did not wholly resign the see, but ceded it on conditions – William was to keep the canonry of Dunblane and other benefices which he had, but James was still to draw the whole revenue of the Bishopric and still to enjoy the patronage of the benefices within the Diocese. Even after 1526 James was designated Bishop of Dunblane, at least once; but in 1534 he appears in a letter as "administrator Dunblanensis".[65]   More surprising still was James' retention of the right of *regressus* – that is, he could, if he so desired, retake his status and authority as Bishop of Dunblane. It is clear either that he was not convinced that he had reached the necessity of retiring through age or ill-health, or that he had not entire confidence in his half-brother; perhaps both. This was a very privileged settlement, and it cost James dearly in papal taxation; 260 florins to begin with; and on 19 January 1526/7, through his procurator, John Towln, he "offered" 800 florins to the Papal Treasury for his common service, because of his retention of the fruits of the Diocese.[66] There is no complaint now by Bishop James, as there was at his provision in 1486, that Dunblane was overtaxed at 800 florins; the tax was accepted. On the same day, and by the same procurator, William offered for his provision another 800 florins in gold. The See of Dunblane was flourishing – in its finances at least.

And that was not the end of taxation for James, though by the time of its imposition James was past caring. On his death came the claim of the Crown to receive the casualty of a year's income of the Bishopric. On 20 January 1545/6, the Queen (then three years of age) in council, James Hamilton, second Earl of Arran, being Governor, granted[67] to Alexander Drummond of Carnock and Matthew Hamilton, Captain of Blackness Castle, for undisclosed payments of course, half the income, for the year following the Bishop's death, of "all lands, annual rents, tacks, stedings, woddis, mylnis, fischeings and possessions pertaining to the bishoprik of Dunblane, males (mails, rents in kind), fermes, proffittis and dewiteis thairof" which pertained "to our soverane lady be the lawis of hir realme and privilege of hir croun throw deceis of the said umquhile James".

James Chisholm may therefore be supposed to have died in the year we call 1545. He leaves the impression of an active and hardworking cleric, who, amid the many demands of King and Parliament was yet diligent in diocesan, and particularly in Cathedral affairs. His administration of its income was competent; he gathered a chapter of considerable note; he was politically sagacious and was steadfast in his allegiance to the Kings under whom he served. For the first time since Michael Ochiltree's bishopric, and even to a larger degree than in his case, the See and Church of Dunblane took an important place in the national life and counted for more than its size and geographical situation might lead one to expect. Doubtless James Chisholm saw no further into the future than the other bishops of Scotland; doubtless they were unmoved by signs which ought to have warned them of the lost visions of the Church; but it is easy to be wise after the event. The life of the Diocese seems to have been active, if not enthusiastic, and the Church in Dunblane was doing as much as its cumbrous system and many abuses would allow. Bishops and lesser dignitaries were often servants of the King and the State as much as of Christ and His Church; many drew the revenues of benefices without fulfilling any church duties and some of them without accepting the appropriate orders; Church and State, bishop and abbot, Church and Pope were often in tension; the levels of moral living, of monastic discipline, and of learning were often low, and were accepted as such, only a few voices being raised in warning. There were outstanding bishops and lesser clergy, of whom and because of whom it could be said, "There is the Church in action at its best, and with all its weaknesses achieving in some measure its appointed task." But exceptional individuals do not make up the life of a Church, though they do raise its tone and inspire better things. The medieval Church never gave itself a chance; taxation by the Papal Camera oppressed it, the Pope gathered too much into his power and in doing so broke down many of the excellent statutes and canons of the Councils, acknowledged weaknesses were not righted, and though there seemed to be clergy enough, only the most miserably paid, the vicars of the parishes, were in close touch with the people. But if those weaknesses are allowed for – and many of the abuses, however scandalous to us, were not so in the eyes of the generality of the faithful – the long bishopric of James Chisholm will be seen as a time of smooth running of the Diocese, increasing income, enlarging endowments, activities in Parliament and offices of State by the Bishop, Dean and Archdeacon at least, adornment of the Cathedral in stone and wood, and in general an air of solid growth, as if the foundations of it all were sure. But, thirty years on, the winds blew and the floods came, and the foundations crumbled. The marvel is that so many saw only the outward prosperity and expected a long, if not a brilliant, future – until a few months, literally a few months, before the vital truths of the Reformers swept over the Church with cleansing and renewing power.

Yet, in the early years of Bishop James, Lollardry made considerable advance. This was the name given to the followers of John Wyclif, who died in 1384, and whose reforming tenets were accepted and promulgated by Jan Hus, who died at the stake in 1415. James Resby, an English priest, described by Bower[68] as "a truly genuine clerk and famous theologian", but of the Wyclifite school, was burned as a heretic at Perth in 1407, and Paul Crawar, a Bohemian follower of Hus, suffered similarly at St. Andrews in 1431[69]; these were the forerunners of the Reformation long before Luther or Calvin or Knox was born. In 1494 the Lollards of Kyle, some of whom were of the aristocarcy of Scotland, were arguing publicly with bishops and other churchmen, and according to Knox they dashed them out of countenance and turned their accusations to laughter. This reads like an exaggeration, and it was thirty years before serious notice was taken in high places of the rising tide of heretical thinking which in another form was to sweep the Roman Church in Scotland to ruin. The burning of heretics could not turn the tide. The Church went lumbering on, satisfied with signs of outward progress; though inwardly crumbling, it was satisfied that it could crush its insignificant opponents.

Martin Luther was born in 1483, and he took his stand against Rome in 1517. Scottish trade with Continental ports gave opportunity of smuggling into Scotland the Reformer's doctrines, assertions, hymns and books. The Act of 1525 against heresy – there had been passed an Act against Lollardry in 1425[70] –

asserted that "the dampnable opunyeounis of heresy are spred in diverse cuntreis be the heretik Luther and his discipillis". It therefore forbade any stranger arriving by ship to bring with him any books or works of the said Luther or to discuss his heresies, under severe penalties. In 1527 the Act was extended beyond incoming strangers to include "all uther the kingis lieges assistaris to sic opunyeounis". This act was repeated in 1535, with the addition that all such books were to be delivered to the ordinary within forty days.[71] Patrick Hamilton, to be mentioned later, of the house of Hamilton, and of royal blood on both sides of his parentage, who had studied at Paris and Louvain, as well as at St. Andrews, where in 1416 it was enacted that all students intending the M.A. degree should take an oath abjuring Lollardry, was sentenced for heresy and burned at the stake in 1528. Others who suffered the like fate were "David Stratoun a gentleman and Master Norman Gourlay, a man of reasonable erudition"; "those two were both hanged and burnt, according to the mercy of the papistical kirk".[72] But the reforming storm continued to gather momentum.

NOTES

1. CAC 84. Many variations of the name occur, some of them weird: e.g. Geyssolm (de Cromnes), Chrisolneus. For the most part I shall use Chisholm.

2. AP II 184. In CAC 217 his provision to Dunblane seems to have created a vacancy also in the Deanery of Moray.

3. ERS IX 435.

4. A. B. Barty: *History of Dunblane, passim*.

5. CAC 297.

6. CAC 338-9, 2 Apr. 1487. See Chapter IX.

7. CR No. 92 states that 11 Jul. 1521 was in the 34th year of his consecration. He must therefore have been consecrated between 11 Jul. 1487 and 10 Jul. 1488.

8. ERS IX 469, 618, 635.

9. The plan was begun with the King's charter, 6 Apr. 1496; it says that Kippen and its patronage had been for long out of the possession of the Abbey (but there is no trace of the truth of this in any record – Bishop James's successful opposition is proof of its untruth). It was only on the resignation of the rector of Kippen, Magister Patrick Coventre, in 1510, that the charter took effect. On 21 Jul. 1510, probably to forestall the Bishop, Patrick instituted the Abbot and one of his canons in the rectory of Kippen by delivering into their hands book, chalice and other ornaments of the high altar; for this institution the Abbot had fortified himself with a papal bull so ordering; he also had the King's charter and its confirmation (23 Jun. 1496); he had a notary present to write a notarial instrument. The Abbot was the villain of the transaction and he so arranged matters secretly that James Chisholm suddenly found ranged against

him Pope, King, Abbot and Earl. It says much for Bishop James's courage that he never wilted.

10. T. No. 883. 10 Jun. 1487.

11. CR 167-8, 168-70, 170-3, 174-5.

12. T. No. 889. AP II 213. 9 Jan. 1491/2.

13. TV II 375 (No. 100) 28 Jan. 1499/1500.

14. See indices of ERS X, XI and XII.

15. *Early Records of University of St. Andrews*, p. 39.

16. RMS II 2230.

17. This anonymous and undated document of eight pages I was kindly permitted by Lord Ancaster to read and annotate.

18. ADCP I 483 4, 23 Feb. 1539/40, at which date he was Dean of Brechin. In 1527, ADCP I 256, he is still Official of Dunblane.

19. RMS II 1702-1722, between 4 Feb. 1487/8 and 27 Mar. 1487/8.

20. "He was ever haunted by the scene of his father's death; and he eased his conscience by continual penance. He wore an iron belt, which he made heavier each year; and he was frequently on pilgrimage to the sepulchre of St. Ninian at Whithorn and to the church of St. Duthac at Tain", Gregory Smith: *Days of James IV*, 55 n.

21. SK 24ff.

22. ADCC I 177.

23. The story is also told in SK.

24. DB II 171.

25. ERS IX 469, 618, 635.

26. ADCC I 184.

27. ADCC II 191.

28. ERS XII 686.

29. Balfour Paul: *Scots Peerage*, II 134, gives the Laird of Trarinzean as Sir John Ramsay, who became Lord Bothwell, and who on death left Bishop James Chisholm as tutor to his son (*Acta Dom. Conc.* XXVI 19). *Genealogy of House of Drummond* asserts that Bishop James Chisholm and Bothwell were half-brothers, by the same mother.

30. RSS I 2838.

31. ERS XIV 480. Renewed 1524, ERS XV 87, and 1529, ib. 577.

32. Boece: *Life of Bishops*. Hat and sword were presented in Holyrood, 31 Mar. 1507.

33. ERS XIII. Preface 180-1. XIV pref. 77, 78, 136, 137.

34. DB III 437.

35. See chapter IX under Robert Lawder.

36. See index of RSS I.

37. ADCP I 42.

38. ADCP I 62.

39. *Foedera* XIII 531. *Rot. Scot.* II 582. 6 Feb. 1515/6.

40. See Index of AP II.

41. AP II 295. cf. also ADCP I 1, 4, 6, 7, 17, 41, 68, 222 for other activities in State affairs.

42. Writs of Yester, No. 378.

43. ADCP I 212.

44. 31 Jul. 1515. SK 30.

45. ATS V xxv. July 1525.

46. DB II 190, year 1519.

47. ATS IV 103. (The pike are stated to have come from the Lake of Menteith, still plenteous in pike.)

48. ATS IV 407.

49. ATS V 256.

50. 2 Oct. 1509. SK 289ff.

51. 10 May 1472. SK 244ff. See Chapter IX under John Hepburn. In 1550, there were difficulties due to resignations, appointment of a chaplain not canonically equipped, his subsequent sponsorship by the Bishop of Orkney as sub-deacon, an intricate story argued in consistorial court, Archdeacon's Court in Dunblane, and elsewhere, too intricate for this book. See SK 396-401. It had a happy ending.

52. 22 Sep. 1509. Charter was confirmed by James IV, 8 Jan. 1509/10, calling it "the charter of his familiar clerk, Master Walter Drummond, Dean of Dunblane"; RMS II 3398. Walter was nephew of the late Magister John Drummond, Dean.

53. RMS III 2139.

54. 20 May 1511. This gift was subject to a liferent; it was confirmed only on 12 May 1587, RMS V 1230.

55. I have found no record of A. B. Barty's statement, in *History of Dunblane*, that Bishop William Chisholm I built and repaired the Altar of St. Blais. This is probably correct; he certainly was its patron.

56. CR 261-4, 264-7. The altars here mentioned are also dealt with by A. B. Barty, *History of Dunblane*, Chapter VIII.

57. CPR XII 524, 817.

58. SK 317-18.

59. RMS III 1257. George Newtoun wrote a life of St. Blane, now lost, but known to have been used by John Colgan in his *Acta Sanctorum Hiberniae* and by Dempster who quotes from it in *Historia Ecclesiastica* – see my *Celtic Church in Dunblane*. A. B. Barty: *History of Dunblane*, 49, says that he wrote also *The Acts of Dunblane Cathedral*, now also lost.

60. ATS III 392. The messenger summoning the four named was John Beg, and he received 10/- for carrying the 4 letters from Edinburgh.

61. F. I 63. This is a book of forms, in which names of places and persons are often annoyingly hidden under initials.

62. F. I 183-4.

63. CR cxxix. 11 Jul. 1521.

64. Brady gives "die 6 June, 1526" and later "8 idus Maii" as the date of William's provision; "8 idus Maii" looks a mistake for "8 idus Junii", which is 6 June. Historians disagree on the relationship of the brothers. Brady first calls them half-brothers and later full brothers. DBS calls William "brother-german" of James. I believe them to have been half-brothers, but the evidence is not conclusive.

65. CR No. 183, pp. 246-7. A facsimile of his signature is given SK 327.

66. Brady I 140, which gives all the financial details here noted.

67. RSS II 1499.

68. Bower: *Scotichronicon* XV, XX.
69. *ibidem*, XVI, XX, where the date is 1433. Knox I 7 gives 1431.
70. AP II 7.
71. AP II 342.
72. Knox I 24-25.

CHAPTER XI

BISHOP WILLIAM CHISHOLM THE FIRST
1526 – 1564

WILLIAM CHISHOLM I accepted at the Pope's hands, and by agreement with his half-brother, provision to a see, in which, on paper at least, the duties, rights and privileges were severely circumscribed.[1] Yet from the moment of William's consecration and induction, James sinks into the background in the public records and seldom appears in them, while William is constantly mentioned, though it was only after James' death in 1545 that William was free to administer the lands and revenues of the Diocese – which he did to his own and his children's advantage and the benefit of his kin. By that time the gusts of heresy were blowing, and it was for William a happy chance that his freedom to deal with the diocesan fruits coincided with the possibility of saving some of these fruits for himself before the storm of reformation came crashing on the Church.

I have come to the conclusion that though James was of stronger personality than William and of altogether finer texture and character, it was William who was the prime mover in James' retiral. I conclude that James yielded to the persuasions of William, that James may have been in temporary ill-health or in some degree of incapacity, but was well enough to lay down stringent conditions, which, however awkward and limiting, William accepted. Whatever William's expectations, it was twenty years before Providence gave him untrammelled liberty in administration. Until then he had no control of the finances, or of the patronage, and he loyally acquiesced in the situation. Better to be half a bishop than a whole canon.

William was consecrated at Stirling on 14 April 1527, the consecrating bishops being Gavin Dunbar of Glasgow, George Crichton of Dunkeld, and brother James.[2]

Within weeks of his provision, William Chisholm was thrust into the full current of political intrigue. In 1526 the young

King was in the custody of Angus, who was influentially supported, but opposed by the Earl of Lennox, who was even more influentially sustained. Lennox with 3000 men tried to rescue the King at Melrose, but failed. The story is told in a letter from Angus to Cardinal Wolsey, 16 September 1526.[3] Despite failure, Lennox took a large army to Stirling, where they had "the assistance and cruel counsale of the archbishops of Glasgow and St. Andrews, the bishops of Dunblane and Orkney, the earls of Lennox, Crawfurde", and others, both prelates and barons. Again Lennox's army failed to rescue the King, this time in Edinburgh. But in the end it was Angus who failed; in 1528, along with a brother, an uncle and others, he was sentenced to forfeiture of life, lands and property.[4] This sentence was uttered not by the whole Parliament, but by a committee of six clerical magnates, including William Chisholm, and five Earls, including Argyll and Arran, all eleven being chosen by the King and all hostile to Angus. Some weeks before this, the King had made his escape to Stirling Castle.

From the first William took his seat in Parliament, and until about 1546 attended most faithfully; even in 1558 and 1560, when painful ill-health was his lot, he struggled to be present. It would be to recount the history of Scotland to detail the dates and decisions of the meetings which he attended. Suffice it to note some of the offices he held and some of the enactments to which he assented. He was appointed to the Privy Council and attended in 1545-7, 1550-3, and again in 1561.[5] In 1553, he was elected one of the twelve commissioners for the Borders to work out a settlement with the commissioners of England.[6] In 1556, with the Clerk Register and the Laird of "Lidingtone", he spent some months at Duns with Tunstall, Bishop of Durham, and the English commissioners, "anent certaine contrawersies betuix the tuo kingdomes, wich they composed and fulley endit."[7] He was a member of the Committee of Causes in 1532, 1542 and 1546, of "the Articles" in 1535, and of the Commission in 1544. In 1542 he voted for the Earl of Arran to be made Governor of the realm; in 1545 he signed the Act for defence of the country; in 1554 he consented to a "bond" (covenant) in favour of Arran, now Duke of Chatelherault; in 1557 he signed the treaty of marriage between Queen Mary and the Dauphin of France; in 1560 he joined in a petition to Queen Elizabeth of England that she should marry the Earl of Arran to ensure peace between their countries. He was Lord of Council, 1530[8]; Auditor of Exchequer 1533 and 1558[9]; he signed the Treasurer's accounts in 1533 twice) and 1550[10]; he received at least 50 letters ("clos", or secret writings) from the Governor of Scotland between 1542 and 1550,[11] each sent by special messenger, on a variety of matters which ranged from the defence of the realm to payment of taxes, from charges of treason against the burgesses of Dundee to an order to "caus thresche corne and bring victuallis to the toun of Edinburght . . . after the first sycht of the Franche navye", from orders to put certain malefactors to the horn to an injunction "for the cursing upon the slaarres of the cardinal". Bishop William was summoned on many occasions to "the convention" (of state), when war threatened[12]; in 1533, with other bishops and abbots, he was commanded "to send their houshaldis to the bordour" within the next quarter,[13] and later in the same year, he was charged, as were all bishops, abbots and even prioresses, with the furnishing of footmen, and all sheriffs with the holding of wapenshaws.[14] With all magnates, clerical and lay, he was bidden by letter in 1537[15] "for their honest preparing agane (= over against) the kingis gracis hame cuming". Queen Dowager, Governor, Parliament and King held him in high regard and placed entire reliance on his wisdom and sense of responsibility, giving him important duties and offices of state and taking him into their innermost counsels.

This royal dependence on him, however, brought him heavy financial consequence. In 1554, a few days after he had signed at Stirling "a registered bond" guaranteeing that the Queen Dowager (James V's widow) and the Duke of Chatelherault (who had just resigned his Governorship) would account for their financial transactions, he was asked to undertake a more exacting and intimate office. The Dowager and the late Governor put no trust in the efficacy of the "registered bond"; it was too widespread and general to satisfy their considerable needs. They asked for curators and Parliament appointed William Chisholm along with the Bishop of Orkney and the Dean of Restalrig.[16] The honour roused in them no enthusiasm, and when they took the oath, *verbum professionis*, they asked it to be minuted that they accepted office only at the special desire of the Dowager and the Duke. What this curatorship cost them is not known, but William Chisholm's friendship with the Queen Regent was shown in two payments made to her account shortly after:

(1) £800, recorded in the year 1554/5 in the books of the Treasurer of Scotland as "received from the queen regent by the hands of William bishop of Dunblane".[17] This may be the sum which Mary Queen of Scots repaid, in part at least, by giving orders in 1561 for £300, and in 1562 for £366. 13. 4 to be given to the Bishop "in complete payment of 1000 marks owing be umquhile hir hienes darrest mother" and "with the bishopis acquitances". But £800 is more than 1000 marks, and the repayments may have been for another loan unrecorded.[18] In any case, Mary took an easy way of repaying her mother's debts, for they were met out of Church revenues, available after the financial débâcle of the Reformation.

(2) £4,400 recorded in 1555 by Astier, the Dowager's French controller, as from the "bishop of Dombelline".[19] No information is available except these facts. The item appears in the Dowager's accounts of income and expenditure for 1555, and is the last item, as if it had been given to balance the expenses, which far exceeded the income. Astier was wrong in his addition of the items, which were only six in number, the only other large sum coming from the Earl of Huntly, who gave £5,008. It would appear that the two large sums, very large for those days, were gifts made to rescue a habitually embarrassed Queen.

But that was not the end of the Queen Dowager's pressure on Bishop William; to the claims of friend were added the claims of tax-collector. £60,000 had been granted her by the Council at Stirling, of which sum she allocated £625 on the Bishop. On 28 October 1557, she wrote to Robert Carnegie[20] as collector of half of the tax that the Bishop of Dunblane had managed to pay only £103. As the Earl of Huntly could not pay his soldiers, she commanded that money be borrowed from any burgh or sheriff. The Bishop had been squeezed dry. So had Huntly.

Though William Chisholm became a notable member of Parliament and its Committee, he was not, after the first few years of his episcopate, or in his later years, in good financial standing with the authorities. He paid his tax of £30 in 1528,[21] and £20 in 1531 and 1532 as his rent of Terrinyeane, rented by brother James and him from the Crown[22]; in 1531 he paid £40, the full tax in lieu of the horses and soldiers which his diocese had to provide for the army.[23] But from 1532 he began to fall behind, and in that year there was engaged "ane boy to rin with ane lettre to the bischope of Dunblane schawing that he would be processit for non payment of the taxt".[24] So threatened, William Chisholm in 1533 paid £88. 6. 8 in full satisfaction, and the collector for the Diocese of Dunblane paid £52. 3. 7 in the same year, probably gathered from the parishes.[25] These payments were made in one of the years when, with eight others, he twice signed the accounts.[26] But matters came to a head again in 1536, when William Chisholm and the Prior of Inchmahome were summoned[27] "to cum and gif comptio of their taxt to the auditouris deput thereto", another summons having been delivered a few days before commanding the Bishops of Dunblane and Dunkeld "to cause their denis cum and gift comptio of their taxt".[28] William Chisholm was again summoned in 1556, 1558 and 1559 for failure to pay his taxes[29]; but he seems to have met his taxes faithfully from 1536 to 1556. It was an unfortunate position for one who as late as 1560 was an auditor of the accounts of the realm; but it is clear that brother James in the early days kept a tight hand on the administration of the episcopal revenues, and that after James' death in 1545 William was short of money at times, because of royal demands and family plans.

Bishop William also found himself at variance with the College of Justice, later called the Court of Session, which James V had founded in 1532. The Bishop was himself a member of the College, which in its early days was not composed wholly of justices trained in law. For its support the prelates were mulcted according to their diocesan revenues,[30] Dunblane's share being £14 per annum. In 1547 the Lords ordered the goods of Bishop William to be distrained for £14 for each of the previous eleven and a half years.[31] William's reply was that he had assigned the vicarages of Dron and Callendreth (Callander) as payment of Dunblane's contribution; he protested that he be "nocht compellit to pay for thir contributioun", or in time of vacancies.[32] It would appear, however, that the two vicars had neither resigned nor died, and the Lords, tired of waiting, claimed that payments could not wait for vacancies. William did not admit the validity of their contention, but consented, of grace, and not of legal authority, to pay the dues until vacancies occurred. He asked that this ex gratia settlement be recorded and he took instruments (asked for official acknowledgment). In this he was clever rather than wise in meeting his obligations by parochial revenues still drawn by beneficed clerics and therefore not available till a vacancy; as a member of the College he must have been aware of the contentions of his brethren and that his defence was weak.

William Chisholm witnessed a considerable number of charters chiefly of the transfer of lands between 1541 and 1559,[33] and others at various dates. These however add little to the history of the Cathedral and may be passed over.

Mandates came to the Bishop in large numbers, and a few to various members of the Chapter. In earlier days, the local patron and the Chapter had important rights in the appointment even to the greater benefices, and the Bishop appointed to the lesser. The story of the struggle for patronage has been briefly outlined in Chapter VIII; it is enough to know that, little by little, the Pope pushed out the patron and the Bishop in the greater benefices, and the King kept urging his claims. An agreement by which Pope, King and local patron were in turn to have the patronage to all benefices, greater or lesser, speedily broke down under the local influence of the King's authority, until in the days of William Chisholm I only the King remained as patron of all benefices. The Pope was ousted except for the final provision to the greater benefices; the Bishop was ousted except for the provision to the lesser. Both Pope and Bishop could refuse to provide the nominee of the King, but this right was exercised only when the appointment by the King was patently unsuitable, and not always even then. In 1535 the Pope admitted the right of the King to nominate to all benefices. From 1531 to 1554 the King issued about twelve such nominations as mandates to benefices in the Diocese of Dunblane, the Pope none, the Bishop none.[34] In the case of Kilmadock, the method is clearly stated: "the disposition is the King's and the provision is the Bishop's". Logie was given in 1532 to a scholar, Robert Robesoun, "as principale of the said parrochin be full richt" and by confirmation of the Bishop.[35] The rise of royal patronage reduced the powers and the status of the Bishop, who was no longer able to choose even the dignitaries of his own Cathedral. The King sent him a Dean in 1536,[36] and a Chancellor and an Archdeacon in 1544.[37]

Letters and mandates and commissions continued to come to

William Chisholm from the Pope. (1) In 1527 Pius II warned him against attacking the privileges of Arbroath Abbey, for the Abbot had complained that the Bishops of Moray and Dunblane, in especial, had been interfering in such matters as the repair of churches and the burdens of vicars in some of their parishes appropriated to Arbroath.[38] When the Bishops sent the facts to Rome, the Pope on 28 August 1527 called the rector of Spot and another to come and explain to him just what these privileges were which the Abbot claimed.[39] This did not close the breach, for in 1532 the Abbot appealed to the Pope to send "apostles" to investigate "the grave charges" made against the Abbey by the Bishops (Glasgow, Dunkeld, Moray, Brechin and Dunblane) in whose dioceses Arbroath held churches in appropriation.[40] (2) About 1536, P. A., a priest of Dunkeld, was accused by the Crown of conspiring in England against the life of James V, and the Pope commissioned the Bishops of Dunkeld and Whithorn to review the case. They took advice from six others of the epis-copal bench, including William Chisholm, and deposed and de-prived the priest.[41] (3) In 1544, along with the Bishops of Moray and Brechin, William Chisholm was authorised by papal bull[42] to admit James Stewart, natural son of James V, as canon of Inch-colm; he is called "clerk", but was not more than fifteen years of age. Trouble arose in Inchcolm later, and in 1551 James Stewart, now Abbot in commendam, sent his procurator "to the personal presence of William, Bishop of Dunblane," with an appeal against John Steill, who was seeking to oust him.[43] (In 1530 James V had petitioned the Pope to allow Steill, then six years of age, to hold a benefice!) (4) In 1555 a bull arrived granting the Priory of Inchmahome to David Erskine, the leading layman of the district, and detailing the steps to be taken by the Bishops of Dunblane and Orkney and another.[44] This was followed by a long instrument naming the properties to be handed over. This was another of many signs that the system of abbeys and priories had broken down; practically everywhere in Scotland these institu-tions were being, or had been, handed over for a payment of cash to neighbouring lairds who had the lands converted into a barony; these, by reason of the upheavals of the Reformation, they ulti-mately possessed in their own rights. In 1445 Inchaffray had become a barony,[45] and in 1551 William Chisholm was given an assedation (lease) of its lands.[46] (5) in 1553 the Bishop of Dunblane was one of the judges in a dispute between the Town Council of Perth and the Blackfriars of the town.[47]

Even yet we have not exhausted the activities of William Chisholm I; indeed, his consuming passion has yet to be expounded. His dealings in land, both in buying and selling, both for the Diocese and for his individual interests, were so many that they must have demanded something of a staff, expert in agriculture and in law. His reputation as the archdespoiler of the Cathedral's endowments in lands is thoroughly deserved. There are extant charters in plenty,[48] in which, with consent of the Chapter, he intromitted with the Church's lands, some of which supported certain of the Cathedral officers. As was by this time customary, and had been for long, in cathedrals, abbeys and priories, William Chisholm I, as did his predecessor James, leased church lands, very often for nineteen years, to neighbouring lairds at an annual rent. It was the easiest way, if not always the most profitable, to provide income for the Cathedral clergy. He adopted a plan which, while it kept him within the Canon Law forbidding the alienation of church lands, yet provided him with considerable sums of money in addition to annual rents, at times increased. For instance, in 1528, he granted a nineteen years' lease to his relative, his full brother in fact, James Chisholm of Cromlix, of the lands of Nether, Over and Middle Cromlix, Auchinlay and Blewbuttergask; but seven years later, with consent of the Chapter, he changed this into a perpetual lease at stated rents for each farm mentioned in the charter. For this perpetual lease James Chisholm agreed to pay, in addition to the rents, 500 marks for the Charter, and Bishop William kept within the Church Law by adding that there was to be no alienation of the lands to any other without his permission. In like manner he leased *in perpetuum* Glassingalbeg and Drumdowlis, for 200 marks and an augmented rent, to Edward Sinclair of Galdwalmore, in 1546; lands to the west of Perth, for an unstated sum and an augmented rent, to Andrew Mersar, in 1563, adding in the charter "as long as the mind of the Supreme Pontiff agrees", for he knew he was sailing rather near the wind; the teinds of many farms, ten at least, in the parish of Dunblane, to Jane Stirling, his natural daughter, second wife of James Stirling of Keir, at a rent of £40 per annum, in 1557; the township and chapel lands of Sauchinthome (which is Deanston) with woods and fishing on the Teith, to John Drummond, at £20 of old rent, with 14/- for 12 capons and 6/- of augmentation, in 1562. All these transactions were with the consent of the Chapter; and only the last two tacks of teinds did not carry with them a stated sum; all of them involved payment of an increased rent. The whole of the church lands were doubtless leased for a period of years; but in the above cases no period is fixed. We get an occasional glimpse of the usual run of leases, as when it is stated (RMS, 19 May 1576) that Bishops James Chisholm and William Chisholm I had leased to William Sinclair of Bankis the lands of Fyndall and Dargall in Muthill, and that William Chisholm II followed their example for an augmented rental, which included 6 score loads of peats and other commodities; in this case, William Chisholm I had, it is stated, given the lease for money paid.

But Bishop William bought and sold lands on his own account and became a considerable landowner in his own right. He bought Ardargy and its "outset" from David Murray in 1538; from James Stirling of Keir, in 1536, "5 mark land" of Glassingall; from the same proprietor in 1540, Strowyehill, which he sold back to Keir in 1563; in 1553 Kippendavie; Wolquhoige in 1549; from George Muschet of Colgart the lands of Lochfield in 1548; from David, Lord Drummond, in 1551 he bought Bordland in Menteith, and from John Menteith of Kers, in 1555, all of West Quarter of Alva. In 1550 he bought back Cagnour, with Loch Culter, Stirlingshire, which his half-brother James had owned and sold, with its grain mill, multures, mill-lands and dependents; in 1553 he gave them to James Chisholm, one of his natural children, but four months later they were bought from the Bishop by the brother of Thomas Charteris, former owner, now deceased. The land-hungry bishop bought in 1543 twelve oxgangs of land of Ochiltree in Lothian for his son James.

Farming was in his blood, and his dealings in land, his own and the Cathedral's, were so successful that his enemies called him "the rich bishop of Dunblane". He required considerable wealth if he was to meet the claims of a needy Queen Dowager and the needs of his considerable family of sons and daughters. In 1542 a marriage contract was drawn between his daughter Jane, called in the contract his "consignes" (blood-relation, cousin), and James Stirling of Keir, who was marrying Jane as his second wife; in this, James Stirling bestowed large gifts of land on Jane, and her father paid £1000 to James and granted a tack of nineteen years of the teinds of many farms, which tack was renewed in 1557 without a terminal date for a rent of £40 per annum. This brought the Bishop into close, but involved, relationship with James Stirling – who had two "fowbegottin" daughters, Helen and Jane. For them the warm-hearted Bishop bought the free tenancy of Beirhome in Keir, and of Kippendavie. With consent of their tutors, William Chisholm sold back these lands to James Stirling, Beirhome in 1552 for £300 Scots, Kippendavie in 1554 for 1000 marks, both amounts to be laid on the Lady Altar of the Cathedral.[49] Lochfield, which he bought in 1548 and gave to his son James for his support, he allowed James to sell in 1552 to his sister Helen, now contracting a marriage with John, son of George Buchanan of that Ilk. Helen and John in the same year purchased Strathyre from George Buchanan, perhaps with the dowry provided by her father.

In other ways the Bishop showed his business acumen and unbounded energy. In 1533, on the death of James Drummond of Duchlage, the heir being a minor, William took over charge and ward of the estate, the giving of the heir in marriage, etc., in place of the boy's uncle George, who renounced the tutorship. As the Bishop's sister-in-law was a Drummond, Jane, wife of James Chisholm, third laird of Cromlix, he may have answered the call of blood; but there were rights and privileges in wardships, and the Bishop's needs were great. In 1552 he bought for £200 the right to compound with criminals for their derelictions within the episcopal territory, for the royal courts welcomed in their still weak organisation the help of local magnates who had the rights of barony and regality.

Like bishop, like dean; William Gordon, the Dean, with consent of Chapter, feued to James Stirling of Keir, in 1549, for an increased rent, the lands of Auchinby, reserving a right of way for horse-drawn carts and other traffic; in 1558 his successor, Roger Gordon, feued to Edward Sinclair of Galdwalmore the lands known as Keirardoch (or Keirblane), a feu later given by the same Dean in 1570 to George Drummond, feuar of Balloch. About 1564 Dean Roger, with consent of Chapter and the chaplains of the choir, sold Cluthybeg (in Findogask) to John Murray of Tibbermore, and in 1558 feued Clevage in the regality of Dunblane to James Mersar of Newton.

The feuing of church land was the usual means of drawing income from it adopted by ecclesiastical owners, but the sale of land was questionable. It may have been due to need of capital, but often it looks as if it was dictated by the uncertainties of the times, when increase of heretical views threatened a reformation. Perpetual leases endangered church property and encouraged expectations in landlords of what might yet fall into their laps. The shadows of future turmoil were being seen, and they were giving birth to widespread and self-regarding dealings in property by clerics and laymen alike.

When we turn to William Chisholm I as churchman, there is little in the records to show that, in spite of his bustling life as parliamentarian, friend of royalty and eager dealer in land, his main concern as Bishop was, as it ought to have been, the care of his church and diocese. Though it was only on James Chisholm's death in 1545 that the administration of the Bishopric fell to him, he was from his provision in 1526 responsible for the advancement of his people in Christian life and grace. In this realm, in which the churchman seems to have been swallowed by the politician and the landed gentleman, it is well to remember the absence of all diocesan records of Dunblane and to withhold condemnation; there is so much we do not know. Maybe he gave his undoubted talents and energies to spheres largely extra-ecclesiastical; maybe he was a diocesan in name largely; maybe there is ground for suspicion that his known activities absorbed him wholly, but a final weighing of the man will be possible only when his episcopal records and diocesan books have been recovered.

The following items are of interest:

A. *Cathedral appointments*

In 1540, when Dean Malcolm Fleming was transferred to be Prior of Whithorn (still called Candida Casa), the Pope on the petition of James V conferred the Deanery on William Gordon, then only a clerk. In 1542, on a like petition, the Pope appointed to the Archdeaconry John Danyelston, the King's groom of the bedchamber (*noster cubicularius*). About the claims of one, Patrick Forhous, controversy raged for some years, for he asserted that he had purchased the Chancellorship of Dunblane at the Papal Court, as well as other benefices. Against his statements the

Lords of Council made proclamation in 1538 at the Mercat Cross of Edinburgh that the rigours of the law would be enforced against him[50]; not only did the law of Scotland forbid such endeavours to seize benefices, but Forhous had taken action against John Chisholm, then in possession. The effort of Forhous to establish himself seems to have continued, for in 1544, on 21 May, the records bear that he was confirmed in the Chancellorship of Dunblane.[51] On the same day John Danyelston was confirmed as Archdeacon.

B. *Cathedral altars*

During William Chisholm I's bishopric, further endowments were added to the altars of the Cathedral, all of them pious benefactions of some clergy of the Cathedral. Details of these and other gifts to the altars as well as the erection of altars will be found in the previous chapter.

Perhaps it was his reactions to the rising demand for drastic changes in the Church which reveal the kind of man he was, his weakness as well as his strength. When parliamentary business brought the necessity of facing the religious issues involved in the approaching reformation, he was wholly at sea, not having given time for serious reflexion on the matters at issue. Yet, throughout his bishopric the growth of the Protestant heresy was so obvious that every churchman ought to have been gravely disturbed. Patrick Hamilton, Abbot of Ferne, was burned for heresy in 1528 at St. Andrews – "the reek of master Patrick Hamilton has infected all it blew upon" recorded Knox in his *History of the Reformation in Scotland*. Norman Gourlay and David Straiton so suffered "beside the Rood of Greenside" in Edinburgh in 1534, and in the same year John MacAlpine, Prior of the Dominicans in Perth, had to flee Scotland for his Protestant beliefs. James Hamilton, of noble birth, having relapsed into heresy, recanted, and in 1537 "is now repentant", reports Theiner (No. 1045). James V asked the Pope in 1538 to appoint David Beaton, St. Andrews, to the sacred purple of Cardinal and the title of Legate, because of his zeal against "infesting heresies"; five in Edinburgh and two in Glasgow were burned for heresy in 1539, George Wishart at St. Andrews in 1546, and Walter Mylne, a priest of 81 years, in 1558, also at St. Andrews. In 1543 the Lords of the Articles declared it lawful for all Scots to possess and read the Bible in English or in Scots; in 1557 "the congregation" of Protestant leaders first appeared, in "Ane Godlie Band" or Covenant. Yet this widespread ferment, both in clerical minds and lay, greatly stimulated by the English Parliament's abolition in 1536 of the authority of the Bishop of Rome, left William Chisholm I as if he were unaware of the threat to his Church. But he was not unaware – for Parliament, which he attended diligently, passed in 1541 acts affirming the honour of the sacraments, the worship of the Virgin Mary, the authority of the Pope and the virtue of images of the saints, denouncing heresy and urging the reform of kirks and kirkmen; as well might a modern churchman plead ignorance of the atom bomb, as William Chisholm I of the upheaval within the Church. Moreover, in 1547 and 1549, the clergy met at Edinburgh in Provincial Council, the Bishop being present at both, and discussed the state of affairs; indeed the rifeness of heresy was the cause of their meeting. Especially in 1549 the Council set down many necessary reforms, and in the preamble stated these as the roots of the evils and heresies of the times, (1) "the corruption of morals and profane lewdness of life in churchmen of almost all ranks", (2) "crass ignorance of literature and of all the liberal arts".[52] These were doubtless contributory causes of heresy, but there were many more – the papal system with its appropriation of parish churches to monasteries, absentee rectors, pluralism, reiterated taxation, papal sale of benefices; there was also the rise of that dawn which is called the Renaissance. Deeper than all other causes was, of course, the discovery of those Biblical truths which have remained the unshaken pillars of the Reformation and of the Churches adhering to it. As preaching had for long been neglected, the Council of 1549 ordained that bishops were to preach four times a year; if any bishops have not been in the habit of preaching, they were enjoined to train and qualify for this exercise.[53] Preaching stations were allotted to archbishops, bishops and dignitaries of cathedrals, abbots, priors and even to the Nuns of North Berwick, the rectory of Kippen being assigned for this purpose to the Bishop of Dunblane. The Council also authorised a course of religious instruction to be prepared for simple folk and took other valuable steps of reform. Consequently Archbishop Hamilton's Catechism was published. But it was all too late, fifty years or more too late. Reform more drastic than the

P

churchmen would allow was coming in spite of them; their own authorities were calling for drastic reforms.[54] William Chisholm I took part in the trial of Adam Wallace for heresy, and along with Cardinal David Beaton and Archbishop Gavin Dunbar of Glasgow, condemned to the fire in 1538 friars Kyllour and Beveridge, Robert Forster, Sir Duncan Simpson and Dean Thomas Forret, Canon Regular and vicar of Dollar, who were destroyed together. Yet, when he had to decide whether to give adherence to the "Scots Confession" when it was accepted by Parliament in 1560, he excused himself, as did the Archbishop of St. Andrews, the Bishop of Dunkeld and two temporal Lords, that as he was not sufficiently acquainted with the book, he was not ready to give his judgment. He said, honestly I believe, that he would agree to what might stand with God's Word, and would consent to reforms of abuses which were not in keeping with the Scriptures; he asked for further time to deliberate on the book. These were reasonable requests, but the churchmen by their neglect of reforms which they admitted were necessary had made such temporising no longer possible. The Bishop of Dunblane had already had ample time and occasion for deliberation on the state of the Church, though not on the "Scots Confession"; but such issues did not lie easy to his mind and concern. He was so moulded that he remained a steadfast Roman to the last. It has to be recognised that by 1559 he was a sick man; he told the Queen Dowager, "in veritie I have bene verra evil at eis in my body".[55] He suffered from stone and gout. On 15 December 1564 Randolph, the English emissary, reported[56] to Cecil that "the bishop of Dunblane lies at the point of death". In that year he died,[57] aged seventy years. Knox called him one of "the chief pillars of the papistical kirk".[58]

NOTES

1. Brady I. 140. William was to retain his canonry of Dunblane and other benefices already held, but James was to retain and administer the episcopal revenues as well as the patronage; he also retained the right of *regressus* (to retake his full bishopric). William paid to the Camera 800 florins for his provision.

2. *House of Drummond* 179, quoted DBS 207.

3. DB IV 113.

4. DB II 241.

5. RPCS I. Index.

6. RPCS I. 150.

7. Balfour: *Annals of Scotland* I 305.

8. Writs of Yester (SHS) No. 459.

9. ERS XVI 225, 286. ATS X 320 (for 1558).

10. ATS VI 143 (1533) and ATS IX 450 (1550).

11. ATS VIII, IX, indices.

12. ATS VI onwards, indices.

13. ATS VI 122-3.

14. 25 Apr. 1533, ATS VI 128-9.

15. c.18 Mar. 1536/7, ATS VI 310.

16. ADCP I 629, 631.

17. ATS X 261.

18. TB 100, 155.

19. "Balcarres Papers" (SHS) Vol. II (1548-57).

20. W. Fraser: *Carnegies of Inveresk* I 34.

21. ERS XV 455.

22. ERS XVI 83, 214-15.

23. ATS V 450-1.

24. 20 Oct. 1532. ATS VI 111; the boy was paid 4/-.

25. ATS VI 146, 148.

26. ATS VI 143.

27. ATS VI 308. Oct. 1536.

28. ATS VI 306. Sep. 1536.

29. ATS X 319, 398, 413.

30. ADCP I 541. Inchaffray, £21; Culross £12; Inchmahome £11. 4/-; Glasgow £42; Paisley Abbey £56; Dunkeld £42; Aberdeen £18; etc.

31. ADCP I 569.

32. ADCP I 575; 12 Jun. 1548.

33. RMS IV 2, 10, 11, 102, etc.

34. The parishes concerned were Abernethy (2), Logie, Aberfoyle, Kilmadock, Chapel of Christ's Well (2), Dunning, Glendevon (2), Balquhidder, Comrie. cf Indices of RSS II, III and IV. In this series of royal presentations there is another William Chisholm who is given the presentation of Cragy in Dioc. of Dunkeld and the rectory of Glendevon (RSS III 603, 739). He may have been a nephew of Bishop William Chisholm I who became Bishop William C. II.

35. RSS II 1222.

36. 20 Nov. 1536. RSS II 2191, when Malcolm Fleming was appointed.

37. CMN 61. 21 May 1544.

38. LAc II 462.

39. *ut supra*, 468.

40. *ut supra*, 510.

41. F. II 49.

42. "Charters of Inchcolm" (SHS) 202, 78.

43. *ut supra*, 203.

44. RBM II 335, 343-349.

45. The barony of Cardenay, CAI No. 146, 27 Jan. 1444/5. The opening of the charter granted by James II parallels the Dunblane charter of James II (see Chapter VIII) in word, phrase and idea, even asserting the claim that his an-

cestors "had dowered the Monastery of Inchaffray with divers possessions". This, as I noted in Chapter VIII, was common form. The possessions are detailed, the rights stated, in much the same way as in the case of Dunblane's grant of barony.

46. ATS X 68.

47. Milne: *Blackfriars of Perth*, 231.

48. It would weary to give the references even to those transactions to be mentioned; they are to be found in RMS, RSS, ATS, SK, CC, FKL, etc.

49. SK 405-6, 407-8.

50. ADCP I 472, 13 Aug. 1538.

51. CMN 61, 21 May 1544.

52. PSSC 85-134.

53. PSSC 98, 121.

54. See Archbishop Hamilton's report on the churches of the Merse, in the Register House's Ecclesiastical Documents, No. 8; also Cardinal Sermoneta's report in 1556 to Pope Paul IV (J. H. Pollen: *Papal Negotiations with Queen Mary*, 528-30); also, the report of De Gouda, Jesuit, to his general in 1562, "it is no wonder that, with such shepherds, the wolves invade the flock of the Lord, and ruin all"; (Pollen: *ut supra*, 138). For earlier admonitions, see James I's letter of 1425 to the Benedictine and Augustinian Orders (AP II 25) and the Act of 1541 anent Reformation of Kirk and Clergy (AP II 370).

55. "Scottish Correspondence of Mary of Lorraine" (SHS) 423.

56. CSP II 100.

57. *House of Drummond*, 179.

58. History I 335 (Dickinson).

CHAPTER XII

BISHOP WILLIAM CHISHOLM THE SECOND
1561 – 1573

O N 2 June 1561, on petition of Mary, Queen of Scots, the Roman Consistory deputed William Chisholm II to be co-adjutor to his uncle, then sixty-seven years of age and suffering severely from stone and gout. He was given the title of Bishop of Massulae (in Numidia), then vacant, and was to succeed his uncle. The necessity of visiting his church titular was waived, and he was to resign it on becoming Bishop of Dunblane; he was allowed to retain the canonry and prebend of Dunblane which he had, and he was given with his uncle's consent, a stipend of £200 from the income of the Cathedral[1]; his canonry and prebend he was to resign one month from the day when he obtained peaceable possession of the Church of Dunblane.

Before his appointment as coadjutor, the Reformation had been achieved, Parliament having ratified the "Confession of Faith" on 17 August 1560. A week later three further acts were passed – one abolished the authority of the Pope in Scotland, one declared to be null and void all acts of the Scots Parliament at variance with the Confession of Faith, and one forbade under severe penalties the secret saying and hearing of mass and the celebration of baptism according to the Roman ritual. The necessity for reformation is not in doubt, as is acknowledged by Roman Catholic writers, both medieval and modern. It would be too much, however, to expect even scholars who belong to the Reformed Church to approve of all the doings of that stormy struggle for the truth of God in Church and State. I am driven to the view that, to go no further back, and no deeper, but for the blindness and over-confidence of the bishops, and the fanatical Romanism of the French Queen Dowager, Mary of Lorraine, who could understand neither the Scots people nor the signs of the times, and who at crucial times broke her solemn promises, the Reformation would have taken another form, within which the best

elements of the Roman clergy would have been able to make a
valid contribution. "The unique feature of the Scottish revolu-
tion", says A. R. MacEwen,[2] "is that it was accomplished swiftly,
peaceably and with little bloodshed." While the Roman Church
in Scotland sent a number of heretics to the stake, these were
few in number when compared with the many victims in England
and other countries. To the credit of the Scottish Reformers let
it be remembered that in spite of their zeal and the severity of
penalties for breaking the new laws, no single execution of their
opponents for religious acts or beliefs can be laid to their charge.
Hume Brown's verdict[3] may stand: "Compared with the tale of
blood and confusion that has to be told of Germany, France,
England and Spain, the history of the Reformation in Scotland is
a record of order and tranquillity . . . It was in the convulsions
attending the change of the national faith that the Scottish nation
first attained to a consciousness of itself, and the characteristics
it then displayed have remained its distinctive characteristics ever
since. It is precisely the combination of a fervid temper with
logical thinking and temperate action that have distinguished the
Scottish people in all the grave crises of their history."

William Chisholm II, the last Roman Bishop of Dunblane, died
a Roman Catholic, as did his uncle, who lived through the early
days of the Reformation. The first mention of William II as
Bishop of Dunblane which I have found is in a letter of 30 March
1565, from Randolph, the emissary of Cecil, English Secretary
of State, to his master: "There came two days since from Flanders
the new bishop of Dunblane." The letter goes on to make derogatory statements and innuendoes about him and his uncle, some
of which at least ring false and others sound grossly exaggerated;
but one statement is true and shows the atmosphere of intrigue
and service of the Roman Church in dangerous conditions, which
marked his tenure of the Dunblane title: "He has brought from
Louvain a holy man of the Jesuit's order, the first that ever in
Scotland durst show his face. This man remains in town (Edinburgh), the prelate hastens towards the Queen."

It may seem strange to many that though the Scots Parliament
accepted the principles of the Reformation in August 1560,[4]
there was still a Roman Bishop of Dunblane, and even stranger
that a coadjutor to him was appointed in 1561 and continued,
after the death of his uncle and until 1573, a Roman Bishop,

drawing, and at liberty to spend, the revenues of his See, with the exception of one third, which from 1567 was allotted to the support of the Reformed clergy. It was only in 1573 that those clergy who would not accept the Reformed Church were excluded and deposed by an Act of Conformity and Supremacy.[5] There are several reasons for this continued toleration of clergy whose beliefs were contrary to the Reformation:

(1) The Act of August 1560 was deficient for the full establishment of the Reformed Church, in that it did not deal with the government of the Church or with its endowments.

(2) The Act of 1560 was itself challenged in validity by Queen Mary when she came to reign in 1561, on the ground that on 6 July 1560, in an agreement called the Treaty of Edinburgh, between England and France, it was conceded to Scotland, at the request and judgment of "the nobles and people of Scotland . . . concerning religion and certain other points on which the Lords Deputies would by no means meddle", that as these were of great importance "they judged them proper to be remitted to the king and queen". In spite of this, the Scots Parliament had passed acts on religion the month following, without reference to the Queen's "intention and pleasure", to obtain which the nobles had engaged themselves that "in the ensuing Convention of Estates some persons of quality shall be chosen for to repair to their majesties and remonstrate (show) to them the state of their affairs, particularly those last mentioned".[6]

(3) When, on 27 January 1560/61, a number of the Lords accepted the Book of Discipline (which embodied recommendations on Church-government and endowment), and promised "to set the same forward at the utmost of our powers", they made this reservation: "Providing that the bishops, abbots, priors, and other prelates and beneficed men, which else have adjoined them to us (this means, who otherwise would have joined us in the reformed Church, but did not), bruik (enjoy) the revenues of their benefices during their lifetimes, they sustaining and upholding the Ministry and Ministers, as is herein specified, for preaching of the Word, and ministering of the Sacraments of God".

For these main reasons the Reformation really left the old Church in being while it laid the somewhat precarious foundations of the new; the old was put into cold storage, the new was born and was breathing vigorously, but was not yet able to take over from the old. Between the two establishments were some clergy who, including three bishops, accepted the Reformation; they belonged to both institutions, receiving their incomes as of old and accepting their creed as of new. It was an anomalous situation, which some of the Roman clergy thought too favourable to them; the Archbishop of St. Andrews and three bishops said, on 22 December 1561, that they would present a quarter of their church incomes for one year, to be at the disposal of the Queen. This was discussed by the Council, which decided that, in the uncertainty as to what was required for the sustenance of the reformed clergy, the maintenance of the Queen and the needs of the realm, one third at least of the revenues of each benefice should be set apart each year until a final settlement was made. This "Assumption of Thirds of Benefices"[7] was decreed on 15 February 1561/2.

Though the Queen made some concessions to the Reformed Church in 1566 and 1567, it was only after her abdication in 1567 that victory was assured to the Reformed faith. In that year, the coronation oath was altered[8] to involve fidelity to the "trew Religioun of Jesus Christ", the Reformed Church was assured of succession to the benefices,[9] and an act was passed[10] ordaining "that the hail thriddis of the haill benefices of this realme sall now instantlie, and in all tymes to cum, first be payit to the ministeris of the evangell of Jesus Christ and their successouris . . . ay and quhill (always and until) the kirk cum to the full possession of their propir patrimonie, quhilk is the teindis". Very much remained to be argued out and bargained for still, which to describe would take us beyond the needs of our present enquiry; but it is relevant that in 1572 an extraordinary General Assembly, called "a convention", meeting in Leith, came to a set of agreed points with the Government. These are known as the "Concordat of Leith". Among other matters, it was settled "that the names and titilis of archebischoppis and bischoppis are not to be alterit or innovat, nor yet the boundes of the dioceis confoundit; but to stand . . . as they did befoir the reformatioun of religioun; at leist to the kingis majesties majoritie, or consent of parliament". The Concordat went on to state the qualifications, method of appointment and spiritual functions of bishops, who were to be "subject to the kirk and generall assembly thairof" and have no authority or duty beyond what superintendents had and exercised.[11]

All this explains why William Chisholm I continued Bishop of Dunblane till he died in 1564, why he could appoint a Roman Catholic Bishop as his "assistant and successor" in 1561, and why that Bishop, his nephew, William Chisholm II, continued to be Bishop of Dunblane till 1573, when all beneficed clergy who remained faithful to the Roman Church and refused their consent to the Reformed faith "salbe *ipso facto* depryvit".[12] It does not explain why William Chisholm II thought it worth while formally to resign his bishopric in 1580, writing from Vaison; it was not his to resign, for he had been deprived.

It will be seen, therefore, that the title of bishop was not entirely empty of content after the Reformation. If he remained Roman, a bishop could not of course legally exercise any of his Roman religious functions, except his own private prayers, but he remained a member of Parliament and Council, was often appointed to parliamentary Committees; he even acted at times in a judicial capacity, and he could continue to live in his "palace", administer the revenues of his diocese, and care for those of the clergy who did not adhere to the Reformed faith; he still drew two-thirds of his income, the remaining third being collected by the Church from 1567, till the Government resumed this task in 1573,[13] on behalf of those qualified and appointed to the various offices of the Reformed Church. There was great scarcity of Reformed clergy for many years, and the General Assembly by enactments at various times authorised other types of temporary and partial ministries, among them superintendents (who took the place and some of the duties of the bishops), commissioners, readers and exhorters. In this exercise the General Assembly was not the sole authority, for the Bishops also admitted clergy to lesser benefices, Deaneries, Archdeaconries and the like.[14] After much discussion in Parliament (the Three Estates) and with many misgivings in the General Assembly, the Assumption of Thirds of Benefices was early accepted by the Church to keep the preachers from starvation. It has been calculated that at the Reformation the Roman Church possessed about half of the land in Scotland, and when a return of the incomes of all benefices had been produced, as the law demanded, it was found that the income of the Roman Church amounted to at least a quarter of a million pounds. Of this income, as has been noted, two thirds were granted by Parliament to the Old Church, now disestablished and in the course of time to lose its title by the death of those who remained in the Roman faith; this was a deplorable settlement for the Reformed Church, but generous to the Roman. Its amount was inspired, not perhaps so much by the generosity of Parliament, largely composed of earls, barons and other landowners, as by a desire on their part to ensure for themselves and their successors the ultimate ownership of the church lands which they had been granted in some form of lease; the zeal of many of the reforming lairds is not above the suspicion of self-interest. In modern times terminable annuities would have been arranged for all clergy who did not conform, and much more would have been thereby saved for the Reformed Church; but in those days when a beneficiary died, the lands from which his income was derived tended naturally to fall into the laps of the landowners, whose lease in most cases became ownership.

The remaining third of the Church's income after expenses of collection had been met amounted to £53,000, when all returns, a tardy business, had been made. Of this sum, a commission of five, all of them Reformed in allegiance, was so mean as to allocate only £24,231 to the maintenance of the Protestant clergy. This parsimonious provision gave stipends between 100 and 300 marks, which were often not fully paid. The remainder of this third was paid into the royal Treasury; but, out of this sum, when pensions to courtiers were made, the Queen's body-guard paid, charitable gifts to penniless nuns and some dispossessed friars given, and Moray, Argyll and many others got their spoil, the Queen would not need much time to count her regal gains.

In these circumstances, very soon after the Reformation there began the break-up of church lands. The way for this had been thoroughly prepared by the transactions of bishops and abbots in the thirty years before the Reformation, William Chisholm I being foremost among his fellows in the traffic. Now the business assumed the proportions of a vast displenishing sale of about a quarter of the lands and farms of Scotland; "sale" is not the word used in such transactions, for sale was forbidden by Church laws, but perpetual or temporary lease for annual rent combined with a preliminary payment was common form. William Chisholm II, his chapter, his dignitaries, canons, prebendaries and chaplains gave lands for money to laymen of means eager to pay the price. And who will blame them? Lands still in their possession at death would revert to the Crown; so alienation by perpetual lease was just prudence, especially when many purchasers were clamouring to buy.

In many cases, for the easing of conscience, alienation of church lands being forbidden by statutes of Church Councils, both general and national, the confirmation of the Pope was asked and often given. For instance, William II, probably in September 1565, perhaps 1566, petitioned the Pope for large powers, which included "to alienate the immovable goods of ecclesiastical benefices by perpetual lease, under pension, tax or yearly rent, not to exceed five ducats only; also to confirm alienations already made".[15] The petition adds that "these faculties are asked for a time only, until some Legate of the Apostolic See be sent for a general reform of the whole Scottish Church, which is now all but extinct". William II may be credited with an honest conviction that the Pope could ultimately redress the temporary uncanonical divergences, though a perpetual lease, if it could be overthrown by a papal legate, should never have been granted. The word "perpetual", however, may only have meant that the lease did not require expensive legal renewal after the customary nineteen years, but continued so long as both parties desired. But though William Chisholm II was in the main honest in his handling of church lands, there were others who were not so scrupulous. In some instances, when a churchman was resisting some greedy seeker after church lands, forgery or force was used, and one villainous Earl of Cassillis tortured and murdered to gain such property for himself.[16] When a Roman bishop died his office was filled generally by a Protestant, who in one instance at least was a layman. He was called bishop, but his function was purely administrative – to allow the displenishment to proceed. This purpose was no longer hidden – one such "bishop", just a lad, of the family of Campbell of Ardkinglass, was presented to the Bishopric of Brechin with power "to dispone and alienate the benefice, as well of the spirituality as temporality of the bishoprick". It was a nauseating business. Such bishops accommodatory the people called "tulchan", which was a stuffed calf-skin placed beside a cow to induce it to yield its milk with gratifying ease and plenitude.

Another course was sometimes taken with church lands and revenues, especially when these belonged to abbeys and priories, whose heads, as many did, accepted the Reformed faith. Their lands were turned into temporal lordships and ended as family property. Other abbacies, having been erected into baronies before the Reformation, were easily transferred when the opportunity came. The provision of a monastery *in commendam* to some powerful churchman or layman worked to the same end, till ultimately the Reformed clergy were left with about one tenth of the property of the Church which had been reformed.

From "Feu-Charters of Kirk-lands",[17] I have noted these Dunblane transactions:

(1) Clevage (1558), lands west of Perth (1563), part of Easter Buttergask (1564), Overardoch (1565), Bridgend, Ramoyle, remainder of Easter Buttergask, Barbush and Leithall, all to James Chisholm of Cromlix (1565); Fundall and Dargall (1567), Tourouchen, etc. (no date), half of Wester Drummaquhence and quarter of Easter D. (1569), all these by William Chisholm I or II according to date.

(2) Glebe-lands and kirk-lands of vicarage of Kippen, by the prebendary (1564); Cluthybeg, by Dean and Chapter (1560); Cur and kirk-lands of Findogask, by the Archdeacon (1576); some part of Glenquhomy, by the Archdeacon (1579); crofts in Dunblane, by the chaplain of St. Blaise's Altar (1564); ruinous manse of the prebend of Monzie by the canon prebendary (1574); property in Dunblane by the Archdeacon (1582); Keirblane by the Dean (1570); waste land in Dunblane by the prebendary of Abernethy (1581); kirk-lands of Monzie by the canon prebendary (undated); Maryland by the Provost of Abernethy (1573); glebe of Strogeich (1564); and others.

These make a formidable list, especially when to them are added the tacks and other transfers of earlier years; they show some of the financial consequences of the Reformation settlement.

William Chisholm II may have visited Dunblane on occasion, if only to supervise the transfer of the Church's property, but no definite record remains of such visits. When he returned to Scotland from the Continent, where he habitually resided, it was not chiefly on the business of the Cathedral and Diocese. He was deeply committed to the effort of his Queen and the Roman

Catholic nobles to undo the Reformation, and to keep close contact with the Pope for the same end. He was a stout Roman and
a very able man, held in the highest regard by Queen and Pope
alike, and it is as the bearer of messages and pleas between Queen
and Pope that he takes a place in international history paralleled
by no previous holder of the episcopal title of Dunblane. His
story belongs much more to the world of political and religious
intrigue and to the church life of Rome and France than to Dunblane, of which he was Bishop only after the Reformation. But I
give its main events in order to complete the picture of the man.

In 1563 Bishop William Chisholm was sent to Rome[18] to carry
to Pius IV assurances of the Queen's loyalty, which had become
suspect when she allowed Archbishop Hamilton of St. Andrews
to be arrested. This must be William II, who was still Bishop
Coadjutor only, for his uncle was too ill to go to Rome. On this
visit the Bishop gave to the Pope a list of the faithful Roman
Catholics among the Scottish nobility, each of whom received
from the Pope a letter of commendation and encouragement.
Again in summer, 1565, he was sent post-haste by Mary, Queen of
Scots, to Rome in order to expedite the papal dispensation
necessary for her proposed marriage to Darnley, who was related
to her within the second of the forbidden degrees. Dispensation
for this degree in the case of princes was reserved to the Pope
himself. Mary's uncle, the Cardinal of Lorraine, had dallied over
the presentation of an earlier petition; so, because of rising discontent among Protestants against the marriage, Mary sent William II, who is recorded as having made a very fast journey; but
he could not overtake the Cardinal, who got the dispensation a
few weeks before he arrived. In any case, Mary was afraid of
growing trouble within the nation and married Darnley on 22
July 1565, some weeks before she knew whether dispensation
would be granted or not. Again, early in 1566 William II was
charged by his Queen and Darnley (now King) to be their orator
(ambassador) to the Holy See, to bear their congratulations to
the new Pope, Pius V, and to ask for money with which to raise
10,000 men for four or five months in order to recover her regal
rights; the Pope was friendly but poor, and gave her much less
than she asked. William II was one of four clergy who assisted
the Archbishop of St. Andrews on 17 December 1566, when he
baptised Prince James, son of Mary and Darnley, in the Chapel

Royal at Stirling. Certainly the most awkward mission given him by the Queen was the fourth, to explain in Paris and Rome her marriage to Bothwell, which took place in the chapel of Holy-roodhouse on 15 May 1567, less than three months after Darnley's murder. This was a Protestant marriage, conducted by Adam, Bishop of Orkney, William Chisholm II being present none the less.[19] He told the French Court and the Pope that it was destiny and necessity, and not her free will, which brought it about. The French said they did not believe this; the Pope was outraged by the dishonourable marriage – "it is not his intention to have any further communication with her, unless, indeed, in times to come he shall see some better sign of her life and religion than he had witnessed in the past".

Bishop William II was also deep in the counsels of the Pope, and the Roman Church. In October 1566 he was sent to Mary at the instance of Vicenzo Laureo, Bishop of Mondovi (later Cardinal Laureo), Papal Nuncio to Scotland's Queen, to carry a suggestion, with which Laureo says that the Bishop of Dunblane agrees, that the quickest way to restore the Roman religion in Scotland was "the punishment of a few seditious wretches"; the Queen should execute with a brave heart this most just punishment, for God's glory.[20] Laureo did not trust the Bishop entirely – "albeit I know he is a true Catholic, pious and very honest, nevertheless . . .", and he sent with the Bishop, and with his consent, the Jesuit father Edmund Hay. Oliver Manare, the Provincial of the French Jesuits, writing on 12 October 1566, about the same mission, is of opinion that William Chisholm's stay in Scotland will be short, "both because of the occupation in which he is engaged, and because he easily changes his mind with the occasion and the need".[21] To her credit, Queen Mary refused to "stain her hands with her subjects' blood".[22]

The reactions of the Scottish Parliament to this twofold activity of William Chisholm II were violent. He was one of the commissioners who had been appointed by Parliament to summon the next, which met in April 1567, and his name is among those who attended it.[23] It cannot have been a very happy occasion for him. Darnley had been murdered and his widow was already preparing the way for her marriage with Bothwell. One Act assured the nation that all who had given their allegiance to the Reformed Church would be undisturbed and unhindered, in accordance with her earlier promise that religious affairs would remain as they were where she arrived in Scotland. Another was sinister; it restored Bothwell, generally accounted one of the murderers of her husband, to her favour, thanked him for his abounding services to her and to the realm, and bestowed upon him his former possessions, of which he had been deprived for complicity in the murderous plot against Darnley. Nevertheless William II was summoned in September of the same year by the Lord Advocate to appear in the Tolbooth of Edinburgh, because, contrary to the law, he had said and heard mass, had administered the sacraments and held communication with the Pope; his alleged licence to do so by the late Queen Dowager was annulled and sheriffs were ordered to proclaim publicly sixty days' warning to him to appear, "because he is furth of this realme"[24]; he was charged with favouring and partaking with the murderers of Darnley; all his tenants were forbidden to pay their rents and dues, and these were arrested until he cleared himself at his trial.

According to a Jesuit source[25] he was tried *in absentia* on 22 November 1567, and sentenced to be deprived of his See and all his property. In 1573 Parliament passed an Act of Conformity,[26] the terms of which were inconsistent with his holding the benefice longer, and in the same year licence was issued to elect his successor to Dunblane.[27] In February 1573/4 the Privy Council forbade, under penalty of death, any dealings with certain ecclesiastics and others, as rebels and outlaws, these including the Archbishop of Glasgow and the Bishops of Ross and Dunblane.[28]

William Chisholm II was probably in Dunblane in the summer of 1565, for on 30 June in that year he wrote a letter, duly witnessed by clerics resident in Dunblane, appointing his brother, James Chisholm of Cromlix, "oure very undoubtit and irrevocable baillie over all the tenants, possessouris and utheris quhatsomevir dwelland within oure said lorschip of Dunblane."[29] The Laird of Cromlix was to be paid £40 yearly from the revenue of the Bishopric. William II was cited to Parliament twice that year, but did not attend.[30] His presence in Scotland in 1567 is proved by his attendance in Parliament that year, but also by his issue of a charter at Dunkeld[31] transferring lands in the parish of Muthill, on intricate and detailed terms, to Malcolm Drummond of Bordland. On 23 May 1567 he granted a charter at the price of 1200 marks, feuing Corscaplie and its teinds to John Charteris of

Kinfawnis, whose wife was Janet Chisholm.[32] Earlier that same month he was present with many magnates when Queen Mary in her foolishness forgave Bothwell for his abduction of her at Dunbar, and because of his good behaviour since, "is minded to promove (promote) him to farther honours".[33] He landed in Scotland "laitly cum fra N." (Netherlands?) in 1569,[34] but there is no sure evidence of his being in Dunblane that year.

Parliament continued to harry him, not as a Roman Bishop of Dunblane, but as one who on public missions was the emissary of the Pope for the restoration of Scotland to the Roman allegiance and in secret journeys and plannings was working for that end. In 1585, when many nobles and others, who had been convicted for "the creull horribill and treasonable murther of our soverane lordis umquhile dearest father" (Darnley), were restored to the King's favour with abolition of the forfeiture they had endured, specially excepted from this generous pardon were the Archbishop of Glasgow, the Bishop of Ross, and "William sumtyme bishope of Dunblane".[35] Shortly after this, King James, in his endeavour to maintain good relations both with Roman Catholic France and Spain and with Protestant England and its Queen Elizabeth, whom to follow on the English throne was the dominating ambition of his life and policy, found it necessary to steer a tortuous political course. How this worked out in the small affairs of his dealings with William Chisholm indicates the twists of policy, the public declarations and the private concessions which he manipulated; James was like a conjuror juggling with a dozen balls, some of which had a propensity for crashing into others; only desperate contortions could at times prevent such a catastrophe. James was often gentle in his dealings with Roman Catholics who broke the law of the land; on the whole, and especially in the early days of his majority, many Roman churchleaders were inclined to believe that he was of their religion at heart and was only waiting the fitting occasion for publicly declaring himself so. It is certain that he had a high regard for William Chisholm, and what Parliament enacted in public James mitigated in Privy Council, as the following outline will make plain:

1585. Parliament excepted William Chisholm II from the general restoration of those who were counted parties to the murder of Darnley; this is noted above;

28 March 1587. King James, for constant affection and faithful service over many past years to his mother, and now continued to him, granted under the Great Seal (RMS V 1173), with consent of the Privy Council, to William, Bishop of Dunblane, contented gratitude in the Articles of Pacification made at Perth on 23 February 1572 and ratified in Parliament in April 1573, as regards the crimes for which forfeiture is imposed, and restored to him his life, lands, benefices, honours and possessions. And he has rehabilitated the said William, notwithstanding the processes of forfeiture and barratry, Acts of Parliament, and expressly the exception contained in the decision of Parliament held at Linlithgow in December 1585.

5 May 1587. James enacted in Privy Council that though Andrew Graham had been elected Bishop of Dunblane in the vacancy, he held his bishopric only until William Chisholm, who had now been restored from the sentences of forfeiture and barratry and reponed in his lands, offices and revenues "for certain good causes and considerations moving his majesty", be fully restored and rehabilitated in Parliament.[36] Meantime Andrew is to have full right to the emoluments.

29 July 1587. Parliament restored William Chisholm, but laid down a condition which William would not even try to satisfy, namely "the same sall nawayes be extendit in his favour qll (till) he have satisfeit Johnne erle of Montrois" and other named, in presence of certain high officers of state.[37]

29 May 1589. The King in Privy Council, while reimposing certain relaxations which William and others had obtained through their residence abroad, dispensed them from giving confession of their faith while outwith the country.[38] It was reported about this time that William had come to Scotland on a mission from the Pope and that he "was well received and permitted to practise in that realm". This may only have been rumour, as it came from England.[39] There seems more truth in another statement in an English agent's report from Scotland that "the bishop of Dunblane returned ill satisfied with the king . . . all hope for the king here (that is, his conversion to Rome) is gone."[40]

Perhaps tiring of his frustrating missions and seeing no hope of Scotland reverting to Roman allegiance, William Chisholm turned his face to Rome and the Continent. He wanted to become a

Jesuit, but his request was refused by authority on the ground that he was more useful to the Church as Bishop. In 1569 he attended the Provincial Council held at Avignon. In that year, or the previous year, he was appointed vicar of Sta. Maria Maggiore and vice-gerent (not vicar general of Rome, as some have asserted) of the Cardinal Vicar of Rome. On 13 November 1570 he was provided as Administrator of the See of Vaison, near Avignon, in France. He was not given the title of Bishop of Vaison, because the Pope still hoped that William II could one day return to a repentant Scotland. The consistorial provision to Vaison's administration, where he was Bishop in all but title, calls him skilled in theology and able to preach in idiomatic French. This office he held for over fifteen years, till on 23 November 1585 Pope Sixtus V granted his request, which his predecessor Gregory XIII had refused, that he be allowed to make his profession in the Grande Chartreuse monastery, near Grenoble. Le Vasseur[41] tells that Chisholm spent his probabtion wearing his episcopal habit. He was succeeded in Vaison by a nephew, also William Chisholm (whom I shall designate as III), second son of James Chisholm, third Laird of Cromlix, who was promoted by the Pope in 1585 from rector of Vaison to Bishop.

In the early days of his probation, William II was sent by the Pope to Scotland in order to bring back a report on the Scottish situation. He reported that the position of the Roman Church there was without hope. In 1587, the General Assembly presented to the King the grievances of the Church, and said in regard to Dunblane that the Bishop, "restored and latelie come home", had been accompanied by a stranger, French or Italian, "supposed . . . to be imployed here in some strange turn", had encouraged the papists and "brought the simple in great doubts, for by his authority he draweth all with him in the old dance. The ministers are hereby despised and troubled in their livings; and the kirks ruined and desolate".[42] It is therefore certain that immediately after his restoration by the Privy Council in May 1587, William Chisholm II returned to Scotland, probably with a Jesuit priest, on his Church's concerns. Early in 1588 it was reported to Walsingham in England that the Scottish-Spanish plotters were expecting the Bishop shortly, for he had gone to Flanders on his way to Scotland on some business with the King himself. The informant, Stafford, promised to keep an eye on the Bishop and hoped to discover his business. There is no record that Chisholm II entered Scotland either in 1585 or 1588; Flanders was near enough for the achieving of his business. Indeed, I think that Stafford was misinformed, and that the man expected was not the Bishop but a relative of the name of Chisholm, who was a secret agent in those days, hand-in-glove with the Spanish plotters. Long before 1588 William II was convinced that he could never return to Scotland as Bishop of Dunblane. There is at Blair's College, Aberdeen, his actual resignation of Dunblane, of date 10 March 1579/80.[43] It was now clear to William II that he could give up thought of Scotland and apply himself to his new commitments with undivided mind.

In the Carthusian Order William Chisholm II won high promotion. He became Prior of the Order, first at Lyons and later at Rome. He probably went to Rome only after 14 July 1591, for on that date John Hay, the Scottish Jesuit, dedicated to William Chisholm, "most religious prior of the Carthusian house of the Holy Spirit at Lyons", his folio edition of *Bibliotheca Sancta*[44] by Sixtus Senensis, a learned scholar and theologian. In the dedication Hay gives ample reasons for the high regard in which William Chisholm was held by his fellows, including the loving care which he bestowed on victims of the plague driven from Avignon, whom he sheltered in his own hospice, "as survivors can testify". The promotion to the Charterhouse at Rome made him *ipso facto* Procurator General of the Order, an office of which he is believed to have been the first holder. When he died at Rome in 1593, he was buried in the cemetery of the Carthusian Church there.[45] The Pope himself was among the mourners present. After the funeral mass, the Pope said to the vicar, "Do not pray for him, but rather for me." A worthy biographical epitaph was inscribed on a monument erected to his memory by his nephew William III, Bishop of Vaison. It gives the date of his death as 26 September 1593. He was sixty-seven years of age.[46]

William Chisholm II is often credited with writing a Latin attack on the Scottish Confession of Faith of 1560, under the title "Examen Confessionis Fidei Calvinianae".[47] In fact, this was written by his nephew, William III. But William II may have written "Discourse of a Scottish to a Spanish Ambassador", an unprinted manuscript in the archives of the Society of Jesus; internal evidence dates it about May 1566.[48] William II is generally credited with compiling lists of the Scottish nobility and bishops according to their Roman or Reformed allegiance. Its date is about 1566; a contemporary copy of it is in the Vatican archives.[49]

The personality of the second William Chisholm is distinct, and only the age in which his lot was cast prevented it from being distinguished. If he had lived in the thirteenth, fourteenth or fifteenth century, his bishopric would have been remarkable, for he was a remarkable man, and it is not likely that a small see in a land on the fringes of the Christian world would for long have satisfied his talents and ambitions. Particularly in the fifteenth century might his gifts have been expected to lead him to high office in the Church abroad. But to a large extent men are governed by the age and country in which they are brought up, and William Chisholm II lived in times which cramped his rightful ambitions. Stormy times confined his possibilities, though not his desires; he was constantly denied that freedom of action which his personality demanded and which would have given him the opportunities of achieving greatness. He held firmly to the Church of Rome, but his times fell in a country where that Church's sun had set, and at a time when intrigue, political ambition and international tensions poisoned the air. As a staunch Roman he could do nothing beyond witnessing to his fidelity – a supreme virtue with its own rewards and consequences, but politically somewhat insignificant. This drove him to the side of those who were doing what they could to overturn the Reformed Church, established by law in 1560, when he was still a canon of the Cathedral. Though these included the Queen and about half of the aristocracy and perhaps a majority of the populace, they were helpless, as the event proved, in reversing the triumph of the new understanding of the Gospel. It is strongly indicative of Popes in the early days of the Reformed Church that William Chisholm II and Bishop John of Brechin (d. 9 April 1566) asked extensive faculties from the Pope[50] as "much needed in the kingdom of Scotland . . . for its salvation of infinite souls who are there perishing". They asked for the powers for a season only, it is true, but in their petition they included the right "to absolve from homicide, heresy, simony, apostasy . . . and other crimes of every nature" . . . to dispense certain monks and mendicant friars, that they might accept benefices, and wear secular dress (other Catholic ministers cannot be found, they say)

. . . to alienate the immovable goods of benefices by perpetual lease up to a limit of five ducats . . . and other faculties of lesser significance. They asked that these powers be given them, as noted earlier, "until some legate of the Apostolic See be sent for a general reform of the whole Scottish Church, which is now all but extinct". In spite of all that had happened and their acknowledgment that their Church had almost ceased to exist, those leaders still hoped for Scotland's return to the Roman allegiance, a hope which others shared. But later the Roman adherents suspected the truth, and finally they knew it. So the staunchest among them carried their strivings underground and kept secret counsels with Rome and even lent themselves to plots, which, though intended for the restoration of the Roman Church in Scotland, would have meant, if successful, the subjection of Scotland to foreign domination as well as the destruction of its Reformed Church. In these subterranean activities William Chisholm II took a ready part, though I believe that his motives were in the main religious and not political; the difficulty was that it was only by political intrigue that the religious cause could hope to gain a speedy victory. A Jesuit report, dated 30 September 1562, says that while the bishops keep quietly at home and "are for the most part destitute of all personal qualifications requisite for taking any lead in such stormy times, the only exception is the coadjutor Bishop of Dunblane. . . . Though holding but a secondary position during the life-time of his superior, he has already made his influence felt . . . having succeeded in confirming a great many people in the faith, and being justly held in high esteem and regarded by all good men."[51] But it is difficult to pardon his approval, for which there is contemporary Roman authority, of the plan which he was sent by Roman Catholic authorities to propose to Queen Mary that the best chance of her recovering lost ground was by the execution of some of the leading nobles among the Reformers. In the eyes of Parliament he was dangerous and a man to be watched; even in the general restoration (1587) of all who had plotted the death of Darnley, Chisholm was still excluded, the only one so rigidly excluded, until he could satisfy the authorities that he had no part in the murder. There is no reason to believe that he even knew of the plot against the King; but being suspect in some matters, he was suspect in all. After about sixteen years in charge of the administration of the Diocese of Vaison, he tired of his Scottish endeavours and entered the Carthusian Order, a disillusioned man. As if to complete the disillusionment the Pope sent him, before he was professed of the Order, while still in his probation, to report on Scotland. What he learned, if he did not see for himself from within Scotland, made it finally acceptable to him that he should leave that realm and enter wholeheartedly on the life of the Grande Chartreuse. In this sphere, his talents found worthier exercise.

The Roman Consistory, in its act appointing him to Vaison, praised abundantly his gifts and graces, not undeservedly. He was a trained theologian and was gifted in languages, speaking idiomatic French, and equipped in Latin and Italian at least. He was a dynamic figure, and sometimes spoke with the tones of such; for instance, in 1571, from Vaison, he wrote to the Laird of Grantully, "You desire to be excused for your sharp writing. The sharpness of it I count nothing, but I will complain to God and our sovereign of the injury done to me by your 'hyct wretting' (insolent writing)." A deserved rebuke, perhaps, but not according to the humility of the saints. He knew where he stood, and stood where he knew. If we cannot find in him much that commands our love, there is much that inspires respect.

NOTES

1. The consistorial act equates £200 Scots with 170 gold ducats of the Camera. Details of this paragraph are culled from Brady, who quotes the act in full.

2. *History of the Church of Scotland* II 144-5.

3. *History of Scotland* II 73-74.

4. AP II 534-5.

5. AP III 72. cf. CSP IV 555, 650.

6. Keith: "History of Affairs of Church and State in Scotland" (Spottiswoode Society) I 298-306.

7. "Thirds of Benefices" (SHS).

8. AP III 23, c. 8.

9. AP III 23, c. 7.

10. AP III 24, c. 10.

11. BUK I 209.

12. AP III 72, c. 3.

13. The government had collected the thirds from 1562 till 1567.

14. See Appendix (post-Reformation appointments). Also SBSH III 1, n. 4.

15. PPN 516-7.

16. J. Cunningham: *Church History of Scotland* I 308/9.

17. FKL, an unpublished MS. in Register House, Edinburgh.

18. Bellesheim: *History of the Catholic Church in Scotland* III 77.

19. *Diurnal of Occurrents* 111-2.

20. PPN 314.

21. PPN 501.

22. PPN cxviii.

23. AP II 546-6-7. In CSP II p. 321, a single sheet "in a contemporary English hand" says that William was appointed a Lord of the Articles on 14 Apr. 1567. This cannot stand against the record in AP II, where his name does not so appear.

24. RPCS I 563, 569.

25. Stevenson: *Mary Stewart*, 146.

26. AP III 72, c. 3.

27. I have therefore fixed 1573 as the end of William Chisholm II's bishopric.

28. RPCS II 334.

29. RMS IV 2910.

30. ATS XI 371-2, 450.

31. RMS V 440.

32. RMS IV 1999.

33. CSP II 573.

34. CSP III 4-5. 15 Nov. 1569.

35. AP III 383. This was repeated, 1587, AP III 467.

36. RPCS IV 163-4.

37. AP III 469.

38. RPCS IV 388-9.

39. CSP IX 363.

40. CSP IX 663. (Report from agent in Scotland to England.)

41. *Ephemerides Ord. Cartus.* III 356ff. Dom. Leo le Vasseur (died 1693) had access to documents since destroyed in the fires (5?) which the Grande Chartreuse has suffered since 1693. He had also the benefit of living traditions.

42. BUK p. 721.

43. This information I owe to the Reverend William James Anderson, M.A., Aberdeen, engaged in research at Blairs. I owe to him also photostats of the resignation which now hang in Dunblane Cathedral Museum. My indebtedness to him is great in other directions also.

44. Lyons, 1591. About 900 pages. The 8 books of Sixtus are issued in one volume.

45. Sta Maria degli Angeli, opposite the railway station; built by Michael Angelo.

46. I also owe much in my study of William Chisholm II to Dom William Curran, librarian of St. Hugh's Charterhouse, Surrey, formerly at Grande Chartreuse, now in Rome, and to Dom Andrew Gray, also of St. Hugh's.

47. Avignon, 1601. French translation, Paris, 1604.

48. Another possible author of it is Yaxley, Archbishop of Glasgow.

49. *Varia Politicorum*, vol. 83, folio 90; quoted in PNN 253ff.

50. Bellesheim: *History of the Catholic Church in Scotland*, III 91; quoted in PPN 516-17. Date is probably Sep. 1565.

51. Nicholas de Gouda, S.J., to the father-general of his order, PPN 113-9; the quotation is from Forbes-Leith: Narratives of Scottish Catholics 75.

THE END

APPENDIX

ABBREVIATIONS

a.	ante, before	fl(s).	florin(s)
ab.	abbot of	fol(s).	folio(s), pages of MS.
adn.	archdeacon of archdeaconry of	*i.a.*	interalia, interalios, among other things or persons
ben(s).	benefice(s) of	ib.	in the same work or author
bp., Bp.	bishop, Bishop of	i.e.	that is to say
bpric.	bishopric of	i.f.o.	in favour of
c.	approximately	i.g.o.	in gift of
cath.ch.	cathedral church of	ill.	illegitimate
cf.	compare	m.	mandate(d), mandatory
ch., Ch.	church, Church	Mr.	magister
chap.	chapel of	n(s).	note(s)
chp.	chapter	nat.	(natural) illegitimate
chr.	chancellor(ship) of	n.p.	notary (public)
cl.	cleric, clerk	O.	Order of (monks, friars)
cn.	canon(ry) of	off.	official (of a cathedral)
cn(s)reg.	canon(s) regular	p.a.	per annum
cn(s)sec.	canon(s) secular	pb.	prebend(ary) of
col.	collated, collation	par.ch.	parish church of
coll.ch.	collegiate church of	p.c.	papal court or camera
c.o.s.	cure of Souls (=pastoral res- ponsibility)	pcr.	precentor(ship) of
		pen.	pension
c.p.	canon and prebendary of, or canonry and prebend of	pet(s).	petition(s)
		pn.	parson(age) of
cpn.	chaplain of	p.(pp.)	page(s)
cr(s).	charter(s)	pr.	prior of
d., D.	diocese of	pro.	provision, provide(d) by or to
dcn.	deacon	prom.	promote(d), promotion
dig(s).	dignity, or dignitary, of (and their plurals)	pt.	priest
		p.v.	perpetual (endowed) vicar- (age) of
disp.	dispense(d), dispensation		
dn.	dean, deanery of	q.v.	"which see"
dom.	dominus, sir	r.	rector(y) of
E.	Earl of	ref.	reference, refer to
ed.	edited, editor, edition	res.	resign(ed), resignation
e.g.	for instance	rsv.	reservation, reserved
el.	elect, elected, election	s.	son of
Eng.	England, English	Sc.	Scotland, Scots, Scottish
excom.	excommunicated, excommu- nication	sdn.	subdean(ery) of
		t.p.	take possession of
ex o.	ex officio, in virtue of his (their) office	tr.	treasurer(ship) of
		U.Ab.	University of Aberdeen
f. ff.	and following page(s)	U.Gl.	University of Glasgow

u.s.	ut supra, as above	Gl.	Glasgow
U.St.A.	University of St. Andrews	Is.	Isles
v.	vicar(age) of	M.	Moray
vac.	vacant, vacancy	O.	Orkney
vl.	valued at	R.	Ross
w.e.p.	with expectation of a prebend	St.A.	St. Andrews
wt(s).	witness(es)		
†	died		
×	between two dates		*Abbeys and Priories*
?	expresses some dubiety	Arb.	Arbroath Abbey
		Camb.	Cambuskenneth Abbey
	Scottish Dioceses	Coup.	Coupar-Angus Abbey
Ab.	Aberdeen	Cul.	Culross Abbey
Ar.	Argyll	Hosp.J.J.B.	Hospital of SS. James and
Br.	Brechin		John, Brackley, North-
C.	Caithness		amptonshire
Db.	Dunblane	Inchaf.	Inchaffray Abbey
Dk.	Dunkeld	Inchma.	Inchmahome Priory
Ga.	Galloway (Whithorn, Can-	Lind.	Lindores Abbey
	dida Casa)	Nuns N.B.	Nuns of North Berwick

THE CLERGY OF DUNBLANE CATHEDRAL

1150-59

　　Bishop　　　M.[1] 1155.

1. As for all the medieval Bps. cf. relevant section of this book.

In Captain Walter Scott's rhyming effusion on *The Right Honourable Name of Scot* (3rd Edition, Hawick 1786), which the author says he had "gathered out of ancient Chronicles, Histories and Traditions of our Fathers", these lines occur on p. 33:

　　　　"Before Alexander the first, his brother Edgar did reign,
　　　　The first that was anointed of Scotland king,
　　　　Reverend John Scot he did surmount,
　　　　Who was bishop of Dunblane, and did the king anoint."

The author gives no reference, but if John Scot was bishop of Dunblane when King Edgar began to reign in A.D. 1097, he belonged to that dimly known period between the passing of the Celtic Church and the organisation of the Roman Church, when an occasional Roman bishop appears here and there. John Scot may have been one of them, cf. Gordon Donaldson: *Scottish Bishops' Sees before David I* in PSAS, 1952-3, pp. 106–17.

1160-69

　　Bishop　　　LAURENCE, *c.*1160 – *c.*1178.

1170-79

　　Bishop　　　SYMON, *c.*1178 – *c.*1196.
　　Deans　　　J. DE DUNBLANE,[1] *c.*1170.
　　　　　　　　THOMAS,[5] *c.*1178 – *c.*1200.
　　Archdeacons　ANDREW[4] OF MUTHILL, *c.*1170.
　　　　　　　　JONATHAN,[2] *c.*1178.
　　Chancellor　NICOLAS, *c.*1170. CR.No. 219.
　　Others　　　MALCOLM,[3] Bp.'s cpn., *c.*1178.

1. wt., CR. No. 218, in agreement between Bp. Db. and Ab. Camb. re Ch. Tulibody. "And the whole Chapter" follows his name; presumably he was Dn.
2. CMN 6–7. Probably became Bp. Db., *c.*1198. LA I 145, 1189×1199, wt., and CL 165, *a.* 20 Mar. 1197/8; wts. as Adn. in both.
3. CMN 6–7, "our chaplain", i.e. Symon's, Bp. Db.
4. CR No. 219, where he is "of Modhel". First recorded Adn. Db.
5. CMN 6–7. Dn. *c.*1198 (CAI No. 3) and *c.*1200 (CAI No. 13).

1180-89

　　　　No new name.

1190-99

Bishops	W.[7] *c.*1196 – *c.*1197.
	JONATHAN, *c.*1198 – 1210.
Archdeacons	JONATHAN,[7] *c.*1196.
	JOHANNIS,[2] *c.*1198.
Canons	MALGIRHE,[1] 1190. CAI Nos. 1, 3.
	MALISE,[5] r. Db., *c.*1196.
Chaplains	MR. WILLIAM DE HALES,[4]*c.*1198.
	HENRY, 1196. C.R. 160–1.
	MALMURE.[1] 1198. CAI No. 3. Bp.'s cpn.
	BEAN,[6] "Magister of Dunblane", *c.*1196.
	CORMAC,[1] pt., Bp.'s. cpn., *c.*1196.
	MAKBETH,[1] pt., cpn. Michael, r. Muthill.
	MALPOLE, Pr. Culdees, *c.*1196. CR. 160–1.
Deacons	GILLEMURE,[1] 1190, CAI No. 1.
	Sir A.,[8] cl. Db., *c.*1198 × 1220.
	MARTIN,[3] "*dapiferus noster*", *c.*1197, CAI 314–15.
	SYTHAKH, Culdee, *c.*1190, CAI No. 1.

1. Note the many Celtic names of this period when many cls. of the old Celtic Ch. were being absorbed into the Roman Ch. Muthill was particularly, and often, named as their ch.

2. CAI No. 3, "Adn. Strathearn". In CL 165 "Adn. Db." He or Jonathan had a son Gilbert, CAI No. 23. CL 165, a. 1198, Johannis is wt. as Adn.

3. The Bp.'s steward, perhaps in minor orders.

4. Ld. C. 425. Also in RPSA 153; Yester Writs, 7; LAc I Nos. 146, 147, 148, 212; CACA I 8–9.

5. CR 160–1. First and only record found of name of bearer of title, "rector of Dunblane".

6. CR. 160–1. Office unknown, but perhaps a chp.

7. CR 160–1 dates this undated cr. as *c.*1210. I have dated it *c.*1196. On this cr. depend the dates of "Adn. Jonathan, my cpn.", Henry cpn., Malise, r. Db., and Bean, Mr. Db., etc. Reasons? (1) *c.*1210, Gilbert was Adn. (*c.*1208–35). (2) before Gilbert, Johannis was Adn. This cr. gives W. as Bp. Db.; see text, ch. III.

8. HMC VII 704b, *c.*1198 × 1220. In minor orders; perhaps Abraham, later Bp. Db. See ch. III.

1200-09

Bishop	JONATHAN, *c.*1198 – 1210.
Dean	THOMAS, *c.*1200, CAI No. 13, cf. 1178.
Archdeacon	G,[2] *c.*1208.
Chaplains	MAURICE ⎫ [1]
of Bp.	GILLECRIST ⎬ *c.*1200.
	PATRICK ⎭
Others	MALGEGILL, Pr. Muthill,[3] *c.*1200.

1. CR 312–3, where Gillecrist and Patrick are each "our cpn.". In CAI No. 10, c.1200, Maurice is again "our cpn." Patrick is "son of Gillemanthach". Gillecrist is also a Celtic name. Maurice was probably Norman.

2. CAI No. 27. Also CAI No. 28 (1210–); in CAI No. 30, he is Gilbertus. Frequent wt. till 1235 (CL 54–57). cf. CACA I 81. Son of Adn. Jonathan or of Adn. Johannis. See 1190–99, n. 2; "Gilbertus filius archidiaconi de Stratheryn" in CAI No. 23.

3. CR 312–3, 398.

1210–19

Bishop	ABRAHAM, c.1212 – c.1225.
Dean	MATTHEW,[5] 1214.
Archdeacon	(GALFRIDUS)[3], 1212.
Canons	INNOCENT ⎫[7] WILLIAM ⎬ c.1214. NICHOLAS ⎭
Chaplains	WILLIAM,[1] Bp.'s cpn., c.1211. PETER ⎫[6] WILLIAM ⎬ c.1214. RALPH ⎭
Others	MACBETH,[2] *rex scolarum de Dumblayn*, c.1214. JOHN and ⎫[4] LUKE ⎬ c.1214. "our clerks", ⎭

1. CAI No. 30.
2. CL 49. See text, ch. III. cf. CL liii–lvi.
3. Reg. de Passelet (Paisley) 229. This is probably an error for Gilbertus, Adn. c.1208–35. I have found no other ref. to an Adn. Galfridus (Geoffrey). CL Index has "Galfrid. Bp. Db.", but this is a slip for "Bp. Dk." cf. HMC VII 704b, dated 1198 ×1220.
4. CMN 11–12; CR 123, 161; LAc I No. 213. In CACA I 80, "Mr. Lucas".
5. LAc I No. 213. Still Dn. c.1230, under Bp. Osbert, CR. 161–2.
6. These 3 wt. as "cpns." in a sentence of Bp. Abraham re teinds of Abernethy. LAc I No. 214. Doutless they were Abraham's cpns. William certainly was, c.1211 (CAI No. 30) and c.1220 (CR 161). Ralph was perhaps Bp. el. Db., c.1225 (but not consecrated).
7. LAc I No. 215. These 3 are designated "canons", wts. in a cr. repeating the sentence (in n. 6 above). As "William cpn. of Bp. Abraham" wts. the cr. as well as "William, canon", there were two Williams.

1220–29

Bishops	RALPH, c.1225 – c.1226, el. only. OSBERT, c.1227 – c.1230. (No other clergy named in records)

1230-39

Bishop	CLEMENT,[6] 1233 — 58.
Deans	MATTHEW, 1230, CR 161–2, cf. 1214.
	MARTIN, "Dn. of Menteith",[1] 1235.
Archdeacons	DOM. G., 1230, CR 161–2, cf. 1208.
	MR. LUKE,[2] 1235.
Chaplains	GILLEBARAN,[3] c.1235.
	PADYN,[4] c.1235.
Others	ALEXANDER ⎫ [5]
	ADA ⎬ c.1230.
	THOMAS ⎭

1. CL 54–57, 7 May 1235. His title seems to imply that he was "rural dn."; there was also a dn. of Muthill, cf. 1272, n. 5.

2. CL 54–57. "Clericus noster" *a.* 1223, CR 123, LAc I 213. Later Dn., *c.*1247, q.v.

3. CL 57–59. Wts. as cpn., 7 April 1239, CL 59–60.

4. CL 57–59. Wts. as "presbyter of Mothel" (Muthill), date and ref. in n. 3 above.

5. wts. as "*servatores nostri*", CR 161–2. May have been in minor orders.

6. See ch. IV. After 1240, the Abbots of Inchaf., Arb., Lind., and Camb., were cns. *ex o.*, Ab. Inchaf. being granted the precentorship (next in authority to the Dn.). Their names are to be found in CAI, LAc, CL and CR. Spottiswode I 213–5 says Clement "gave divers lands and rents to the church of Culros", but without refs.

1240-49

Bishop	CLEMENT, 1233 — 58.
Deans	W., 1240, CAI No. 67.
	MR. LUKE, c.1247, CAI No. 75.
Archdeacons	MR. LUKE, 1240, CAI No. 67.
	MR. DUNCAN,[1] 1248 × 1258.
Precentor[2]	NICOLAS, 1240, CAI No. 67.

1. Duncan takes the place of Luke, prom. dn. He wts. as "Adn. of Strathearn", CL No. 28.

2. As Ab. Inchaf. was a dig. of Db. Cath., I shall enter his name in this fashion. The student will find the names of the other cns. *ex. o.*, who were members of Chp. Db. Cath. as indicated in n. 6 of 1230–39, but I shall not enter them in this Appendix. I shall however call attention to any necessary corrections in their names, dates, etc.

1250-59

Bishops	CLEMENT, 1233 — 58.
	ROBERT DE PREBENDA, 1258 — 84.
Dean	ROBERT DE PREBENDA,[1] 1255 — 58.
Canon	MR. RICHARD STIRLING,[2] 1259.
Others	Three unnamed cls., 1259, CPR I 367.

1. CPR I 318–9; T. No. 66. Papal cpn., 1256, CPR I 334. The first pluralist noted in D. Db.; a mild example, but a portent.

2. CPR I 367. As the name Stirling is found in over 30 different spellings, I use the modern spelling throughout, except when the old spelling would be of interest. So with other names. Here it is "Strivelin".

1260-69

Bishop	ROBERT DE PREBENDA, 1258 – 84.
Dean	DOM. HENRY, 1266. CAI No. 4 of Appendix (p. 157). Brackley D.116.
Officials	MR. RICHARD DE STIRLING, 1266, CAI p. 157. Brackley D.116.
	MR. B., 1269, CAI p. 159.
Canons	MR. WILLIAM DE LACORNERE,[1] 1263.
	DOM. JACOBUS, r. Balquhidder, 1266 – c.1275, CAI Nos. 95, 96, 100, 102, 104, 105.

1. CPR I 416, 10 Dec. 1263. See ch. V. Obviously of Norman or French origin.

1270-79

Bishop	ROBERT DE PREBENDA, 1258 – 84.
Deans	DOM. J.[2] (JOHN), 1271.
	MR. THOMAS,[3] c.1272 – 90.
	DOM. DONALD,[5] dn. Muthill, 1272.
Canons	MAGISTRI RICHARD,[1] GILBERT and J. DE LOGY,[2] 1271.
	MR. JOHN DE ROGLYN,[4] 1273.

1. CAI No. 98. In CAI No. 102, c.1272, he is "Richard de Stirling". In CAI No. 118, 1287 he is "late v. of Strogeith". In Bagimont he is "Mr. R. de Stirling" (1st year) and "Mr. Richard" (2nd year). His tax each year is 32d; his pb. (not named in B., but it was Strogeith) was worth £1. 6. 10 p.a. T. No. 264.

2. J. de Logy, CAI No. 98; Mr. John de Logy in CAI No. 99, both 98 and 99 being dated 1271. In B. he is taxed 14s. 10½d., and so his unnamed pb. was worth £7. 8. 9 p.a. T. No. 264. In CAI No. 100, also 1271, he is "Dom. Johannis at that date dn. of Strathearn and r. of Glendevon". He was very soon succeeded by Thomas, as Dn.

3. CAI No. 102, c.1272. Still Dn. 1282/3, CAI No. 112. On 15 Jul. 1274, CAI No. 104, commissioned by Pope to recover the possessions of Inchaf. Still Dn. c. 1290, and wt., HMC VII 705a.

4. CR 24–5. Rutherglen still often called Ru'glen. Note that the designations "de Roglyn", "de Stirling", etc., in case of a cl. means generally only his place of birth or upbringing, not that he had an estate. I suspect that many a Norman cl. adopted a Scottish place-name for strategic reasons.

5. CAI No. 102, wt. as "dean of Metthel", which I take as Muthill. Probably a rural dn. cf. Martin, 1235, n. 1.

1280-89

Bishop	WILLIAM, 1284 – 96.
Precentor	HUGH, c.1282.
Archdeacons	MR. AUGUSTINUS, 1283, CAI No. 112.
	W. DE MONROS, 1287, CAI No. 118.
Official	unnamed, 1280, HMC VII 705a.
Canons	ALPIN ⎫[1]
	W. DE STIRLING ⎬ 1287, CAI No. 118.
	ROBERT DE DUNDE ⎭

1. One of the wts. who saw Inchaf.'s crs. proving its patronage of Strogeith, in addition to the three cns., the Bp., Adn., etc., was "Moynache filius alpini". Alpin was el., confirmed and consecrated Bp. Db., in 1296.

1290-99

Bishops	WILLIAM, 1284 – 96.
	ALPIN,[1] 1296 – 1300.
Dean	JOHN,[2] 1296.
Precentor	THOMAS, 1296.
Archdeacon	WALTER,[3] 1292.
Chancellor	PETER, 1296, T. No. 355.
Treasurer	GEOFFREY,[3] 1292.
Canons	JAMES KARDEN,[5] c.1294.
	MICHAEL DE DONO,[6] 1296.
	WILLIAM DE GOSFURD,[4] 1296.
Chaplain	SIR MICHAEL,[7] c.1290.

1. T. No. 355 gives full details of his el., with names of digs. and cns. who composed the electoral college. See ch. VI. cf. SDI II 115–8.

2. T. No. 355. Still Dn., 24 Aug. 1302, CL 177.

3. T. No. 355. Walter, Adn., and Geoffrey, Tr., were appointed, 1292, collectors of the tenth in Scotland for the Holy Land, Rot. Scotiae I 7b. This six-year tenth was granted to King of England when Scotland had no king and was ruled by Guardians.

4. T. No. 355. In 1309, T. No. 387, he is "cn. Db. presbiterus" (pt.). In CPR II 53, he had 5 prebends (in Db., Gl., Carlisle, York and Lincoln dioceses). See ch. VI. He is the first notorious pluralist recorded in Db. The Pope, 20 Mar. 1308/9, after making many arrangements for him, wrote "No one is therefore to oppose our abolition, remission, donation, collation, provision and dispensation."

5. Dempster: Eccles. History, quoted in A. B. Barty: History of Db., p. 25, "of ancient lineage, and of great talent", author of "some noteworthy theological volumes."

6. Cn. in T. No. 355, 1296. In HMC VII 705a, c.1290, there is a cr. in which a wt. is "Sir Michael, cpn.; "other wts. are of Db., e.g. Mr. Thomas, dcn. (perhaps here meaning Dn.) of Db. and Allan of Kynbuc. Michael was therefore probably cpn. before he was cn.

1300-09

Bishops	NICHOLAS[1] I, 1301 – 07.
	NICHOLAS[2] II (DE BALMYLE), 1307 – 19.
Dean	One unnamed,[3] 1307.
Precentor	MAURICE,[4] 1307 –
Archdeacon	MAURICE DE STRATHEARN,[5] 1306.
Canons	NICHOLAS DE BALMYLE, elected Bp. 1307 ⎫
	WILLIAM DE EGLISHAM, 1307 ⎬ T. No.
	HENRY DE STIRLING, 1307 ⎭ 386.
	ADAM DE MORAVIA.[6]
Canons ex	WILLIAM, Ab. Lind., 1307.
officio	MICHAEL,[7] Ab. Camb., 1307.

1. He was Ab. Arb. and cn. *ex o.* when appointed by the Pope. T. No. 369. Spottiswode says he gave half of Ch. of Strowan to Inchaf. But he did not know that there were two Bishops called Nicolas in succession.

2. Before el., he was cn. Db., T. No. 386.

3. T. No. 386, present with 3 cns. named (Nicholas de Balmyle, William de Eglisham, Henry de Stirling) and 3 cns. *ex o.* (abs. Inchaf., Lind., Camb. – Ab. Arb. absent) when Cn. Nicholas de Balmyle was el. There is no other known record of Ab. Lind. being cn. Db. *ex o.*, and no record of his being granted cn. Db., but it was probably *c.*1240, in Clement's general settlement. This lack of record is probably due to CL being an incomplete collection of Lind. crs.

4. T. No. 386. Succeeded Nicholas de Balmyle as Bp. Db.

5. CR 81. Previously v. Clackmannan.

6. RDD 355, 1307 × 1318. On 15 Oct. 1328, he is Bp. el. Brechin, DBS 180. Chr. of Scotland, 1331/2 – see ERS, and CACA I 240-1. From 1328 to 1349 he was Bp. Br., DBS 180/1.

7. I have entered these because there is no other known record of their being abs. of their monasteries. cf. CL 306.

1310-19

Bishops	NICHOLAS DE BALMYLE, 1307 – 19.
	(ROGER DE BALNEBRICH,[3] el. 1319.)
	(MAURICE,[3] Ab. Inchaf., 1322.)
Archdeacon	WILLIAM,[2] 1315.
Canon	ROGER DE WEDALE,[1] 1312.

1. CPR II 102, 23 Sep. 1312, given m. by Pope. CACA I 146 suggests him as cl. of same name who appears as r. of Kinnell in crs. 67 and 92 in CACA I, and also, *c.*1300, in No. 69 of crs. in General Register House; also, as pb. Mortlach wt. on 15 Dec. 1321 (RA I 47). *c.*1391, REM 117 in retrospect refers to R. de W. who got grant of Domus Dei of Elgin. He may also be found in CACA I 150, 151, where a 1440 notarial instrument cites a cr. of 1300, in which R. de W. was wt.

2. CR 270/1, 19 May 1315, where he is also cn. Dk.

3. See ch. VI.

R

1320-29

Bishop	MAURICE,[1] 1322 – 47.
Dean	DONALD, *c.*1322 – 28, CACA I 224–5.
Precentor	Ab. CRISTIN, *c.*1320.
Official	MR. WILLIAM DE ECFORD,[3] 1322.
Canons	WALTER DE DUPPUL, c.p. 1329, CPR II 285.
	JOHN DE LEYS,[2] c.p. 1329, (v. Abernethy).

1. In the long vac., 1319–22, King of England urged Pope to pro. Friar Richard de Pontfreynt, O.P., BC III 689. cf. T. Nos. 216, 217. CPR II 222.

2. CPR II 203. Pluralist. In 1329, c.p. Dk., c.p. Db., had pen. of 100 sh. from Db., pen. of 3 marks from St.A., and was given by Pope in addition a cn. Gl. w.e.p. In 1331, CPR II 363, Pope pro. him to c.p. M. In 1332, CPR II 384, domestic cpn. to James, Bp. St.A., and pro. r. Kynkell (d. St.A.).

3. CACA I 224. Only recorded ref. to this Off. Db. Dr. D. E. Easson refs. to one of this name, DRR 340, 347, as procurator of Dunfermline 1311 and 1314/5, and as Off. of Adn., Gl., and rural dn. of Kyle, M. 401.

1330-39

Bishop	MAURICE, 1322 – 47.
Precentor	WILLIAM.[2]
Canon	MALCOLM DE INVERPEFFRY,[1] 1332.

1. CPR II 386. He was M.A. Had no pb. in D. Db., but was r. Strathbroc (d. St.A.), cn. Gl. w.e.p. and is now pro. by Pope to c.p. Dk. Pluralism was increasing in the ch. of Sc., and continued to grow.

2. Conjectured between Cristin and Symon de Scone, as Ab. Inchaf. cf. CAI pp. 252–3.

1340-49

Bishops	MAURICE, 1322 – 47.
	WILLIAM, 1347 – 61.
Archdeacons	WILLIAM DE IHETEME,[2] 1344.
	WALTER DE COVENTRE,[2] 1345.
Canons	WILLIAM,[1] 1347.
	KESSAN, 1347, CPR II 258.
	MR. MALCOLM DE DRUMBREC,[3] 1349.
Others	NICHOLAS DE KYNBUCK,[4] 1348.

1. Bp. Db. same year, T. No. 576.

2. William de Coventre, scholar and diligent pluralist, became Bp. Db., 1361. Here are details of his ecclesiastical and scholastic progress:

1333, "determinant" (intending a degree) in U. Paris – Auctarium Chart. Uni. Paris. I (cf. DBS 204n).

1345, CPR Pet. I 89–90, "of D. Db.", M.A., Lic. Civil Law, pets. for Adn. Db., vac. by reason that William de Iheteme, since deceased, accepted Adn. Dk. and held both offices without papal disp. (CPR III 198 and CPR Pet. I 89, tell that Wm. de I. resigned his Adn. Db. to become Adn. Dk. But Walter de C. could not wait to verify the facts.) His pet. says he is c.p. R., c.p. Abernethy, cn. Dk. w.e.p.

1345, pro. Adn. Db., but his expectation of pb., Dk., is annulled, CPR III 198, CPR Pet. I 89, CL 292.

1348/9, CPR Pet. I 145, he "a Scot, of D. Db. . . . envoy of U. Orleans" asks for Dn. Ab., though he has the above offices; says he is willing to resign his expectation of a pb., Dk. Granted.

1348/9, CPR III 290, CPR Pet. I 149, pro. Dn. Ab., and again told to resign expectation of pb. Dk. His Adn., Db., has not been mentioned in any pet. since 1345, which means that it had not taken effect.

1349, CPR III 351, he is D.C.L., Dn. Ab., and is allowed to enjoy income of Dn. for 5 years while he studies civil law at a university. He is still only sub-deacon, and not in pt.'s orders.

1350, CPR III 390, he is D.C.L., M.A., L.C.L., and Dn. Ab. Pope rsv. for him a ben. (D. St.A.) worth 27 marks with, or 20 marks without, c.o.s.; he is to res. Dn., but was still Dn. Ab. in 1353 and 1361, see below. He is still c.p. R. and Dk.

1350, Professor in Orleans U., SHS Misc. II 101.

1350, CPR I 413, T. No. 589, is at Rome as procurator in res. of Roger, Bp. R.

1353, envoys of U. Orleans, pet. i.f.o. Walter de C. (himself an envoy) for c.p. M. w.e.p. The petition as in duty bound mentions that he is Dn. Ab., c.p. Dk. and R. (he has evidently res. his c.p. Abernethy). CPR Pet. I 241. CPR III 480.

1357, CPR III 435. disp. to hold Dn. Ab. and named ben. (D. St.A.).

1361, Walter de C. has now taken pt.'s orders, and is prom. from Dn. Ab. to Bp. Db., and is consecrated. CPR Pet. I 325. As soon as he is pro. Bp. Db. he sends 3 petitions to the Pope:

(1) CPR Pet. I 375, i.f.o. Michael de Monimusk, L.C.L., for Dn. Ab. This is another eager pluralist, not so successful as Walter. Walter in this pet. describes himself as "Dn. Db., c.p. Db., Br. and R." Prom. from Dn. Db. to Dn. Ab., on his becoming Bp. Db. Now Adam de Tiningham (D. St.A.), papal sub-collector for Scotland, hammers at the papal door for Dn. Db. – CPR Pet. I 379.

(2) CPR Pet. I 375, 409, i.f.o. his kinsman, Andrew Ox, to be given the Ch. Inverarity (D. St.A.) vac. by Walter's consecration as Bp. Db. (Inverarity was a preserve of the De Coventres – a. 1345, held by John de C. who res. it; 1345 by William de C. (d. Db.) L. Civil Law, who was also c.p. R. and Abernethy, CPR Pet. I 89; in 1361, Walter de C. held it, and res. on becoming Bp. Db.)

(3) CPR Pet. I 375, i.f.o. William Emerici (Mercer) to obtain Walter de C.'s c.p. Dk. William Emerici had "the Ch. of St. Modoc, D. of Db." (Editors of several of the records think this is St. Madoes, which was not in D. Db. I think it is Kilmadock.)

3. CPR Pet. I 175–6, 1349, Malcolm de Drumbrec was cn. w.e.p.; also v. Tarvas (D. Ab.) and was petitioning the Pope for c.p. C. He was a cl. (D. Ab.).

4. CPR III 297, 1348, was "of D. Db.", petitioned for ben. i.g.o. Bp. St.A. Other refs., CPR Pet. I 142, and CAI No. 132, where in 1358 he is Adn. Db. In 1360, Sir Nicholas de Kinbuck, Adn. Db., and others gave account of the third contribution towards the King's ransom from the Stewartry of Strathearn, ERS II 43.

1350-59

Bishop	WILLIAM, 1347 – 61.
Archdeacon	NICHOLAS DE KINBUCK,[1] 1358.

1. See n. 4 under 1340-9. In CAI No. 132, 11 Apr. 1358, as Adn., he confirms an agreement between Db. and Inchaf. of 1266 re Nesgask (= Findogask, Gasknes or Gask) which was Adn.'s mensal. In ERS II 43 he is designated Dom. a title increasingly used by cls. of all ranks.

1360-69

Bishop	WALTER DE COVENTRE,[1] 1361 – 71.
Deans	MICHAEL DE MONYMUSK,[2] res., 1361.
	ADAM DE TININGHAM,[3] 1361.
	HENRY DE DUNBLANE,[4] c.1366 – c.1380.
Precentors	SYMON DE SCONE, a.1365.
	JOHN, 1365.
Archdeacon	ANDREW, 1365, CAI No. 135.

1. See n. 2 under 1345.
2. CPR Pet. I 375. In 1361, he res. and became Dn. Ab.
3. CPR Pet. I 379, 1361, he is pro. Dn. Db. See n. 2, under 1345. A most diligent petitioner for papal privileges – in CPR Pet. I, between 1344 and 1380, when he was consecrated Bp. Ab. there are 12 pets. by, and papal concessions to, him. In the course of these we learn that he was secretary of William, E. Douglas, cl. of the King and Queen of Scots, a member of the Pope's household. In 1378, as Dn. Ab., he petitioned i.f.o. 4 kinsmen, one nephew and one cpn. "who has served him faithfully for 20 years".
4. For this dn., see n. 9 under 1381.

1370-79

Bishops	WALTER DE COVENTRE, 1361 – 71.
	ANDREW, 1372 – 80.
Precentors	WILLIAM, 1370 – 73.
	JOHN DE KELLY, 1373 – c.1380.
Archdeacons	DAVID BELL,[2] 1375.
	MAURICE DE STRATHEARN,[1] 1378.
Treasurer	MICHAEL MANYSON,[3] a.1379.
Canon	DOUGAL (Bp. 1380).
Others	JOHN DE BALNANYS,[4] "of the D. Db.".

1. CPR Pet. I 556-9. Before holding this dig. he was v. Clackmannan.
2. CCS II 75. In 1377, ERS II 554, he was collector of royal taxes in Strathearn. Earlier refs. speak of him as "cl. of the wardrobe". When Adn. he is "cl. on probation of our Lord the King working in the office of the cl. of the wardrobe", 1375, and draws his salary, £40, "from the start of this account" CCS II 85. This is not the David Bell, cn. Inchaf., who became Ab. Holyrood, etc. CAI p. 253.
3. CPR Pet. I 541-2, noted as dead at 1379. Died as p.v. Abernethy (D. Db.) vl. £10, which office he had held for one month only.
4. CPR Pet. I 542. Pets. for ben. i.g.o. Lind., though he has a pb. Abernethy. Granted by Pope.

1380-89

Bishop	DOUGAL, 1380 – 1403.
Dean	DAVID DE STIRLING,[9] 1381.
	One unnamed,[1] probably D. DE S. above.
Precentor	WILLIAM DE CULROS, 1381.

Canons   ROBERT DE CARDUN,[5] 1380.

DUGAL DE LORNE,[6] 1380.

DONALD,[7] 1380.

DAVID DE STIRLING,[9] 1381.

Others   ANDREW DE KYLE,[3] 1380.

JOHN ENERICI,[4] 1380.

THOMAS FABER,[8] 1381.

WILLIAM DE KIRKINCOLAYTH[10] (Kirkintilloch), 1387.

Students from Dunblane[2] at U. Cologne, 1389 – 1559.

1. In 1384, 1386, 1388 (twice), and 1390, Dn. Db. (unnamed) received £5 for his labours in the office of the chamberlain of the King, "by grace of the auditors" – ERS III 245, 677, 684, 688, 694.

2. J. H. Baxter in "Sc. Notes and Queries", 1931, p. 104, notes that 1389 × 1559, the Register of U. Cologne records 55 students from D. Db. (38 from St.A., 12 from Gl., 3 from Dk., 1 from the Hebrides, 1 from R.) There may be others among those recorded simply as "from Scotland".

3. CPR Pet. I 552. Bp. Ab. pets. i.f.o. him a cn. Db., w.e.p. Andrew is a pt., "who with very great pains and miseries has followed the papal court in Italy" – an expensive and often heart-breaking business for men of no influence. Granted by Pope: but we hear no more of Andrew.

4. This should read Emerici – see n. 2, 1345. Same ref. as n. 3 above, Bp. Ab. asks for John E. of D. Db. a ben. i.g.o. Lind. Granted.

5. DBS 70n. In 1379/80 he is "student in arts at Paris", and has c.p. Db. and Dk. Robert II pets. for his being given a cn. M. w.e.p. These were to support him in his studies, his work in the 3 ds. being done by cls. paid by him, or just neglected and left to vs., paid from teinds.

6. CPR Pet. I 554. He is of d. Ar., c.p. Db. and Dk. Pets. for ben. i.g.o. Bp. St.A. Cpn. and secretary of Robert, E. Fife and Menteith, second son of King of Scotland, who pets. in his favour, saying he has studied canon and civil law for 3 years, to receive a cn. Db., w.e.p., *though he is already c.p. of the same*, and has Ch. Kilmor (D. Ar.). Strange request! Stranger still Pope should write "granted". In CR 168–170, 174–5, Bp. James Chisholm told Ab. Camb. that he could not be twice c.p. in the same chp. and cath.; but the Ab. did manage to be c.p. of Kippen and of Kincardine (in Menteith), both in D. Db.

7. CPR Pet. I 554, "son of Giles of Strathearn", pt., c.p. Db., asks for cn. Dk. w.e.p., 1380.

8. CPR Pet. I 559, 1381, Robert, King of Sc., pets. i.f.o. this cl. for a cn., Db., w.e.p.

9. CPR Pet. I 556, 1381, is col. to Dn. Db. by Pope *proprio motu* (of his own accord) with the annexed c.p. void by death of Henry of Db. He was therefore Dn. and c.p. Db. I have found no other trace of Henry of Db., but as Adam de Tiningham was still Dn. Db. in 1365, and was probably transferred to Dn. Ab. shortly thereafter, I have put Henry de Db. as Dn. Db. tentatively *c.*1366. In 1366, David de Stirling res. Culter (D. Gl.) CPR Pet. I 519. In 1381, Robert II of Scotland petd. for David de S. his cpn. for a cn. Gl., w.e.p. CPR Pet. I 559. For another David de Stirling, see n. 9 under 1420.

10. In 1387, CPR Pet. I 569, Matthew, Bp. Gl., pets. i.f.o. William de K. for a cn. Db., w.e.p. He has the Ch. Kirkinclayth, but is ready to resign it. (May be Kirkintilloch.)

1390-99

Bishop	DOUGAL, 1380 – 1403.
Dean	DONALD DE BUTE,[1] 1394.
Precentor	WILLIAM FRANKLYN, – 1398.
Archdeacon	FINLAY COLINI,[2] 1400.
Treasurer	EUGENIUS DE DUMBARTON,[8] 1394.
Canons	FINLAY COLINI,[2] 1394.
	RICHARD KNIGHT,[10] 1394.
Chaplain	MAURICE,[5] 1394.
Others	NIGEL CAMPBELL,[6] 1391.
	GILBERT DE STRATHEARN,[3] pt., 1394.
	JOHN DE SPYNY,[4] 1394.
	JOHN LANG,[7] pt., 1394.
	ROBERT CANTORIS,[9] 1394.

1. CPR Pet. I 615, 1394. (1) Robert, Duke of Albany, pets. in his favour for a cn. M. w.e.p. (2) Donald de B. is pro. to Dn. Db. In 1381, Bp. Whithorn pets. in his favour for ben. i.g.o. Dunfermline Abbey, though he has Ch. Struan (D. Dk.), CPR Pet. I 564. In 1390, CCS II 174, Dn. Db. draws £5 for diligence in office of *camerarius* (chamberlain). In 1403, still Dn., and cn. Ab., pets. for a cn. Dk. w.e.p., CPR Pet. I 631. In 1406, 1407/8, 1408, he is auditor of accounts in the Royal Treasury, while still Dn. ERS IV 1, 40, 64, CCS IV 1, 35, 40, 64. See 1400-1409, n. 4.
2. CPR Pet. I 615, 618. Finlay is c.p. Db., p.v. Abernethy, and has the bens. of Ferlyn (d. Db.) and Hospital of Ochtirogle (d. St.A.), vl. 100 francs, in 1394, when Robert, Duke of Albany, King's brother, pets. for him, who is his cpn. and B.C.L., for a cn. Dk. w.e.p. Ferlyn was Erolyn, a chap. attached to Abernethy, when the latter was appropriated to Arb. (Reg. Vetus. No. 241); when Erolyn became a par. ch. (Errol), it was in D. St.A. In 1400, CPR Pet. I 615, he is Adn. Db.; also in 1401 (CPR Pet. I 618). Spottiswode calls him Finlay Dermoch.
3. CPR Pet. I 615, 1394, Robert, Duke of Albany, pets. for this pt. (D. Db.) for a ben. i.g.o. bp. Gl. He "has studied canon law for 3 years". Granted.
4. CPR Pet. I 613-4, 1394, John de Spyny is "a scholar in arts", and pets. for a cn. Db. w.e.p. Granted.
5. Bp. Dougal asks for his cpn. Maurice, in 1394, pro. of a cn. Db. with rsv. of a pb. though he has a p.v. in d. Db. CPR Pet. I 591-2.
6. CPR Pet. I 576, 1391, Nigel C. (d. Db.) pets. for Ch. St. Mary, Arran (Kilmory), D. Sodor. Same year and ref. Denis Bricii Abothill, pt. D. Down (Ireland) pets. for ben. i.g.o. Bp. and Chp. of Db., or of Inchaf. This was granted by Pope, but I have found no trace of Denis in Scotland.
7. CPR Pet. I 589-590, 1394, Bp. Dk. pets. i.f.o. John Lang, pt. for ben. i.g.o. Bp. and Chp. Db. Granted.
8. CPR Pet. I 615-6, 1394, King Robert III pets. i.f.o. Eugenius de D., Tr. Db., for ben. vl. 40 marks i.g.o. Paisley Abbey or Ab. Kilwinning though Bp. Db. has pro. him to Tr. Db. Granted. He again pets. 1405, for E. de D., his cpn, for ben. in Db., vl. £10. Granted. CPR Pet. I 630. This is repeated in 1406, CPR Pet. I 622-3.
9. CPR Pet. I 613, Robert III pets. 1394 in "Roll of the Coronation" (installation of Pope Benedict XIII, an Avignon Pope) that R.C. be pro. to a ben. i.g.o. Bp. and Chp. Db. Granted.

10. CPR Pet. I 616, 1394, Richard Knight is an interesting person. Was a soldier, a *miles* (hence his name, Knight), who became a pt. and was secretary to Robert Stewart, Duke of Albany, E. Fife and Menteith. Also Lic. in Arts, had studied canon law for many years, had often laboured for the Ch. So states the pet. 1394 of Duke of Albany asking for Richard K. a ben. vl. 60 marks, i.g.o. Bp. St.A., though he has Ch. of Comrie, D. Db., and chap. Tannadice, D. St.A. Granted.

1400–09

Bishop	FINLAY DERMOCH (FINLAY COLINI[5]), 1403 – 19.
Dean	DOM. GILBERT DE OCHTERTYRE,[1] *c.*1400.
	DOM. DONALD DE BUTE, [4] 1394 – 1408.
	GILBERT,[1] 1409, RBM I 258.
Archdeacon	FINLAY DERMOCH,[2] 1400, CPR Pet. I 615.
Others	ANDREW DE FULLARTON,[3] 1403.

1. RMS II 187. Probably the same as Gilbert, Dn., *c.*1420 (Carnegies of Inveresk II 508–510). As Donald de Bute was Dn. 1394–1408, Gilbert de O. may have been rural dn.; cf. ns. on 1394; but RMS II 187, an undated cr., but before 1403 he is named dn., and with John Rolloc is cl. of Robert, E. Fife and Menteith. He may have become Dn. on death of Donald de B. If he was Dn. *c.*1420, he must have died or res. about then, for Michael Ochiltree became Dn. in 1420.

2. See n. 2 under 1394. Also ch. VII.

3. CPR Pet. I 628. M.A.; in Roll of pets. presented by U. Paris, where probably he won his degree, for a cn. R. or Db. w.e.p. Granted.

4. ERS IV 1. Chiefly notable for his service to the state. See n. 1 under 1394. Wt. in 6 crs., 1406/7, at Culross, Perth and Stirling; in one of the Perth crs. (RMS I 895) Robert, Duke of Albany, E. Fife and Menteith, Governor of Scotland, founded a chap. in Stirling Castle: RMS I 891, 894, 895, 896, 902, 913.

5. Colini (son of Colin) may mean that Finlay was of the Argyll family, Lords of Lorne, in which Colin was a common name.

1410–19

Bishop	WILLIAM (STEPHAN), 1419 – 29.
Archdeacon	THOMAS DE GRAHAM,[1] *a.* 28 Feb. 1419/20.
	JOHN BUSBY, 1420.
Canon	MICHAEL OCHILTREE.[2]

1. CSSR 181; CSSR II 38–39 and n. At date noted he exchanged with John Busby, who was c.p. Duffus (d. M.).

2. CSSR 3. See ch. VIII. Some additional details are here given:

1418. B. Dec., pt. D. Db., has read for 3 years in canon law, is c.p. Strogeith (D. Db.) vl. £14 of old sterling. Has disp. as son of a pt. James I, in prison in England, pets. for "his familiar" to get a ben. i.g.o. Bp. or pr. St.A. or Ab. Dunfermline, though he is c.p. Db. and p.v. Strogeith.

2 May 1419. Now also c.p. Monzie, d. Db., and pets. for c.p. Obny (now in Auchtergaven), D. Dk., unlawfully detained by William Croyser, "who bears himself as a priest", CSSR 38–39.

26 Jun. 1419, repeats above pet. CSSR 81.

1 Jul. 1419. James I pets. again for M.O., giving more details. M.O. is "familiar, domestic and commensal of himself, his father and his mother" (i.e. of Robert III and Queen Annabella Drummond). His B.Dec. is of Paris, and he

intends to go on to the Licentiate; asks for additional bens. and a dig., and to hold two incompatible bens., "because in these parts bens. are contiguous and extremely lean in fruits". Also to hold Monzie and Strogeith for life. Let it be done for 5 years, says Pope, CSSR 82–3.

15 Jan. 1419/20. John Feldew tells Pope that "a certain priest" called Michael de Ochiltree, by virtue of an earlier expectative grace (right granted by Pope to expect a ben. not then vacant) had accepted the p.v. of par. ch. Stirling (£20 sterling). But a pt., Patrick Scot, detains it by authority of the patron (Dunfermline Abbey). John F. pets. for it, and the Pope says "Let it be done". CSSR 147–8. The result is recorded, 4 Feb. 1419/20, CSSR 160–1, – Pope allows Patrick, chap. Duke of Albany, Governor of Sc., to resign Inverkeillour, and M. de O. to resign Stirling, and both to exchange bens. Stirling is now vl. 40 marks sterling in absence, and 60 marks in case of residence.

25 Nov. 1420. Michael O. is now Dn. Db. The Dn. was a non-elective major dig. with c.o.s. and he was pro. by the Bp. on death of Donald de Bute. Then he obtained a c.p. Db. (though the statutes of the Ch. forbade such to be held by the Dn.). In pet. to Pope, M.O. mentions that he has Strogeith, and his c.p. Db. was Monzie. Now he asks for permission to hold them together for life. CSSR 235. The Pope says "for 5 years". When M.O. on 13 Dec. 1420, again pets., "when all ordinary burdens are deducted, the fruits are so scanty that they are notoriously insufficient for the fitting sustentation of the Dean"; but again the Pope says "for 5 years". CSSR 237.

11 Mar. 1420/1, CSSR 245/6, John Stewart's intrusion into the Dn.; also

9 May 1421, CSSR 253, M.O.'s pet. for the issue to be expedited; also

22 May 1421, CSSR 260, John Stewart's claim that the Pope had pro. him; these brought M.O. to Rome to urge his claims ("let it be done as he asks, i.e. as John S. asks", says the Pope) –

these 3 last entries are dealt with in the first pp. of ch. VIII.

20 Apr. 1422. Ingeram Lindesay, pt. D. St.A., of noble race, B.Dec., asks for M.O.'s c.p. Db. since M.O. had been prom. (a false rumour) to Bp. Sodor. Explanation of rumour is in early pp. of ch. VIII; CSSR 297–8 and n. (Ingeram L. became Bp. Ab. – DBS 122, BCPS 315 etc.)

20 Apr. 1422, CSSR 298/9, John Stewart having been repelled though son (ill.) of Robert III, born 1390, John de Keremor, B.Dec. asks to be made Dn. Db. (see early part of ch. VIII). On 23 Apr. 1422, and 27 Apr. 1422, John de K. (being at Rome) sends in further pets., unsuccessfully, CSSR 302–3. To every one of the petitioners the Pope wrote "Fiat".

But, April 1424, the Pope pro. M.O. officially to Dn. Db., which he had held de facto since 1420. Now he is B.C.L., and "Almoner General of James, King of Sc." He is given right to hold various types and numbers of bens. though he is c.p. Dk. and Db., as well as Dn. Db. CPR VII 376–7.

1425, M.O. obtained par. ch. Inchmagranach (D. Dk.). Pope adds that recently he had pro. M.O. to p.v. Tibbermore (D. Dk.) to hold for 3 years. CPR VII 391–2, 406.

Sep. 1427. The 3 years are ending; so Pope disp. M.O. to hold Lilliesleaf (D. Gl.), which he seems to have exchanged with Tibbermore, for life, along with c.p. Inchmagranach. CPR VII 546–7.

27 Apr. 1427. M.O. still dn. when m. to settle a thrice-appealed and thrice-lost suit at Rome. CPR VIII 106–7.

11 May 1427. M.O. still Dn. when m. to collate Gilbert de Bannory to Ch. Db. CPR VIII 100-1. See 1420-29, n.5.

22 Jun. 1429. M.O. is made Bp. Db., and res. Inchmagranach. CPR VIII 97. I have documented M.O.'s career at length; the ways of a pluralist are worth

finding out, sometimes, for the light they cast on the inner workings of the Roman Court. Though pro. Bp. 1429 he was still unconsecrated 10 May 1430 (RGB I 157–9). The earliest record of M.O. designated Bp., is on 12 Apr. 1431, CPR VIII 368–9.

Spottiswode calls him "a wealthy prelate", says "he purchased to his see a great part of the forfeited lands of Strathearn, adorned the Cathedral, built the bridge of Knaig at Machante, with the Church of Muthill".

1420-29

Bishop	WILLIAM (STEPHAN), 1419 – 29.
	MICHAEL OCHILTREE,[3] 1429 – 47.
Dean	MICHAEL OCHILTREE,[3] 1420 – 29.
Precentor	DONALD, 1420 – 29.
	JOHN LANGE, 1429 – c.1430.
Chancellor	ADAM DE PORT,[5] died c.1423.
	DONALD GELESON,[5] c.1423.
	WILLIAM CLERK,[5] c.1423 – 29.
	GILBERT DE BANNORY,[5] 10 Jun. 1429.
	JOHN WILLIELMI,[10] 1423 – 25.
Treasurer	DOM. WILLIAM DE ATHRAY, 1422, RBG I 148–157.
Official	One unnamed,[1] 1420.
	MALCOLM JOHANNIS,[2] 1425.
Canons	DAVID DE STIRLING,[9] 1420.
	WILLIAM DE CADZOW, 1422; RBG I 148–157.
	MALCOLM JOHANNIS,[2] 1423.
	ALAN STEWART,[6] 1423.
	ROBERT DE CRANNACH,[7] 1424.
	JOHN DE DALRYMPYL,[8] 1429.
Notaries	WALTER AWENERE,[4] cl. and n.p., 1422, RBG I 148–157, 1430, *u.s.* 157–159.
Others.	MALCOLM LAWTFUT, 1420, cl.
	WILLIAM DE FOULIS, 1422, pt. ⎫ [8]
	(cl. in 1425, CSSR II 95–96.) ⎬ RBG I 148–157.
	JOHN MACKISON, 1422, pt. ⎭
	WILLIAM BURGES, 1422, pt.
	MALCOLM JOHANNIS,[2] 1423, cl.

1. This Official, without name, was m., 1420, to resv., col. and assign a ben. i.g.o. Inchaf. A., to Malcolm Lowtfut, cl., D. Db. CPR VII 167–8.

2. CPR VII 252–3, 1423, on death or res. of John Roleris, v. Kippen, was presented to Bp. Db. for vac. Kippen. He was son of a pt. As this was not stated in this appointment, technical difficulties arose after he had possession of K. These, including payment of 30 fls. to *Camera* (CAC 88), were rectified.

1429, is cn. and Off. CPR VIII 100–1.

4 May 1430, is Off. and r. Kippen. RBG I 157–159. Some confusion here, for in 1432, CPR VIII 437–8, he was p.v. K., also B.C.L. and has been "Official

General of the episcopal court of Db." for seven years – which makes him Off. in 1425.

1432. CPR VIII 437, already disp. to hold 6 mutually compatible bens., plus K., plus officialate Db., is now disp. to "hold any other bens. . . . of any number and kind, compatible with one another and the aforesaid . . . to res. them, or . . . exchange as often as he pleases". cf. CPR VIII 438. The Middle Ages were not shocked, as we are, by such rampant pluralism, which, bad enough in Sc. and Eng., was much worse on the Continent.

14 Mar. 1423–4. Present in Roman Court, and acted as proctor for Ingeramus Lindesay (see in n. 2, 1410–19), cn. Br. Brady II 359.

3. See n. 1410–19. Michael O.'s payments to Papal *Camera* on his pro. to Db. are as follows:

12 Jan. 1430/1, offered by his proctor, Ingeram Lindsay (formerly petitioner for M.O.'s cn. of Db., now chr. M.) 370 gold fls. (1 fl. = 8s.) for his common and 5 little services, payable in 2 terms, each of 8 months. CAC 106. Same day, paid 100 fls. CAC 13–14.

1 Oct. 1431. Paid 85 fls. and also 36 fls. 25s. CAC 229.

2 Oct. 1431. Paid 97 fls. 9 s., this and the two sums the day before, by hands of Cosmo and Laurentius de Medicis, international bankers. CAC 14–15.

11 Dec. 1431. Paid 100 fls. and 2 fls. 8s. 4d., by above Ingeram (proctor at Rome for several Sc. cls. at various dates). CAC 229.

4 Jul. 1430. There is a receipt for payment by Thomas Crappeman, for William, Bp. Dk., for 12 fls. 25s. and for 1 fl. 46s. 2d. Dr. Annie I. Dunlop thinks, probably correctly, that this is an error for Michael O., Bp. Db., who still owed for one of the 5 little services. One William was consecrated Bp. Dk., 1430, but he never got possession of the see. CAC 227 and n.

13 Nov. 1449, two years after his death, his bankers, Antony de la Casa and Society, paid 1300 fl. "for his common service of the Ch. of Db." CAC 271. There is some unknown factor behind this; a legacy to Pope would not have been so entered. It looks like an additional assessment, due perhaps to the rumours reaching Rome of Db.'s large accession of wealth by James II's cr. See chps. VIII and X.

Michael Ochiltree as Dn. Db., CSSR 235, CSSR II 109–110, 115, 120, 166.

4. First notice of a notary public (n.p.) in D. Db. Such were in minor os., though later the office was borne by some rs. and vs. Their numbers grew, until the Ch. had to regulate their training and qualifications. Still they increased, and being really in most cases laymen, though they were in lowly os., are often called in the records "married cls.". They served the Ch. well, and were the forerunners of lawyers in certain legal work. The name is still in use, and every parish minister in Sc. today is legally able to exercise some notarial functions.

5. Adam de Port and Gilbert de Bannory, as chrs. Db. were p.vs. Kilmadock, CPR VIII 100–1. Gilbert was son of a pt. On death, c.1423, of Adam de Port, no appointment was made for years, so that the office was rsv. to Pope to fill. But Bp. Db. col. William Clerk (1425, CSSR II 99.) and he was in possession for about 6 years. This irregularity being discovered, William C. was removed from office. One Donald de Geleson seems to have held the office for a time after death of Adam de P. There is no record of this appointment, but he is recorded as dying and leaving a vac. Pope m. 3, including Dn. Db., and Malcolm Johannis, Off., to assign Gilbert de Bannory, prt., D. Gl., master of the Poor Hospital of Strathblathan (Strathblane) by papal authority, though not yet in possession of it, cf. CAC 97–8. In 1429, 3 cns. Gl. were m. to remove Robert Storm, col. uncanonically by Bp. Gl., from the Poor Hospital, and assign it to Gilbert de Bannory, CPR VIII 102. Patrick de Port, CPR VIII 143, 1429, pr. Inchma. (cf. n. 1, 1430–39) had died; may have been a brother

of Adam de Port. "Port" probably refers to Port of Menteith, and may have been their birthplace.

6. TV VI 73. Alan Stewart was natural son of Walter, E. Atholl and Caithness. On 22 Mar. 1422/3, his father pets. for him to be given further bens. in addition to c.ps. of Menmorr (D. Ar.) and Logie (D. Db.) and Cruden (D. Ab.). Res. Logie, 1430, CPR VIII 368–9, VII 102–3.

7. Before 1424, CPR VII 371, Robert de Crannach, M.A., was pro. to cn. Db. w.e.p. and to a dig. of Db., as well as to a ben. i.g.o. Ab. Arb. Pope now pro. him (back-dating it to 1418) to cns. Dk. and M., a pb. in each to be rsv. to him, plus a dig. in one of them. A notorious pluralist; B.C.L. and M.A.; receives many further grants, e.g. 1425 (CPR VII 405), 1426 (CPR VII 441), especially 4 Jul. 1430 (CPR VIII 176–7). May 1432, when in Rome, acts as proctor (CPR VIII 420). 23 Dec. 1435, Dn. Db., had seat in Council of Basle (see Ch. VIII), etc., see Indices, CPR VII, VIII, IX.

He was one of a family of cls., Crannachs:
  (1) David de C., sdn. and cn. Dk., brother of
  (2) John de C., Bp. C., later Bp. Br., envoy of James I to Pope Martin V. David and John were brothers of
  (3) Robert de C., Dn. Db., Adn. M., etc., etc.
  (4) William, Ab. Inchaf.

8. CPR VIII 143, 1429, cn. Db., was instituted by chp. Db. as vicar-general *in spiritualibus*, during the vac. before Michael O. was pro. Bp. Db. As such he confirmed el. of Patrick de Cardros as Pr. Inchma., after death of Patrick de Port. Pope confirmed this, by giving m. to 3 (including Dn. Db., and John de D.).

9. This was another David de Stirling from the cl. who became Dn. Db., 1381. When, 29 Jan. 1419/20, this D. de S. cn. Db., was presented by a lay patron to the Bp. Db. to be admitted c.p. Balmanno, in Coll. Ch. Abernethy, Bp. refused, and confirmed another presented by other patrons. De de S. got himself instituted by others. Pets. Pope to pro. him to the c.p. *Fiat ut petitur* (Let it be done as asked) CSSR 158, 180.

10. CSSR II 86–7, appointed by Bp. Db., and therefore doubtfully. In a pet. against him, he is called "alleged pt. of Br."

1430-39

Bishop	MICHAEL OCHILTREE, 1429 – 47.
Dean	JOHN STEWART,[5] 1430, res.
	ROBERT DE CRANNACH,[5] 1430.
Precentor	ROBERT BETON, 1430.
	WILLIAM DE CARMIELE, 1430.
	JOHN TRELOCH, 1430 – 45.
Chancellor	ANDREW JUVENIS,[1] 1430.
	LAURENCE PIOT,[4] 1431.
	ROBERT DE CRANNOCH,[5] c.1435, res. 1440.
Canons	ANDREW JUVENIS,[1] 1430.
	DONALD MACMACHTANE,[2] 1431.
	LAURENCE PIOT,[4] 1431.
	NICHOLAS DE OTTERBURN,[3] 1432.
Chaplain	DOM. JOHN MALCOLM; SK 211–2.
Notary	ANDREW ANCOLSON, cl. and n.p.; SK 211–2.

1. CAC 102. On 20 Dec. 1430, he paid through a proctor at Rome the annates (income for first year) due by him for Chr. Db. (to which a c.p. Db. are annexed, vl. £20 sterling) void by death of Adam de Port. Andrew Juvenis (or Young) was col. 5 Dec. 1430. It would seem that the col. of Gilbert de Bannory (cf. 1429) did not take effect, though he paid annates (CAC 97–8). cf. n. 5, 1420–9.

2. CAC 106. Got a bull, 16 Jul. 1431, anent c.p. Logie (vl. £8 sterling). £ noted as = $2\frac{1}{2}$ fls. (gold of the Camera). 15 Jul. 1437, CPR VIII 628, he is M.A., D.C.L., Dn. Dk., r. Weem (D. Dk.), cn. Db., pb. Logie (D. Db.), c.p. Invernochty (D. Ab.) Died a. 1445 CPR IX 444; some think in 1440. In Apr. 1431 Robert de Cardo tried to take possession, but res. – CPR VII 102–3, VIII 368–9. Donald M. was at Council of Basle, BCPS 492. See ch. VIII. When Dn. Dk., he began to build at his own expense "the costly bridge over the Tay . . . near Dunkeld"; in 1440, CPR IX 110, the faithful were promised relaxations of penance if they gave aid. Son of a pt.

3. CPR VIII 453, in which Nicholas de Ottieburn is M.A., and L.C.L., pcr. Gl., c.p. Gl., c.p. Db. (pb. being Balquhidder vl. £4). Earlier he had rsv. of a cn. Dk. with rsv. of a pb. and dig., Gl. or Dk. Also, 1432 p.v. Mearns (d. Gl.) but this he had to res. when he became pcr. Gl. and c.p. Balquhidder (of lay patronage). Pcr. vl. £15; c.p. Gl. vl. £60.

4. CPR VIII 335–6, one of a family of pluralists; in CPR VIII and IX the movements of Laurence, Alexander and Patrick Piot are almost beyond human patience to follow. They were kinsmen of "divers nobles and barons of the realm of Sc." CPR VIII 610–11.

May 1431, CPR VIII 335–6, Pope states he had recently pro. Laurence to Chr. Db., and p.v. Tibbermore (D. Dk.) and several others in Dk. and Br. He is also cn. M. He was M.A. He had the ear of the Pope – in 1437, CPR VIII 620–1, got c.p. Moneydie (D. Dk.) in a disputed settlement, and in Feb. 1437–8, CPR VIII 674–5, in a dispute about Kilmany (D. St.A.) James Lindsay, cn. Gl., M.A., of a race of barons, is to have, says the Pope, in all expectative graces granted to him, precedence over all other expectants except (1) members of the Pope's household, (2) Laurence Piot. From the many entries in CPR VIII, it is clear that in 1437, L.P. was c.p. Moy (D. M.), c.p. Balquhidder (D. Db.), (these last 2 vl. £16), v. Kilbarchan (d. Gl. vl. £16), had rsv. of c.p. Ellen (d. Ab.) vl. £8, pro. of c.p. Logy (d. Ross) vl. £16, of Dn. R. (£30) about which he is litigating, and of a cn. Gl., and a ben. St.A.

5. CPR IX 131. For Robert de Cranach, see n. 7, 1420–9. Col. Dn. 7 Jul. 1430, CAC 101.

CPR VIII 177, 6 Jul. 1430, Robert de C. is to get Dn. on death of Donald de Bute or res. of John Stewart, cl. The papal information was in this case out of date: Donald de Bute died c.1408 and there had been two Dns. before John Stewart.

1440–49

Bishop	MICHAEL OCHILTREE, 1429 – 47.
	ROBERT (LAWDER),[10] 1447 – 66.
Archdeacon	WALTER STEWART,[8] 1447 – 73 or 74, when he died.
Chancellor	ALEXANDER DE LICHTON,[2] 1440.
	MR. JOHN CHRISTINI,[3] 1447.
Official	One unnamed, 1445, CPR IX 441, 444, 498, (3 ms.)
	MR. JOHN CHRISTINI,[3] 1447.

Canons	WILLIAM GORDON,[1] 1440.
	JOHN OCHILTREE,[6] 1443.
	PATRICK LETHE,[9] 1444 – 47.
	JAMES OCHILTREE,[5] *a.* 1445.
	ROBERT DE LAWDER,[7] 1447.
	JAMES WISHART,[9] 1447.
Notaries	WILLIAM DE ABERNETHY, pt., 1446, RBG I 14.
	DOM. JOHN ROBERTI, SK 222–3, 1448; RMS II 291, 1449.
	JOHN DE ATHERAY, pt., 1449 AP II 61, (cf. n. 3, 1455).
Others	MR. JOHN SPALDYNE,[4] v. of Db., 1448, SK 220.

1. SHR No. 25 p. 330. Cn. Db., incorporated 9 Sep. 1440 in Council of Basle, BCPS 489. Matriculated at U. Louvain, 1434.

2. CAC 127. Robert Crannoch has res. and Alex. de L. is now, 4 Nov. 1440, Chr. Db. He paid 25 gold fls. as total annates, CAC 234, 266. He is M.A., and I.U.B. (=Bach. of both Laws, Canon and Civil); c.p. Duffus (D. M.) c.p. Lethnot (D. Br.), Adn. C. (not in possession) which he is ready to res. on obtaining Chr. Db., CPR IX 131. His plurality was very great. Also there was a Duncan, a Henry, and a John Lichton (=Leighton), probably 4 brothers; cf. CPR IX. CAC 234 reads "Alex. de Tulach (more correctly Lichton)".

3. SK 222–3, 5 Sep. 1448, John C. is "*officialis et cancellarius*". In 1449, RMS II 291, held both offices. In 1447, RMS II 640, he is official only.

1457, cn. Db. LC 143.

1460, SK 230–1, cn. Db.

1456, Official and Chr. PSSC 235–7.

A useful cl., Mr. John Cristison! Christini is Christie, Cristinson, Cristison, etc.

4. The only medieval v. Db. whose name we know.

5. Perhaps a brother (or a nephew) of Michael O., Bp. Db. pt., D. Db., B.C.L., of noble but ill. birth; p.v. Monzievaird, Muthill and Kippen, all D. Db., in succession. A restless soul, see ch. VIII. CPR IX 497–8, 498.

6. CAC 132. John O., cl., D. Db. On death of Donald Macnachtane, c.p. Logie (see n. 2, 1431), there is a contention for Logie, in which Patrick Lethe obtained possession. But Pope decides for John O., CPR IX 383. But in 1444/5, Pope changes his mind, and gives Logie to Patrick Lethe (Leiche). As there is no mention of his being ill. (or of his noble birth), John O. may be of a different family from Michael and James O. His name is given as OUTHRE, which may be Guthrie, CPR IX 444. The others are spelt Ouchre, etc.

7. CPR X 298–9, 310–1, Bp. Db. same year, 1447. How long he had been cn. is unknown. At 1447, he was also c.p. Cardross (D. Gl.) CPR X 291–2.

8. CPR X 15. Walter Stewart was kinsman of James II and grandson of Robert III; his father is reported to have been a dcn., CPR XII xxxii. Had generous papal disps., including pro. to Adn. Db. He is to have preference over all others for a c.p. Gl. and Dk., and for a dig. of one of them, and rsv. of a ben. St.A., CPR X 82–83. Brother of Robert Stewart, CPR X 14, 15, cn. M., and M.A. Walter is also M.A.; on 16 Nov. 1447, is absolved from excom. for simony (for second time); penance enjoined; rehabilitated, CPR X 359. He must have been at Papal Court at this time. In 1451, r. Minto (D. Gl.) and receives further graces, CPR X 174. Dead by 8 Oct. 1454, CPR X 260. Mrs. Dunlop, in "James Kennedy, Bishop of St.

Andrews" p. 97, quoting the MS. Reg. of Supplications (421 fol. 158, 29 Nov. 1447) shows that Walter Stewart was postulated to the Bpric. of Db. by Dn. and Chp. in 1447 on death of Michael O. Mrs. Dunlop says that Robert Lawder was pro. at instance of the King of Sc., though Walter was related to him (though out of wed-lock). Walter was compensated by wider and higher graces. In 1459 he was Adn. St.A. In 1474, he was in minor orders only – an acolyte, though he was also a papal cpn., CPR XIII 33, 34.

9. CPR IX 444, Patrick Lethe res. Logie, 23 Nov. 1447. Same date, James Wishart, B.C.L. res. p.v. Symington, D. Gl. They exchange bens. CPR X 292. Still cn. 16 Jun. 1464, CPR xi 510/1, where he is sub-delegated as judge in a dispute, in which one of the m. judges, having an interest, delegated his place to Patrick Lethe. Evidently the exchange did not take place.

10. Spottiswode says that Robert Lauder founded divers pbs. and cns. in Cath. Db., but gives no details.

1450-59

Bishop	ROBERT (LAWDER), 1447 – 66.
	(THOMAS,[11] 1459.)
Dean	HENRY MURRAY,[2] res. 1455.
	WILLIAM SCOT,[2] 1455. (£12 with c.o.s.)
	JOHN DONALD,[10] d. 1458.
	ANDREW MOSCHET,[10] 1458.
Precentor	NICHOLAS FECHIL,[8] 1458 – 62.
Chancellor	MR. JOHN CRISTINSON,[7] 1458.
Treasurer	MR. JOHN DE ATHERAY,[3] 1455.
Official	MR. JOHN CRISTINSON,[7] 1459.
Canons	JOHN CRISTINI,[7] 1457.
	MALCOLM DRUMMOND,[4] 1457.
	PATRICK REDE, 1450 × 1455, HMC III 417–8 (Abercairney MSS.).
Chaplains	DOM. PATRICK OGYLL,[9] 1455. SK 228.
	DOM. LUKE ARNOT, 1459, SK 230–1.
Notaries	GAVIN BRADY, 1456. (ref. lost).
	JOHN DE SPENS,[5] pt. and n.p., 1457.
	JOHN SCOT,[6] pt. and n.p., 1457.
Others	Chaplains of the Choir,[1] 1450.

1. They were granted £5 yearly for ministering to the Perth Justices of Ayre on their outward journeys, ERS III 512. This sum came from fines. ERS V 418.

2. Both Henry Murref (Murray), Dn. Db., and William Scot (p.v. Stirling) res. and exchange bens. CPR XI 249, 279, both dated 4 Dec. 1455.

3. SK 228, CS 184. Also tr. 1463, RMS II 978, and 1466, CC III 396. Probably the n.p. of 1449. See ch. IX. Dead by 1470.

4. CS 184; also 1461/2, CAI No. 150. Also Malcolm de Drummond, cn., in Abercairney MSS., HMC III 417–8. The first of many of the name among the clergy of Db. Cath.

5. CS 184; also 1472, SK 247; RMS II 1675 (13 Jul. 1470); RMS II 2325 (1471).

6. CS 184; also 1461/2, CAI No. 150, and 1468, SK 242–3.

7. LC 143. cf. 1447 (n. 3) and 1460 (n. 2); HMC III 417–8 (chr.) MSS. of Abercairney.

8. See chp. IX.

9. cf. 1462, when still cpn.

10. CPR XI xxvi.

11. In RMS II 1062, Thomas, Bp. Db., appears as wt. This is only known ref. No room for him in episcopal succession. In 1459 Robert Lawder attended Parliament. Probably a mistake for Thomas, bp. Dk., 1452–76; he also was a Lawder.

1460-69

Bishops	ROBERT (LAWDER), 1447 – 66.
	JOHN HERSPOLZ or HEPBURN, 1466 – 86.
Dean	JOHN DRUMMOND,[1] 1462 – 95.
Precentor	GEORGE MERREFF[7] (MURRAY), 1467 – 89.
Chancellor	JOHN CRISTIE,[2] 1460.
Official	JOHN CRISTIE,[2] 1460.
Canons	JAMES KENNEDY, *a.* 1465, (his pb. was Abernethy), CPR XII 485, CAC 154.
	ALEXANDER LUMSDEN[3] (Abernethy), 1465.
	HUGH DOUGLAS[4] (Abernethy), 1467.
	MARTIN WAUS,[5] 1468.
	[THOMAS STRATON (v. Dow),[6] 1469.]
Chaplains	DOM. PATRICK OGIL (cf. 1455 n. 9) and
	DOM. GILBERT HUNTER, CAI No. 150, 1461/2.
	Four chpns. of Innerpeffray.[8]
Notaries	THOMAS LAYNG and ROBERT MARSHALL, 1463, RMS II 978.
	DONALD ADE, pt., n.p., 1465, PSSC 235–7.
	JOHN SCOT, pt., n.p., 1468, SK 242–3 (cf. n. 6, 1457).

1. Early Records of U.St.A., p. 39. Entered as "determinant", 1462, and paid 7/6 for his term's fees. Already Dn., an appointment which supported his studies, and had no relation to the orders necessary for his work or of the Dn.'s duties. cf. n. 6, 1470–9.

2. SK 230–1; for 1462, CAI No. 150. For 1465, cf. PSSC 235–7. See under 1440–9, and 1450–9, where he is cn., Off., and Chr.

3. CPR XII 485, 607. Col. and pro. c.p. Abernethy on res. of James Kennedy. Was of noble birth by both parents. Made papal acolyte, 1466, CPR XII, 387. Paid 17 gold fls. as annates for c.p. Abernethy, 1466, CAC 244, 282. On 18 Dec. 1465, CAC 151, res. at Apostolic See p.v. Cadder (D. Gl.) and same day got two bulls giving him pension of 10 marks Sc. from p.v. of par. ch. of Legerwood, D. St.A., assigned to him by bull of 26 Nov. 1465, CAC 151. R. of Flysk, D. St.A., when, on 14 Mar. 1468/9, he granted a pen. of £10 Sc. p.a. from fruits of Flysk, along with cn. Db. and pb. Abernethy, which he holds, to William Ferguson, p.v. Cramond (D. Dk.) CPR XII 636. 23 Jul. 1466, on own request, is made perpetual administrator of Cistercian nunnery of S. Berwick. During the wars, the nuns had fled, and Jedburgh Abbey took possession. Authorised to recover possessions, expel Jedburgh, and dispose of fruits, without alienation of goods, CPR XII 256. In a last

bull of Paul II, he got a pen. from Gl., CPR XII xxxv. In 1466, he paid his annates for c.p. Abernethy, CAC 154. He was at Rome in 1466, CAC 158, for he paid annates in name of John Lathrisk for c.p. Banchory–Devenick, D. Ab.

4. CPR XII 607. Hugh D. is of royal lineage and of a race of earls. James Kennedy's res. of 21 Nov. 1465 of Abernethy, while at the Apostolic See, caused a vac. which was filled by Hugh Douglas, cn. Ab. (Abernethy had several pbs., being collegiate).

5. CPR XII 812–3. Martin Waus (Vaus, Was, Vars, Wores, etc.), Dn. C., was at Rome on 16 May 1463, when he paid annates for a friend, CAC 145–6. 15 Jul. 1473, Dn. R., papal collector in Sc., CAC 174, when he is again in Rome and promises to pay annates for another. Sep. 1480, still Dn. R., paid annates for Bourtie, D. Ab., to which he had been pro. on res. of Thomas Waus (about this time there were in the Sc. Ch. George, Alexander, David and Thomas Waus, but their relation to Martin is unknown), CAC 200.

1463, paid 28 fls, as total annates of Dn. C., CAC 241. On 19 Apr. 1485, paid 21½ fls. as annates for c.p. Bourtie, CAC 255, 295.

7 Oct. 1475, still Dn. R., is appointed Nuncio and collector in Sc., CAC 329. Of noble birth by both parents. James III pet. in his interests, CPR XII 548. 1476, Chr. Gl. (Records of Burgh of Stirling). Was M.A., and received many disps. CPR XII 552, xxvi.

6. CPR XII 356, 11 May 1469, p.v. Dow, Db., which he is to resign when he obtains pr. Monymusk, vl. £55 sterling. 11 May 1470, pro. to Monymusk, CAC 164–5. But Dow was in D. Dk., and not in D. Db.

7. See ch. IX.

8. The status of Innerpeffray, about which there have been various views, is settled by a writ in IWC. P. 22 describes original cr. by John, Lord Drummond, 3 Feb. 1459/60, giving "to the 4 cpns, appointed for serving the altar in honour of the Virgin Mary in the Ch. of Innerpaffray of a yearly annual rent of 40 marks Sc., to be uplifted from the lands of Innerpaffray". Another cr., 3 Feb. 1505/6, confirmed under Great Seal, 4 Feb. 1505/6 "for the maintenance of 4 cpns. to the 4 altars situate in the Ch. of Innerpaffrey and with houses and a yeard to every one of the cpns.", along with fuel from the common moor, and "four soums grass and an horse". In 1581 William Lindsay (was) "provost of the College Kirk of Inner-paffray" p. 25 u.s.; later called William Lindesay "provost or chief cpn. of the Ch. of the Virgin Mary of Innerpaffray". In 1594, William Lindesay gave to James Drum-mond of Innerpaffray 12 acres of land and 4 yards (gardens) and the lands of Kirkhill in Monzie, "reserving to himself and successors (evidently he alone is left) a chamber when he resides there" (p. 25 u.s.); in the same year James VI erected Innerpaffray into a barony under Great Seal i.f.o. James Drummond; but in 1581, p. 25 u.s., James is "commendator of Inchaffray and baron of Innerpaffray".

1470-79

Bishops	JOHN HEPBURN, 1466 – 86.
Dean	SIR JOHN DRUMMOND[6] (1462 – 95).
Archdeacon	ALEXANDER RATE,[1] 1474 – 79, when he died.
Chancellor	MR. HENRY BOYES,[3] 1473.
Treasurers	JOHN LOCKHART,[4] 1470.
	WILLIAM ELPHINSON,[4] 1476.
Officials	JOHN DE OCKERBURN, 1470, CPR XII, 788–790.
	JOHN FRASER,[7] 1476.

Canons	Dom. David Luthirdale,[8] 1473.
	Dom. William Ingeram (Comrie), 1476, RS 259.
	Robert Brun,[2] 1478.
	Dom. John Hastings,[9] 1478.
Chaplains	Dom. John French, cpn. to altar of Virgin Mary (in Nave), 1472. SK 244–6, HMC X 65.
	Dom. William Patonson, 1472, SK 244–6.
	Dom. William Ingeram, 1476, cf. cns. above.
Notaries	Thomas Ancolsone, 1471, SK 243–4.
	Dom. James Darow,[5] cpn. and n.p., 1474.
	Dom. Robert Redhuch, cpn. and n.p., 1474, SK 248–9.
Others	John Liell, pt. 1471, LS 194; CC III No. 434.
	John Moffet,[10] commissar of Db., A.Aud. 34.

1. CAC 178. "A continual commensal member of the Pope's household", CPR XIII 103–4. Pro. to adn. 30 Apr. 1474 on death of Walter Stewart who had been Adn. since 1447, see 1440–9, n. 8. Paid annates 16 Jul. 1474, £32. Officially the vl. was £20, but had increased.

1476, CPR XIII 220, he "has to go to divers parts of the world on his own business and is of noble birth; even absence is not to affect his membership of the papal household or his privileges as a commensal (precedence, safe-conduct for himself and a retinue of 4). Details of journeys unknown.

1472, CPR XIII 873, pro. archpriest of Ab.; and Adn. Ab., in CPR XIII 16.

1473 and 1475, proctor at Apostolic See for 3 Sc. churchmen, CPR XIII 340, 347, 462.

30 Apr. 1474, still litigating at Rome about above Adn. Ab. (he was r. Dunotter for life), was col. Adn. Db., to hold this with Dunotter, Adn. Ab., and 3 other incompatible bens. CPR XIII 33.

1474. Col. cn. Gl. w.e.p. and a non-major elective dig. CPR XIII 278. This because St.A. had not granted Pope's request that he be given a ben., 1 Jan. 1471/2, when he was also made cn. Br.

26 Dec. 1474. Pb. Renfrew (£30 sterling) CPR XIII 38.

7 Jan. 1474/5. Col. Dn. Dk. (£50 sterling) CPR XIII 40.

31 Jan. 1474/5. Licence to res. or exchange any ben. without further licence from Pope, on condition that he reports such to the cls. of Papal Camera (for taxation). CPR XIII 41.

8 Jun. 1475. Indult to have a portable altar. CPR XIII 220.

20 Jun. 1475. Indult for life to visit by deputy his Adns. Ab. and Db. and to receive procurations (fees in lieu of hospitality) in money, 30 silver *gros turnois* (= 2½ gold fls. of Florence) per day, CPR XIII 43. Same day, Off. Db., and 2 others are to see to these visits by deputy, CPR XIII 43.

20 Oct. 1475. His Dn. Dk. contested by James Lewinton. Pope pro. James to Bpric. Dk. and again col. Alexander Rate to Dn. CPR XIII 47.

24 Aug. 1479, noted as having died beyond the Apost. Court, after retiring from membership of papal household, CPR XIII 619.

Yet, up to 8 Jun. 1475 at least, CPR XIII 220, he is designated acolyte, and therefore unfit canonically to discharge the duties of any of his bens., digs., offices. A persistent and monstrous pluralist. He may never have been in Db.

2. CAC 192, 15 Apr. 1478. Pb. unreadable in MS. At this date, he obtained 2

bulls, authorising a pen. of £5 sterling out of its fruits. On 13 May 1478, CAC 194, he is cn. Br. and pays annates for his pb. Panbryde (£12 sterling), now united to a c.p. Br. which he already holds.

3. BC IV 1403. On 9 Feb. 1473/4, being at Rome, he offered in name of John Layng, Bp. el. Gl., 2500 fls. for his common and 5 customary services. (For these, fully described, cf. CAC xlix ff.)

16 Feb. 1473/4, CAC 247, Henry Boyes, pt. St.A., M.A., still at Rome, paid annates, 22 fls. for p.v. Linlithgow, D. St.A. (£20 sterling) void by pro. of John Layng, to See of Gl. Pro. to Linlithgow 1474, CAC 177. Still Chr. Db. 1478, LAc II No. 119.

4. CAC 164. John Atheray has died and John Lockhart, pt. D. St.A., is appointed. Promises to pay annates within 6 months of uplifting fruits, vl. £18 sterling.

6 Jul. 1470, CPR XII 742–3, opposed by David Ray, cl. Cause went to Rome; after enquiry John L. was pro. For reasons unknown, except "to end litigation" between David Luthirdale (see n. 8 below) and William Elphinston, both contestants for Adn. Dk., and to allow David to possess it in peace, John L. res. tr. to Bp. John Hepburn, who pro. William Elphinston, who obtained possession. In recognition Pope gave John L. a yearly pen. for life of £10 Sc. from par. ch. of Tealing, D. Dk., which is united with the Adn. Dk. (£28), to be paid by David L. and his successors – CPR XIII 506, 10 Aug. 1476. This was reinforced by 2 bulls, six weeks later. This was obviously a pre-arranged plan, and so profitably did it work out for John Lockhart that he made a practice of resigning bens., to which he first made claim, and so he gathered considerable income for his "good nature".

18 Jan. 1477/8, John Lockhart got pen. of 10 silver marks from p.v. Bathgate (d. St.A.), after giving up his claim to it, CAC 186, CPR XIII 545.

23 Jan. 1477/8, John Lockhart got £4 p.a. for life from Lasswade, "by occasion of a certain concord", CAC 186; CPR XIII 542, where date is 20 Feb. 1476/7.

Same date, £10 Sc. (=£4 sterling) from Kirkmichael, D. Gl., owing to his res. CAC 186. William Elphinston, Tr. Db., has been given r. Kirkmichael, and the pen. was granted on 14 Dec. 1476, CPR XIII 558.

William Elphinston, M.A., M.Dec. became Bp. Ab. 1484, instigated the founding of U. Ab. by Pope Alexander VI, 10 Feb. 1494/5 and was its first Chr. James III appointed him Chr. of Sc., and James IV Keeper of the Privy Seal. A very great man.

5. James Darow, SK 248–9, pt. St.A., n.p. CS 185; in 1477 cpn. and n.p., RMS II 1326, 2388. On 1 Jul. 1478, the community of Stirling conferred on him the Altar of the Holy Rood in the par. ch. there, for life, on his resigning the Altar of St. Katherine, RS 264. In 1485, cn. Db. and n.p. RMS II 1622. A gifted and learned "lawyer". The late Thomas Miller, minister at Bonnybridge, used to discuss his greatness with me, and has written on him in Juridical Review, vol. xxxvii, 162–177, and xlv, 32–48. See chp. IX.

6. Dn. from 1462–95. RMS II 2230 gives latest known date, 20 Jan. 1494/5. In 1485, 1489, 1491 he took successful legal action in defence of his teinds and lands, ADCC I, 106, 107, 110, 198; A. Aud. 116. With him begins a Drummond monopoly of Dn. Db., parallel with that of the Chisholms in Bp. Db. "The Family of Drummond" which Lord Ancaster kindly allowed me to examine says he was second son of Sir Walter Drummond of Cargill and Stobhall, was also r. of Kinnoul as well as Dn. Db. A hardy and bold churchman who thrust himself into the Dn.; hence "You take it as the Drummond took the order". A papal knight. Tutor to his nephews when his brother Malcolm died. Had several children and grandchildren "for albeit they were ecclesiastical persons . . . yet very few outwent them in the propagation of their kind; of these sons several families about Db. had their beginning".

Dn. John Drummond had a son William, "familiar cl. of James V", r. Forteviot, who succeeded his father as Dn. Db. William D. had a son Malcolm, who was n.p. It will be convenient to gather here some details of other members of the Drummond family connected with Db. Cath.:

Malcolm, brother as above of Dn. John Drummond, had as his second son, *Walter Drummond*, a man of great ability, r. of U.St.A., later Dn. Db. (Register of Paisley Abbey, 153, 437). In 1496, Chr. Dk., and Cl. of Register and Council of Scotland, under James IV. He was proprietor of Sackentowne (par. Kilmadock), which was changed in name to Deanston, after him. Also cpn. Forgandenny, and r. Forteviot, ADCC I 121 (1489) and I 307 (1493). cf. 1457, n. 4.

Walter Drummond of Deanston, had a son *John D.*, who succeeded his father as Dn. Db., and r. Kinnoul. See 1516, n.6., and 1530–1539, n. 8. This John Drummond and his father Walter, both Dns. Db., were buried in the Drummond Aisle of Db. Cath.

7. RS 260. In 1476, DB III 108, Provost of Abernethy; also in 1482/3, RMS II 1558.

8. ATS I 1. Auditor of the King's Accounts. From ERS VIII, we learn that he was

Auditor, 1473 (p. 138), 1475 (p. 266), 1476 (p. 326), 1477 (p. 401);

cl. of accounts, 1473 (p. 149), 1475 (p. 281); 1472 (p. 186) he was paid £6. 4. 10;

cl. of household accounts, 1477 (p. 401);

Chamberlain of Linlithgowshire, 1474–1478 (pp. 212, 303ff, 331ff, 401, 510). In 1479, his successor gave in Luthirdale's accounts, p. 601.

His fee was £10 p.a., with extras for transport, etc. By liberality of the King he received payments for his household (1476, pp. 375, 379).

Adn. Teviotdale, 1475 (p. 266);

Adn. Dk., 1476 (p. 326), 1477 (p. 401), 1478 (p. 510).

His signature is reproduced, ATS I 75.

9. CS 185–6. John Hastings, cn. Db., appears in James Darow's protocol book, with others, appointed procurators by and for John Spaldyn, Dn. Br., p.v. par. ch. Dundee, in Spaldyn's house in Stirling. Juridical Review, vol. xlv, p. 37.

10. This was the deputy of the Off. Db. Cath. He presided, when so authorised in the Off.'s commissary court.

1480–89

Bishops	JOHN HEPBURN,[4] 1466 – 86.
	JAMES CHISHOLM, 1487 – 1526.
Archdeacons	JOHN CANT,[1] c.1480 (res.).
	ANDREW PURWES,[1] 1480 (res.).
	DUNCAN BULLY,[1] 1480.
Canon	SIR JAMES DAROW,[2] 1485.
Notaries	JOHN BONER, 1480, CPR XIII 103-4.
	DUGALD COSOUR, 1485, RMS II 1622, 1301, etc.
	JOHN ADAMSON, pt., n.p., 1488, RBG I 33; SK 267–8.
Others	JOHN EDMONSTON,[3] cl., 1481, CPR XIII 108.

1. CAC 203, where Duncan Bully is pt., D. St.A., M.A. John Cant and Andrew Purves are known only from the ecclesiastical involutions of Duncan B., which are extraordinary, and run thus – Alexander de Rate, familiar of the Pope, is dead; though pro. Adn. Db., he never had possession, cf. 1474, n. 1. Duncan B. was pro.

Adn. Db. at Rome, 15 Aug. 1480, and on 3 Aug. 1481 promised annates within 6 months, Adn. Db. being vl. £20 stg.

3 May 1474. CPR XIII 34–35, D.B. has been for 4 months cn. Gl. and r. Renfrew (vl. £20 stg.), without taking stipend, for 7 years cn. Ab. and r. Methlick (vl. £16 stg.), for a year cpn. Altar of Holy Rood in Stirling par. ch. (vl. £3½ stg.). All these he res. and was col. to r. Kinnell (d. St.A.), which he retained for 2–3 years, but Pope told him to resign as inadequately disp. for defect of birth. Pope rehabilitated him and col. him again to Kinnell D. St. A. (is this Kinkell?), vl. £16.

15 Aug. 1480, CPR XIII 103–4, D.B. sent a most involved pet. to Pope – Adn. Walter Stewart had died, Alexander Rate, having res. Adn. Db. a. death, Bp. Db. appointed John Cant, cn. Abernethy, who res. without gaining possession. Bp. Db. then appointed Andrew Purwes, who then exchanged it with Duncan Bully for the r. Kinnell. Pope calls the matter to himself, and m. 3 cls. to assign it to Duncan "whether void by deaths of Walter and Alexander or by the res. of Walter, Alexander, John Cant and Andrew, or in any other way". Pope disp. Duncan as son of a pt. and a married woman, to be prom. to all, even holy, orders.

6 Nov. 1490, at Stirling, at the uniting of the Altars of Holy Trinity and of St. Thomas in par. ch. Stirling, "compeared a venerable man, Mr. Duncan Bully, Adn. Db., as patron of the 2 altars". They were united "because the annual rents of the same were destroyed by the burning of the town, so that they were unable to sustain 2 cpns., but one only". Then he instituted a discreet man, Sir Robert Symsoun, cpn., "by delivering the horn of the altar". Among the wts. are two of the name of Adam Bully (perhaps Duncan's relatives); one, Adam Bully, had in 1479 added an endowment to the Trinity Altar in Stirling. CS 48.

2. RMS II 1622. See 1474, n. 5.

3. CPR XIII 108, 4 Dec. 1481, a pen. of 70 marks Sc. (=£9 stg.) was granted to him from fruits of Inchma., because he had withdrawn his litigation to allow David Henrisoun to enjoy the pr. To be paid half yearly in the City of Db.

4. Spottiswode says that he had a long dispute with Ab. Inchaf., and that he was buried in choir of Db. Cath.

1490–99

Bishop	JAMES CHISHOLM,[10] 1487 – 1526.
Deans	MR. JOHN DRUMMOND,[3] 1462 – 95.
	MR. WALTER DRUMMOND,[4] 1497 – 1512.
Sub-dean	DOM. JAMES BELCHES,[9] 1498, RMS II 2474, 1497, HMC X 67.
Precentor	LAURENCE OLIPHANT,[1] 1495 – 1513.
Archdeacon	HENRY ALANE.[2]
Officials	MR. WILLIAM FORBES, 1494, RMS II 2230.
	HENRY QUHITE,[8] 1498.
Canons	MR. WALTER SMALL, 1491, A. Aud. 149.
	MR. WILLIAM FOWLAR,[5] 1491.
	SIR JOHN FRESALL (Balquhidder), 1498, RSS I 203.
	JOHN BRUS (Balquhidder), 1498, on res. of John Fresall, RSS I 203.
	DAVID REDEHUCH (r. Aberfyle, became r. Glendevon), a. 1500, RSS I 595.
	JOHN MALISON (Kippen), 1496, RMS II 2306.

Chaplains	JOHN KILGOUR JOHN SMART[6] (also n.p.) THOMAS ROW THOMAS CUMNOK	} 1499 RMS 2474.
Notaries	DOM. JOHN SMART,[6] 1498. JOHN DECURRY, 1495, IWC 70.	
Others	LAURENCE OLIPHANT,[1] cl., 1495. RICHARD SINCLARE JOHN OF ROW	} bailies[7] of Db.

1. CAI 255. On 16 Nov. 1495, pro. Ab. Inchaf. for first six months as commendatory, i.e. drawing income but, being only a cl. (minor orders), unable to fill the whole work of Ab. After that, having taken orders, he became Ab. CAI 337. Son of first Lord Oliphant. Fought and died at Flodden, 9 Sep. 1513. In Dec. 1495, offered 100 gold fls. for his commend of Inchaf. – (Brady).

2. ERS X 413; ATS I 206. Still Adn., 1497, RMS II 2338. Last ref. to him as Adn., 1503, wt. to a Keir cr., SK 277–279. He was a more diligent servant of the State than of the Ch., as the following refs. from ERS show:

X 20, 1488, "cl. of accounts"

X 420, 1494, cl. of the royal household.

1491–1501, acts for comptroller and receives the accounts.

X 710, 12 Dec. 1492, r. Ruthven; James IV in a letter calls him "cl. of our comptis of our household".

X 711, 718, 745, 753, 1492–95, royal commissioner of lands.

X 573, 1496, called "Adn. Dk." This may, or may not, be a mistake for Db.; cf. David Luthirdale, 1473, n. 8, who held two adns. Probably neither did any work in either.

X 537, for 1495, X 604, for 1496, he is auditor; also

XI 283, for 1501, and XII 1, for 1502.

ADCC II 35, 340–4, 446–7, 251, 284, 458, Lord of Council in 1496, 1499, 1500.

ADCC II 251, 284, 458, for 1498, 1500, Lord of Exchequer.

RSS I 513 (1500) one of commissioners to manage for 3 years the estates forfeited by John, Lord of the Isles.

In 1497 (ERS XI 48, 51, 60, 64), 1498 (XI 117, 125), 1501 (XI 361) he received payments for his work as acting comptroller.

In 1498, XI 123, he is given clothing for Christmas by the King's bounty.

In 1499 (XI 229) he is repaid £38. 15. 1 which he had lent to the household. Same year (XI 247) his salary as cl. of household is £10 p.a. with £10 (XI 256) as cl. of the household's books. Same year (XI 248, 258), £30 and £45 for his labours in the Treasury.

1497–1500, lets Crown lands on 18 occasions, XI 392–451, and 1502–1504, on six (XII).

1503 (XII 182), £10 as cl. of expenses, and £20 for his labours in the Exchequer (XII 185).

3. RMS II 2230. cf. 1462, n. 1, and 1470, n. 6.

4. RMS II 2367, 11 Jul. 1497. Walter was nephew of John D., whom he succeeded as Dn. He was private secretary to James IV.

In 1498, RMS III 53, "Cl. of Rolls and Register and Council".

Frequent wt. to crs. between 1496 and 1501, e.g. RMS II 2346; see index. Last recorded appearance is 29 Mar. 1511/2, CR 130.

Chr. (probably of Dk.) 1494, RMS II 2354, and 1469.

22 Sep. 1509 or 1510, RMS II 3898, Walter D. endowed cpn. Altar of St. Nicholas (original Santa Claus) in Db. Cath. (in S.E. of nave), ch. X.

As Cl. of Rolls etc. above (=Lord Cl. Register) 1498, wts. documents, ERS XI 163 etc.

1499, is given a fee (£22) and a gown, ERS XI 195, gives an obligation (XI 269) in 1500, gets free of customs 8 barrels of salted salmon (the duty was 32/-) XI 270, and is given £37 for certain expenses, 1501, p. 362.

1497, a commissioner of Crown lands, ERS XI 387.

1503, given licence to pass to the Court of Rome and other parts beyond the sea, with protection, RSS I 999.

His early ecclesiastical history is dated thus:

2 Jan. 1477/8, paid annates by proxy for Inchma. CAC 190;

7 Mar. 1477/8, CAC 214, paid annates by proxy for Ch. of Fettercairn;

4 Jan. 1482/3, CAC 293, paid annates by proxy for p.v. Aberdeen.

Lennox Papers II 125, show him r. Forteviot and Kinnoul.

"Early Records of Uni. of St.A." show Mr. Walter D. el. r. of the U. on date in 1487, 1488, 1489, 1496, 1510, 1511. D. E. Easson suggests that he may be the determinant (undergraduate) of that name in U.St.A. 1467, and licentiate in same year.

ADCC II Index has about 100 refs. to W.D., dn. Db.; 7 to him as cl. register on sederunt of Lords of Council; 14 on sederunts as Lord Auditor; 2 as Lord of Exchequer; 2 as parliamentary commissioner, and others.

4 Nov. 1499, he appears as Cl. Register, witnessing a royal grant, but also as Dn. Dk. CC IV 624ᴬ. This may be a mistake for Db., though it is difficult to say that in those times he could not have been dn. of two cathedrals.

1 Apr. 1511 he signed as Dn. CR 170–173.

5. On 26 Aug. 1491, William Fowlar, cn., gave certain rents in Forrester's Wynd, Edinburgh to endow a cpn. to serve Altar of St. James the Apostle, in Ch. St. Giles. RMS II 205. His original seal is in Db. Cath. Museum.

6. SK 271–1. John Smart appears as n.p., RMS II 2474, where the 4 who sign as cpns. (see under chaplains 1499) are probably cpns. of Db. where the cr. was drawn up.

7. ADCC I 407. First mention of baillies in Db. These were deputies of the official in his consistory court.

8. cf. 1506, n. 4.

9. "Schir James Belchis" had a "chalmer" (office, chambers) in Db., in 1497, SK 270, 314.

10. Spottiswode calls James Chisholm a severe censor of the corrupted manners of the clergy. Also says that he recovered many lands and possessions sacrilegiously taken; this is not evident in the records.

1500-09

Bishop	JAMES CHISHOLM, 1487 – 1526.
Archdeacon	JOHN DOBY,[1] 1506.
Official	MR. HENRY QUHITE,[4] 1506.
Canons	JOHN CHISHOLM,[2] 1509.
	JAMES WILSON[6] (Monzie), 1509.
	WALTER FORBES, 1509, RMS II 3398.
	JAMES EDMOUNSTOUN (r. Aberfoyle), 1500, RSS I 595.

Chaplains	DOM. JOHN CHISHOLM.[2]
	DOM. WALTER MENTEITH ⎫ 1506 RMS II 2969.
	DOM. THOMAS REOCH ⎭
	DOM. JOHN FRASER,[5] 1509, RMS II 3398.
	SIR THOMAS MYLLAR ⎫ cpns. of Altar of Vir-
	and ⎬ gin Mary, Keir Aisle
	SIR ARCHIBALD BALCOMY ⎭ 1509, HMC X 68.
Notaries	ANDREW NORTOUN,[3] 1506, RMS II 2969; called Mortoun, 1509, SK 289–91.
	JOHN CHISHOLM,[2] 1509.
	THOMAS ROW, (also cpn.), SK 289–91; see cpns. 1490–99.

1. RMS II 2971, 3078, M.A. Still Adn. in 1512, when he paid £20 towards the contributions from the whole Ch. to the King. The only other payment from d. Db. was from Inchma. P. (£100). Total from Ch. Sc. was £4275. 10. 9 – ATS IV 396. In 1511, however, Bp. Db. paid his whole tax, £166. 13. 4; total from Ch. £31,338. 11. 8 – ATS IV 172–3.

2. RSS I 1858. cf. 1506 when John Chisholm was cpn.; in 1509, SK 289–91, cn. On 27 Apr. 1510, given pen. of 40 marks yearly during King's will "for his gude and thankful service done and to be done to the King's grace". RSS I 2053. See n. 7, 1515.

3. Nortoun, still n.p., 1510. CR 167–8.

4. RMS II 2969. Henry Q. (or White) still Off. 1521, RMS II 242, and 1527, ATS V 317, when he gets a letter from King to be in Edinburgh on 2 Mar. 1526/7 "for the sessioun" (forerunner of Court of Session). 7 May 1498, he was "forspekar" for James, Bp. Db., in a land case (Bennie, unsuccessfully claimed by Ab. Lind. against Bp. Db.), ADCC II 191. Henry Quhite was counsel in court, for on 14 June, 1498 Walter Forbes is still off., ADCC II 218. H.Q. was Off. in 1506, RMS II 2969, and on 2 Oct. 1509, SK 289/9.

5. This may be the John Fresall, cn., 1498, which may mean Fraser.

6. SK 289–91. Cn. 1510, RMS II 3398; 1511, CR 170–3; 1512, RSS I 2390, when presented to Glendevon if/when vac. occurs.

1510-19

Bishop	JAMES CHISHOLM, 1487 – 1526.
Deans	JOHN DRUMMOND,[6] c.1510 – 15.
	SIR JOHN CHISHOLM,[7] 1515.
Precentors	(CARDINAL PETER (ACCOLTI) *in commendam*, res. 1514).
	(ALEXANDER STEWART DE PITCAIRN, commendator, 1514 – 1537).
Archdeacon	PATRICK BLACKADDER,[4] 1513 × 1528.
Canons	JAMES BELCHES,[5] 1510.
	DOM. WILLIAM MURRAY,[3] 1515.
	MR. PATRICK COVENTRE (Kippen), 1510, CR 167–8.

Chaplains	DOM. JOHN FORFAR,[1] 1512.
	DOM. JOHN LAUDER,[1] cpn. Altar of St. Stephen, Martyr, Db. cath., 1512.
	DOM. JOHN REDE,[2] cpn. to Bp., 1517.
Notary	JOHN BROUNE, 1516. RGB I 50,

1. Before 1512, John Forfar gave a croft in Db. as additional endowment of choir in Cath. (later Robert Braidfut likewise gave a holding) – RMS V 1230, which is also ref. for John Lauder, cpn., 1512.

2. At date, 10 Dec. 1517, John Rede, cpn. was presented to v. Glendevon. RSS I 2952.

3. ERS XIV 92, 1515, William Murray was cn. Db., and customs officer of Stirling. So, 1516, 1517, ERS XIV 189, 261. In 1514, ERS XIV 51, he is only customs officer.

4. DB II 171. Only ref.; was murdered; cf. ch. X.

5. RMS II 3398: cf. 1498, n. 9. Sdn., 1518, SK 270-314. In 1511, was c.p. Db. pb. unknown, CR 170-3.

6. RSS I 2390. This John Drummond was nat. son of Dn. Walter D., and succeeded his father as Dn. Db., and r. Kinnoul – Lord Strathallan's MS. Life of the Drummond family; in 1514, Lord Strathallan says, John D. as r. Kinnoul was forced by his uncle, Lord John D., elder brother of Walter D. of Deanston (who was John D.'s father), to conduct the marriage in Ch. Kinnoul of Archibald, E. Angus, and Margaret Tudor, widow of James IV. There was nothing uncanonical in the marriage; but it is interesting to note that Lord John D. was grandfather of Archibald, E. Angus, and father of Margaret D., whom James IV wanted to marry. If James IV and Margaret D. had been married privately, this marriage of Margaret Tudor would have been within the forbidden degrees and have required absolution.

7. ADCP I 62, 12 Dec. 1515 and 13 Dec. 1515, which detail contest for Dn. with Mr. Gilbert Strathauchin. 3 Aug. 1517, ADCP I 99, v. Dunning.

1520-29

Bishops	JAMES CHISHOLM, 1487 – 1526.
	WILLIAM CHISHOLM I, 1526 – 64.
Archdeacon	GEORGE NEWTON,[7] 1521
Chancellors	MR. ANDREW MAKBREK,[4] 1520.
	ANDREW AITON,[1] † 12 Nov. 1528.
Official	One unnamed,[9] 1525, 1526. He was Henry Quhite
Canons	WILLIAM CHISHOLM,[3] 1526 –
	DOM. JOHN CHISHOLM,[8] 1527 – 1532, when he became Archdeacon. RMS III 466.
Chaplains	Nine cpns. of the choir,[2] 1522.
	DOM. THOMAS WATSON, 1st cpn. of Keir, 1522, SK 317-8.
Notaries	DOM. RICHARD STIRLING, 1521, RMS III 242.
	JAMES BLAKWOD,[5] 1522.
	ANDREW SYM, 1522, SK 317-8 (1539, SK 363-4).
	ROBERT LEIRMONTH, 1522, SK 317-8.
Others	JAMES GRAY,[6] pt. 1520, and n.p.
	JOHN P., pt., F. I 54-55.

1. Also r. Spot, as his epitaph in the Eng. College at Rome declares (I owe this to Professor J. H. Baxter) – "Andree Aiton, nobilis Scoti, patria Fifensi, Dunblanen. ecclé. cancellarii, rectoris de Spot, viri optimi, fide et integritate insignis, literarumque culti et ornati in maxima bonorum et fortunarum expectatione functi lamentabile sepulchrum lacrȳs bene merenti posuit. Vixit annis XXXII, mensibus octo et diebus XV. Obiit die XII Octobris MD xxviii." For Aytons of Denmuir, see Anderson: The Scottish Nation, I 170. cf. "Notes and Queries" series 3, vol. viii, p. 246, for notes by one, Rawlinson.

2. SK 317–8. Bp. James Chisholm on 14 May 1522 endowed 9 cpns. of choir, and col. Thomas Watson, cpn., to the first cpn. of Keir within the said choir. Done in chp. about 11 o'clock forenoon, in presence of 5 wts., and 3 n.ps. Three wts. are cpns. of choir – Dionisius Row, William Anderson and Robert Akinhead. The 3 n.ps. were practising in D. Db., and are recorded in other refs., especially James Blakwod and Robert Leirmonth, both of notable Db. clerical families.

3. He was given indult to hold the cn. after he became Bp. Db. Brady: Succession I 140. v. Muthill, 1522, HMC X 70.

4. RMS III 384. May have been brother of Alexander M., burgess of Perth, whose cr. of purchase of land he wt. On 1 Aug. 1526, Alex. sold half the land, and again the Chr. is wt.

5. SK 317–8. James Blakwod appears as v. of Strowan, wt. on 18 Jan, 1532. RMS III 1257, and at other dates until 1539.

6. He transcribed an early "Chronicle of Scots and Picts", which is dated c.1187. Gray's MS. is No. 34–7–3 in Nat. Lib. of Scotland, and is the only copy known. See Skene: "Chronicles of Picts and Scots" p. lii, pp. 148f. Skene says Gray copied the Chronicle very badly, but nobody else is known to have copied it at all and the original is lost. Gray's MS. contains more than the Chronicle; e.g. some Sc. vernacular verse (printed by Sc. Text Society, 1918). It consists of 82 folios, with many blanks; cf. T. Innes: Critical Essays II 627–32. Innes added a list of contents (not wholly correct) on fol. 80. Of James Gray, Innes says – "he was a person of character in his time, being successively secretary to the first two Archbishops of St.A. after Patrick Graham" (1466); to wit, to William Schevez (1478–97) and to Prince James (Stewart, D. Ross), second lawful son of James III and brother of James IV (James Stewart was Abp. St.A., 1497–1503). Innes thinks he is the same James Gray who is recorded in the Panmure MS. of Scotichronicon as having illuminated its second volume, Magnus Macculloch also claiming his share in the illumination. The claim is dated at Edinburgh 9 Jan. 1479/80.

7. CR 122, 11 Jul. 1521, assisted at installation of Alexander as Ab. Camb. He wrote "The Acts of Dunblane Cathedral" now lost. This would have been an illuminating document. See A. B. Barty: History of Dunblane 49. Also c.1531, n. 4.

8. This John Chisholm, cn. 1527–32, Chr. 1532– must be a different cl. from John Chisholm (though most probably of the same family), who was Dn. Db., 1515, n. 7, and v. Dunning (1517).

9. ADCP 220, Off. Db., is on Privy Co., 1525. On 12 Feb. 1525/6, the unnamed Off. Db., with others, is joined with the Lords of the Secret Council and Ministers of Court, ADCP 238.

1530-39

Bishop	WILLIAM CHISHOLM I, 1526 – 64.
Deans	DOM. WILLIAM DRUMMOND,[8] 1532.
	MR. MALCOLM FLEMING,[1] 1536.
	WILLIAM GORDON,[1] 1539.

Sub-Dean	MALCOLM CHISHOLM, 1532, RMS III 1257. Also n.p.
Precentor	(GAVIN DUNBAR, Archbishop of Gl., Commendator of Inchaf., 1538 – 1547.)
Archdeacon	GEORGE NEWTON,[4] † c.1531.
	DOM. JOHN CHISHOLM,[3] 1532 – 42.
Chancellor	MR. JOHN CHISHOLM,[10] 1534.
Treasurer	PATRICK MURRAY, 1535, CC V 1105.
Official	MR. HENRY QUHITE,[11] 1530.
Canons	DOM. JAMES WILSON,[6] 1531 (Glendevon).
	"RECTOR OF LUNDY",[5] 1539. Logie is meant.
Chaplains	Twelve of choir,[4] 1532.
	DOM. DAVID GURLAW,[9] Bp.'s cpn., 1532.
	EWEN THOMSON, 1535, CC V 1105.
	STEPHEN CULROS, cpn. Trinity Altar, 1534, CR 264–7.
Notaries	THOMAS ANNAND, cl. 1531, SK 242–3.
	JOHN BANNATYNE, cl. 1531, CC VI 1066.
	MALCOLM CHISHOLM, 1532 (see under sub-dn., 1532).
	WILLIAM MORISON and ROBERT ADE or ALDIE (IWC pp. 57/8), 1532, RMS III 1257.
	STEPHEN CULROS[7] and THOMAS GILLESPY, 1532, RMS III 1233, 2036.
	JOHN QUHITE, 1533, RMS III 1339.
	WILLIAM GILL, 1533, RMS III 1342.
	ANDREW STOBY (?), 1535, CC V 1105.
	PATRICK WRYCHT, 1538, RMS III 1879.
	ALEXANDER SINCLARE,[12] cl., n.p., 1538, CC VI 1177.
	ANDREW SYM,[2] 1539.
	THOMAS LEIRMONTH, 1539, RMS III 2042.
	THOMAS BISHOP, 1539, RMS III 2042.
	ROBERT LEIRMONTH, 1532, RMS III 1257 (cf. 1522, n. 2).
	WILLIAM LITSTER, IWC p. 58.

1. 20 Nov. 1536, RSS II 2192, William Drummond is dead, and the King presents Mr. Malcolm Fleming. 17 Jan. 1538/9, Malcolm Fleming is being prom. to Pr. Candida Casa, and James V asks Paul III to prefer to Dn. Db. William Gordon, (who was only a cl.). T. No. 1046. cf. 1540–49, n. 6.

2. cf. Andrew Sym, n.p. 1522; cf. 1522, n. 2. 1539, n.p. SK 363-4. On 18 Jan. 1431/2, he wts. as v. Comrie, RMS III 1257.

3. RMS III 1257; still Adn., 1539, SK 363-4. Succeeded George Newton, who must have † c.1531 (see n. 4 following). cf. 1521, n. 7. In 1510, John Chisholm was v. Dunning RMS IV 3398, cf. 1527, n. 8. In 1538, cpn. St. Serf's, Dunning, RSS II 2463 (Ch. Dunning has fallen in status). His nat. son, James, was legitimated 1 Feb. 1553–4, RSS IV 2362. John C. † 1542, see 1540-9, n. 1. In 1538, F. II

50–55, one John C., res. provostry Dunglass and was given a pen. He may have been the Adn. Db. See n. 10, below.

4. RMS III 1257, 1532. Names of 12 were Malcolm Drummond, William Anderson, Stephen Culros, John Mason, Constantius Symmer, James Forsyth, John Wricht, Alexander Ferguson, John Beir, Andrew Ewinson, James Burale, Robert Akinheid. Malcolm D. leads the list, because he is Mr., a graduated Master, the others are all Dominus (Sir). It will be seen that Stephen Culross is also noted as n.p. Among cpns, and n.ps. names of Chisholm and Drummond appear, as also Leirmonth and Blakwod – Db. clerical families.

Robert Akinheid, cpn. choir, was also cpn. Altar St. Nicholas the Bp., in Db. Cath. As such he feus to Robert Leirmonth, citizen of Db., lands and ruinous small house near Holmehill (between the croft of Adn. Db., called Glenquhome, his wood and the common road to Traimyill (Ramoyle), etc. These adjoined R.L.'s own garden, the cpn.'s own holding occupied by Robert Cairns, the baker, and the spring called "Phillip's Well" (a draw-well in Kirk Street, see A. B. Barty's "Dunblane", p. 251); the rent, 24 sh. p.a. RMS V 2139.

The names of the 12 are given in John Stirling of Keir's cr. granting rent of £12 from Keir and other lands detailed for money paid to him by the Adn. Db., George Newton. George N. had died and his executors (John Chisholm, Adn. Db., Malcolm Chisholm, Sub-dn. and n.p., and Robert Leirmonth, n.p.) paid over the sum which George Newton had deposited for safety with the Minorites of Stirling. This sum was in return for a daily mass to be sung at the High Altar of Db. The King confirmed the cr., 8 Feb. 1532–3, and is granted one silver penny of rent p.a., RMS III 1257. For George Newton, as author of a lost "Life of S. Blane", see J. H. Cockburn: The Celtic Church in Dunblane.

George Newton's name on documents clearly dated 26 Mar. 1533 and 4 Mar. 1534–5, CR pp. 264–7, is not easily explained; for in the above endowing cr., 18 Jan. 1532/3, and in the confirming cr. of 8 Feb. 1832/3, he is "the late" (quondam). Those crs. dated later than his death may have been prepared beforehand, and dated after his death.

5. RMS III 1923, 4 Mar. 1538/9, there is mention of "the rectors of the par. ch. of Lundy in the D. of Db.", within which parish lay the lands of Gogar. Lundy is probably a mistake for Logie, in which Gogar lies.

6. CR 261–4. Still cn. 1539, SK 363–4; cpn. and n.p. in 1530, RSM III 969. Still r. Glendevon, 3 Jul. 1546, cr. 2241 in Nat. Lib. of Sc. In IWC he wts. transumpt of sasine, 25 Apr. 1540, as "cn. Db., and prebender of Logie and commissary of Db."; subscribed with seal by William Blackwood, commissary cl.

7. RMS III 2036, A.D. 1532. Stephen C. was also a cpn. choir. The n.ps. are increasing in number; many were cls. in minor positions, cpns., cns., pts., vs., who so eked out their small resources. Popes tried to regulate the number and the qualification of n.ps., but this was difficult in a country so far from Rome.

8. On 7 May 1532, RSS II 1221, Dn. William Drummond's nat. son, John, was legitimated. On 24 Nov. 1536, RSS II 2194, the late Sir William Drummond, Dn. Db., "quhilk wes borne bastard" also "decessit bastard". He could therefore make no will. His goods fell to the King, who gave them to Henry D., perhaps another and older nat. son of Dn. William D., if there was such.

9. Sir David Gurlaw, 1532, Bp. Db.'s cpn., ATS VI 123, received from King's Tr. 10 sh. for riding furth of Db. to the King in Drynane (Drymen) with despatches sent hastily from the Council. In 1537, he got £10 from the goods of late Dn. William D., ATS VI 295; see n. 8 above. He was pt. in 1539, SK 363–4; wt., 1542, SK 378–9, as Gourlay; cf. 1562, "others".

10. CC V 1105, 10 Feb. 1534/5, shows that the Chr. and the Adn., though both of the same name, were different men, for both appear as wts. in this cr. Also, they

were both different from Dn. Sir John Chisholm, q.v. 1515, n. 8. The Adn. was still in that dig. in 1539, SK 363–4. First record of the Chr. is CR 264–7, 1534; in 1535, RMS III 1487.

11. *Henry Quhite* (White), a landed proprietor of generous instincts, was also a cl. of the highest legal capacity and reputation. 1 Jun. 1530, CR 261–4, he is cn. M., Db., and Br., r. Sanct Modoc and Off. Db. In 1535, pb. Logie CC V 1105. In CR 261–4, he is also hereditary lord of Auchnaguff; he granted to Camb. the third part of Kintulach with third of its mill (all in par. Dunbarney) to endow a cpn. with 17 marks p.a. to say "masses for ever for Henry Quhite's soul". The cpn. he founded was that of Trinity Altar in Db. Cath. (26 Mar. 1533, 4 Mar. 1533/4, CR pp. 264–7), the first cpn. being "Schir Stevin Culrois" (see n. 7 above). A strange proviso was that if the Bp. Db. absented himself "fraudfully", the endowed stipend will not be paid by Camb., but the Ab. shall be bound to find as good a stipend for the discharged cpn. Ab. Inchaf. is to hold the endowment for the annual payment. This is the agreement (one of the earliest such written in Sc. tongue) to which Bp. James Chisholm attached his seal as "administrator general of the fruits of the Bpric. of Db." ADCP I 256, 349, 368, 373, 408 show his importance in the Session and among the Lords of Council. On 23 Feb. 1539/40, he is instructed to attend when he feels able and to draw his full salary as pen., ADCP I 483–4, when he is called "Dn. of Br." In 1532, ADCP I 373, he is r. of Finavon. He was Off. Db. in 1527, ADCP I 256.

12. In CC VI 1177, Andrew S. is described "cl., of D. Db., n.p. and cl. of the court of the officialate".

1540-49

Bishop	WILLIAM CHISHOLM I,[10] 1526 – 64.
Dean	WILLIAM GORDON,[6] 1539
Sub-dean	JAMES BLAKWOOD,[8] 1546.
Precentor	(JOHN HAMILTON, 1547 – 51, *in commendam* Ab. Inchaf.; in 1547 he was aged 12).
Archdeacon	JOHN DANYELSTON,[1] 1542.
Chancellor	PATRICK FORHOUS,[7] 1544.
	JAMES KENNEDY, 1546, cf. 1550, n. 2.
Treasurer	WILLIAM MURRAY,[4] 1547.
Canons	MR. JAMES KENNEDY, 1542, SK 375–6, 381–2.
	SIR GEORGE WAWANE,[2] 1542.
	MR. WILLIAM CHISHOLM,[11] pn. Glendevon, after 1546, BA fol. 297b.
Chaplains	DOM. WILLIAM DRUMMOND, 1541; RSS II 4384; RMS III 2531.
	DOM. ANDREW DRUMMOND,[3] 1548.
	SIR JAMES BLAKWOD,[8] cpn. Altar Virgin Mary in Keir Aisle, res. 1549, HMC X 73.
Notaries	SIR THOMAS BROWNE, pt., CC VI 1304.
	ALEXANDER SINCLAIR,[5] 1546.
	WILLIAM BLAKWOOD,[9] 1542, SK 378/9.
	PETER WRIGHT, 1544, IWC 59.
	WILLIAM KINROSS, 1548, IWC 66/7.

Others   FINLAY PHILIPSONE ⎫
              JOHN BONKYLL   ⎬ baillies of the bp., 1544,
              JAMES GRAHAME   ⎭   CC VII 1344.

1. T. No. 1062, 21 Nov. 1542, when James V pets. Pope to appoint "our chamberlain", John D. to Adn. Db., vac. by death in this month of John Chisholm. This would not only gratify the King but be for the good of Db.

John Chisholm, late Adn., was ill.; his goods fell to Crown, which sold them to Archibald, E. Argyll, Lord Campbell and Lorne. RSS III 1034.

2 Mar. 1553/4, James and Jonete Danyelston, nat. children of John D., Adn. Db., were legitimated, RSS IV 2456.

2. George Wawane (Gavin) was wt. along with Mr. David Gourlay, Bp. William's cpn. (1532, n. 9) and others, to contract of marriage between James Stirling of the Keir and Jane Chisholm (here called "consignes", female cousin, though she was daughter, of the Bp.; cf. "Genealogy of the Drummonds", 179). The terms of the contract give the matrimonial arrangements in such circles in the Middle Ages – Db., 5 Mar. 1541/2, SK 378/9:

(a) James Chisholm, Laird of Cromlix, in whose home Jane had been brought up, is to obtain disp. for 3rd degree of consanguinity and 4th of affinity between the parties.

(b) James Stirling to infeft Jane in his lands of Cadder, and thereafter contract the marriage.

(c) For this, James Chisholm of Cromlix is to pay him £1000 (Jane's dowry, equal today to about £50,000), which he will apply in redeeming his lands.

(d) James Chisholm is to cause the Bp., with consent of Chp., to lease to James S. and Jane, the teind sheaves of the Keirs and 8 other properties, which the said James (i.e. Stirling) had "brukit" (enjoyed) for 14 years.

(e) The Bp. to support Jane and her husband in all ordinary expenses for 5 years, and James is not to sell or wadset (pledge) his lands without the Bp.'s consent.

Many wts., clerical and lay, are given.

Parties sign – James Striveling of ye Keir.
          James Cheshelm wyt my hand.
          Jane Cheisholme wt my hand.

Receipt for the above £1000 follows.

The whole is entered in the books of the Offs. and commissaries of St.A. *principalis*, Lothian, Gl. and Db. – all by William Blakwood, n.p.

Jane was second wife of James Stirling, who divorced his first wife, heiress of Cawder (also Janet) and kept her lands. Jane Chisholm became the mother of Sir Archibald Stirling and of James Stirling, who were killed in Db., in a quarrel about land, by one George Sinclair.

3. RSS III 3029, Andrew D.'s nat. son was legitimated 16 Nov. 1548.

4. CC VII 1399B. He was tr. 1549, RMS V 1548; 1563, RMS IV 2153. See also SK 410/1.

5. Alexander Sinclair, 10 Dec. 1538, was "cl. D. Db., n.p. and cl. of the court of the officialate", CC 1177. As "Alexander Sincles" he was n.p. in a cr. (MS. in Sc. Nat. Library. Ch. 2242, 3 Jul. 1546). He may have been related to Edward Sinclair who, in the cr. above, was granted Glassingallbeg and Drumdroulis by Bp., Dn. and Chp., Db., for 200 marks.

6. MS. cr., 2241, Sc. Nat. Library, 3 Jul. 1546. Signature (with others) reproduced in BFDC 1957. On 22 Nov. 1546, Privy Council ordered him to hand back to Ab. Crossraguel his leases of the Abbey's lands and emoluments before 20 Dec. 1546 (i.e. in 4 weeks) RPCS I 52. Kin to James Gordon of Lochinver.

7. CMN 61. A notorious impetrator. cf. ADCP I 472; contrary to Sc. laws he had purchased the Chr. Db., from the Pope, and had tried in 1538 to oust John Chisholm from the dig. He managed finally to be confirmed as Chr. Db. in 1544.

8. James Blakwod was cl. to chp. of Db., 1556, when he acquired Shanraw and other lands from Bp. William C. I., Barty: Hist. of Db., 76. He was "subdecanus Dunblanen", when he signed MS. cr., 3 Jul. 1546, No. 2241 in Sc. Nat. Library. Other signatories were Bp. William C. I, William Gordon, Dn., John Danelston *mea manu*, James Kennedy, Chr.

9. See 1530–9, n. 6, where in 1540 he was commissary of Db.

10. Had been pn. Glendevon, cf. BA fol. 297b. Spottiswode calls William C. a wicked and vicious man who utterly despoiled the benefice. He says he was the brother of James C., his predecessor.

11. cf. 1530–9, n. 6; 1550–9, n. 9.

1550-59

Bishop	WILLIAM CHISHOLM I, 1526 – 64.
Deans	WILLIAM GORDON,[2] 1539 – c.1557.
	MR. ROGER GORDON,[3] 1557 † c.1587.
Sub-deans	JAMES BLAKWOD,[2] 1550.
	EDMUND CHISHOLM, 1551, SK 410–1.
Precentor	(ALEXANDER GORDON (Commendator of Inchaf.), 1551 – 64.)
Archdeacon	GEORGE WAWANE,[2] 1550.
Chancellor	JAMES KENNEDY,[2]1550 (cf. J.K. cn.1542, chr.1546).
Canons	JOHN HAMILTON[2] (Kippen), 1550.
	(he is "JOHN HAMMILL",[4] 1551.)
	SIR JAMES WILSON,[9] 1551 (Logie).
	ANDREW STRATHENRY[6] (Monzie), 1555.
	JOHN FORFAR,[1] 1557.
	WILLIAM SHAW, 1557, SK 410–1.
	ALEXANDER CHISHOLM,[7] 1555 (Comrie).
Chaplains	SIR JOHN DONYNG, cpn. Ch. St. Mary, Inverpeffray, 1551, LACC fol. 142 r.
	SIR JOHN FORFAR,[1] 1552, cpn. Altar Virgin Mary.
	SIR WILLIAM BLACKWOOD,[1] 1550, cpn. Altar Virgin Mary.
	DOM. MATTHEW MUSCHET ⎱ cpns. 1550, SK 398.
	DOM. GEORGE ROSS ⎰
	SIR ANDREW LAUDER ⎱ 1556, cpns. of the choir, SK 410; RMS IV 1066.
	MR. ALEXANDER ANDERSON ⎰
	SIR WILLIAM BLAKWOD[1] ⎱ cpns. 1557, SK 410–1
	JOH LEIRMONTH ⎰ (n.ps. 1550, see below).
Notaries	JOHN GRAHAME, 1550, CC VII 1475; 1562 RBM II 357–8; 1577, CS 102.

Notaries   JOHN LEIRMONTH[8]
(also cpn. above)   ⎫
WILLIAM BLACKWOOD[5]   ⎬ 1550, SK 396–8.
ANDREW BLACKWOOD   ⎭
JOHN MORISON, 1550, SK 398–9. 1572, IWC 61/2.
ROBERT DON, 1558, IWC 60.
ANDREW STRATHENRY[6] (c.p. Monzie, 1555), RMS
IV 1058.
DAVID BOUSIE and GEORGE COCK, 1558, IWC 66/7.

Others   WILLIAM DRUMMOND,[2] sacristan.

MR. JOHN SINCLAIR,[9] 1551   ⎫ LACC, are commis-
SIR JAMES WILSON,[9] 1552   ⎬ saries or commis-
⎭ saries general.

SIR WILLIAM CUSTNY ⎫ 1553, LACC, commis-
SIR JOHN WRYCHT   ⎬ saries.

1. SK 410–1. John Forfar inducted to cpn. Altar of Virgin Mary by Bp. William on 25 Jan. 1549/50, res. 3 Feb. 1549/50. Bp. then col. Sir William Blackwood (n.p., see n. 5), presented by James Stirling of Keir, the patron, SK 398. William B. was only a cl. and therefore not canonically equipped, but Keir dispensed him so long as the chapel is served by a suitable cpn. "These things were done in the Archdeacon's Court within the City of Db. about 9 a.m. in presence of, etc." On 14 Mar. 1549/50, William B. was prom. sub-deacon by Robert, Bp. O., at Jedburgh (D. Gl.), on the "commission of the Lord Commissary General of Gl., vicar general of remote areas, the See of Gl. being vac.". After diligent examination in knowledge, morals, and other requisites, he was "by the laying on of our hands prom. canonically to the sacred order of sub-deacon". SK 399/400, where he is first called "acolyte of D. Db."

But Mr. Abraham Crichton, Provost of Douglas and Off. St. A. in Adn. Lothian, had obtained the cpn. in Db. from the Pope. However, 7 Dec. 1551, in consistory court of St. Giles, Edinburgh, about mid-day, before wts., he renounced his right to the cpn. of St. Mary in Db. Cath., having no desire to molest W.B. now in peaceable possession of it. SK 400/1. John Forfar is cn., 2 May 1557, SK 410–1.

2. SK 401–2, 23 Mar. 1549/50, Dn. William G. and Chp., to augment income sell lands of Auchynby (between Langrig to N. and E., Kippendavie to S., and Drummagone to W.) with consent of Bp., to James Stirling of Keir, for 13/4 Sc. already paid, and 40/- still due. J.S. is to pay 4 marks yearly to Dom. William Drummond, sacristan of the Cath. (also called sacritan, RMS V 2210) and successors. Right of way is reserved for "wenis and cairtis" (waggons and carts) for inhabitants. This cr. is signed by Bp. William, Chr. James Kennedy; James Wilson, r. Glendevon; John Hamyltoun, pb. Kippen; George Wawane, Adn. Db.; James Blakwod, *sub-decanus* Db. (sub-dean also, SK 410/1, 1557, and RMS IV 1993). James Kennedy, still Chr., 12 May 1557, SK 410–1. Dom. George Wain (Wawane) Adn. Db., was incorporated, 1551, as student in St.A. (Early Records of U.St.A., 254). Still Adn. 19 Feb. 1556/7, SK 412–3. In 1533, 1535, without designation, CR 264–7. John Hamyltoun, frequent wt., CACA II, always as John Hammill, cn. Db. – cf. p. 205. See n. 4 below. J.K. still Chr. 1562, BA fol. 315b.

3. SK 410–1. Noted as "the late", 12 May 1587, RMS V 1234. On 8 Feb. 1569/70, with consent of Chp., feus Keirblane – confirmed 27 Jul. 1587, RMS V 1302. With S. Blane's name in Keirblane, note Kingairth in Strathearn, RSS IV 3020 dated 28 Jun. 1555.

On 28 Feb. 1558/9, Roger Gordon, Dn. Db., CC VIII 1773, wt. a cr. selling r. and v. of Girthtoun (by Bp. Galloway, to repair his kirk) to John Gordaun of Lochinver (perhaps his father or brother). In 1550, feued Dean's yard. IWC 99.

4. CACA II 205. John Hammill is John Hamyltoun (1550, see n. 2), cn. Db., and pb. Kippen, for as Hammill he is pb. Kippen, 16 Nov. 1552, and later, in "Rental Book of Cupar-Angus" (Grampian Club). I have found no ref. in wh. he appears as Hamylltoun, except SK 401–2 above. Dr. Easson suggests that he may be John Hummyle, cpn., wt. 30 Jul. 1523 ("Blackfriars of Perth"), who appears as steward of Cupar Abbey, June 1555 (Rental Book of Cupar II 254) and who had a pen. from teinds of Bendochy, 1562 (ib. I 362); this is possible, but the different areas made it unlikely.

5. William Blakwod was in all likelihood the principal notary and cl. of the consistory court of Db. LACC, the MS. book of the court 1551–5, calls him "scribe" (fols. 77 v. and 115 r.) and "notarius publicus" (fol. 223 v.). He is not called "commissary" (chairman, judge of court) in LACC. Most of the book seems to be in his handwriting; it corresponds closely with marginal notes written and authenticated by the signature "Willelmus (or W.) Blakwod", all through the book. Examination has not yet found him described in the book as "registrar", the corresponding Eng. title of his office. But, on 30 Aug. 1569, at Stirling, RPCS II 22, 26, it is recorded that he produced the Register Book of Db. and satisfied the Privy Council. But so important was this register that on 7 Sep. 1569, the Council demanded sureties from two burgesses of Stirling that W.B. would not abuse it, and would produce it to all interested parties. The book is now in the General Register House, Edinburgh. W.B. remained a staunch Roman Catholic. See chp. IX.

6. Andrew Strathenry, combined his c.p. (Monzie) with n.p. RMS IV 1058, 1157, SK 410–1.

7. Alexander Chisholm, c.p. Comrie, on death of John Sinclair, r. Comrie. RSS IV 2914. In 1564, his son, Malcolm, was legitimated – at cost of 40/-, ATS XI 285–6. On 16 Mar. 1578/9, RMS V 1288 informs us that he adhered to the Reformation and that his wife was Jonete Buchanan. Still r. Comrie, 1 Jun. 1582, RMS V 534. In 1562, BA fol. 297b, reported that he had set pn. to John Comrie of that ilk for 40 marks.

8. LAAC fol. 405 v, the Bp. ratified his appointment as procurator fiscal of the consistorial court, on 19 Oct. 1554.

9. LACC. Sir James Wilson, pb. Logy (from 2 Jan. 1550/1) and Mr. John Sincler (from 7 Jan 1551/2) presided in consistory court in the earlier part of the period covered by the book. Both are termed commissary or com. general. James Wilson was r. Glendevon, from 1531 (RMS III 242). On 20 Jan. 1543/4, Mr. William Chisholm, probably later Bp. William C. II, was presented to the Bp. to succeed James Wilson, r. Glendevon, when he res. or dies, etc. But James W. lived on, and did not leave Glendevon till at least 1546, when in Charter 2241, in Sc. Nat. Library, he is r. Glendevon still. He was not cn. when r. Glendevon.

1560-69

Bishops	WILLIAM CHISHOLM I, 1526 – 64.
	WILLIAM CHISHOLM[12] II, 1561 – 73.
	ROBERT PONT,[10] 1562, first minister of Db. after the Reformation.
	THOMAS DRUMMOND, minister, 1564.
	MR. ROBERT MONTGOMERIE, minister, 1567 – 72, TB 251.

Dean	ROGER GORDON,[5] 1557 – 70.
Sub-dean	ELMOND (EDMOND) CHISHOLM, 1562, BA fol. 298b.
Archdeacon	MR. JAMES CHISHOLM,[11] 1566 – 82.
Treasurer	MR. WILLIAM MURRAY,[2] 1547 – 80.
Canons	ROBERT SEYTOUN (Logie), 1567, RMS IV 2378.
	JAMES ROLLAND (Balquhidder), BA fol. 308a.
Chaplains	Six, of the choir,[4] 1562.
	DOM. JOHN LEIRMONTH, cpn. Altar St. Blaise, 1561, TB 14; 1572, RMS IV 2056.
	SIR JAMES FINLAYSON, cpn. Altar St. Nicolas, 1561, TB 14; 1567, TB 255. Also 1562, BA fol. 305b
Notaries	ANDREW KER, 1567, CC X 2100.
	ANDREW DRUMMOND,[9] cl., n.p. 1565, CAI pp. 163–5.
	JAMES DRUMMOND, cl., n.p. 1565, CAI pp. 163–5.
	JAMES BLAKWOD,[3] 1566, LC 803.
	BALTASER SPENS, 1566, pt., n.p., CC IX 2058; 1576, CC IX 2379.
Others	JOHN MUSCHET,[6] 1565, commissar-cl.,[8] RMS IV 2910.
	JOHN LEIRMONTH,[1] v. of Db., 1567.
	DUNCAN NIVEN,[7] *"ludimagister scole Db."* 1567, RMS IV 2378.
	DAVID GOURLAY, chamberlain of Bp. Db., 1562, BA fol. 285b, cf. 1532, n. 9. BA fol. 297b, he is v Abernethy.
	JOHN MORISOUN, servant of Bp. Db., BA fol. 285b. cf. notary of same name, 1550. It fell to J.M. to present the details of d. Db.'s income under Act of Assumption, 1562.

1. RMS IV 2056. John Leirmonth, cf. 1550, n. 8, also under cpns. 1557. sold land to James Blackwood, 2 May 1567. On 23 May 1567, wt. as "John Leirmonth, v. of Db.", RMS IV 1999. In 1564, was cpn. of S. Serf's Chap. in Dunning, LC 803, having succeeded John Chisholm, v. Dunning, 1510, RMS II 3398, Dunning having meantime been reduced from v. to chap.; RSS II 2463. In minor orders; adhered to Reformed Church and prospered out of ch. offices as a layman and notary. Still cpn. S. Blaise 1572, RMS IV 2056.

2. RMS IV 2153. cf. 1549, n. 4. On 14 Oct. 1563, he was cpn. (endowed) of Altar St. Catherine in St. A. The lands of this chap. in "the Adn.'s Aisle" or "Aisle of St. John the Evangelist", in Ch. of St. A. he feued in 1563 for "a large sum of money". Still Tr. Db., 16 Mar. 1579/80, RMS V 1288. In 1568, he is Sir William Murray of Tullibardin, Tr. Db., TB 255. He was collector general of the thirds of benefices, 1567–8, and designated knight, TB 195.

3. Throughout LC notaries of Db. appear in great numbers right on to 1749. The first who appears as "writer" in Db. is "Thomas Hambell", on 19 Oct. 1613,

LC 1692. On that same day, same ref., appear as baillies "John Blacvod, citizen of Db. and John Broune there".

4. RMS V 842, 6 Sep, 1562, cpns. of choir (now 6) and Bp. Wm. C. II feued land to John Drummond, son (nat.) of Malcolm D. Their names are James Forsyth, Robert Henderson, Alex. Anderson, Thomas Rob, Robert Sinclair, Wm. Johneson. One of the wts. is Duncan Niven, cf. n. 7. But 1562, BA fol. 317b, 9 cpns. are given, there being added Edmund Chisholm, William Drummond, and Arch. Lauder.

5. ATS XI 309. Dn. 1557, n. 3. 1562, BA fol. 299a, dn. Still Dn. 1570 – FKL II 152. V. town and parish, Db., BA, U.S.

6. RMS IV 2910, 30 Jun. 1565, wt. to appointment by Bp. Wm. C. II of his brother, James Chisholm of Cromlix, as bailiff of Bp.'s lands at £40 p.a. Same date wrote a notarial instrument at Db., ERS XIX 406.

7. RMS IV 2378, 1567. cf. n. 4 above. His title is schoolmaster. Still living 1 Jun. 1582, wt. in RMS V 534. In a 1562 cr., RMS V 842, wt. without title. Also a notary, 1563, IWC 100.

8. RMS IV 2910, 30 Jun. 1565. Title of officer in the consistory court, responsible for taking notes, writing minutes, recording sentences, etc. Perhaps successor to William Blackwood, q.v. 1550, n. 5.

On 24 Dec. 1574, James Pont, commissare of Db., is wt., LC 904. Also 1581, LC 1022, and 1584, CC XII 2724. J.P. was brother of Robert Pont, first Reformed minister at Db.; cf. n. 10 below.

9. CAI 163–5, 3 Nov. 1567, wt. as "v. of Strageith", CC X 2100.

10. Robert Pont became a very distinguished leader of the Reformed Ch. See his life in "Dictionary of National Biography". Had son Zachary (CC XII 2724), and another, Timothy, who became minister at Dunnet and was Sc.'s earliest cartographer, a very remarkable man (cf. BFDC 1951). See n. 8 above.

11. In 1566, v. Findogask and Strathblane, TB 255. cf. 1572, n. 4. In 1562, BA fol. 289a, rental of adn. Db. was 320 marks, with first charge a pen. of £50 to Robert Danielson, pn. Dysert; £8 to v. pensioner.

12. cf. ch. XII.

1568. The Bp.'s rents were ordered by the superintendent of Fife (who had Strathearn under his care) "to be left in the hands of Johne master of Grahame" for 407 marks, TB 249; 1569–72, "assigned to Earl of Mar", TB 249.

1570-79

Bishop	ANDREW GRAHAM,[6] first Reformed Bishop, 1573 – 94.
	ROBERT MENTEITH, minister, 1572 – 8.
	ANDREW YOUNG, minister, 1578 – 1614.
Sub-dean	DOM. EDMUND CHISHOLM, 1571, RMS IV 1993, cf. 1557.
Archdeacon	MR. JAMES CHISHOLM,[4] 1572.
Canon	WILLIAM SCOT[1] (Monzie), 1573; v., 1592, LC 1246 reader, 1568 – 72, TB 254.
Chaplains	JAMES STIRLING,[2] younger of Keir, cpn. Altar of St. Mary, 1574.
Notaries	MR. THOMAS AITKEN, cl., n.p., 1571, CC X 2236
	ROBERT FOGO,[5] cl., n.p., 1572, CC X 2264.
	JOHN HENRYSON, 1571, IWC 95.

Others   Students.[3]

MR. WILLIAM SHAW,[7] chamberlain of Db., 1577, RMS IV 2643.

1. RMS V 425, 15 Jan 1572/3. W.S., pb. Monzie, with consent of Dn. and Chp. (could they be gathered at this date?) feued his ruined manse, with garden in city of Db., to John McKilvoire, reserving to himself "a decent room and stable" as often as he comes to Db. Rent, 13/4. John Merser promised to spend 300 marks on repairs in next 4 years, if W.S. will repay him if the lease is later cancelled. cf. FKL II 94. Adn. James Chisholm, a wt.; cf. n. 4 below.

2. SK 42, 423, 20 Dec. 1574, James Stirling of Keir, patron of the altar, presented the income to his son James, "for support of his entertainment at the sculis". William Blakwod, previous cpn., did not conform to the Reformed Ch. – "his non-comperance befoir the superintendent or commissioner of the diocye to gif his attestatioun to his fayth and obedience to our soverone lord and his auctorite at the tyme appointed by the act of parliament maid thair upoun". This is stated in the act of presentation by the patron.

3. After the Reformation, the income of chaplaincies was often given to students at the Universities, e.g. "Early Records of U.St.A." 298, 301, 305, to one Robert Bannatyne, the income of chap. St. Michael in Crieff, 1573, 1576, 1577. cf. also, same ref., 298, 301, 307, in which the mails (rents) of Deanston were bestowed; they were common of the "choristaris in Db.", £20.

4. James Chisholm, CC X 2239, was also r. and p.v. of Tarbolton, the kirklands of which, 28 acres in all plus houses, yards (or gardens) he rented, on 19 Jan. 1571–2. In 1571, along with Wm. Melrose, minister at Findogask, he complained to Privy Council (RPCS XIV 110) against Laurence, son of Earl of Errol, as one of a party who destroyed the manse of Findogask, which was mensal to Adn. Db. Still Adn., 1579, FKL II 93; 1582, FKL II 194, RMS V 534.

5. Robert Fogo, cl., n.p. also, 1584, CC XXII 2766/68.

6. Said by some to be son of Lord Graham. Sometime v. Wick. Consecrated Bp. Db., 1573.

7. RMS IV 2643. In 1557, there was a cn. of this name, cf. SK 410–1. If this is the same man, he perhaps refused to conform and became executive officer of the Laird of Cromlix, see 1565, n. 6.

INDEX

D.C. stands for Dunblane Cathedral